A Unifying Enlightenment

Scientific and Learned Cultures and Their Institutions

Editor

Mordechai Feingold (*California Institute of Technology*)

VOLUME 30

The titles published in this series are listed at *brill.com/slci*

A Unifying Enlightenment

Institutions of Political Economy in Eighteenth-Century Spain (1700–1808)

By

Jesús Astigarraga

BRILL

LEIDEN | BOSTON

Cover illustration: Francisco de Goya, *Junta de la Compañía de Filipinas*, c. 1815. https://commons.wikimedia.org/wiki/File:La_Junta_de_Filipinas.jpg.

Library of Congress Cataloging-in-Publication Data

Names: Astigarraga, Jesús, author.
Title: A unifying enlightenment : institutions of political economy in eighteenth-century Spain (1700-1808) / by Jesús Astigarraga.
Description: Leiden ; Boston : Brill, [2021] | Series: Scientific and learned cultures and their institutions, 2352-1325 ; volume 30 | Includes bibliographical references and index. | Summary: "This book contains a systematic study of economic institutions during the Spanish Enlightenment in the area of print culture, education and the organisation of financial matters at state level. The book is a fresh interpretation of political economy's contribution to the development of the European Enlightenment. Far from being a straightforward intellectual phenomenon, this new science played a crucial role in both the circulating and institutionalisation of Enlightenment culture and the process of political unification and articulation undergone by the Spanish monarchy, which culminated in a constitutional culture."– Provided by publisher.
Identifiers: LCCN 2020039277 (print) | LCCN 2020039278 (ebook) | ISBN 9789004442382 (hardback) | ISBN 9789004442894 (e-book)
Subjects: LCSH: Spain–Economic conditions–18th century. | Spain–Commerce–History–18th century. | Enlightenment–Spain–History–18th century.
Classification: LCC HC385 .A78 2021 (print) | LCC HC385 (ebook) | DDC 330.946/054–dc23
LC record available at https://lccn.loc.gov/2020039277
LC ebook record available at https://lccn.loc.gov/2020039278

Typeface for the Latin, Greek, and Cyrillic scripts: "Brill." See and download: brill.com/brill-typeface.

ISSN 2352-1325
ISBN 978-90-04-44238-2 (hardback)
ISBN 978-90-04-44289-4 (e-book)

This book is printed on acid-free paper and produced in a sustainable manner.

To a@,
To a,
To Inés.
To my mother.

Contents

Preliminary Note

This book is the result of a research process of *long durée*. Entirely original material rubs shoulders with other work that has already seen the light of day in the form of previous versions of articles and chapters in books, normally in languages other than English. Some of the earlier material formed part of a wider research project that was completed in 2017 and for which the author was awarded a Ph.D. in History by the Complutense University of Madrid. However, there were many other incentives for writing the book and it has benefitted from finding numerous allies along the way. It has also had the enormous good fortune to come to fruition in an eminently international framework, under various research projects (HAR2016-77344-R: Spanish Ministry of Economics, 2017–2020, and H26_17R: Aragon government, 2017–2019), backed up in recent years by research visits to universities in France (Paris 1), Italy (Venice, Florence and Naples), Britain (Oxford), Belgium (ULB and KU Leuven) and Germany (Hamburg). However, the most inspiring ally of all has been the large and varied universe of researchers and teachers with whom the author has had the opportunity to converse over the years. It is not easy to compile a detailed and thorough list of all the scholars who have been involved in this research via different channels, but this does not excuse me from expressing my profound gratitude to them all. Some deserve a special mention here: María Victoria López-Cordón (Complutense University of Madrid), whose teaching never failed to leave its mark on the direction of the aforementioned doctoral thesis, and Javier Usoz (University of Saragossa) and Juan Zabalza (University of Alicante). My relationship with these two academics has been one of constant collaborative research that goes far beyond obtaining specific academic results. In fact I owe them an even greater debt; both have co-authored some of the articles and chapters included here, if in somewhat revamped form. The academic dialogue, in the best sense of the term, which I have enjoyed with Javier Usoz throughout these years, has been decisive in underpinning the book's definitive interpretive direction, and his habitual altruistic and generous attitude only redoubles my gratitude towards him. The same can be said of Ernest Lluch, who supervised my earlier doctoral thesis in Economics; the content of this book follows in the wake of his teachings. The serenity that comes with the passing of time does not free us from the obligation to remember his tragic murder in Barcelona by the terrorist organisation ETA in November 2000 as it really was: an absolutely pointless act of merciless cruelty. In a different sense, and beyond the imperative to create a fair and living memory in defense of so many innocent victims, the book's own history has been marked by other shadows: it was finished at the height of the international crisis created by Covid-19, when once again pain and death scarcely gave us time to rethink how specific values and ideas from the Enlightenment could be decisive in reshaping our immediate future. Fortunately, shadows of one sort or another have been always been offset by Maite and Valentín, who are always present, and, more particularly, by Katia Fach's brilliance and her sharp and shrewd long and short term view of circumstances, and our daughter Inés, an unfailing source of optimism and happiness. Without them my work would not have taken the form of this book.

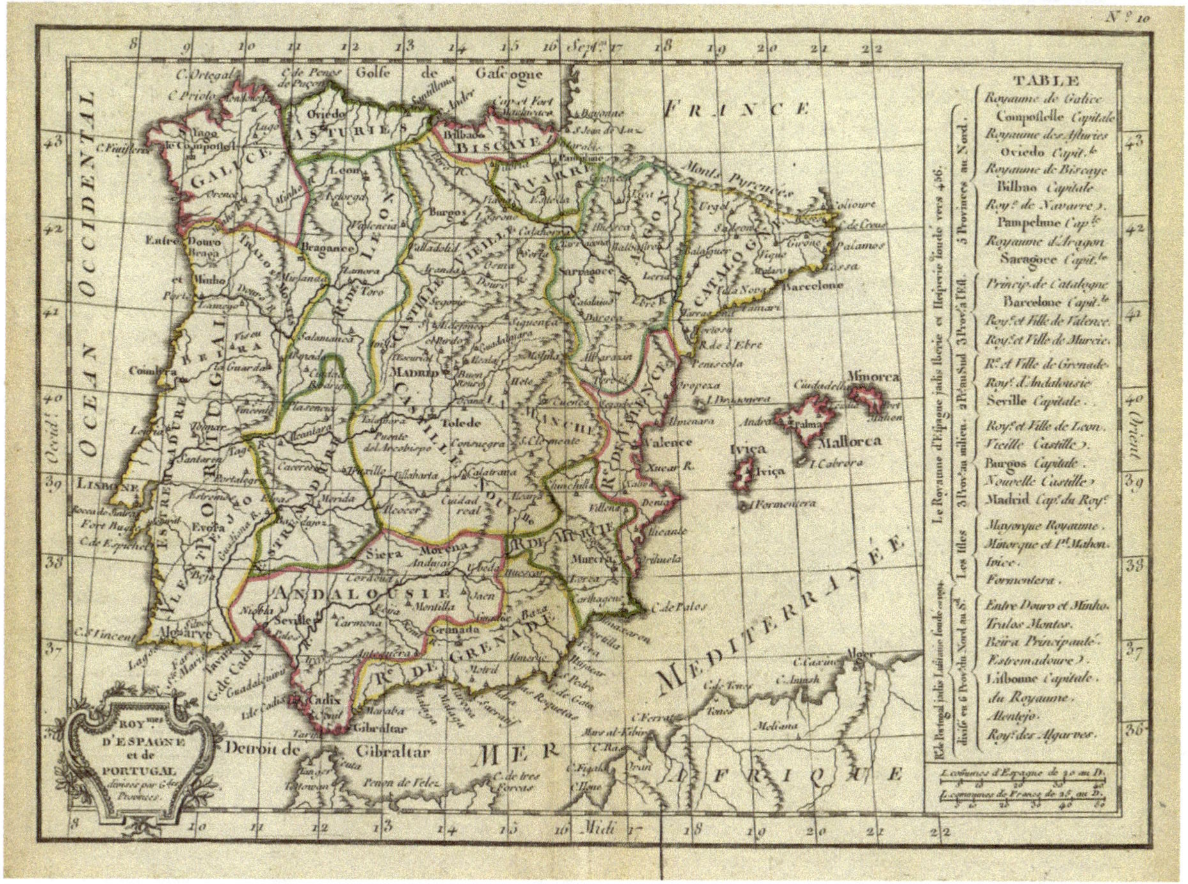

Map of Spain and Portugal by Charles Francois Delamarche and Jean Lattre, 1800.

Introduction

On the 17th of April 1806, barely two years before the uprising on the 2nd of May 1808 which marked the outbreak of the Peninsula War (1808–1814), Simón de Aragorri (1720–1806) died in Madrid.[1] Possessor of an immense personal fortune, his will included an unusual clause concerning a legacy to one of his great nephews: whoever was responsible for his education was "urgently" required to ensure that he was instructed in the "science of political economy."[2] This stipulation would only have had implications at private level had they come from someone whose life had been less eventful than Aragorri's. Born into a French Basque family, he learned at a very young age how to exploit his homeland's porous borders to create a varied array of businesses that were mainly based on brokering between Spain and France and other European markets. In 1753 he moved to Madrid, where he initially specialised in financial and monetary transactions as well as trading in goods with the Royal Service, which he channelled through his trading house "Aragorri and brothers." By the end of the 1750s he had become one of the Spanish navy's major suppliers of provisions and his commercial interests subsequently spread into other fertile areas: the colonial and grain trades. Meanwhile, he also acted for one of Madrid's main savings banks, becoming the Spanish representative of the *Caisse d'Escompte* in Paris and cornering the profitable business of exporting American silver. By these means Aragorri amassed one of the largest fortunes in Spain at that time, whose future survival he wished to entrust to political economy.

Aragorri was as skilled at entering the most influential political circles in Spain as he was in business. His life overlapped with the reigns of the first four Bourbon monarchs: born in 1720, when Felipe V was on the throne (1700–1746), during the reigns of Fernando VI (1746–1759), Carlos III (1759–1788) and Carlos IV (1788–1808) he displayed an unusual talent for rising from the world of commerce to the highest echelons of political power. He first gained the trust of Leopoldo de Gregorio, Marquis of Esquilache (1699–1785) and Jerónimo Grimaldi (1710–1789), influential ministers in Carlos III's first government; then Pedro Pablo Abarca de Bolea, Count of Aranda (1719–1798), Miguel de Múzquiz (1719–1785), José de Gálvez (1720–1787), Pedro Rodríguez, Count of Campomanes (1723–1803), José Moñino, Count

1 The websites referenced in this book were available at the time of printing.

2 Josep M. Delgado, *Dinámicas imperiales (1650–1796)* (Barcelona: Bellaterra, 2007), 218.

 | DOI:10.1163/9789004442894_002

of Floridablanca (1728–1808) and Pedro de Lerena, Count of Lerena (1734–1792), followed by the powerful Manuel de Godoy (1767–1851), during the reign of Carlos IV. Backed by his enormous wealth, he was a kind of power behind the throne for forty years, securing some of the most significant economic reforms of his day. Aragorri was influential in the passing of a law to liberalise the grain trade in 1765; he was personally involved in the 1765 and 1778 regulations concerning free trade with the colonies; he had links with people in positions of responsibility in the Havana trading company (1740); he developed the Philippines company (1785), the last of the chartered companies in the eighteenth century, and he participated in the reform schemes of the first economic society in Spain, the Sociedad Bascongada (1763), founding a *fanderie* for laminating iron and a company for manufacturing and preserving fish in the Basque Country. In short, he had a finger in many pies and according to Alexander Humboldt was possessed of a "lively sharp intelligence," contributing to financing the Crown with one hand while pulling out chairs for ministers so that they could sit down to sign reforms with the other. His rise did not go unrecognised; in 1769 he was raised to the nobility and became Marquis of Iranda, meanwhile consolidating his influence with the Treasury through his appointment as honorary minister of the Treasury Board. In 1795, now in his twilight years, he was designated state councillor. During the following years, before failing health forced him to retire to the country at the end of the century, this "highly skilled courtier," who had received "an excellent education and travelled widely," converted his luxurious Madrid mansion, near the King's palace, into a type of salon, which according to contemporary witnesses was frequented by courtiers, high ranking officials and diplomats.

Iranda was undoubtedly a unique figure in the Spanish Enlightenment, just as unusual as the clause in his will. Although apparently insignificant, in reality the clause represented a veiled recognition of an entire era. Over and above his unquestionable astuteness for exploiting sets of political and economic circumstances, Iranda was a first-hand witness to political economy's emergence among the senior government officials, politicians and merchants of his generation as an indispensible language for understanding the country they served and attempting to reform it. At the time of his birth there were virtually no signs of an active economic culture in Spain. The country was struggling to recover from the recent War of Succession (1700–1714); there were a handful of trade consulates, a few merchants' handbooks and fewer translations in circulation. The generation headed by Gerónimo de Uztáriz (1670–1732), devoted to building the new King Felipe V's economic programme on the legacy left by the *arbitristas*, was just beginning to emerge,[3] and other than some limited manifestations of print culture, there were no signs of an institutionalised economic culture. The scenario was radically different when he died: merchants' handbooks, treatises and translations of texts dealing with political economy had not only increased exponentially, but in the sphere of print culture, the trade and economics press was flourishing, while the first teaching manuals and commerce and economics dictionaries were starting to appear. Spain had also built up a dense network of economic societies and trade consulates, as well as founding university chairs in political economy and commerce, a state bank and an official agency for economic development and statistics. In short, the country had witnessed the blossoming of an institutionalised economic culture, of which there was no trace at all when Aragorri took his first steps; not only was he present at its birth, but he also contributed personally to its maturity. Like Law in Louis XIV's France, Aragorri moved towards political economy during Carlos III's reign as a means of rising from trade to politics.[4] He had reasons to be somewhat dazzled though: he had learnt about trade and finance with his brother in the office of the modest family business in San Sebastian.

This book deals with the emergence of these economic institutions during the reigns of the first four Bourbon kings in Spain, from the start of Felipe V's regency (1700) to the abdication of Carlos IV (1808). A mainstream approach to the notion of institutions has been taken. The New Institutional Economics perspective, which views institutions as sets of formal and informal contracts, rules and conventions through which societies organise their economic affairs and establish their coercive powers, has not been adopted in any strict sense. The raw material is the institutions that grew up around political economy in eighteenth century Spain and used education and print culture to fulfil three crucial aims: promoting economic growth, instigating the circulation of information about this new science and organising the management of state financial and economic affairs within the government. The focus is therefore on institutions that enjoyed their own legal statutes — which is to say, their creation was expressly acknowledged by the political establishment —, together with others that took institutional form because they were longstanding features of society. These categories include various expressions of Enlightenment

3 Reyes Fernández Durán, *Jerónimo de Uztáriz (1670–1732). Una política económica para Felipe V* (Madrid: Minerva, 1999).

4 Jesús Astigarraga, "Un nuevo sistema económico para la Monarquía española. Las *Reflexiones sobre el estado actual del comercio de España* (1761) de Simón de Aragorri," *Revista de Historia Industrial* 52 (2013): 13–44.

sociability, such as economic societies; government bodies dealing with economic and commercial issues like the Board of Trade, the trade consulates and the statistics agency; educational institutions such as the political economy and commerce chairs, and, finally, in the print culture sphere, magazines with economic content — whether specialised or not — , merchants' handbooks, teaching materials and political economy and commerce dictionaries.[5]

The approach chosen for this study has been used in international research with notable success over the last decades. Alfred William Coats is one of the central referents, although for later periods than those discussed here. This work is therefore closer to the numerous research studies into the history of economic institutions in the European Enlightenment, which have normally approached the topic at national scale, and among which the joint projects on Italy headed by Guidi and Augello are especially inspiring.[6] As a result of these studies, more is known about the history of political economy chairs, commerce dictionaries, the press and economic societies in different European countries than ever before. Against this backdrop, this work explores the relationship between economic ideas and institutions. Political economy was an essential component of the changes ushered in by the Enlightenment; changes that were both technological and institutional, and that together gave rise to the modern concept of economic growth.[7] Changes of this nature logically required the creation of a new set of institutions. However, as Robertson stresses, the *long* European Enlightenment was essentially an intellectual movement which was characterised by certain distinctive values, beliefs and ideas.[8] Institutionalised economic culture was one more expression of this intellectual movement, and in Spain's case it was largely prompted from abroad. The economic institutions that blossomed there were the outcome of a process of acclimatising foreign experiences to the Spanish context, which is why it is so important to analyse the sequence linking: the international circulation of Enlightenment ideas, their acclimatisation to Spain and their conversion into institutions.

---

5 Other manifestations of informal enlightened sociability institutions such as gatherings, coffee houses and salons are not addressed in this book; on this issue, see María Ángeles Pérez-Samper, "Luces, tertulias, cortejos y refrescos," *Cuadernos de Estudios del Siglo XVIII* 10–11 (2001): 107–53, and María Victoria López-Cordón, "Vida privada, asuntos públicos," in *Felipe V y su tiempo*, ed. Eliseo Serrano (Zaragoza: IFC, 2004), 447–76.

6 Massimo Augello and Marco E. L. Guidi. *Economisti e scienza economica nell' Italia liberale (1848–1922). Una storia istituzionale* (Milan: F. Angeli, 2019), I, VII-XXXVIII, 3–19.

7 Joel Mokyr, *The Enlightened Economy. Britain and the Industrial Revolution, 1700–1850* (New Haven-London: Yale University Press, 2009), 30ff.

8 John Robertson, *The Case for the Enlightenment. Scotland and Naples, 1680–1760* (Cambridge: CUP, 2005), 28–44.

Insofar as the institutions represented the fermentation of certain ideas, attention needs to be paid to the fundamental changes that have taken place over recent decades in the study of political economy during the general Enlightenment movement. Most importantly, the field has been freed from the fossilised interpretations nurtured by the History of Economic Thought. The traditional interest in approaching the topic as a series of schools of economic thought — Mercantilism, Physiocracy or Classical School —, each with supposedly greater explanatory power in the area of economic analysis, has given way to an approach that makes political economy an essential component of modern political theory, especially in the sphere of the rivalry for international trade.[9] In effect, from the 1740s and 1750s onwards, enlightened thinkers in Spain became aware that the country's future depended on surviving in a global market made up of competing trading nations, and that this had become the key to modern politics.[10] As Hutchison stressed, it was during these decades that the boom in interest in political economy observed all over Europe began to be assimilated in Spain,[11] starting a cumulative process that had a dramatic effect on the shape of other coterminous disciplines, especially political science.[12] The interest that in Spain nobles, merchants and bureaucrats showed in the new science, which was depicted as a systematic and coherent body of ideas and laws, also extended to its most representative institutions: in 1752 the first journal with economic content appeared and in 1763 the first economic society was founded, which was indistinguishable from its peers in other European countries. As, first, Venturi and, then, Robertson showed, political economy was certainly "the most important" of all the "connecting discourses" of the European Enlightenment.[13] As in other countries, the key to the arrival of these innovative ideas in Spain was the prolific traslations task undertaken by Enlightenment protagonists which began to proliferate during the 1750s and

---

9 Istvan Hont, *Jealousy of Trade. International Competition and the Nation-State in Historical Perspective* (Cambridge-London: Harvard University Press, 2005), 1–155.

10 Antonella Alimento, "La concurrence comme politique moderne: la contribution de l'école de Gournay à la naissance d'une sphère publique dans la France des années 1750–1760," in *L'économie politique et la sphère publique dans le débats des Lumières*, ed. Jesús Astigarraga and Javier Usoz (Madrid: CV, 2013), 213–27.

11 Terence W. Hutchison, *Before Adam Smith. The Emergence of Political Economy, 1662–1776* (Oxford: Blackwell, 1988), ch. 10.

12 Steve L. Kaplan and Sophus A. Reinert, "The Economic Turn in Enlightenment Europe," in *The Economic Turn. Recasting Political Economy in Enlightenment Europe*, ed. Steven L. Kaplan and Sophus A. Reinert (London: Anthem, 2019), 6–9.

13 Franco Venturi, *Utopia and Reform in the Enlightenment* (Cambridge: CUP, 1971), 123–26; John Robertson, "The Enlightenment Above the National Context: Political Economy in Eigtheenth-century Scotland and Naples," *The Historical Journal* 40, no. 3 (1997), 672.

1760s.[14] This cannot have been an easy task because these men had been educated according to classical Scholasticism patterns, which made it extremely difficult for them to access the new knowledge. Indeed, throughout the eighteenth century, the political economy crossed language, political and cultural barriers. It crossed denominational barriers too, no small matter in Catholic Spain, with its religious orthodoxy; this science was eventually accepted from the Catholic south to the Protestant north, and encouraged the rise of secular culture.[15] Its significance in this sense becomes even greater if the enormous asymmetry between the international spread of treatises on "politics" vis-à-vis those on "economics" is borne in mind; this was definitely a feature of the Enlightenment as a whole, not only in Spain, and is partly explicable by the fact that throughout the eighteenth century "economics" was one of the preferred languages of "politics."[16]

Economic institutions also spread, although its creation involved additional difficulties regarding the circulation of ideas. Economic societies, chairs and press on political economy proliferated because of similar factors to those driving the flow of ideas; factors such as patriotism, the desire for the public good and emulation.[17] Emulation needs to be understood in the context of the renewed debate between "rich and poor countries,"[18] although this was now mediated by the emergence of political economy, which was at the service of a new international order that was peaceful, balanced through trade and

14 For an overview, see María Jesús García, "Translation in Enlightenment Spain," in *Routledge Companion to the Hispanic Enlightenment,* ed. Elizabeth Franklin Lewis, Mónica Bolufer and Catherine M. Jaffe (Abingdon-New York: Routledge, 2020), 258–70. The best work on political economy's translations during the Spanish Enlightenment is Vicent Llombart's, "Traducciones españolas de economía política (1700–1812): catálogo bibliográfico y una nueva perspectiva," *CROMOHS* 9 (2004), http://www.fupress.net/index.php/cromohs/article/view/15644/14764.

15 Margaret Schabas, *The Natural Origins of Economics* (Chicago: University of Chicago Press, 2005), 39–41.

16 For an interpretation of the contribution of political economy to the development of the Spanish constitutional culture, see José María Portillo, "Constitucionalismo antes de la Constitución. La economía política y los orígenes del constitucionalismo en España," *Nuevo mundo-Mundos nuevos* 7 (2007), https://doi.org/10.4000/nuevomundo.4160.

17 On the significance of patriotism, see John Shovlin, *The Political Economy of Virtue. Luxury, Patriotism and the Origins of the French Revolution* (New York: Cornell University, 2006), 5ff. On emulation and the important role played by translations, see Sophus A. Reinert, *Translating Empire. Emulation and the Origins of Political Economy* (Cambridge-London: Harvard University Press, 2011), 13–72, and on this issue in the Spanish context, Gabriel B. Paquette, *Enlightenment, Governance, and Reform in Spain and its Empire, 1759–1808* (New York: Palgrave MacMillan, 2008), 30ff.

18 Hont, *Jealousy of Trade*, 267–322.

inclined to foster the economic development of nations. This science therefore emerged as a new way of imagining a world of peaceful competition between rival trading states, a new geopolitics based on the "spirit" and "balance" of trade, in which, from the Treaty of Utrecht, international trade treaties aimed to establish themselves as its main guardians.[19] Economic institutions were the cornerstones of this new geopolitics, which focussed on the importance of economic development that was separate from the imperatives of war and military obligations. Spanish men of letters and elites committed themselves firmly to acclimatising these European economic institutions, which were markers of success in other countries, to Spain. As discussed later in this book, they looked to Germany, Italy, Holland, Belgium, Switzerland, Portugal, Ireland, Russia and, of course, Britain, where a system of public information that encouraged innovation operated; once the Glorious Revolution was over, the appearance of economic institutions was fostered by both its parliamentary system and its politicised and relatively unrestricted public sphere. However, as these economic institutions eventually also took root in countries with absolute monarchies, the cultural mediation from France, which was of course essentially political, was key in constructing the cultural identity of the Spanish economic Enlightenment;[20] but, as Spanish historiographers have been insisting for decades, this does not in any way imply identification with the French model. In any event, the authors' emphasis on using intellectual history to explain the development of economic institutions was also motivated by the current state of the historiography of eighteenth century Spain. By comparison with the progress made in social, economic and cultural history, the Spanish Enlightenment requires a considerable boost from studies of intellectual history, especially since in Spain innovation's main added value was its adaptive element.[21]

---

19 Antonella Alimento and Koen Stapelbroek, "Trade and Treaties: Balancing the Interstate system," in *The Politics of Commerce Treaties in the Eighteenth Century. Balance of Power, Balance of Trade*, ed. Antonella Alimento and Koen Stapelbroek (Cham: Palgrave MacMillan, 2017), 1–43.

20 This represented a notable shift with respect to Spain's previous influence on French absolutism; see Jean-Frédéric Schaub, *La Francia española. Las raíces hispanas del absolutismo francés* (Madrid: Marcial Pons, 2004).

21 Jesús Astigarraga, "Admirer, rougir, imiter. Spain and the European Enlightenment," in *The Spanish Enlightenment Revisited*, ed. Jesús Astigarraga (Oxford: VF, 2015), 5–7. A very useful instrument for this approach are provided by the cultural history: Peter Burke, *Cultural Hibridity, Cultural Exchange, Cultural Translation: Reflections on History and Theory* (Cambridge: Polity, 2010). A more rigorous analysis of foreign sources nourishing the Spanish Enlightenment will prompt a notable change in Sánchez Blanco's negative account on it — *Europa y el pensamiento español del siglo XVIII* (Madrid: Alianza, 1991) and

This work also explores the role played by Enlightenment economic institutions in structuring the state. All over Europe this was constructed through the imposition of royal sovereignty on increasingly broad and unified spaces and institutions. In Spain the process underwent a radical transformation in the eighteenth century as a result of the War of Succession. The political structure of Habsburg Spain, which survived until 1700, was based on a composite plural country with federal characteristics and political bodies that were organised relatively horizontally.[22] Although Castile's political tradition contained embryonic centralising and standardising ambitions, under the Habsburgs few attempts were made to dissolve this composite monarchy's inherent political pluralism. Economic institutions were thus based on large territorial units, mainly the Crown of Castile, with its dominions in the Americas; the Crown of Aragon, consisting of Aragon, Catalonia, Valencia and Majorca; and the Kingdom of Navarre and the Basque provinces, all of which had significant economic, monetary and fiscal autonomy. As is well-known, even before the end of the War of Succession, relatively new political formulas in the institutional and political history of Spain began to be tested. In their ultimate aims, they resembled formulas promoted by elites in other countries, some of which, such as Britain and Holland, had republican elements. Local particularities, with their heterogeneous institutions and legislatures, were considered dysfunctional, and centralisation and homogenisation therefore emerged as the best foundations for political and economic progress. The policy developed by Felipe V was a response to this. The successive implementation of the *Nueva Planta* decrees in the Crown of Aragon — first in the Kingdoms of Valencia and Aragon (1707) and then in Catalonia and Majorca (1715–1716) — represented a change of political model from the horizontal "composite" structure of the Habsburgs to the more centralised and vertical structure of the Bourbons, the executive administrative pattern of which was more streamlined and started to focus on the *Secretarías*.[23] However, this did not mean that a fully centralised

---

El Absolutismo y las Luces en el reinado de Carlos III (Madrid: Marcial Pons, 2002) —, which had excessive influence on Jonathan Israel's interpretation of Spain: *Democratic Enlightenment: Philosophy, Revolution, and Human Rights 1750–1790* (Oxford: OUP, 2011), 374–410. Mónica Bolufer has recently offered a fairer balance: "The Enlightenment in Spain: Classic and New Historiographical perspectives," in *Routledge Companion to the Hispanic Enlightenment,* ed. Elizabeth Franklin Lewis, Mónica Bolufer and Catherine M. Jaffe (Abingdon-New York: Routledge, 2020), 3–15.

22 John H. Elliott, "A Europe of Composite Monarchies," *Past & Present* 137, no. 1 (1992): 48–71.

23 María Victoria López-Cordón, "Secretarios y secretarías en la Edad Moderna: de las manos del Príncipe a relojeros de la Monarquía," *Studia Historica. Historia moderna* 15 (1996): 107–31, and "Instauración dinástica y reformismo administrativo: la implantación del sistema ministerial," *Manuscrits* 18 (2000): 93–111; María Teresa Nava, "El poder y su

uniform state was achieved; the long period of economic and demographic growth that took place from around 1720 to 1790 was possible in spite of the fact that both political authority and the domestic market were heterogeneous and fragmented. One of the most revealing issues was that the *única contribución, catastro, equivalente* and *talla,* taxes that were levied in Aragon, Catalonia, Valencia and Majorca, respectively, differed significantly from their Castilian equivalents because they were mainly direct. This meant that different regions had different tax rates and that industry and trade received differing levels of incentives. Elliot identified another additional problem;[24] the asymmetry between the seat of political power and the centres of economic growth. Carlos II and the Hapsburgs had left a burdensome economic legacy: an impoverished, backward and commercially weak monarchy that was dependent on foreign powers. The first signs of recovery appeared before the War of Succession in the Mediterranean and Cantabrian areas: agricultural techniques were more advanced here than inland and trade began to recover its traditional vitality. Having established itself as the seat of political power and economic decision-making after the war conflict, Castile now had to provide these new centres of economic growth with representation, as regional economics had fallen silent. In short, as the Spanish economic treatises — from Ustáriz (1724) to Jovellanos (1795) — showed, achieving a centralised uniform economic system remained a major problem for Bourbon absolutism in Spain.

In recent decades there have been many studies exploring the reasons behind Spain's inability to solve this problem in the eighteenth century. The most relevant from this work's perspective argue that it was due to flaws in the design of its absolutist structure. Comín and Yun explained from a fiscal-military state point of view that, although Spain lacked universal nationwide taxes, as did Britain, its fiscal revenues were larger in the eighteenth century than is normally supposed, yet still insufficient because the continuing existence of regional differences and social hierarchies prevented it from broadening its tax base.[25] Torres, on the other hand, suggested that the problem was Spain's inability to construct a sufficiently efficient "war machine." Unlike France and

precio: los orígenes de la Secretaría del Despacho de Hacienda (1700–1724)," in *Gobernar en tiempo de crisis*, ed. María Victoria López-Cordón and José Manuel Nieto (Madrid: Sílex, 2008), 109–32.

24 John H. Elliott, *Imperial Spain 1469–1716* (London: 1963). Spanish trans., *La España imperial, 1469–1716* (Barcelona: Vicens Vives, 1986), 410–11.

25 Francisco Comín and Bartolomé Yun, "Spain: from Composite Monarchy to Nation-State, 1492–1914. An Exceptional Case?," in *The Rise of Fiscal State: a Global History 1500–1914*, ed. Bartolomé Yun, Patrick K. O'Brien and Francisco Comín (Cambridge: CUP, 2012), 248–53.

Britain, Spain's sovereign public debt policy was extremely restrained in the last decades of the century, which limited its spending power, including on the military.[26] Even more importantly, especially in comparison with Britain, it lacked the appropriate administrative and political instruments to mobilise adequate fiscal and financial resources and to obtain sufficient support from society: the "moral economy" of collaboration between private and public interests was weak in Spain.[27] The main stumbling block was therefore lack of authority, and this pertained to the fact that Bourbon power was not strong enough to develop coercive means to put its fiscal and financial decisions into effect and thus protect its markets and support the expansion of trade.[28] Of course, this was not unrelated to the nature of the Bourbon administration itself. Far from benefitting from more efficient models of bureaucracy, the Spanish government was hindered by its dynastic-patrimonialist component,[29] as well as by the slow pace at which the process to centralise the Treasury, a key area, unfolded. This was not only due to the moderate nature of the reforms; the Treasury was forced to appropriate military networks to control a structure through which to carry out its revenue-raising and spending functions, and even so it had to wait until the middle of the century before the General Treasury emerged as an authoritative body and accounting unit in the management of revenue and, especially, public expenditure.[30]

The lack of a unified domestic market was an additional problem. The centralising urge inherent in the *Nueva Planta* decrees materialised only slowly,[31] and this merged with the patchy unfolding of the market integration process.

---

26 Rafael Torres, *El precio de la guerra. El estado fiscal-militar de Carlos III (1779–1783)* (Madrid: Marcial Pons, 2013), 403–08.

27 Agustín González Enciso, *War, Power and the Economy Mercantilism and State Formation in 18th Century Europe* (London-New York: Routledge, 2016) and "Between Private and Pubic Interests: the *Moral Economy of Collaboration* in Eighteenth-Century Spain," in *The War Within. Private Interests and the Fiscal State in Early-Modern Europe*, ed. Jöel Félix and Anne Dubet (Cham: Palgrave Macmillan, 2018): 171–93.

28 Rafael Torres, *La llave de todos los tesoros. La Tesorería General de Carlos III* (Madrid: Sïlex, 2012), 14–17.

29 Pablo Fernández Albaladejo, *Fragmentos de monarquía* (Madrid: Alianza, 1992), 353–412, and "Dinastía y comunidad política: el momento de la patria," in *Los Borbones. Dinastía y memoria de nación en la España del siglo XVIII*, ed. Pablo Fernández Albaladejo (Madrid: Marcial Pons-CV, 2001): 485–532.

30 Torres, *La llave*, 74ff., 99–125; Anne Dubet and Sergio Solbes, *El rey, el ministro y el tesorero* (Madrid: Marcial Pons, 2019), 223ff.

31 See, for example, John Lynch, *Bourbon Spain, 1700–1808* (Oxford: Basil Blackwell, 1989). Spanish trans., *La España del siglo XVIII* (Barcelona: Crítica, 1991), 64–195; Henri Kamen, *The War of Succession in Spain, 1700–1715* (London: Weidenfeld & Nicolson, 1969). Spanish trans., *La Guerra de Sucesión en España* (Barcelona: Grijalbo, 1974), 337–90.

In contrast to a school of historiography that delays the start of this exercise until the nineteenth century, Llopis showed that it was a lengthy affair that began before the seventeenth century,[32] and Grafe confirmed this, with nuances.[33] However, although this integration certainly took place, in the eighteenth century it achieved a regional dimension at best. Ringrose made a detailed study of the fact that the eighteenth century witnessed the appearance of a group of economic regions that did not match the old historical kingdoms exactly but were instead structured around urban centres.[34] According to Pérez Sarrión, this century was decisive in the emergence of these polarised and specialised economic areas, which blossomed through exploiting their respective comparative advantages and were structured around one or two cities, normally ports, with stable markets and a wide hinterland.[35] Nonetheless, the single uniform market never really materialised; in other words, during the eighteenth century trade functioned better in the interior of certain regions than between them. Moreover, the old fragmentation persisted between some maritime markets that were well integrated into the international economy but lacked links with domestic internal markets and whose trade penetration was generally weaker. However, this was not due only to the factors that were traditionally put forward, such as internal customs barriers, low population density and high transport costs; according to Grafe again,[36] this "slow, incomplete and haphazard" integration was a consequence of the jurisdictional fragmentation deriving both from the existence of the usual Ancien Régime corporate groups — the Church and the guilds — and specific territorially-based institutions in the shape of cities and semi-autonomous historical regions, which retained their sovereign rights and conditioned the system of government in Spain even more than the cities did.

However, what the all these interpretations appear to overlook is that Spain's political configuration was conditioned by a further essential factor: economic policies and reforms. This issue is particularly relevant to the last thirty years

32 Enrique Llopis, "España, la 'revolución de los modernistas' y el legado del Antiguo Régimen," in *El legado del Antiguo Régimen en España*, ed. Enrique Llopis (Barcelona: Crítica, 2004), 32–39, and Enrique Llopis and Sonia Sotaca, "Antes, bastante antes: la primera fase de la integración del mercado español de trigo, 1725–1808," *Historia Agraria* 36 (2005): 225–62.

33 Regina Grafe, *Distant Tyranny. Market, Power, and Backwardness in Spain, 1650–1800* (Princeton-Oxford: Princeton University Press, 2012). This work employed the unusual method of using the price of cod as a measure of integration instead of the price of grain.

34 David R. Ringrose, *España, 1700–1900: el mito del fracaso* (Madrid: Alianza, 1996).

35 Guillermo Pérez Sarrión, *La península comercial. Mercado, redes sociales y Estado en España en el siglo XVIII* (Madrid: Marcial Pons, 2012), 35–48, 63–66.

36 Grafe, *Distant Tyranny*, 117–18.

of the eighteenth century, a period that was dominated by the aforementioned Count of Campomanes, Attorney General — *Fiscal* — of the Council of Castile and the main ideologist behind the economic reforms in this decisive stage of the Spanish Enlightenment.[37] Although it has been argued that these reforms were exclusively war-oriented (to guarantee success in armed conflicts) and fiscal (to increase tax revenue to strengthen the sovereign politically), Llombart has argued convincingly that their overriding aim was to promote economic development in the nation as a whole.[38] In reality, public expenditure to achieve this goal was residual in eighteenth century Spain and was still overwhelmingly patrimonial and military.[39] But this was not the case in other European countries: Britain, for example, devoted proportionately less to wars than countries under Bourbon rule, while increasing expenditure on improving the empire's economy.[40] In other words, during the eighteenth century the state was not only moulded by war; it was also shaped by economic development, thanks to specific policies designed to promote this, and as these policies' source of inspiration was political economy, this was also an essential factor in structuring the state. During the forties and fifties political economy emerged in Spain as a systematic body of principles and laws which aimed to disclose the rules of international competition so that "trade jealousy" could be tackled successfully and Spain could reinvent itself as a new "trading empire" and thus regain its longed-for splendour.[41] The key lay in boosting the different productive sectors of the national economy, which furthered the populace's wealth and material well-being.

For its part, the state was essentially based on the premise of centralisation, and Enlightenment political economy as a science was in fact formulated on the basis of this premise. Debates about the market and the role of the state, which cut across all European economic literature, from Melon's *Essai* (1734) to

37 On his political figure, see Concepción de Castro, *Campomanes. Estado y reformismo ilustrado* (Madrid: Alianza, 1996), 127–212, particularly; on his profile as a political economist and a policy maker, see Vicent Llombart, *Campomanes, economista y político de Carlos III* (Madrid: Alianza, 1992).

38 Vicent Llombart, "La política económica de Carlos III: ¿fiscalismo, cosmética o estímulo del crecimiento?," *RHE* 11 (1994): 11–39.

39 The most up-to-date analysis are Torres, *La llave*, 76–84, and Dubet and Solbes, *El rey*, 404ff.

40 Steve Pincuss and James Robinson, "Wars and State-Making Reconsidered," *Annales: Histoire, Sciences Sociales* 71, no. 1 (2016): 5–36.

41 Fidel J. Tavárez, "La invención de un imperio comercial hispánico, 1740–1765," *Magallánica* 2, no. 3 (2015): 56–76, http://fh.mdp.edu.ar/revistas/index.php/magallanica/article/view/1509/2215.

book v of Smith's *The Wealth of Nations* (1776), took as their starting point the existence of a hierarchy that was established on the basis of an economic and political agent — the sovereign — with authority and decision-making powers in financial and economic matters throughout the country as a whole, and therefore with the authority to establish an orderly policy of state intervention. Using criteria from the German tradition, this centre determined not only the policies for creating the constitutional order within which economic actors could act freely (*Ordnungspolitik*), but also the policy process that supported the express intervention of the sovereign in order to achieve specific economic objectives (*Prozesspolitik*). However, the centre in which economic decisions were formulated actually had to be created: it was a political construct. It is therefore not surprising that, as Paquette argues, *regalism* as a political programme aimed at eroding the privileges of the Church, the guilds and regional institutions should have intertwined with political economy to become two of the main axes of Bourbon reforms.[42]

The arrival of European Enlightenment political economy in Spain, from Uztáriz (1724) to Jovellanos (1795), helped to structure a programme with features that set it apart from previous economic culture.[43] There was no centralising criterion under the Hapsburgs because of the country's pluralist composition; however, the Enlightenment actually shaped the first programme in Spanish history that was modulated for all national territory on the basis of this criterion. The aim was to complete the centralising absolutist project that had been chosen at the crossroads of the War of Succession and which lay down that economic structuring was a key factor for achieving political articulation. Two courses of action were required: firstly, creating political and government entities to centralise economic decision-making and, secondly, shaping a single domestic market that would end the trading, customs and fiscal differences between regions. Centralisation facilitated the creation of hierarchies, which is to say, an adequate structure for transmitting information and the orderly implementation of decisions, while also enhancing rationalisation: it enabled the court to rise above the interests of corporations and privileged regional

42 Paquette, *Enlightenment*, 62–63. Niccolò Guasti is essential reading on this topic: *Lotta politica e riforme all'inizio del regno di Carlo III. Campomanes e l'espulsione dei gesuiti (1759–1768)* (Florence: Aliena, 2006).

43 The best guide to Spanish Enlightenment political economy is a set of studies compiled by Enrique Fuentes Quintana, *Economía y economistas españoles. Vol. III. La Ilustración* (Barcelona: Galaxia Gutenberg-Círculo de Lectores, 2000), especially that by Vicent Llombart, "El pensamiento económico de la Ilustración española," 7–89.

bodies so that its measures could be shaped in accordance with the criterion of "the public good."

However, what sets the Spanish Enlightenment apart is the fact that, in practice, its economic programme was never structured around a single centre — the court — but was instead polycentric. This was, firstly, because of the blossoming of an economic culture linked to the old historical kingdoms and, secondly, because the court itself encouraged the creation of decentralising economic institutions. At the same time, this economic programme was wholly standardising and homogenising. Given a choice between absolutism and the relativism of economic laws, the Spanish clearly had leanings towards the latter, and political economy's ability to adapt to different contexts was praised as a great virtue. The fundamental cause of the Spanish Enlightenment's lack of homogeneity was therefore the regional factor. This is clearly shown by the numerous political economy treatises that appeared in the different historical kingdoms after the sixties. The urge for centralisation that characterised the Spanish Enlightenment's economic programme thus entailed neither renouncing decentralisation nor a strictly rationalist standardisation or homogenisation in a narrow sense. Together with the continuation of socio-economic practices, structures and networks associated with the old historical kingdoms, the Enlightenment's very nature provides a further explanation. The movement faced a twofold challenge: creating a central state-level power around the sovereign that acted on the basis of a criterion that was more in line with general interests, while guaranteeing both the recognition and exercise of authority, the key factor for implementing court decisions. This entailed devising institutions to involve the regions, local authorities and elites in the developing of a shared programme. This issue was particularly pressing given Spain's situation at the beginning of the century: a society divided by a bloody war, with vestiges of civil conflict, and an economy that was paralysed because of the conflict and also because of a long process of decline. The key issues were not so much centralisation and homogenisation but managing to unify the different heterogeneous parts that made up the country around a common project and aims. This was the ultimate purpose of the Spanish Enlightenment's economic programme. Although the programme naturally involved numerous centralising and homogenising criteria, above all it was inclusive, both with respect to the regions and their authorities and elites: most of all, it was unifying. Collaboration was emphasised in order to achieve political economy objectives, which emerged as priorities: lifting the country out of the state of stagnation and impoverishment in which it was languishing, through wealth creation and the enhancement of the populace's material well-being, essential conditions for attaining the Enlightenment ideal of "public happiness." In fact, the institutions discussed in this book were designed so that economic development should also serve this unifying purpose.

It would be dishonest to conceal the fact that the problems addressed here are closely related to Spain's current political situation, specifically because some of its old territorial entities — at the time of writing, mainly Catalonia — are part of the new democratic Spain that was structured around the 1978 Constitution. This issue ignited a lively historiographical debate in which one of the major themes is precisely the impact of the Enlightenment and Bourbon reforms on Catalonia. It is not possible to go into detail here and, in any event, Fernández Díaz's excellent recent work renders this unnecessary.[44] The debate initially focussed on the nature of the War of Succession and the consequences of Felipe V's absolutist politics for Catalonia. One of the main currents of thought, represented by authors such as Fontana, Albareda and Lluch,[45] has extended the influence of the old nationalist Catalan historiography into the present day. To these writers the War was not only an international conflict with its roots in the issue of succession, but, as Lynch had already noted, it was also a civil conflict.[46] It solved Spain's political organisation between the first Bourbon monarch's absolutist unitary model and the Hapsburg's constitutionalist pact-based "federal" model, which, according to Elliot, lay concealed behind the dual Castilian and Aragonese political tradition of previous centuries.[47] Felipe V's victory tipped the balance in the former's favour. The suppression of the Catalan constitutions in 1715–1716 not only undermined Catalonia's cultural identity, but also prevented the region — and Spain as a whole — from moving towards a constitutional and economic model that could have eventually developed into a political reality similar to Holland or Britain, instead of being subsumed into an absolute, dynastic-patrimonialist and authoritarian state with the result that Catalonia became a mere "province," neglected by central power. As these authors emphasise, however, Catalonia did gradually accept the new political situation, especially after the 1725 Treaty of Vienna and then during the 1740s, when *austracismo*, both internal or in exile, gave

44 Roberto Fernández Díaz, *Cataluña y el absolutismo borbónico. Historia y política* (Barcelona: Crítica, 2014).

45 Some of the major landmarks in this historiographical current are as follows: Joaquín Albareda, *Felipe V y el triunfo del absolutismo. Cataluña en un conflicto europeo (1700–1714)* (Barcelona: Generalitat de Catalunya, 2002) and *La guerra de Sucesión de España (1700–1714)* (Barcelona: Crítica, 2010); Josep Fontana, *Historia de Catalunya: La fi de l'Antic Règim i la industrialització (1787–1868)* (Barcelona: Edicions 62, 1998); and, finally, Ernest Lluch, *Las Españas vencidas del siglo XVIII. Claroscuros de la Ilustración* (Barcelona: Crítica, 1999).

46 Lynch, *Bourbon Spain*, 37–45; on the War, see Kamen, *The War of Succession*.

47 Elliott, *Imperial Spain*.

its last gasp following the death of Carlos VI. Nonetheless, this "persistent and purified" *austracismo*, to quote Lluch, which was shaped by Ramón de Vilana Perlas (1663–1741) and Amor de Soria (1659?-1748?), found its expression in subsequent decades through a set of political initiatives that combatted Bourbon centralism and coalesced into a sort of "Catalan alternative."[48] During Carlos III's reign the economic projects set up under the auspices of the Barcelona Board of Trade and guided by Romà, Capmany and Caresmar preserved Catalonia's distinct and separate personality in some way.[49] However, to Fontana and Albareda, the gap between Catalan and Castilian Enlightenment schemes was difficult to bridge: with its hierarchical, militarised and aristocracy-based power structure, which lacked political participation channels for Catalonia, Bourbon reformism damaged not only the Principality but also, once again, the whole of Spain.

Fernández Díaz qualifies this paradigm, with its emphatic conclusions, as *filoaustracista* — or Austrophile — and it has also been harshly criticised. Without denying that the *Nueva Planta* would have been a traumatic experience for Catalonia, García Cárcel explained that "vertical" Spain's victory over "horizontal" Spain buried the very possibility of finding a path between absolutism and constitutionalism to conciliation.[50] Arrieta, in turn, recalled that neither Catalonia nor Spain was wholly *austracista* or Bourbon, and that Felipe V's standardising project was less strict than was maintained: the Basque Country and Navarre retained their ancient *foral* — charter territory — privileges and Catalonia kept its private law institutions.[51] Speculating about Spain's future had the old *foral* institutions been retained was unreasonable, as Fernández Albaladejo recalled, especially if no attempt was made to ascribe some of the features of modernity that they doubtlessly lacked at that time to their present-day versions.[52] It was therefore necessary to attempt a complex-free

48 Lluch, *Las Españas vencidas*, 62–92; for more details, *La alternativa catalana (1700–1714–1740)* (Vic: Eumo, 2000), and *Aragonesismo austracista (1734–1742). Conde Juan Amor de Soria* (Zaragoza: IFC, 2000).

49 See, especially, Ernest Lluch, *El pensament econòmic a Catalunya (1760–1840)* (Barcelona: Edicions 62, 1973).

50 Ricardo García Cárcel, *Felipe V y los españoles: una visión periférica del problema de España* (Barcelona: Plaza y Janés, 2002), 112–13, 192–200, 218–22.

51 Jon Arrieta, "L'antitesis pactisme-absolutisme durant la guerra de Successió a Catalunya," in *Del patriotisme al catalanisme: societat i política (segles XVI-XIX)* (Vic: Eumo, 2001), 105–28, and "Austracismo, ¿qué hay detrás de ese nombre?," in *Los Borbones. Dinastía y memoria de nación en la España del siglo XVIII*, ed. Pablo Fernández Albaladejo (Madrid: Marcial Pons-CV, 2001), 177–216.

52 Fernández Albaladejo, *Fragmentos de monarquía*, 301–02.

assessment of the impact of Bourbon reforms on Catalonia, and the most useful basis for this is Vilar's interpretation. In his opinion the *Nueva Planta* did not represent the end of the Catalan nation; instead it eliminated unhelpful vestiges of the past and gave rise to a sustained period of economic growth, which had the effect of deepening the phase that began in 1690–1705. Bourbon political authoritarianism, with its bastions of centralisation and standardisation, was therefore not incompatible with Catalonia's economic dynamism. Its cornerstones were Catalonia's enterprising society and a well-designed economic programme — industrial protectionism, participation in the domestic market, free circulation of trade with the Indies and maintenance of Spain's monopoly in the American colonies — which would have been impossible without vigorous support from the court in Madrid.[53] Other authors like Martínez Shaw,[54] as well as Fernández Díaz himself, later followed a similar path. According to the latter, the relationship between Catalonia and the rest of Spain was more one of cooperation than confrontation.[55] The reform projects instigated by Fernando VI and Carlos III were welcomed unhesitatingly by the Catalan ruling classes and the yearning for the old constitutions was not translated into the political will to reinstate them. Hence, the change of political model represented by the *Nueva Planta* did not only promote economic growth, social development and the renewal of Catalan culture in a general sense, but it also made dual patriotism possible, as Capmany describes so well: "Catalonia is my homeland, Spain is my nation."

This second historiographical line, with all the nuances detailed above, thus highlights the eighteenth century consolidation of a type of "win-win" relationship between Catalonia and the rest of Spain: the latter was able to articulate a unifying economic programme with a major stronghold in Catalonia, whose economic upturn, unique in the entire Hispanic context, can only be explained on the basis of collaboration from the court in Madrid. However, the *filoaustracista* interpretation has dealt a heavy blow to this notion: it has led to the Spanish Enlightenment being completely dismissed because it opted for a false path to the modernisation of the state, which was absolutism; Bourbon reformism had many despotic and few enlightened elements.[56] The

---

53 Pierre Vilar, *La Catalogne dans l'Europe moderne* (Paris: SEVPEN, 1962), I, 79–82, II, 419–23.

54 Carlos Martínez Shaw, "La Cataluña del siglo XVIII bajo el signo de la expansión," in *España en el siglo XVIII*, ed. Roberto Fernández (Barcelona: Crítica, 1985): 55–131, and, on the various regional economic growth patterns, "Las vías del desarrollo regional en la España del siglo XVIII," in *El mundo hispánico en el Siglo de las Luces* (Madrid: SEESXVIII, 1996): I, 176–92.

55 Fernández Díaz, *Cataluña*, 441–549.

56 Fontana, *Historia de Catalunya*, 112–13, 117, 137, for example.

assessment of Bourbon reforms that prevailed in the Spanish Enlightenment mainstream has also been discredited. Since the seventies a group of highly respected authors — Lynch, Domínguez Ortiz, Maravall and Elorza, among others[57] — have promoted an interpretative consensus by identifying these reforms with the expression of "enlightened absolutism" in Spain. This has been understood as a period of modernisation, differentiated from absolutism in the strict sense precisely because the corridors of power had been penetrated by an enlightened ideology that changed the ways of thinking about the country and inspired an incisive reform policy that reached all regions of the country to a greater or lesser degree.[58]

Although this historiographical debate is far from closed, the central place occupied by Catalonia has had a notable distorting effect. In reality the debate was about the territorial structuring of the country as a whole, and it has tended to conceal the fact that the tensions between the centre of Spain and the peripheries involved more players in the eighteenth century. The ancient historical regions have all experienced problems in this respect one way or another, so restoring a comprehensive overview is essential now. Along with the economic and intellectual reform programme unfolded by the court in Madrid during the Spanish Enlightenment, other programmes existed at sub-state level, which recent historiography has qualified as "regional:" it is as natural to talk of a Catalan, Aragonese or Basque Enlightenment as it is a Spanish Enlightenment.[59] Based on the first studies to interpret the Spanish Enlightenment almost as a mere court phenomenon, French-inspired, with its roots,

57 For a summary of this generation, see Antonio Elorza, *La ideología liberal en la Ilustración española* (Madrid: Taurus, 1970), 18–41.

58 H. M. Scott, "Introduction: The Problem of Enlightened Absolutism," in *Enlightened Absolutism. Reform and Reformers in Later Eighteenth-Century Europe*, ed. H. M. Scott (Michigan: University of Michigan Press, 1990): 1–35. Paquette's study contains some relevant nuances on the careful use of this oxymoron in Spain's case — always more suitable than "enlightened despotism" — owing to the regalist component, that is, the defense of the authority of the monarchy against the Church (*Enlightenment*, 14ff.).

59 Fuentes Quintana, ed., *Economía y economistas*, 577–606, 613–76. For a brief summary, see Llombart, "El pensamiento," 51–60. Lluch opened the series with his study on Catalonia: *El pensament*. See, on Galicia, Fausto Dopico, *A Ilustración e a sociedade galega. A vision de Galicia dos economistas ilustrados* (Vigo: Galaxia, 1976); on Valencia, Pablo Cervera, *El pensamiento económico de la Ilustración valenciana* (Valencia: Generalitat Valenciana, 2003); on the Basque provinces, Jesús Astigarraga, *Los ilustrados vascos* (Barcelona: Crítica, 2003); on Aragon, Javier Usoz, *Pensamiento económico y reformismo ilustrado en Aragón (1760–1800)*. PhD. Zaragoza: Universidad de Zaragoza, 1996; on Navarre, Jesús Astigarraga, "Estudio Preliminar," in *Ilustración y economía en Navarra (1770–1793): el pensamiento económico de José María Magallón y Francisco Javier de Argáiz*, ed. Jesús Astigarraga (Vitoria: Gobierno Vasco, 1996), XIII-CXXX.

according to Sarrailh, in a "select minority" of men of letters and politicians with links to the power of the monarchy, or, in Herr's words, essentially activated by this power through a series of "Enlightenment channels,"[60] another more inclusive interpretation has emerged through contributions from the historical regions: there has been a shift from an interpretation based on a "single centre" — Madrid and its powerful court — to one that is polycentric.

In other areas of Europe, such as Italy and Germany, the polycentric component was clearly a consequence of the fragmented political structures in different states or principalities, which had a decisive impact on the way in which Enlightenment ideas were received and applied there. The vestiges of the old *foral* Spain that remained after the War of Succession, even outside the Basque provinces and the Kingdom of Navarre, conditioned the geographical distribution and entrenchment of Enlightenment culture there. The country's real political structure would have been more pluralist than its absolutist and supposedly unified substratum revealed. The first manifestations of the Enlightenment, which centred on the activities of isolated groups of thinkers known as *novatores,* retained this important regional component even after the Bourbons came to the throne; figures such as Gregorio Mayans (1699–1781) and the highly significant Valencian *novatores* hub are perfect illustrations of this. The emergence of the institutionalised political-economic culture, as a continuation of these first expressions of cultural change, was partly connected to the regional element. The clearest example here is the Sociedad Bascongada: the first economic society in Spain, it was created far away from the court in Madrid on the initiative of politicians with links to the *Juntas* — the *foral* Boards — in the three Basque provinces, with the aim of setting up an advisory body for the *Juntas.* It is well known that the monarchy itself promoted the decentralisation of the Enlightenment via the founding of economic societies after 1775 and then by the spread of trade consulates during the 1780s. However, it is highly symptomatic that in the reign of Carlos III, before this official political programme was launched, a number of books were devised that were expressions of political economy's acclimatisation to the old historical regions. Influential figures in local politics, such as Count of Peñaflorida in the Basque Country and Count of Aranda and the Count of Fuentes in Aragon, lent their weight to the process, and in the 1760s Anzano in Aragon, Narros in the Basque

60 Jean Sarrailh, *L'Espagne éclairée de la seconde moitié du XVIIIe siècle* (Paris: Impr. Nationale, 1954). Spanish trans., *La España ilustrada de la segunda mitad del siglo XVIII* (Méjico: FCE, 1957), 110–51; Richard Herr, *The Eighteenth Century Revolution in Spain* (Princeton: Princeton University Press, 1958). Spanish trans., *España y la revolución del Siglo XVIII* (Madrid: Aguilar, 1964), 129–65.

Country, Ramos in the Kingdom of Valencia, Olavide in Andalusia and Romà y Rosell in Catalonia became the first spokesmen for these "regional" economic Enlightenments, which were extremely active in the period prior to the *Cortes* of Cadiz. These and others authors that continued developing this regional economic focus — Arteta, Generés and Asso in Aragon; Sisternes in Valencia; Cornide in Galicia; Foronda in the Basque Country; Caresmar and Capmany in Catalonia — authored a series of economic treatises whose content referred to the situations in the Principality of Catalonia, the Basque provinces and the Kingdoms of Valencia, Aragon, Galicia and Navarre for the first time since the arrival of the Bourbons. They were written from a regional perspective and aimed to address the specific economic problems in these areas. Political economy thus displayed its ability to adapt to different contexts, which explains why it became the driving force behind the decentralisation of the Enlightenment in Spain.

This factor endowed the economic Enlightenment in Spain with a certain polycentric structure, which was only affirmed when the court in Madrid pursued its country-wide programme of economic societies and trade consulates. The programme's success was positively influenced by the Enlightenment's social composition: López-Cordón argued that the Spanish Enlightenment was essentially the work of men of letters, bureaucrats, publicists and other crown servants with links to institutions, both official — ministries, courts and municipal councils — and quasi-official — economic societies or consulates—, and this explains its intensely pragmatic nature.[61] This all helped to give the acclimatisation process a significant regional component; in some cases, such as the Basque provinces and Catalonia,[62] proposals with doctrinal and reforming bases that did not always match the official programme designed at court were put together, while in others, like Aragon and Valencia there was greater harmony between the two.[63] In any event, the regional element did not mean that the Bourbon reforms met with strong opposition in the strict sense. Contrary to the assumptions of the Catalan *filoaustracista* current of thought, they were received with more cooperation and complementarity than confrontation in Spain as a whole, such that the "regional" Enlightenments in fact

61 María Victoria López-Cordón, "The Enlightenment and its Interpreters: Nobility, Bureaucrats, and Publicists," in *Routledge Companion to the Hispanic Enlightenment*, ed. Elizabeth Franklin Lewis, Mónica Bolufer and Catherine M. Jaffe (Abingdon-New York: Routledge, 2020), 203–17. Franco Venturi underlined the parallel with Italy: "Economisti e riformatore spagnoli e italiani del'700," *Rivista Storica Italiana* 74 (1962): 532–61.

62 See, respectively, Lluch, *El pensament*, and Astigarraga, *Los ilustrados vascos*.

63 See, respectively, Usoz, *El pensamiento económico*, and Cervera, *El pensamiento económico*.

contributed to the political structuring of the new Bourbon monarchy, which had been devised by the centre around a set of reforms designed to operate on a country-wide basis. They carried the official Enlightenment programme to the most far-flung areas in the country and enabled local elites to become involved in a process of receiving and transmitting information and support for the reforms. Above and beyond the issue of jurisdictional fragmentation, the underlying idea was that this centralised project could only succeed if it went hand in hand with some manifestation of decentralisation. This complex interpretation becomes even more so if the colonies are included in the picture, as the economic institutions did not take on an imperial dimension until much later: the process did not come to fruition until the very end of the eighteenth century, when economic societies and consulates were first founded in enclaves across the Atlantic and a local press began to emerge. However, although little may be known about the transfer of economic and political culture from peninsular Spain to these areas nowadays, and there were exceptions, the country played the role of "centre," mediating between Europe and Latin America, where there would have been a different reception and adaptation process. To sum up, the Spanish Enlightenment was polycentric in nature, and its next of kin was the Enlightenment in the Italian states that Venturi described in such detail.

Underlying this analysis is the notion that it is possible to interpret the appearance of an institutionalised economic culture in Enlightenment Spain through the interpretative outlines provided by the national context.[64] In accordance with this, taking the correct approach to the Enlightenment phenomenon would require breaking it up in such a way that the notion of the Enlightenment singular would give way to that of Enlightenments plural, defined in national, political (republican versus monarchical) denominational (Catholic versus Protestant) and other terms. It is well-known that the cost of this historiographical tradition, these days vigorously represented by Pocock, has been the deconstruction of the Enlightenment's unitary sense. At the same time, however, it has undeniably helped towards a better understanding of the players and contexts that received Enlightenment ideas, as well as the great importance of local movements such as those in Scotland and Naples. Nonetheless, the validity of focusing on national context when interpreting the appearance of an institutionalised economic and political culture in Spain is debatable.

64 Roy S. Porter and Teich Mikula ́s ̌, eds., *The Enlightenment in National Context* (Cambridge: CUP, 1981). To Porter the idea of a unitary Enlightenment was a type of "hallucination" (4–5). The fact that Spain was once again ignored in this work needs to be highlighted.

Firstly, the approach is anachronistic: it projects the nation-state structure that became entrenched in the two subsequent centuries onto the eighteenth century; in Spain's case, this would require extending "national contexts" to the Latin American countries created in the first decades of the nineteenth century, still under the effect of the Enlightenment. Together with this, as shown above, the raw material of the Spanish Enlightenment was the myriad of centres, issuers and receivers; it would therefore be necessary to divide up the national dimension into smaller "sub-national" components, thus creating a kind of Russian doll-type fragmentation dynamic. Finally, the national context approach is of questionable usefulness when addressing political economy's emergence as a science. This process was the outcome of research involving many nations and generations, which cannot be separated from its cosmopolitan component.[65] If it is possible to talk of the existence of a specific Spanish Enlightenment political economy with its own unique institutions it is because this discipline had already coalesced in other countries. The political economy of the Enlightenment in Spain was a fusion of this non-native culture with the Spanish tradition, represented by Scholasticism and mainly *Arbitrismo*; however, above all, it involved the acclimatisation of these foreign ideas and institutions to the Hispanic context. The birth of Spanish economic culture in the eighteenth century was therefore a product of intellectual and institutional interconnection. In short, as Venturi said, it was the fruit of the fusion of the Enlightenment's patriotic and *local* aspects with the cosmopolitan and *universal*. If the Enlightenment is reduced to a multitude of movements and unconnected independent local centres, along Robertson's lines, we not only abolish the idea of the Enlightenment, but we abort the very essence of the birth of political economy as a science with no specific nationality that took root in most European countries. Spanish economic culture was thus the local expression of a general Enlightenment movement. This can be analysed without the need to renounce the notion of a single and indivisible Enlightenment;[66] that is to say, in line with Robertson, on the basis of a notion of the Enlightenment that accepts a common framework of ideas and aspirations whose main motivation is the material improvement of the human condition.[67]

⁖

65 Robertson, "The Enlightenment," 667–97.

66 See Israel's works on this position, although the main intellectual innovations are attributed to five countries (Holland, Great Britain, France, Germany and Italy): *Radical Enlightenment: Philosophy and the Making of Modernity, 1650–1750* (Oxford: OUP, 2002), 140–41, and *Democratic Enlightenment*, 6–7.

67 Robertson, *The Case*, 28ff.

The structure of this book is relatively simple. It is organised chronologically to respect the order in which the different institutional manifestations discussed appeared. Too much weight should not be attached to the fact that the merchants' handbooks and the press are dealt with separately; there were practical reasons for this, although the fact that many publications had educational purposes and numerous handbooks provided information beyond the strictly trade-related has been borne in mind. This is also applicable to the distinction made between handbooks and commerce dictionaries: in this case the boundary has been drawn according to whether the contents were organised in alphabetical order or otherwise. Chapter 1 therefore deals with the first phase of the publication of handbooks for merchants (1699–1760) and the discussion is resumed in chapter 9, which is devoted to the next phase (1760–1808). The origins of the economic press are covered in chapters 2 and 3: the former discusses the periodical published in the 1750s by the journalist Graef and the latter details the initiatives that developed in the following decade, which was known as the Spanish press' "spectator phase." Chapter 4 focuses on the appearance and spread of economic societies and trade consulates, as well as the different ways these societies spread and popularised information about economics and agriculture. Chapter 5 covers political economy and commerce dictionaries. The university chairs founded to teach these disciplines are covered in chapter 8. Finally, Chapters 6, 7 and 10 deal with different magazines with economic content that appeared between 1780 and 1808 during the "golden age" of Spanish press. The book is closed with an epilogue describing the future awaiting the economic institutions discussed here.

CHAPTER 1

Merchants' Handbooks (1699–1759)

Educate, Inform, Reform

1 Introduction

The sixteenth and seventeenth centuries witnessed an explosion in the production of merchant's handbooks throughout Europe.[1] These works had antecedents in mediaeval abacus books and the Italian *pratica della mercatura*.[2] Their content varied enormously, including equivalence tables, compendiums and guides to legislation. They were best symbolised by the commercial arithmetic and accountancy handbooks used in offices, private schools and other informal teaching institutions for the training of merchants and accountants. While their economic content may have been absolutely basic, these books played a key role in spreading commercial knowledge throughout society. They contained both *propositional* knowledge — weights and measures, foreign exchange and currencies, trade geography, trade law and ethics — and *prescriptive* knowledge — applied arithmetic and accountancy, trade practices and vocational training — about trade. They also assiduously included guides to learning arts and crafts.[3] From the beginning of the sixteenth century onwards they flourished as a significant expression of print culture, as trade expanded to the colonies and access to information — and the consequent reduction in transaction costs — became the best guarantee of commercial success. In Britain publications of this type formed an own genre during the decades of change in the seventeenth and eighteenth centuries, and production spiralled

1 The number of volumes were published in the period 1500–1549 (around 1.400) contrasts with the more than 1900 works published between 1650 and 1699 (around 1.900); see Johan Hooch, Pierre Jeannin and Wolfgang Kaiser, eds., *Ars Mercatoria. Handbücher und Traktate für den Gebrauch des Kaufmanns, 1470–1820* (Paderborn: Schöningh, 1991–2001), 1, 364ff, 2, 646ff, and, in the same work, by Wolfgang Kaiser, "Ars Mercatoria. Möglichkeiten und grenzen einer analytischen bibliographie und datenbank," 3, 1–36; also, additionally, Johan Hoock, "Discours commercial et économie politique en France au XVIIIe siècle: l'échec d'une synthèse," *Revue de Synthèse* 108, no. 1 (1987): 58–60.

2 Joseph A. Schumpeter, *History of Economic Analysis* (New York: OUP, 1954), 156–57.

3 Arthur H. Cole, *The Historical Development of Economic and Business Literature* (Boston: Baker Library, Harvard Graduate School of Business Administration, 1957), 8–10.

 | DOI:10.1163/9789004442894_003

from then on.[4] Nevertheless, *Le parfait négociant* (1675) by the French custom inspector Jacques Savary played a highly significant role in their internationalisation; accepted as the standard format for merchants' handbooks, it not only established its own genealogical line in France — La Porte, Larue, etc. — but also crossed national borders.[5] At the same time, competition soon appeared in the shape of handbooks covering Dutch commerce, which was thriving: the *Traité général de commerce* (1700) by Samuel Ricard, *Le négoce d'Amsterdam* (1723) by his son Jean-Pierre Ricard and similar volumes from other French authors, such as Huet and Le Moine de l'Espine. All this stimulated in the eighteenth century Europe the production of handbooks on trade, *commerce*, *commercio* and, also, *comercio*, because Spain made a frequently forgotten but not insignificant contribution to this international print culture movement.

2 From Pérez de Moya to Corachán

Commercial arithmetic in eighteenth century Spain had changed little for two centuries. This was especially true of that devised in Hapsburg Spain during the monetary stage referred to by Hamilton as "bronze," which was dominated by economic decline and monetary chaos, mainly because of the autonomy enjoyed by the old Spanish kingdoms.[6] The treatises of the period matched the three large monetary areas then active: Castile, to which the Basque Country was linked, Navarre, and the lands of the Crown of Aragon, each with its own specific features.[7] The handbooks from this long period were reissued on a large scale in the eighteenth century. One in particular was responsible for

4 Natasha Glaisyer, *The Culture of Commerce in England, 1660–1720* (Suffolk: The Boydell Press, 2006), 100–42; James Raven, *Publishing Business in Eighteenth-Century England* (Suffolk: The Boydell Press, 2014), 180–205.

5 This *Colbertist vade mecum* was reissued some thirty times before 1800 and was translated, at least partially, in England, Holland, Germany and Italy. Its content was also disseminated via compilations and dictionaries: see Johan Hoock, "Le phénomène Savary et l'innovation en matière commerciale en France aux XVIIe et XVIIIe siècles," in *Innovations et renouveaux techniques de l'Antiquité à nos jours*, ed. Jean-Pierre Kintz (Strasbourg: Oberlin, 1989), 113–23; Hoock, Jeannin and Kaiser, *Ars Mercatoria*, vol. II; Cole, *The Historical*, 15–16.

6 Earl Hamilton, *War & Prices in Spain, 1651–1800* (New York: Russell & Russell, 1947): 9–35. Regarding Spanish hanbooks of this period, see José María López Piñero, *Ciencia y técnica en la sociedad española de los siglos XVI y XVII* (Barcelona: Labor, 1979), 168–78, and Elena María García Guerra, "Los manuales de mercaderes y contadores durante la Edad Moderna," in *Las Enciclopedias en España antes de l'Encyclopédie*, ed. Alfredo Alvar (Madrid: CSIC, 2009), 319–33.

7 Grafe, *Distant Tyranny*, 132–33.

transferring knowledge of commercial arithmetic from the late Middle Ages to the Enlightenment: the *Aritmética práctica y especulativa* (1624) by Andalusian churchman and University of Salamanca graduate Juan Pérez de Moya (1512?-1596). A model of Renaissance scientific culture, the treatise presented mathematics as both a science and an art at the same time. Together with astronomy, music and geometry, they belonged to the elite group of the liberal arts, and side by side with rhetoric and dialectic made a decisive contribution to promoting the common good: "art is no use to deceive, but to excuse deceit;"[8] without these arts, Spain, as all the monarchies, would endure "perpetual confusion."[9] Their application in the mercantile sphere had undeniable advantages at moral level as they were useful for "restraining mean-spirited traders;" however they were also useful in a political sense as they underpinned contracts, inheritances, taxes and other elements on which civil order was based; they were, in short, indispensable to society. Mathematics illuminated the "known and granted" principles of this civil order, which was not natural but man-made, and thus could only be accessed via education. Mathematical reasoning and its applications to the commercial sphere went hand in hand in the Moya´s *Aritmética*, whose chief purpose was to train mathematics teachers.

Moya's book covered numeracy, literacy, practical geometry, progressions, square numbers and square roots (books I, II, III, IV and V). It dealt with both basic arithmetic and with algebra (book VII) and contained plenty of examples of mathematical theory applied to the mercantile world. Book I included examples of *juros* — state bonds — , *censos* — secured annuities — and interest rates as well as currency, weights and measures conversions. Moya was therefore able to use these units of measurement in his subsequent books, and his applied approach extended to algebra. Book VI was devoted to teaching the mental conversion of Castilian currency, and book VIII to the coins, weights and measures of the ancient world and their equivalence with Castilian coins. This magnificent treatise culminated in an eloquent dialogue between two students on the usefulness of mathematics, which included all kinds of recreational arithmetic exercises (book X). The text's didactic virtues were thus enhanced, and the approach was characteristic of a man as Moya, who probably worked as a private mathematics tutor and designed his book to disclose his knowledge.

Moya's shadow fell over three other prestigious sixteenth and seventeenth centuries merchants' handbooks that were reissued in the eighteenth century.

8 Juan Pérez de Moya, *Aritmética práctica y especulativa* (1562; Barcelona: Rafael Figueró, 1703), 350.

9 Pérez de Moya, *Aritmética*, 344.

Written by Seville-based Valencian Jerónimo de Santa Cruz, Jerónimo Cortés (?-1615), also from Valencia, and Andrés Puig, a Catalan, these works were responsible for extending the life of the Crown of Aragon's splendid tradition in applied arithmetic.[10] They were actually teaching materials, although Santa Cruz was probably a merchant, unlike Puig and Cortés who were both mathematicians. In contrast to Moya's book, which was limited to Castile, they were tailored for use by merchants in the contexts in which they were written: Valencia-Seville (Santa Cruz), the city of Barcelona (Puig) and the Kingdom of Valencia (Cortés).

Their approach to theory was unusual. Cortes' handbook included no mention of algebra, and geometry was not incorporated until the 1724 edition. Santa Cruz did not cover algebra either, but he began with a chapter about numbers, which Moya's book lacked. Puig's work was undoubtedly the most theoretical: two of the six sections of his book were devoted to algebra, yet they barely touched on its applications in the mercantile world. What shaped these handbooks' distinguishing features was in fact the dialectic between theory and its fields of application. Santa Cruz included numerous examples taken from Valencia and Seville merchants' books, but his *Dorado* was fairly limited in the field of applications to trade. Unlike Moya, he only included practical examples in the chapters on basic mathematics, as more advanced mathematics "rarely arise in the art of trading."[11] Somewhat unusually, his examples still applied to lost enclaves of the Spanish Empire, such as Flanders, and included the treatment of anaesthetics (chapter XI). Santa Cruz aimed to use these examples to train accountants and merchants in whom mathematical training "shone out," but also to instruct the assayers in the *Casa de Contratación* — House of Trade — in Seville; for this reason space is devoted to the treatment of precious metals (book II, chapters IX, X) and his book was used as a guide in the *Casa* for decades.

The desire to "make skilled accountants" also pervaded Puig's *Aritmética*.[12] While his book included uses of the accounting and auditing procedures typically employed by Madrid army suppliers,[13] their applications were mainly limited to "merchants and traders" in Barcelona, particularly those in the textile trade. In this sense Puig's book contrasts sharply to Cortés' handbook,

---

10 Vicent L. Salavert, "Introducción a la historia de la aritmética práctica en la Corona de Aragón en el siglo XVI," *Dynamis* 10 (1990): 63–91.

11 Miguel Jerónimo de Santa Cruz, *Dorado contador* (1594; Madrid: Joaquín Ibarra, 1754), 240.

12 Andrés Puig, *Aritmética especulativa y práctica y arte de álgebra.*(1672; Barcelona: Giralt, 1715), 144.

13 Puig, *Aritmética*, 146.

which was aimed at "dealers and merchants of all kinds."[14] The latter included innumerable examples including the militia, the clergy, rural agents and a wide range of craftsmen and retailers (silversmiths, tailors and many more), thus providing a snapshot of the rich social stratification of Valencian trade. These examples covered the exchange of agricultural goods (rice, oil and wheat) inside the Kingdom of Valencia and the sales and purchases that took place with Aragon, Majorca, Andalusia and other areas of Hapsburg Spain. However, the book was chiefly oriented towards the interests of wholesale trade, especially textiles and silk, the two branches in which the region specialised. It showed Valencian trade's large hinterland and the diversity among its merchants and their forms of association, including the most long-established: a whole chapter was devoted to merchants' companies and delegates.[15] This rich variety provided the book's raw material and was also to be found at teaching level. Unlike Puig and Santa Cruz, Cortés' book was a genuine compendium of mathematical conversations, problems and games, and he restored the teacher-pupil dialogue method in the final chapters.

The marked differences between the regions are also behind the disparate treatment of currencies, weights and measures in these handbooks. Moya confined his discussion of this question to Castile, with the odd brief incursions into Portugal, and Santa Cruz did much the same. However, Cortés and Puig broadened the scope of Moya's book VI and gave it an interregional dimension.[16] The requirements of the intensely internationalised Valencian and Catalan trading worlds led them to include detailed foreign currency equivalences as well, which were almost entirely absent from Moya's work. Their source was mathematics tutor Oberto Cantone's *Uso prattico dell'aritmetica* (1599), coming from the commercial world of Naples.[17]

Moya's stamp was less visible in Juan Bautista de Corachán's handbook. His *Aritmética*, published in 1699, can therefore be considered the starting point for a new type of merchants' handbook during the Spanish Enlightenment. A philosophy teacher with a doctorate in theology, Bautista de Corachán (1661–1741) held the University of Valencia chair in Mathematics and was a

14 Vicent L. Salavert, "L'aritmetica practica de Geronimo Cortés i la vida mercantil al País Valencià a les darreries del segle XVI," *Estudis. Revista de Historia Moderna* 8 (1982): 105–24.

15 Jerónimo Cortés, *Aritmética práctica muy útil y necesaria para todo género de tratantes y mercaderes* (1604; Zaragoza: Herederos de Diego Larumbe, 1724), book II, ch. XXIV.

16 Cortés, *Aritmética*, book IV. In books II and III of Puig's work, Catalonia is the epicentre for calculating exchange rates in the main European markets.

17 Cortés, *Aritmética*, 528; Puig, *Aritmética*, 155. Cantone was cited — in his edition of Venice, 1675 — in 1731 by José García Caballero.

member of the city's *novatores* circle, one of the most active nuclei during the *early* Spanish Enlightenment.[18] *Aritmética* thus covered the rich local university heritage of the teaching of and pursuit of mathematics as a core element in the new philosophy. Every aspect held traces of Corachán's modernising teaching work. His book was also excellent at theoretical level, which lifted it above more practical guidance handbooks such as that written by his countryman Valencian Cortés. He also stated his sources clearly, which was unusual in literature of this type; these included references to both classical mathematics treatises and others produced in Spain during the sixteenth and seventeenth centuries, including some written by his teachers at the University of Valencia — the censor of *Aritmética* was the prestigious cartographer Tomás Vicente Tosca —. The "Proemial" of Corachán's book was remarkable; it was devoted to the history of mathematics, as Cortés book was, but with less detail, and included a historical inquiry into the currencies, weights and measures of the classical world. The book stood out both for its academic tone and its usefulness to scholars of "Sacred Scriptures, historians and lay authors."[19] Its main audience, however, was mathematics teachers: Corachán presented his bare theses "with all mathematical rigour, so that beginners can understand them without forgetting that teachers have to read them."[20]

The handbook's academic hallmark was visible in other aspects, such as its desire to educate. The seven books were packed with exercises and concluded with an appendix containing "number games," and everything was related to trade. Although Corachán actually supported a single weights and measures system, he detailed the coins, weights and measures that were in general use in Castile and the Crown of Aragon at the beginning of his text. While some of his examples did refer to commercial usage in Kingdom of Valencia, this was not the defining feature of his handbook, which aimed to be used outside

18 López Piñero, *Ciencia*, 444–49. On Corachán, see José María López Piñero and Víctor Navarro Brotons, *Història de la ciéncia al País Valencià* (Valencia: Generalitat Valenciana, 1995), 236–26. The doubts raised by his work's lack of innovation have been settled by Jesús Pérez Magallón: *Construyendo la modernidad: la cultura española en el tiempo de los novatores (1675–1725)* (Madrid: CSIC, 2002), 126–31. Other brief insights into the world of the Spanish *novatores* are to be found in Antonio Mestre, *Despotismo e Ilustración en España* (Barcelona: Ariel, 1976), and Antonio Lafuente and José Luis Peset, "Las actividades e instituciones científicas en la España ilustrada," in *Carlos III y la ciencia de la Ilustración*, ed. Manuel Sellés, José Luis Peset and Antonio Lafuente (Madrid: Alianza, 1988), 31–34.

19 Juan Bautista Corachán, *Aritmética demostrada teórico-práctica, para lo matemático, y mercantil* (1699; Barcelona: Pablo Campins, 1735), Prólogo.

20 Corachán, *Aritmética*, Prólogo.

the Kingdom's borders. However, its ambitious theoretical framework was in one sense also its main weakness. The chapters devoted to numeracy were very well-balanced in terms of illustrating theory with examples devoted to the "ordinary treatment of purchases, sales, profits, bartering, companies, etc. [that] is called mercantile, because it mainly benefits merchants."[21] However, like Puig's handbook, this balance disappeared when the author embarked on the topic of advanced mathematics. Corachán's arguments in favour of the use of decimal nomenclature were pioneering and his handbook even contained logarithms, "one of this century's great inventions." The two last books lacked examples though: the algebra was of little use for "merchants' dealings." Inasmuch as Corachán demonstrated the infinite possibilities of the noble art of mathematics in its applications to harmony and music, he alienated potential readers. In spite of this, *Aritmética* was reissued in 1719, 1735 and 1757, although the second edition carried a warning that the monetary equivalences had become obsolete. While the series of Cortés and Puig's handbooks had already come to end (1724 and 1745), Santa Cruz and Moya's works fared differently; the fact that Santa Cruz's book ran to five editions in the eighteenth century — the last in 1794 — can be explained by the fact that it was used in the *Casa de Contratación* in Seville. The reissue of Moya's book is proof of its importance as a model for other handbooks, and its influence can be seen not only in the thirteen editions throughout the century — the last was in 1798 —, but also by the fact that its internal structure dominated similar handbooks in Spain. In short, commercial arithmetic from the time of the Habsburgs was still very much alive in Spain during the 1700s.

3 From Corachán to Bordázar

Trade handbooks continued to appear during the War of the Spanish Succession. Felipe v first dealt with the monetary chaos the War created — both sides issued coins during the conflict, and French money was legal tender on the Bourbon side —; then, through the *Nueva Planta* decrees, by removing customs barriers between Castile and Aragon and suppressing the regions' commercial and monetary independence, he took the first steps towards a unified monetary system. An important symbol of this reform was the 1730 creation of the Currency Board, which was immediately merged with the Board of Trade, thus assuming jurisdiction for all money-related affairs. Debased coinage from

21 Corachán, *Aritmética*, Prólogo.

the War and billon coins from the Habsburg period had been withdrawn in 1718 and 1726, with the aim of replacing them with new copper coinage for use in all provinces. The years from 1709 to 1738 witnessed an uninterrupted chain of legislative measures intended to stabilise the monetary system and thus to resolve a strategic issue: harmonising the provision of silver for trading in the domestic market with its exportation, which was vital for clearing the chronic annual shortfall in the Spanish balance of trade. These stabilising measures were essentially a continuation of Carlos II's 1680 and 1686 reform in Castile, when to prevent the inflation of billon coinage it had been withdrawn from circulation, and the dual silver coinage system was introduced. The system was institutionalised under Felipe V in 1709 and 1716 with the creation of a division between silver that was "old" or "national" and exportable, and "provincial" silver whose purpose was to pay large domestic trade sums and which had an intrinsically lower value than the first (25%). Other laws stabilised the two silvers with gold and copper billon, which was often used in the retail trade.[22] As Hamilton and Vilar maintained, these measures established a monetary period that was characterised by "stability" and "recovery." It will continue throughout the limited and continuist monetary policies adopted by Fernando VI (1746–1759).[23] The period was not one of genuine unification, however: in Grafe's words, "the Castilian reforms rather than a decreed formal unification of the monetary standard provided a stable monetary anchor."[24]

This scenario had a significant effect on merchants' handbooks. In addition to their traditional commercial literacy function, they became a key instrument in the transmitting of information about the reforms and their effects on monetary equivalences. Spain had problems for the dissemination of information: unlike Britain, it had no parliamentary body to publicise its laws and it differed greatly from other absolute regimes like France, which had both an active press and a centralised and highly hierarchised Board of Trade and General Treasury. So, literature for merchants in this period showed in Spain its versatility within print culture by taking government measures to

22 Hamilton, *War,* 36–54; Pierre Vilar, *Oro y moneda en la historia, 1450–1920* (Barcelona-Caracas-Méjico: Ariel, 1969), 329–39; Antonio Miguel Bernal, *España, proyecto inacabado. Costes/beneficios del imperio* (Madrid: Marcial Pons, 2005), 318–22; Pérez Sarrión, *La península,* 279–92; Grafe, *Distant Tyranny,* 132–37. According to these authors, various laws re-valued gold coins vis-à-vis silver coins (1726), "national" silver coins vis-à-vis "provincial" coins (1728) and silver vis-à-vis billon (1737). The growing silver deficit, which was due to its massive exportation, forced the creation of gold coinage of little nominal value, whose exchange rate with billon was fixed, and was a supplement to silver (1738).

23 Hamilton, *War,* 58–62.

24 Grafe, *Distant Tyranny,* 137.

the public and thus coming out in support of real sovereignty. This is evident from the period's most important texts, beginning with those written by the metal assayer García Caballero, a true inspirer of Felipe V's first monetary reforms.[25]

The function was facilitated by the fact that handbooks published after the War retained their local dimension. Beyond the slow pace at which the desire for centralisation inherent in the *Nueva Planta* decrees materialised, the problem of the lack of a unified Spanish market left its mark on the Spanish merchant's handbooks. The urban systems, around which the specialised economic regions were structured, emerged as the main places for the production of these books; they were published in Saragossa, Valencia, Barcelona, Seville, Cadiz, Bilbao and Madrid, cities in which trade information was more easily accessible — including by word of mouth — and which were also centres of print culture, as well as of the territorial structure of the Spanish Treasury,[26] and consolidated the trading networks that dominated activity in these economic regions. Generations of handbooks dealing with special features of urban or regional trade usage were thus established, following a sequence that began with the Habsburg heritage and remained unbroken throughout the century.

However, the value attached to this legacy altered significantly in the 1720s and 1730s. As we have seen, the earlier manuals, from Moya to Corachán, were arithmetic treatises and were structured accordingly; their commercial content was usually either fairly vague or simply non-existent. The handbooks produced during these two decades were characterised by complaints about this model's shortcomings for training merchants properly, although there was no clear connection among their authors. One of the first authors was priest and jurist Manuel de Zubiaur (1660-?), whose *Aritmética*, published in Bilbao in 1718, was backed by a dedication to Spanish nobleman Joaquín Ponce de León,

25 See, among others, José García Caballero, *Breve cotejo, y balance de las pesas, y medidas de varias naciones, reinos, y provincias, comparadas, y reducidas a las que corren en estos reinos de Castilla* (Madrid: Viuda de Francisco del Hierro, 1731), 186ff.; José Tramullas y Ferreras, *Prontuario y guía de artífices plateros* (Madrid: Herederos de Francisco del Hierro, 1734); Antonio Bordázar de Artazu, *Proporción de monedas, pesos y medidas, con principios prácticos de aritmética y geometría para su uso* (Valencia: Imprenta de Antonio Bordázar, 1736), 96–9, and *Reducción de monedas antiguas, y corrientes de toda Europa, sacada del libro de monedas, pesos, y medidas, escrito por Antonio Bordázar de Artazu* (Valencia: Simón Faure, 1736); Bernardo Muñoz de Amador, *Arte de ensayar oro y plata, con breves reglas para la teórica y la práctica, en la que se explica también el oficio de ensayador y marcador mayor de los reinos* (Madrid: Antonio Marín, 1755), 7–12.

26 Dubet and Solbes, El *rey*, 337ff.

Duke of Arcos.[27] The book was aimed at commercial mathematics teachers employed in the milieu of the Consulate of Bilbao, an institution with which Zubiaur had close links.[28] The *Aritmética*'s defining feature, however, was its extreme simplicity: it was a brief compendium of basic numeracy and was perfectly suited to Bilbao's trade usages and the flourishing activity in exporting Castile wool and Basque iron to the main European markets that was developing there. The handbook included calculations for breakdowns, freight and other aspects of consular activity.[29] There were also numerous examples of currency conversion, not only Spanish, but also the international currencies that "flowed" in local trade. Finally, given Biscay *foral* status, pupils were taught how to calculate duties on the goods when they passed through *puertos secos* — interior customs — en route for Castile.[30]

The same desire for simplification pervaded Francisco Javier García's *Aritmética*. Published in 1733, it was designed to teach Aragonese merchants how to operate in the new customs-free trade which opened up with Valencia, Catalonia and Castile following the *Nueva Planta* decrees, and how to circumvent the customs barriers that still existed with Navarre. The book had a significant social function; as well as being a teacher himself, García also examined teachers in Saragossa and his text seemed to be designed to dominate mercantile education in the city, to whose governors it was dedicated. The content was organised so as to teach the rudiments of commercial arithmetic "so basic that an expert will be annoyed by such trivial, while he who lacks it will be delighted,"[31] and thus took the form of a dialogue between teacher and pupil. However, its six books actually followed the same structure as the old handbooks and included geometric applications for surveyors and algebra. This suggests that the handbooks' social prestige was still linked with the inclusion of advanced mathematics sections, even if this limited its potential educational impact.

Juan Antonio Taboada's two handbooks were a case apart. They were geared towards the Madrid and Castile commercial context and the first, the *Antorcha luciente* (1729), aimed to explain the 1728 *Pragmática* — Law — and prevent the frauds committed in coin handling in Madrid trade, which the book

27 Manuel de Zubiaur, *Aritmética práctica para instruir la juventud* (Bilbao: Antonio Zafra, 1718), 8.

28 José Manuel Barrenechea, "Estudio Preliminar," in *Moral y economía en el siglo XVIII*, ed. José Manuel Barrenechea (Vitoria: Gobierno Vasco, 1995), XL-LIII.

29 Zubiaur, *Aritmética*, 369–78.

30 Zubiaur, *Aritmética*, 351–68.

31 Francisco Javier García, *Aritmética especulativa, y práctica, y arte mayor, o álgebra* (Zaragoza: Luis de Cueto, 1733), Al lector, unpaginated.

describes very well. Its content was later subsumed into the *Antorcha Aritmética* (1731), which was more general but also full of recriminations. Some pointed the finger at "certain amateur enthusiasts of the art of arithmetic;" others were aimed at teachers, who had been wrong to underestimate the value of practice, "master key of trade;" and, finally, "ancient and modern" authors such as Moya and Cortés were accused of producing long-winded and confusing books that were full of words that sounded strange "to ordinary people."[32] While these books' content was easily accessible to mathematicians, astrology and geometry teachers it was "almost impossible" for accountants and merchants to grasp. For these reasons the *Antorcha Aritmética* was practical, simple and avoided difficult vocabulary. There was no chapter on algebra, as this was not considered useful to merchants; however, a long section was devoted to the coins, weights and measures used in Castile (book III), and three chapters were devoted to teaching charge accounting and special transactions data, the uses of bill of exchange handling in Madrid and, finally, the rules governing the sale of Segovia wool via Bilbao.[33]

The fact that the 1730s was the most prolific decade for the production of merchants' handbooks during the first half of the century can be explained by the measures for monetary stability enacted between 1726 and 1736. Compendiums, tables and news, referring to these measures and the new monetary equivalences, abounded during this period, written by authors from all walks of life who presented themselves as genuine servants of the King (Crean, Aparici, etc.). It was in this context that the most important handbook of the decade was produced: the *Proporción de monedas, pesos y medidas* (1736) by Valencian Antonio Bordázar de Artazu (1671–1744).[34] Bordázar came from a family of printers that were very close to Valencian *novatores* and were committed to spreading their writings — his father had issued Corachán's handbook —. In the 1740s he made an unsuccessful attempt to found a mathematics school in Valencia. His multidisciplinary education led him to write books on spelling, to attempt to improve topography in the Kingdom of Valencia and to teach mathematics, geometry and architecture free of charge, all of which left a clear mark on his handbook. The book's publication was a well-thought out operation. The censor was Gregorio Mayans, one of the great figures of the *early* Spanish Enlightenment, and an unusually long endorsement by Juan Nebot arguing for the use of mathematics in the civil sphere also featured as a

32 Juan Antonio Taboada y Ulloa, *Antorcha aritmética práctica, provechosa para tratantes y mercaderes* (1731; Madrid: Imprenta de José Otero, 1784), 133–34, 142, 151.

33 Taboada, *Antorcha aritmética,* 209–24, 224–36, 370–416.

34 On Bordázar, see López Piñero and Navarro Brotons, *Història,* 226–32.

paratext.[35] Nebot had made a direct contribution to the introduction of Cartesian philosophy and atomism to the University of Valencia and had links to both Corachán and Tosca, the cartographer, who had been his teacher at university. Nebot cited Benito Jerónimo Feijoo (1676-764) to attack Aristotelian physics and other prestigious scientists, such as Boeerhaave and Wolff, to argue in favour of the primacy of mathematics in natural philosophy and their value as the "spirit of the republic;" no-one should "trade in civil life without arithmetic, statistics and geometry, which number, weigh and measure fairly, proportionately and appropriately."

Nebot's text established direct links with Bordázar's prologue. It not only detailed the applications of the different branches of mathematics and geometry, but also put forward an idea that pervaded the whole book: the unchanging mathematical rules that established the proportions between different units of measurement were in opposition to those of a "purely civil and political nature," which depended on the vicissitudes of commerce and the sovereign's decisions. This was especially the case with the proportion of coins, weights and measures in civil dealings, the theme of his book, and he thus managed to avoid any theoretical explanation of the mathematical rules. Designed, in short, to "use what had been learnt," his book was limited to presenting the preliminary principles with "concise and purely practical doctrine." It was organised into three treatises, the first of which concerned arithmetic. The second dealt with practical geometry; it was unusually long and presented the subject matter as a field that was open to innumerable applications by surveyors and craftsmen among others, over and above trade.[36] The third dealt with coins, weights and measures. The change with respect to previous handbooks was substantial; this work was less verbose and more dealt with arithmetic more concisely yet without foregoing an ambitious technical goal: the treatises on arithmetic and geometry were rounded off by logarithms and the use of a compass and trigonometry respectively.

The third treatise was the longest and most innovative. It devoted to the history of mathematics and coins of the ancient world set up a dialogue with Corachán's handbook. However, having previously explained that separating the extrinsic and intrinsic values of currency was counter to "the best policy,"[37] Bordázar openly defended Felipe V's monetary legislation. The book also included the most comprehensive equivalence tables to be published

35 Bordázar, *Proporción,* VII-XIV.

36 It included a long section on the builders' police by Juan Torija; Bordázar, *Proporción,* 164–74.

37 Bordázar, *Proporción,* 92, 96–99.

so far; his author systematically researched the coins, weights and measures used in all Spain's old kingdoms and those in current use and their foreign equivalences. He presented them with their values prior to the 1728 reform, including the main European markets and some in Asia.[38] The choice of sources undoubtedly enhanced the quality of his handbook: his monetary equivalences were connected with Dutch treatises through Ricard's *Le négoce d'Amsterdam*. The aim was to make a contribution to the proper training of merchants as well as, like Corachán and the generation of economists in the times of Felipe v (Santa Cruz, Uztáriz, Ulloa and Zavala, among others), to move towards a monetary and customs union. In 1741 Bordázar presented the King with a proposal for introducing a new standardised system of measurements in Spain.

4 The Financiers' Revolt

In the face of the desire for altering the handbooks' content, other authors demanded an entirely different approach. Dubet identified a distinctive type of commercial literature in eighteenth century Spain. It was aimed at a diverse amalgam of financers, treasures, accountants, suppliers and other similar economic actors who lacked a specific corporate entity but whose training required something different from what the user handbooks provided.[39] This issue was expressed in the clearest possible terms in Martín de Ezpeleta's *Libro de cuentas* (1704). Ezpeleta was an accountant from Navarre and had powerful patrons — his book was dedicated to the Bishop of Gerona —. His *Libro* was inspired by the problems he encountered during his inspection work at Saragossa General Hospital in 1695. Having had to face the fact that the solutions to these problems were not to be found in "in any book" of accounts, least of all in those "endless arithmetic books, that cover everything but with general rules,"[40] he decided to put together a book with a radically practical bent. As the paratexts stated, the work deliberately eschewed the classic mathematical

38 The monetary reform of May 1737, which once again realigned the value of silver vis-à-vis gold, immediately invalidated Bordázar's monetary calculations, obliging him to publish a pamphlet containing the new equivalences (*Reducción*).

39 Anne Dubet, "Les calculs des gens d'argent: des traités d'arithmétique pour marchands et financiers en Espagne au XVIIIe siècle," in *Des marchands entre deux mondes,* ed. Jean-Pierre Clément, Béatrice Pérez and Sonia V. Rose (Paris: Université Paris Sorbonne, 2007), 323–38.

40 Martín de Ezpeleta, *Libro de cuentas extraordinarias* (Zaragoza: Gaspar Martínez, 1704), unpaginated.

sequence, only resorting to it — and then always the most basic form — when it was required to solve specific problems raised by his inspection work, which ranged from the conversion of *censos* — secured annuities — and the different currencies in use in Spain to the Castilian wool trade. The book was written in Aragon at the height of the War of Succession and, although the imminent political changes rendered much of its content redundant, Ezpeleta was far from being forgotten. His *Libro* was taken up by the unorthodox Taboada and also lit the flame that led to the writing of a generation of books with their own defining features.

It was no accident that this flame grew stronger during the 1730s, when the publication of standard trade handbooks was at its height. Three texts appeared between 1734 and 1736, written by Valero Verdebel, José Fernández de Anuncibay and Félix García de la Fuente. Verdebel was the Count of Aguilar's chief accountant, and his book, *El contador moderno* (1734), had the backing of Agustín Luyando Montiano (1697–1764), a major authority on politics. It was unmistakably the work of a highly experienced accountant and Verdebel elaborated on the important social function of bookkeepers as bastions of contract compliance and thus genuine servants of the King, who would ensure that his laws were not open to "exception and alteration by his subjects."[41] However, its content was most precise. His aim was not to establish the "basic principles" of accounts,[42] as much as to tackle the "usurers" and "deceptions" arising from the measures of 1705 and 1727, which had reduced interest on *juros* — state bonds — and *censos* — secured annuities — from 5% to 3%. This issue was by no means extraneous to the other two texts: Fernández de Anuncibay's *Pláticas de aritmética* (1734) and García de la Fuente's *Voz aritmética* (1736) were both rooted in the Castilian economy — the former was from Avila and lived in Segovia, while the latter was from Salamanca, where he doubtlessly worked as an accountant — and had very similar internal structures. Their early chapters covered basic arithmetic, after which matters not covered in user handbooks were addressed. In Aunucibay's book the "rule of three" used in basic algebra in Spain was applied to practical issues such as the valuing of *juros* — state bonds —, sales tax and tithe and excise collection, bids, wills and asset distribution among heirs. Meanwhile, the last of the teacher-pupil conversations of which the book consisted were devoted to typical operations between accountants, guardians, stewards and asset managers. These undertook to explain annuity rates and the division of

41 Ezpeleta, *Libro de cuentas extraordinarias*, 119–20.

42 Valero Verbedel, *El contador moderno* (Madrid: Antonio Sanz, 1734), Prólogo, unpaginated.

goods resulting from wills. A long conversation discussed the lease of taxes, bids and auctions; yet another dealt with excise collection, including exact instructions for participating in markets and trade fairs and for training gem merchants' apprentices.[43] In a similar vein, García de la Fuente devoted two entire books to information on annuities and related issues, aimed at helping Salamanca harvesters to calculate tithes and taxes, as well as geometry rules for measuring land surface.[44] Adopting a very practical stance, he also dealt with typical problems in rural property management and included minutely detailed accounts relating to the administration, apportioning of income from entailed estates, and wills.

García de la Fuente's book was the inspiration for Diego Guardamino's *Prontuario* (1757). The author was a granary accounting agent whose work was endorsed by the Marquis of Campo de Villar, General Superintendent of Granaries. It was clear from the content that the works by great mathematicians from the old Habsburg kingdoms — Cortés, Tosca, Corachán and Puig — were very much alive, but were also obsolete: Guardamino focussed on correcting their information on weights and measures with the aim of providing a guide for the proper management of the kingdom's granaries. A few years previously, in 1743, army treasury and Crown of Aragon official Andrés de León had cited Ezpeleta in his work *Extracto*. The book was dedicated to his superior Manuel Horcasitas and its content was mainly military: it was full of random information on fortifications, the time reckoning of military salaries, war invalids and new conscripts. It also included coin reconversion tables to "learn by heart" and techniques for reading fractions. Compiled using information gathered "over more than ten years" from "practical and prudent men,"[45] the book took the deconstruction of user handbooks to its limits. It illustrated perfectly the ancestry of these books on trade, which were carved from experience and were essentially instruction manuals. Rather than transmitting basic knowhow, their social function was to list and communicate a set of methods, work routines and technical knowledge that were well-established enough to be circulated throughout society and applied immediately in multiple commercial activities.[46]

---

43 José Fernández de Anuncibay Urreta Basurto, *Pláticas de aritmética y palestra de contadores* (Madrid: Juan Muñoz, 1732), 264ff., 269ff.

44 Félix García de la Fuente, *Voz aritmética práctica para todos* (Salamanca: Imprenta de Santa Cruz, 1736), 122–30.

45 Andrés de León, *Extracto de reducciones de monedas, de pesos, de medidas y de números quebrados* (Zaragoza: Joseph Fort, 1743), 83.

46 Dubet, "Les calculs," 337.

5 Other Channels of Mercantile Information

The publication of accounting books and treatises on metal assaying increased in the eighteenth century. The first were extremely informative and contained tables of the most basic trading operations as well as the usual currency, weights and measures equivalences. They were similar to the primers, containing Christian doctrine, calendars and the basics of literacy, about which their authors usually agreed. In contrast to the user handbooks, they aimed to foster the social advancement in treasuries and trading houses of those who "cannot count."[47] At the same time, they provided "a rest" for trained merchants, as they enabled them to calculate more quickly. These books had a legacy from the seventeenth century *Arte subtilísima* (1680) by University of Salamanca teacher Antonio Rodríguez. Written for a "civil" audience and focussing on Castile, it was first distributed during the first three decades of the century. Books of this type were easy to adapt to changes in the law. In 1731 the original was tailored for the 1728 and 1731 monetary reforms by Pedro Enguera (or Henguera), a mathematics teacher and master builder from Madrid. Various editions were published consecutively with the aim of increasing trust among the readership, a tactic that was effectively repeated for the 1778 monetary reform and resulted in a new series of editions. The *Arte*'s longevity was thus increased. It became the most reissued text among treatises for merchants in the eighteenth century, boasting two dozen print runs and continuing into the next century.

Other accounting books that were geared towards local requirements appeared outside Castile. In 1716 Bartolomé Villar, an Aragonese churchman and teacher of "the trade deal" based in Valencia, published a *Libro de cuentas.* He was motived by the region's complete lack of commercial arithmetic teachers, which were essential for "the truthful exercise of deals and contracts."[48] His book was therefore designed for "all kinds of merchants." Although it provided information on the nearby market in Teruel, its framework was the Kingdom of Valencia, especially the capital. Like Cortés' handbook, which was still in

47 "If you can read and say the numbers, you can follow any deal or contract," said the heading of Bartolomé Villar's *Libro de cuentas para todo género de mercaderes* (Valencia: José García, 1716). Felipe Medrano's booklet on purchasing in ounces, arrobas and pounds had the same purpose (*Tablas de reducción,* 1748), as did that by Andrés de Ávila, which was full of educational information about fractions and currency conversions: *Modo fácil para la cobranza, y pago de cualquiera cantidades en los cuatro reinos de Castilla, Aragón, Valencia, y Cataluña* (Valencia: Tomás Santos, 1769), 110–17.

48 Villar, *Libro de cuentas,* unpaginated.

print, this work used commercial tariff and equivalence tables to transmit the richness of local trade and the transactions between the city of Valencia and its surrounding area. In other cases, the city authorities themselves took the initiative. In 1769 Andrés de Ávila, a Valencia city council official, published a book of international currencies, weights and measures equivalence tables for use by local merchants.[49] However, it was the silk industry that was the real commercial arithmetic specialist in Valencia. While it was Carlos Bernardo de Quirós that established the bloodline in 1740, the most comprehensive tables were the work of arithmetic teacher Mariano Badelles. Their purpose was to instruct treasury officials and wholesale and retail merchants, especially silk traders, in bill of exchange operations and converting the coins and weights used in the old kingdoms. The *Descanso de comerciantes* (1754) reappeared later in a series of new editions, in some cases expanded, thanks to mathematics teacher Manuel González de la Torre, and stock exchange broker and guild master Mariano Torralba. The series continued until the end of the century with González de la Torre's *Libro de Cuentas* (1794) whose absolute simplicity was again undescored: to use it, it was not "necessary to know arithmetic or the art of counting."[50] However, Valencia's centuries-old commercial arithmetic was brought to an end by the decline in the silk industry in the final years of the century.[51]

Further proof of the great versatility of accounting books was to be found in the nearby *Principado* — Principality — of Catalonia, where some texts of this type were published in Catalan. In 1746 Francesc Ifern, teacher and churchman — he was presbyter and beneficiary of Gerona cathedral — published a compendium of basic arithmetic for use in commerce in Catalan, for the reason that the most widespread texts were incomprehensible to many merchants as they were written in Castilian Spanish.[52] Alternative editions were issued in Gerona, Barcelona and Tarragona, at the end of the century, and reflected the fact that Catalan was used in commercial spheres in a large part of the region. However, the success of Ifern's text was surpassed by *Llibre facil de comptes fets*, which was published anonymously, probably, for the first time, in Gerona in 1703. Although it appeared under various titles, it was actually a translation of *Le Livre des comptes faits* (1669) by François Barrême,

---

49 Ávila, *Modo fácil.*

50 Manuel González de la Torre, *Libro de cuentas hechas útil para toda clase de personas* (Gerona: Jaume Bró, 1750), 4.

51 Cervera, *El pensamiento económico*, 43–44.

52 Francesc Ifern, *Compendi breu de las quatre reglas generals de la arismetica practica* (1746; Gerona: Narcís Oliva, 1753), "Al benévolo lector," unpaginated.

a French mathematician and *protégé* of Cobert. The tables in the Catalan version aspired to cover all the Principality's productive activities, not only for merchants, shopkeepers and treasury officials but also for *entrepreneurs*. However, the parts of the book specifically related to the military were in Castilian Spanish, and in fact some complete editions of the book were published in Castilian in Barcelona. They were produced in alternate years there and in Gerona, which suggests that they were used by different productive agents, such as merchants and farmers. The book's long and fruitful life cycle lasted until the nineteenth century and bears witness to the fact that texts of this type were both simple and cheap to produce as they were published as smallish pamphlets with relatively few pages.[53] They would also have been a fail-safe business, which explains why they were issued by publishers such as Jaume Brò and Narcís Oliva in Gerona as well as by book merchants: Madrid book merchant Francisco Asensio published in the 1750s several coinage equivalence tables that were adapted to the 1737 law.

The treatises devoted to assaying precious metals with the aim of striking coins described the rules and techniques to be followed by mints to achieve the degree of fineness required by laws.[54] The cash value of the coins, and therefore the amount of gold and silver that was put into circulation and extracted abroad, depended on these laws. Therefore, these treatises were strategic for the Royal Treasury, which had incomes from seignioriage rights, and also for Spain, as the main international producer of precious metals. However, the traditional "mining monoculture" employed in the colonies, and other flawed economic policies, had turned the country into a type of "safe storehouse" from which these metals were then distributed all over the world.[55] The treatises thus echoed complaints about the planners of these damaging policies.[56] They began with the *Quilatador de oro, plata y piedras* (1572) by León-born silversmith Juan de Arfe y Villafañe (1535–1602) and reached the eighteenth century by means of a book about mining entitled *Arte de los metales* (1640) by

53 As it is mentioned in the *Tyrocinio aritmético, instrucción de las cuatro reglas llanas* (Zaragoza: José Fort, 1738). This brief booklet of basic mathematical rules was the first handbook written by a woman: the Aragon-born María Andrea Casamayor. She had to hide under a male pseudonym (Casandro Mamés de la Marca y Araioa).

54 On the extensive literature on Royal Mints in Spain, see, especially, Glen Murray, "Guía de los marcos acuñados y ensayadores de la Casa de Moneda de Madrid," *Numisma* 233 (1993), 295–387; Francisco de Paula Pérez Sindreu, *La casa de la moneda de Sevilla* (Seville: Universidad de Sevilla, 1991); and, on the Crown of Aragon mints prior to the *Nueva Planta*, Albert Estrada-Rius, *La casa de la moneda de Barcelona* (Lleida: Pagès, 2015).

55 Muñoz de Amador, *Arte*, 7; on this issue, see Bernal, *España*, 236–45.

56 Muñoz de Amador, *Arte*, 7ff.

Andalusian churchman Álvaro Alonso de Barba (1569–1662), which achieved an unusually high circulation for a Spanish technical book in the seventeenth and eighteenth centuries.[57]

As they were a manifestation of sovereignty, the contents and authors of these treatises were strictly controlled. They were written by silversmiths whose alacrity for mineral testing and mathematics had led them to join the closed professional body of assayers and coin stampers at the Royal Mints. The ancient Council of Castile prerogative to appoint these experts had been given to the Board of Trade, which became responsible for all coinage-related issues from 1730 onwards; this institution was now not only charged with nominating these experts,[58] but the treatises they produced also required its approval before publication, which explains why there were so few: Javier García Caballero (1713, 1731), José Tramullas y Ferreras (1734, 1743) and Bernardo Muñoz de Amador (1741, 1755). The first two were senior officials at the Royal Mint in Madrid, while the third performed the same role in Barcelona before moving to Madrid. From 1720–1760, their main functions revolved around the mints in Seville,[59] which produced most metals, and Madrid. Their status as Board of Trade employees accounted for the fact that their books were dedicated to Patiño (García Caballero) and Ensenada (Tramullas), who were their presidents.

The publications on metal assaying were official, and it is no surprise that they flourished under Felipe v's reforms. The functioning of the mints was prescribed by the ordinances of 1718, 1728 and 1730; while the first ceded the minting monopoly to the state, the last centralised the creation of all silver and gold coinage on the peninsular in the mints in Madrid and Seville, while all copper coins were to be struck in Segovia. The remaining mints in Castile were now closed; those in Aragon had already been shut down. The aim was to promote monetary unification, the centralisation of the mints and the mechanisation of their work, both in Spain and in the colonies, especially the replacing of the hammer technique with screw presses. The works also publicised the royal decrees establishing the values of gold and silver in carats and monies; in short, they were a firebreak for the monetary policies put in place by Felipe v,[60] who their authors considered the real architect of this much called-for protectionist

57 Álvaro Alonso de Barba, *Arte de los metales en que se enseña el verdadero beneficio de los de oro y plata por azogue, el modo de fundirlos todos, y cómo se han de refinar y apartar unos de otros* (1640; Madrid: Bernardo Peralta, 1770); Bernal, *España,* 236–37.

58 Muñoz de Amador, *Arte,* 211–12.

59 Bernal, *España,* 304–07.

60 Bernardo Múñoz de Amador, *Proporción aritmética-práctica de la plata* (Madrid: Antonio Marín, 1741).

policy. Proper enforcement of these laws was also essential from the international law perspective to guarantee fair trade with other countries.[61]

García Caballero (¿-1744) produced his first treatise in Seville in 1706 at the height of the War of Succession, although it was not published until the end of the conflict, in 1713, five years after the author had attained the position of chief assayer at the Madrid Mint, a strategic point for the development of laws. García Caballero dedicated his book to Felipe V, hoping that it would permanently replace Arfe's treatise on training assayers and coin stampers. A quarter of a century later he was still chief assayer and published an excellent historical investigation aimed at combatting the array of weights and measures and promoting unifying policies. Behind this lay support for the new King's reforms, in which the author had played a key role.[62] He also countered classical Castilian sources on the value of Spanish coins and their international equivalents, accusing Covarrubias, Moya and Juan de Mariana (1536–1624), author of the most influential history of Spain, of being over-theoretical. His books were not isolated cases, however. Metal assaying required guides and tables that publicised the changes in the law among silversmiths; as the assayers were the arbiters of these changes, the treatises assumed the central social function of combating fraud. Barcelona author Tramullas produced three noteworthy books on the issue which were commissioned by the Board of Trade to publicise the royal measures and persuade goldsmiths to respect the laws and their guild regulations (1732). It was simply a matter of tackling the manufacturers' "greed" and the gold and silver coin stampers' "lack of intelligence."[63] Tramullas was particularly well-qualified for this; not only was he chief assayer, he was also the Crown of Aragon's silversmiths' workshop inspector. One of his works was censored by the Salamancan Muñoz de Amador (¿-1759), who wrote the main overview of this remarkable types of books in 1755. He was already a highly experienced professional; having started out as a silversmith, he was recognised as an assayer in 1736 and joined the Madrid mint ten years later. His *Arte de ensayar*

61 García Caballero, *Breve cotejo,* 2. A further example of proximity to treatises with legal content, which made reference to the international law and included information about national and international monetary equivalences, is: José Manuel Domínguez Vicente, *Discursos jurídicos sobre las aceptaciones, pagas, intereses, y demás requisitos, y cualidades de las letras de cambio* (Madrid: Herederos de Juan García Infanzón, 1732), 491–516.

62 García Caballero, *Breve cotejo,* 8, 186ff.

63 José Tramullas y Ferreras, *Guía, y desengaño, de artífices plateros, y marcadores de oro, y plata* (Barcelona: Herederos de María Martí, 1743), Prólogo, unpaginated. He also published a text on equivalences between Catalan and Castilian coins: *Puntual correspondencia, y reducción verídica de la moneda de vellón de Cataluña a la de Castilla, y la de Castilla a la de Cataluña* (Barcelona: Herederos de María Martí, 1743).

oro y plata (1755) was dedicated to Juan Francisco Gaona, Count of Valdeparaíso. It was a compilation of theory and practice in the vein established by Arfe and Alonso de Barba and culminating with García Caballero, Tramullas and Portuguese expert Roque Francisco, all of whom he had followed "to the letter" within the framework of recent ordinances and laws.[64] Due to his thorough knowledge of the tradition he produced the eighteenth century's best summary of the assayer's craft, to which he dedicated one of the *Arte*'s three books.

Carlos III's accession to the throne in 1759 ratified the internal diversity hidden by merchants' handbooks. The publications by Miguel de Hualde and Pedro Cantos Benítez (¿-1763), issued barely five years apart, were good reflections of this. The first was the work of a Carmelite priest from Navarre, written in the form of a dialogue between an administrator and a lay accountant — the author himself —, and was pervaded by the age-old Scholastic concern over achieving justice in civil affairs.[65] By comparison, the second was a much better reflection of the arrival of a new political era and contained a splendid discourse on Spanish monetary history from ancient times to the Bourbons. Its political intent was clear: to show the long history of the Council of Castile, to which it was dedicated, as the supreme body of the regime. Cantos attacked the naturalist interpretation, which held the arts and sciences, particularly jurisprudence, to be worthless: the latter was essential for maintaining the laws of society and for ensuring that the government fulfilled its obligation to maintain "peace, utility and justice."[66] In this scheme of things, the currency emerged as proof of the Spanish monarchy's centuries-long relevance. It is therefore clear that the real audience was not merchants but the new political elites that had gathered around Carlos III: it was published in 1763, just four short years after the start of his reign.

6 Final Remarks

The merchants' handbooks published in Spain during the first six decades of the eighteenth century were on the whole collections of rudimentary and stale

64 Muñoz de Amador, *Arte*, 4, 12–13.

65 See the first of the three booklets in Miguel de Hualde's work, *El contador lego, especulativo y práctico, sobre varios asuntos de aritmética civil y astronómica* (Madrid: Francisco Javier García, 1758).

66 Pedro de Cantos Benítez, *Escrutinio de maravedises y monedas de oro antiguas, su valor, reducción y cambio a las monedas corrientes* (Madrid: Antonio Marín, 1763), 11–14. In the second part of the book he discussed old Spanish coins, mainly from Roman times, with the aim of tackling the conversion of their prices and contracts vis-à-vis current coins.

knowledge about mathematics and economics. Not only were they lacking in innovation — Moya's work cast a long shadow over them all —, but were simple repetitions, plagiarism or pastiches, whose limited originality was masked only by pretentious titles and little mention of sources. However, outside the intellectual history context, they had considerable social and cultural significance. They proliferated because in a state like Spain there was no alternative that was capable of covering essential social functions: thanks to their enormous versatility, they not only provided training in commercial arithmetic but also contributed to the spread of information, the reduction of transaction costs, the passing on of professional techniques and the struggle against fraud. This functional diversity explains why they appeared in so many formats, a factor that in itself makes them unique within the body of print culture. Nonetheless, this diversity fell short of that in Savary and Ricard's handbooks, which explains why Spain not only lacked a Board of Trade with the political capacity of France's and a trading centre with the power of Amsterdam, but also because the low level of internationalisation and the highly fragmented market, the handbooks tailored to town or regional dimensions were more useful than national or universal *vade mecums*.

At this point, the question arises as what type of audience the authors of the handbooks were addressing. The first readers were undoubtedly their sponsors. A further glance at the dedications reveals their writers' close proximity to nobles, clerics, senior officials and political authorities who may have had family, or other links to the world of trade or finance. Patronage was not only based on the authors' desire to promote themselves in the world of trade, finance or government, but also on the authorities' interest in protecting such literature as a personal contribution to the nation: these books underpinned "the fabric of society" and the "public good," thus providing a service to the King.[67] On the basis of this initial readership, it is possible to speculate as to their wider audiences: Zubiaur wrote his book for mathematics teachers; Fernández Anuncibay for "new trainees;" Atienza to bypass teachers; Coll y Alsina for his merchant son. Everything therefore points to a highly diverse audience, which also accounts for the wide variety of formats used. It has been noted that some texts were aimed at specialised professionals such as assayers, while others were written for social groups with low levels of literacy. Given the complexity of most of the books, however, most readers must have been educated adults,

67 Eduardo Crean, *Cálculo general de todos los cambios corrientes en estos reinos de España, con Francia, Inglaterra, Holanda, Portugal e Italia; compuesto en once cuadernos de tablas* (Madrid: Francisco Martínez Abad, 1737), unpaginated.

mainly experienced mathematics teachers, merchants and financers, who could use them in their schools, business offices and private houses.

Nevertheless, their usefulness extended far beyond the actual readership. These books were a unique expression of the significant explosion of print culture in the eighteenth century,[68] capturing on paper not only arithmetic and notions but also trading techniques and routines. Their introduction into offices and libraries meant that this became available to merchants and policy makers. As there were no regulated institutions for commercial training, official statistics or regular press, they were guarantees that knowledge would be handed on from one generation to another, accumulated and spread, if only, quite certainly, at local level. In addition, as Maravall recalled, the simple requirement to train social groups to respect the rigour of mathematical rules was in itself a feature of modernity.[69] Even more important was this body of literature's connection with the struggle for social dignity of commerce. In spite of proposing "a short voyage through the immense sea of numbers" (Corachán), commercial arithmetic was "the energy of other sciences" (Nebot); the "shining beacon" that guided nations (Santa Cruz); the "master key of trade" (Taboada); the set of "rules that accountants use, like painters use colours" (Santa Cruz); and, finally, "a type of criterion for measuring truth" (Moya). These books presented the mechanical activity of trade, which was stigmatised through social suspicions and misgivings over its religious legitimacy, as being interwoven with the "most subtle" noble and liberal art of mathematics. Thus, when in mid-century the "science of commerce" was conceived in Spain as a powerful weapon for political action, the battle to dignify trade became intertwined with the idea that merchants that had been trained by means of a regulated system and suitable handbook were an indispensable asset for the republic. In Campomanes' words, they were the "beacons of political economy," the type of individuals that stimulated the flow of blood in the state "as the heart does, pumping the blood around the human body."[70]

---

68 See, for example, Thomas Munck, *The Enlightenment. A comparative Social History 1721–1724* (New York: OUP, 2000). Spanish trans., *Historia social de la Ilustración* (Barcelona: Crítica, 2001), 115–53.

69 José Antonio Maravall, *Antiguos y modernos. La idea de progreso en el desarrollo inicial de una sociedad* (Madrid: Sociedad de estudios y publicaciones, 1966), 565–67.

70 Pedro Rodríguez de Campomanes, *Apéndice a la educación popular* (Madrid: Antonio de Sancha, 1775–1777), IV, XI-XII.

CHAPTER 2

Graef's *Discursos Mercuriales* (1752–1756) and the Origins of the Economics Press in Spain

1 Introduction: Graef and the *Discursos Mercuriales*

On 1 October 1752 the first issue of the *Discursos mercuriales* (DM), produced by Juan Enrique Graef (1710-?), was published. This periodical has been studied in depth,[1] and its eminent place in the history of Spanish journalism is due to its undeniable pioneering nature.[2] Founded during the reign of Fernando VI (1746–1759), Graef's journal represented a significant step forward in the creation of a relatively autonomous press that was both moderately critical and open to a "public" interested in "political" issues. It was also the first publication in Spain whose title explicitly referred to political economy, initially appearing under the title of *Discursos mercuriales económico-políticos*; its permanent name, *Discursos mercuriales. Memorias sobre la agricultura, marina, comercio, y artes liberales, y mecánicas* was coined three years later. For this reason it undoubtedly constituted the starting point of an economic press that would slowly but irreversibly emerge in Spain during the second half of the eighteenth century.

The little information available about the journalist Juan Enrique Graef (or Graaf), refers to his Flemish origins and the fact that he was one of many foreign experts recruited by the powerful minister Ensenada to boost the modernising of the Spanish economy during Fernando VI's first government. Before

1 The main source of this chapter is Jesús Astigarraga, "*Oikonomia* y 'Comercio' en la versión española del *Journal Oeconomique*: los *Discursos mercuriales* (1752–1756) de Graef," *Cuadernos de Historia Moderna* 42, no. 1 (2017): 239–60. A complementary work on Graef and his newspaper is Francisco Sánchez Blanco, "Los *Discursos mercuriales* (1752–1756) de Juan Enrique Graef," *Estudios de Historia Social* 52–53 (1990): 477–89, and "Introducción," in *Discursos Mercuriales económico-políticos (1752–1756)*, ed. Francisco Sánchez Blanco (Seville: Fundación El Monte, 1996), 19–76.

2 See mainly Juan Sempere y Guarinos, *Ensayo de una biblioteca de los mejores escritores de Carlos III* (Madrid: Imprenta Real, 1785–1789), IV, 176–98; Paul-J. Guinard, *La presse espagnole de 1737 à 1791. Formation et significance d'un genre* (Paris: Centre de recherches hispaniques, 1973); María Dolores Sáiz, *Historia del periodismo en España. Vol. 1. Los orígenes. El Siglo XVIII* (Madrid: Alianza, 1983); Inmaculada Urzainqui, "Un nuevo instrumento cultural: la prensa periódica," in *La República de las Letras en la España del Siglo XVIII*, ed. Joaquín Álvarez Barrientos, François Lopez and Inmaculada Urzainqui (Madrid: CSIC, 1995), 125–216.

 | DOI:10.1163/9789004442894_004

arriving in Spain Graef had studied navigation in Le Havre de Grâce (France) and had travelled widely in Europe. However, his summons to Spain may have been owing to his skills in economic development, specifically in farming and linen manufacturing; in 1744 he was living in Galicia and helping Gerónimo de Uztáriz's son to grow flax for making linen,[3] Ensenada's policy of recruiting foreign experts clearly gave rise to cultural transfers not only in scientific and technical fields but also in the political economy domain.[4] Graef was in fact a self-proclaimed professor of "the theory of commerce," an expression that seemed to allude less to any official training in the field than to his having cultivated a "propensity for trade" through "continuous reading, the different countries that I have seen and interacting with all kinds of people."[5] Once settled in Spain, Graef was able to travel throughout the peninsula, and in the 1750s he was living in Madrid, where he was involved in certain controversies arising between the capital's merchants and in fledgling institutions such as the Academy of San Fernando (1752), while at the same time working on the DM. The periodical had two phases: October 1752, and from October 1755 until July 1756.[6]

The DM's hesitant and meagre trajectory should be viewed in relation to the political career of Zenón de Somodevilla, Marquis of Ensenada (1702–1781), who was probably its driving force. The DM was published during the period in which the Marquis, in his position as the Secretary of the Treasury, the Americas, the Navy and War (1748–1754), was the strong man of Fernando VI's government, together with José de Carvajal (1702–1781). The possibility that the DM could have been "the voice and diffuser of the Minister's policies"[7] can be veiled deduced from the exhaustive *Representación* which Ensenada presented to Fernando VI as a government programme in November 1751.[8] Carrying out his reforms required shaping "opinion" in some way, especially given what

3 DM, no. VIII, 81ff.

4 Other similar cases to Graef were those of the French engineer Carlos Le-Maur, who translated *Elemens du commerce* (1754) by Forbonnais (*Elementos de comercio*, Madrid: Imprenta de Francisco Xavier García, 1765), and the Irish-born Bernardo Ward, author of the *Proyecto Económico* (c. 1762; Madrid: Joaquín Ibarra, 1779).

5 DM, no. I, paragraph LI.

6 Graef could have been the editor of the later *El duende especulativo sobre la vida civil* (Madrid, 1761); but this first "spectator" to the history of Spain was concerned with criticising customs and had no economic content.

7 Sánchez Blanco, "Introducción," 58. On Ensenada, see José Luis Gómez Urdáñez, *El proyecto reformista del marqués de Ensenada* (Lérida: Milenio, 1996), and, on Carvajal, José Miguel Delgado, *El proyecto político de Carvajal* (Madrid: CSIC, 2001).

8 SEV, XII, 260–82.

turned out to be ultimately insurmountable resistance from the nobility and clergy to the post-1749 implementation of Ensenada's main project: the land cadastre for the Crown of Castile and the *única contribución* or single tax.[9] However, the Secretary's influence was even greater in the discontinuation of the DM. When Ensenada was ousted in July 1754, the periodical remained as a type of channel of expression for related sectors, and praise for Ensenada's land cadastre and other reforms continued through to the last issue in July 1756. Four months later the new Minister for the Americas, Ricardo Wall (1694–1777), withdrew Graef's printing license, thus effectively silencing any opposition to the policies of Fernando VI's second government. The international economic context had changed enormously by then as a result of the outbreak of the Seven Years War: Graef was in favour of prolonging Ensenada's characteristic policy of neutrality.[10]

The DM was not an official newspaper; in his day only the *Gaceta de Madrid* (1697) and the *Mercurio Histórico y Político* (1738) enjoyed this status. Rather, the publication explored formulas that were new to Spain and were drawn from more highly-developed cultural nations. In response to those who accused him of "profaning the mysteries of the government"[11] or even of "political sacrilege," Graef argued the advantages of airing political and economic matters, and the DM thus laid the foundations for the emergence of a new "space," structured around an educated readership who was interested in these semi-clandestine "political" matters.[12] Issues relating to "commerce" figured prominently.[13] Together with education, the best way of combating the social prejudices against

9 Gómez Urdáñez, *El proyecto*, 177–88; on the Ensenada's reforms on the organization of the Royal Treasury, vid. Dubet and Solbes, *El rey*, 308–13.

10 José Luis Gómez Urdáñez, *Fernando VI* (Madrid: Arlanza, 2001): 95–124; Delgado, *El proyecto*, 81ff.

11 DM, no. 1, "Al Excmo. Señor Marqués de la Ensenada." This spirit was also evident in the periodicals of Rousset de Missy, to which reference is made later: *Magazin des evénements de toutes sortes, passés, présents, et futurs* (no. 1, 6 of August 1742, 1) conceived under the maxim "*post tenebras lux.*"

12 J.-H. Witthaus, "Los *Discursos mercuriales* de Juan-Enrique Graef. Acerca de la constitución de la esfera pública a mediados del siglo XVIII," in *Redes y espacios de opinión pública*, ed. Marieta Cantos (Cadiz: Universidad de Cadiz, 2006), 51–65. As in France, Graef fought against the politics of secrecy: James van Horn, *The Rise of the Public in Enlightenment Europe* (Cambridge: CUP, 2001). Spanish trans., *La aparición del público durante la Ilustración europea* (Valencia: Universidad de Valencia, 2009), 96; Robin J. Ives, "Political Publicity and Political Economy in Eighteenth Century France," *French History* 17, no. 1 (2003): 1–4.

13 Graef could have been inspired by authors such as Melon or Forbonnais, who were already known in Spanish enlightened circles. On the arrival in Spain of the Melon's *Essai* (1734) via Teodoro Ventura de Argumosa' *Erudición política* (Madrid: 1743), see Jesús Astigarraga,

commerce was to follow the British example of encouraging the publication of "political" journals. The political authorities must have been the chief beneficiaries of these writings: in reality, they would not have been able to access the information necessary to take appropriate government action without the help of "selfless men" with whom "they could talk freely and represent without pressure and without flattery."[14]

However, this new space, which was at once both tentatively autonomous and critical of political power, also had very clear limits. On the one hand, Graef's initiative was designed to be a type of "patriotic" firewall against foreigners such as Montesquieu, who distorted the undeniable virtues of the Spanish character. On the other hand, there were Ensenada's policies, of which Graef seems to have thorough knowledge, probably acquired through privileged channels close to the minister. The DM took on a semi-public format; it became a "political object" or what is commonly referred to as a "national interest."[15] The first target readers were political authorities and courtiers, who were greedy for reliable information so as to be able to establish appropriate policies to promote all the branches of "commerce;" political diseases "originate from what is not known and its entire health depends on it being known."[16] Graef not only defended the huge political commitment required by the Castilian land cadastre, but also lavished eloquent praise on Boulainvilliers in his references to his quest to transform French mayors into "immediate instruments" to solve the "public calamity."[17]

The "commerce" question filled the pages of the DM from the outset; even so, the publication suffered many vicissitudes and the first print run, which began in October 1752, was interrupted after two issues. The second run consisted of twenty instalments, one published every two months between 1 October 1755 and 21 July 1756.[18] Given that the exact reasons for this double launch of the DM are not known, the most plausible hypothesis is that this was due precisely to its disparate treatment of the subject of "commerce." As we shall see

---

"La dérangeante découverte de l'autre: les (més)aventures de *l'Essai politique sur le commerce* (1734) de Jean-François Melon dans l'Espagne du XVIIIe siècle," *Revue d'Histoire Moderne et Contemporaine* 57 (2010): 91–118.

14 DM, no. I, 12.

15 DM, no. XVI, 754.

16 DM, no. I, paragraph I.

17 DM, no. XV, 660–61. This spirit was fairly similar to that of Ward's *Obra pía* (1750) and *Proyecto económico* (c. 1762). Both these texts recommended creating a "political map" of the Kingdom to instruct ministers.

18 While these twenty issues contained around 110 texts in the form of memoirs, speeches, letters and ripostes, the DM did not carry book reviews.

in greater detail later, the publication was launched in September 1752 with a somewhat radical *Discurso Preliminar* based on natural law. The *Discurso* met with disapproval, not only from theologians, but also from the political authorities, who were obliged to spearhead the Spanish monarchy's essential shift towards "commercial policy." It is highly likely that the *Discurso*'s approach did not please those at the heart of the court who scrutinised the publication's initial contents, and printing was therefore quietly ceased after the second issue. When publication restarted three years later in October 1755, the opening *Discurso Preliminar* was far more tempered and in line with official political culture. However, as a result of this double launch the publication's economic content maintained an unequal balance between *Oikonomia* and the theoretical and political "science of commerce."[19]

2 The 1755 *Discurso Preliminar*

The main reason behind the conservative and official tone of the 1755 *Discurso Preliminar* is that it was written not by Graef but by an anonymous author who was undoubtedly very close to Ensenada. Its content bristled with references to authors who were well received in court circles, the journal's natural target readership: Fleury, Moreri, Bossuet, Dubos, the *Mémoires de Trevoux* and, of course, Feijoo. These sources were used in a lengthy historical narrative aimed at weaving an apologetic defence of the Spanish nation and culture. Spain's unquestionable under-development did not justify foreigners treating the Spanish as "Goths and barbarians whose conceit and arrogance is a scandal of humanity,"[20] but it did motivate an investigation into the causes of this backwardness. To Graef the main problem lay in Spain's scant regard for the productive arts that fell under the heading of "commerce:" agriculture, industry, the navy and trade. The 1755 *Discurso Preliminar* was thus imbued with a defence of this scientific, utilitarian and practical culture, which had mainly originated in Britain and was spreading rapidly through enlightened circles in Europe: in a nutshell, knowledge was the main lever for wealth.[21]

19 On the meaning of "science of commerce" in the French context, not always interchangeable with that of political economy, see Paul Cheney, *Revolutionary Commerce. Globalization and the French Monarchy* (Cambridge, Mss-London: Harvard University Press, 2010), 2ff.

20 DM, *Discurso Preliminar* (1755), 6.

21 Joel Mokyr, *The Lever of Riches* (New York-Oxford: OUP, 1990). Spanish trans., *La palanca de la riqueza* (Madrid: Alianza, 1993), 109ff., 143–44, 299–301. This *Baconian* backdrop was fairly similar to what Genovesi sought to introduce in the Naples under *Carlo di Borbone*

Graef believed that this notion should take hold in Spain, as a matter of urgency. In his view, simple emulation was the key; that is "imitating the efficiency and desire of foreigners to right wrongs."[22] One of his priorities was reforming the universities that had expelled Scholasticism from their halls and incorporated the new scientific culture. Another was to link Spain into the dense network of academies and "erudite" societies that were spreading across Europe, with their new criticism and discussion-based methods of sociability, academic chairs and original mechanisms of social emulation through awards and experiences.

Graef identified neglect of the useful arts as the main cause of Spain's backwardness, pointing to the nobility as being primarily responsible for the fact that Spaniards were — together with the Polish — the last "bystanders of the fortune of the other industrious Europeans."[23] Spanish society was held back by an intolerable sense of honour for the nobility; due to their countless inherited "extravagances," the noble class "wishes us to live in isolation and leisure." The chief antidote for Spain's secular backwardness was thus the creation of an active noble class, which would be brought up and educated to become involved in all the productive arts related to commerce and manufacturing, a project that was also supported by the most influential economic writers of the day, from Uztáriz and Zavala to Ulloa. However, this would require a decisive policy for the public protection of the useful arts, similar to those implemented by the main European sovereigns. Graef indirectly proposed Ensenada as minister of continental rank for these policies for the productive arts.[24] Everything had to be resolved within the framework of a political project based on enlightened absolutism: initiatives from the sovereign and the nobility around a patriotic programme to rehabilitate the useful arts should be combined. However, the form of government in Spain meant that this programme required additional efforts; unlike monarchies, republics and the "mixed" British system favoured participation in public matters and their constitutions thus fostered greater appreciation of the development of the arts, among which a prominent place was occupied by trade.

---

during the same period with his *Discorso sopra il vero fine delle lettere e delle scienze* (1754); see Robertson, *The Case*, 353–54; Reinert, *Translating empire*, 191–94.

22 DM, *Discurso Preliminar* (1755), 31.

23 DM, *Discurso Preliminar* (1755), 31.

24 On the dissemination of practical knowledge during Ensenada's ministry, see Gómez Urdáñez, *El proyecto*, 236–62.

3 The Chief Source of the *Discursos*: The *Journal Oeconomique*

When publication of the DM resumed in October 1755, Graef probably became its main author, although he must have had the help of a second writer due to his "scarce knowledge" of Spanish;[25] in any event, Graef essentially worked as a translator. Always inspired by the virtuous effects of emulation, he strongly defended the social usefulness of translations, particularly in a country such as Spain, which was paralysed by a century-long cultural delay. In 1752 he stated that it had taken him "more than eight years" to collect the material for his periodical; material that in the case of the "theory of commerce" had been published six years earlier.[26] However, these statements do not tally with a basic analysis of the DM's hidden sources; the materials from external collaborators and those drawn from certain French journals that were fairly well-known in Spain at that time — such as *Mémoires de Trevoux* — were clearly a minority in comparison to those taken from the *Journal Oeconomique* (JOE, 1751–1767).[27]

The JOE was a magnificent exponent of the intense emergence of enlightened thought in France in the 1750s. From the first issue in 1751 its *leitmotif* was a scientific and utilitarian orientation, following in the footsteps of the iconic first volume of Diderot-D'Alembert's *Encyclopédie*, which had been published a few months earlier. Graef's overall design for the DM is more than likely to have imitated the format of the monthly French publication. The two journals showed many similarities: their semi-public nature, their formal characteristics and the same multidisciplinary content, which ranged from fine arts and commercial geography to engineering and natural science, all with a Baconian undercurrent. Not only was the detailed description of the contents of the DM similar to that in the JOE,[28] but a good part of its memoirs, including the most original in the Spanish context,[29] were taken from JOE and translated before appearing in the DM. The JOE was without doubt Graef's main source for the

25 DM, no. XVI, 754.

26 DM, *Discurso Preliminar* (1755), paragraphs LI, LII.

27 On the JOE, see Jean Sgard, *Dictionnaire des journalistes (1600–1789)* (Grenoble: 1976, http://dictionnaire-journalistes.gazettes18e.fr/journaliste). This source, together with the Sgard's *Dictionnaire des journaux (1600–1789)* (Paris: 1991, http://dictionnaire-journaux.gazettes18e.fr/journal), has been consulted in this book in relation to the press outside Spain.

28 Cfr. DM, *Discurso Preliminar* (1755), 53ff.; JOE, 1 January 1751, 5ff.

29 There is a detailed comparison in Astigarraga, "*Oikonomia* y comercio," 246–49.

DM — essentially the Spanish version of the iconic French enterprise — a fact that did not go unnoticed by other Spanish journalists.[30]

4 *Oikonomia* in the *Discursos Mercuriales*

The DM's economic content was disparate and heterogeneous and appeared to lack any preconceived plan.[31] However, if it could be said to be characterised by a *filo rosso*, it was undoubtedly *Oikonomia* or *Oeconomie*. This subject matter increased the JOE's influence over the DM; deemed the pioneer on economic issues in France,[32] the former's content veered away from its original affinity with *Oeconomie* and began incorporating the "(political) science of commerce"[33] after coming under the influence of the Gournay circle in 1754.[34]

30 See CGH, II, 218. Nifo and Saura will make use of the JOE in their subsequent journalistic ventures.

31 The DM also published discourses on legal economics (insurance, privateers or mail), banking, fishing or mining. Trade geography was also present in news about different European enclaves (Genoa, Russia, Minorca or Leipzig) and colonies (in general, the British colonies as a whole). Its suggestions regarding hospice policy had already been proposed by Ward in his *Obra pía* and seem to have been taken from the Spanish translation of Joshua Gee by Benito de Novoa, following the French version by Jean-Baptiste de Secondat: *Consideraciones sobre el comercio y la navegación de la Gran Bretaña* (Madrid: Imprenta de Juan de San Martín, 1753), 64ff., 110ff.

32 Philippe Steiner, "Les grandes revues économiques de langue française au XVIIIe siècle (1751–1776)," in *Les revues françaises d'économie politique XVIIIe-XIXe siècle*, ed. Luc Marco (Paris: L'Harmatan, 1996), 35–37, 46–52, and *La 'science nouvelle' de l'économie politique* (Paris: PUF, 1998), 13–14. On the Italian case, see Massimo Augello, Marco Bianchini and Marco E. L. Guidi, eds., *Le riviste di economia in Italia (1700–1900)* (Milan: F. Angeli, 1996). In Britain commerce had already appeared as a "national political issue" in the press, dating back to the controversies between *The Mercator* and *The British Merchant* with the signing of the 1713 French-British trade treaty; see Perry Gauci, *The Politics of Trade: the Overseas Merchant in State and Society, 1660–1720* (Oxford, OUP, 2001), ch. VI. However, beyond the specialized press, on topics about commerce in newspapers published in London and in provinces, vid. Glaisyer, *The Culture*, 143ff, and Raven, *Publishing*, 165–73. Finally, on the pioneering role of the United Provinces during the *early* Enlightenment, see Israel, *Radical Enlightenment*, 145ff.

33 Arnaud Orain. "Le *Journal Oeconomique*, le cercle de Gournay et le pouvoir monarchique: quelques preuves matérielles d'un lien organique," *Dix-Huitième Siècle* 45 (2013): 567ff.

34 The recent and extensive literature on this circle does justice to its crucial role in the dissemination of economic thought throughout Europe; see Loïc Charles, Frédéric Lefebvre and Christine Théré, eds., *Le cercle de Vicent de Gournay* (Paris: INED, 2011), and, complementarily: Catherine Larrère, *L'invention de l'économie au XVIIIe siècle. Du droit naturel à la physiocratie* (Paris: PUF, 1992), 95–193; Simone Meyssonnier, *La balance et*

Georges-Marie Butel Dumont took advantage of his role as editor of the JOE to steer it towards the stances taken by this highly reputable circle, after which it began to publish summaries of books by Herbert, Plumard de Dangeul and Duhamel de Monceau, followed by a section on "extracts from English periodicals" to divulge the work of Gournay's favourite British authors (Gee, Hume and Tucker) and supporting freedom of the arts and of the grain trade.

Oeconomie was the "central science" of both the JOE and the DM from the start.[35] In one of the latter's first issues Graef published an insightful report on the "*Principios de la Economía, fundados sobre la ciencia natural y sobre la física*."[36] Presented anonymously as an original article, it was in fact written by Linneo and was taken from the JOE in which this work had played an essential role in guiding its main direction. In the *Principios,* Linneo, the Swedish botanist and zoologist, addressed the *Oeconomie*'s relationships with the natural sciences and physics, that is, the administration of a property through these sciences. It took a classic approach to economics — or economic science — , that is, to quote Graef, as "a science that uses the elements to teach us how to use natural things;" hence economics' affinity with physics, botany and similar disciplines. Adopting the scientific standards expounded in these fields would improve the exploitation of natural resources, as well as bringing about a closer association between theory and practice. The main aim was to achieve the efficient exploitation of the three branches of the natural world: metals, agriculture and livestock, which constituted the basis of states' power. In short,

---

l'horloge. La genèse de la pensée libérale en France au XVIIIe siècle (Paris: Les éditions de la passion, 1989), 161–275; Antoin Murphy, "Le développement des idées économiques en France (1750–1756)," *Révue d'histoire moderne et contemporaine* XXXIII, (1986): 521–41; Reinert, *Translation empire,* 142ff.; Jean-Claude Perrot, *Une histoire intellectuelle de l'économie politique* (Paris: EHESS, 1992); Takumi Tsuda, "Un économiste trahi, Vincent de Gournay (1712–1759)," in Jacques-Claude-Marie Vincent de Gournay, *Traités sur le commerce de Josiah Child avec les Remarques inédites de Vicent de Gournay*, ed. Takumi Tsuda (Tokyo: Kinokuniya Company, 1983), 445–85. No summary of the situation in Spain is available.

35 The discourses that structured this perspective are: no. III, "Principios de la economía, fundados sobre la ciencia natural y sobre la física" (1–25); no. III, "Cultivo del lino" (45–62); no. IV, "Tratado de la agricultura en general, de la naturaleza de los granos y de su conservación y gobierno" (1–24); no. V, "Continuación sobre la agricultura y anatomía del grano y su vegetación" (19–35); no. VIII, "Continuación sobre el cultivo del lino" (73–90) and "Principios de las labores del campo, huertas y jardines, para los doce meses del año" (139–59); no. XI, "Extracto de una carta escrita por un profesor de Suecia sobre el estado de la historia natural" (387–92); no. XIII, Examen de las tierras para la labranza" (489–507); no. XV, "Discurso sobre el modo de regar los campos y de mejorar las tierras" (653–80); no. XVIII, "Mejora del cultivo de las tierras" (945–66).

36 DM, no. III, 2.

Graef maintained that "natural history is the basis of economics" and referred to the existence of an "economic natural science."[37]

The *Oeconomie*'s line of thought was underpinned by a series of very conservative ideas based on the divine origin of natural resources. It favoured practical vision over theory and was spread through the classical metaphors on nature such as harmonic bodies, describing trade as a circulation system similar to blood. A particularly prominent metaphor was the equating of the apparatus of the state with a family, and this type of analogy was also used to liken public and domestic finance or parents and benefactors and paternalistic political authorities. All a father's "economic" virtues were also possessed by the head of state: sobriety, prudence and the rejection of luxury, which coincided with the etymology of the word "economics" as a "prudent manager." In fact, in the DM Graef addressed an agent, to whom he repeatedly referred as "wise," "judicious" a "prudent" "manager" and "industrious." As such managers had to run their estates on the basis of respect for the principles of this "economic natural science," which merged with physics and the natural sciences, it was therefore appropriate to promote their education in new rural academies through informative texts with an emphasis on grain farming, which was one of *Oeconomie*'s essential branches.

In fact, in the DM, *Oeconomie* was essentially projected on an agrarian-based economy and most of the papers it carried were dedicated to agriculture.[38] Their *filo rosso* was the discontent caused by the fact that agriculture had been forgotten in Spanish politics, as well as in the main economics texts of the 18th century. Graef was a pioneer in the capturing of the agrarian turn characterising the European Enlightenment: his tacit criticism of Uztáriz and Ulloa's tradition is clear here. This was particularly serious, given that the agricultural sector was undoubtedly a better guarantee of national power and wealth than commerce or manufacturing: according to Jean-Baptiste Duhalde, the archetype of Chinese agriculture operated powerfully vis-à-vis the strength of the trading republics.[39] However, Graef's periodical also provided a conservative perspective in this respect. The DM was not open to the Anglo-French

37 DM, no. XI, 388. On Linneo and his conception of economics as a component of natural philosophy, see Schabas, *The Natural*, 29–35, 40–42.

38 Approximately thirty per cent of the articles in the DM were related to agriculture and were either reflections on the principals of the farming economy or experiences and practical regulations for the promotion of raw materials, fruit, etc. They accounted for about forty per cent if the news relating to other frontier sciences and arts such as the natural sciences, botany, mining and fishing are added. On agromania in 1750s France see, Shovlin, *The Political Economy*, 51–58.

39 DM, no. VIII, 73–4.

"new agronomy" encouraged by Tull and Duhamel de Monceau, despite the fact that this had been covered in both the JOE and Duhamel de Monceau's *Traité* (1750), which was translated into Spanish in 1751.[40] Far removed from all this, the sources of Graef's agricultural *Oeconomie* were the agronomic treatises based on Spanish and French geoponic tradition. The best expression of this is Alonso de Herrera's lengthy unfinished discourse, which was published between January and July 1756 and focused on sixteenth century Castilian agronomy. Meanwhile, although the DM alluded to different French naturalist philosophers, such as Buffon, Linneo and Reaumur, and sought to rehabilitate the Spanish tradition initiated by Feijoo, its allegiance was closer to French treatises on traditional agriculture, specifically those by Vallemont, Liger and Pluche, Spanish translations of which were already in print.[41] The fact that the treatise by Pluche, a Jansenist philosopher, constituted a basic element of the DM once again highlights the way the journal fitted perfectly into the political culture of the time: Esteban de Terreros published a full version of Pluche's lengthy natural history treatise between 1753 and 1755,[42] which was one of the most important translations in 1750s Spain.[43]

40 Henri-Louis Duhamel de Monceau, *Tratado del cultivo de granos* (Madrid: José Ortega, 1751). The version produced at Campomanes' behest included the translation from Arabic of two chapters of Abu Zacharia's agricultural treatise; Llombart, *Campomanes*, 66–67. The real diffusion in Spain of the "new agriculture" promoted by Duhamel, Patullo, etc. began later, during the sixties.

41 For the Spanish translations by Louis Liger (1728), Pierre Lorrain de Vallemont (1735) and Noël-Antoine Pluche (1753–1755), see Ernest Lluch and Lluis Argemí, *Agronomía y fisiocracia en España (1750–1820)* (Valencia: Alfonso el Magnánimo, 1985): 9–14.

42 Nöel-Antoine Pluche, *Espectáculo de la naturaleza, o conversaciones acerca de las particularidades de la historia natural* (Madrid: Gabriel Ramírez, 1753–1755); it was republished in 1755–1758, 1771–1773 and 1785. Terreros, a Jesuit, was a mathematics teacher at the Real Seminario de Nobles de Madrid. In his "Translator's Prologue" (I, 1753, unpaginated), he described the technical difficulties involved in the translation and he intensified the conservative nature of Pluche's book even more. It is no accident that the cycle of translations of Archbishop Fénelon's *Les Aventures de Télémaque* (1699), published in Spain in the 1750s, should begin then. This "great metaphor" of the art of governing, with its virtuous, austere, peaceful and agraniarist message, was also both a best seller and a long seller in Spain; vid. Marco E. L. Guidi and Marco Cini, eds., *Le avventure delle 'Aventures'. Traduzioni del 'Télémaque' di Fénelon tra Sette e Ottocento* (Pisa: Edizioni ETS, 2017), 145–57, 159–90; on Fénélon, see Lionel Rothkrug, *Opposition to Louis XIV. The Political and Social Origins of the French Enlightenment* (Princeton: Princeton University Press, 1965), 234–98, and Hont, *Jealousy*, 25–27.

43 For an overview, vid. Françoise Étienvre, "Traducción y renovación cultural a mediados del siglo XVIII en España," in *Fénix de España*, ed. Pablo Fernández Albaladejo (Madrid: Marcial Pons, 2006): 93–117.

Although the DM was essentially influenced by the JOE, when the latter fell under the influence of the Gournay circle, the DM's stance did not shift, a fact that is clearly reflected in its treatment of the thorny question of the grain trade. In January 1756 Graef announced the publication of a discourse on the topic, to include a reflection on measures to avoid shortages and taking a critical standpoint vis-à-vis its free export.[44] The approach echoed Herbert's *Essai* (1753), which had already been reviewed in the JOE. However, the discourse was never finished, and when Graef returned to the subject months later, he expressed his opposition to the organising of the grain trade through private warehouses, feeling that this would reduce prices and bring labourers to ruin.[45] The liberalising of trade, one of the hallmarks of the Gournay circle, therefore represented a threat to the *Oeconomie* of a "prudent manager" and for this reason the DM did not endorse the Gournay circle and its emphasis on starting to combine "freedom" with "protection,"[46] in spite of the fact that around the same time the first translations of Herbert and Plumard de Dangeul's books had begun to circulate in Spain.[47] All this was a reflection of the persistence of a conservative, paternalistic and Catholic agrarian approach.

5 From *Oikonomia* to the "Science of Commerce:" The *Discourse on Commerce in General* (1755–1756)

Graef began publishing a new *Discurso* — or *Tratado* — *sobre el comercio en general* in the DM's second issue in November 1755.[48] This was the longest discourse in the whole publication: not only were there three additional instalments, but it was intended to be read together with the 1752 *Discurso Preliminar*,[49] of which it was undeniably a continuation. These two *Discursos* seem to have been based on two main sources. The first were the reflections on the "political" science of commerce supported by the Gournay group; however, they were not spread by the JOE when Butel Dumont was editor, but in the

44 DM, no. IV, 3.

45 DM, no. XV, 657–58.

46 Murphy, "Le développement," 521–41.

47 Francisco Quintana, *Dos discursos sobre el gobierno de los granos, y cultivo de las tierras* (Madrid: Francisco Xavier García, 1755). The translation was instrumental in nature and undertaken to support the agricultural reform of 1756–1757 which gave rise to the liberalisation of domestic trade and a moderate opening up to foreign trade.

48 DM, no. IV, 25–78; no. IX, 176–202; no. XIV, 617–32; no. XX, 1104–117. The *Discurso* was never finished.

49 DM, no. I, *Discurso preliminar* (1752).

economic writings of Gournay's most conspicuous disciple, François Véron de Forbonnais, specifically *Le Négociant Anglois* (1753).[50] The second source was Jean Rousset de Missy,[51] a Huguenot journalist and historian in exile in the Netherlands. Graef was particularly indebted to his extensive writings, especially the gazettes published in Amsterdam after 1741 under the title of *Magazin des événements de toutes sortes, passés, présents et futurs* and reissued with different titles throughout the 1740s. The most relevant were two series published after the Aachen Treaty (1748): *Le Vrai patriote hollandais* (1748–1750) and *L'Epilogueur moderne* (1750–1755).

Graef's *Discurso* took a new approach to *Oeconomie*, and at its heart was the meaning of "commerce." His analysis was connected with natural law and the law of nations, the legal tradition created by Grocio, with which someone like Graef, who was Dutch, was undoubtedly familiar.[52] The 1752 *Discurso Preliminar* explained that when all countries had substantiated their autonomous political status in the form of kingdoms or states, existing law found its form of organisation in the *Jure Naturae et Gentium*; this was an allusion to Pufendorf's work, which seemed to inspire Graef, and whose aim was the greater "desirability of all individuals of a state." This went beyond conventional legal science, and while it was able to inform about positive right and the history of laws, it was not capable of specifying the regulatory link between laws and the common good. While the "digests and *pandectes* and their commentators" emerged "*ad infinitum*," natural rights and the laws of nations clearly showed

50 François Véron de Forbonnais, *Le négociant anglois, ou traduction libre du livre intitulé: The British Merchant, contenant divers mémoires sur le commerce de l'Angleterre avec la France, le Portugal et l'Espagne* (Dresde: 1753). This was a partial translation of *The British Merchant*, a series of articles compiled by Charles King and published between 1713 and 1714 in the periodical with the same title. Forbonnais understood this book to contain the "healthy maxims of commerce" (*Le négociant*, I, XXVI); however, it was more than a simple translation, as Forbonnais used it to present his epistemological method, together with his rejection of a navigation act, his "commercial monarchy" project and his way of interpreting international relations; vid. Antonella Alimento, "Beyond the Treaty of Utrecht: Véron de Forbonnais' French Translation of *the British Merchant* (1753)," *History of European Ideas* 40, no. 8 (2014): 1044–66.

51 On Rousset de Missy, vid. Margaret Jakob, *Radical Enlightenment. The Origins of Freemasonry: Facts an Dictions* (Philadelphia: University of Pensilvania Press, 2006): 62ff.; Dieter Gembicki, "Le journalisme à sensation: *L'Epilogueur moderne* (1750–1754) de Rousset de Missy," in *Le Journalisme d'Ancien Régime* (Lyon: Presses universitaires de Lyon, 1982): 241–55; Christiane Berkvens-Stevelinck and Jeroom Vercruysse, eds., *Le métier de journaliste au XVIIIe siècle* (Oxford: VF, 1993).

52 A decade before Graef, José del Campillo recommended including natural law and the law of nations in the Spanish education system, following Heineccio's moderate book: *España despierta* (c. 1743; Oviedo: 1993), voice "letrados y leyes."

the path towards achieving the greater usefulness of the state and its subjects; thus, "they enlighten us in order to enjoy it better than the civil laws of the ancient emperors."[53]

In defence of this legal tradition, Graef appealed to authorities on humanism and *iusnaturalism,* such as Lipsio, Klock, Grocio, Pufendorf and Schelius. He did not hold back in declaring that, thanks to the implementation of this tradition, the ubiquitous role of theologians had been limited to that of simple consultants on matters of conscience. In the civil and criminal fields this sphere had passed into the hands of jurists and lawyers, and in the ecclesiastic field to canonists. However, the problem of modern politics was different to that of the old disputes between the theologist-politicians and the *juris*-politicians. According to Graef, none of the legal traditions of the "theological state" or of the "law of nations" provided access to what he called the "policy of commerce." In Spain matters concerning this policy unfortunately remained in the hands of theologians and jurists, but in practice neither of them was capable of dealing with them, as both lacked the necessary precise knowledge. The outcome of Graef's reasoning was a sturdy disparagement, not only of theologians, but also of the *juris*-politicians who dominated the bureaucratic machinery and who would undoubtedly have been the DM's first readers, and consequently those who were probably keenest to interrupt its publication. Graef's final message was that they were not qualified to lead the forced shift of the Spanish monarchy towards the "policy of commerce;" in short, to accept that commerce had become the fundamental element of modern politics.

Behind these arguments were very specific political interests related to the reform of the Spanish Board of Trade, the main state body for stimulating economic growth. However, the Board never managed to silence criticisms of its structure and composition; these began in 1720 and involved prestigious writers such as Uztáriz.[54] The Board came under attack for two main reasons: firstly, instead of having the same status as the councils and ministries, it was merely a treasury advisory committee with limited executive powers and poorly-defined competences; secondly, the eight to twelve members of its managing Board did not hail from the merchant or professional classes but were instead civil servants recruited from the councils, mainly from the Councils of Castile, the Indies and, after 1730, the Treasury; they had legal backgrounds and devoted very little time to the Board's affairs. The need for reform

53 DM, no. I, *Discurso Preliminar* (1752), paragraph XLIV.

54 Uztáriz called for the creation of a "Main Board or Trade Council," made up of individuals who were "intelligent and skilled" in trade; *Teórica y práctica de comercio y de marina* (1724; Madrid: Aguilar, 1768): 410. On this issue, see ch. IV and X above.

was clear. In fact, Graef's *Discurso* coincided with the time when the Board first opened up to new specialists from the world of commerce, among whom the two most important were Bernardo Ward (¿-1759) and Francisco de Craywinkel (1713–1772).[55]

In his *Discurso sobre el comercio en general,* Graef continued to outline what he called the "philosophy of commerce," seeking to persuade readers that this was the only "political medicine" that could cure the battered Spanish monarchy. The central theme was clearly Pufendorf's principle of the sociability of commerce.[56] Commerce constituted a "smooth, charitable and glorious" means of underpinning political society. Insofar as it was an activity dedicated to the creation and appropriation of wealth, he assumed a "society of free and independent men," who had the liberty to attempt to create their own wealth through reciprocal agreement. This implied the right to the peaceful enjoyment of goods: the ideas of national power and the universal monarchy based on military superiority had become obsolete. It also implied the rejection of any political community of slaves or one governed by a tyrant: as the government seized the wealth in both these types of society they were irremediably poor. In contrast, commerce was the chief mechanism for attracting wealth, which both contributed to well-being and formed the basis of the state's opulence and power. Commerce had become an essential tool, not only for expanding this power, but also for simply maintaining it, thus emerging as an inescapable activity for achieving the political objective of public happiness; in short, the cornerstone which Graef called "true politics." This justified its attracting not only merchants, but also statesmen. Once again, Graef accused these "pseudo politicians," "backstreet politicians," "promoters of crackpot schemes," "clerks" or "vain politicians" of not knowing the most elementary rules of commerce. It was their incompetence that frustrated the possibility of reforming the stagnant Spanish monarchy and introducing the management of this key element into state policy.

Graef's recognition that commerce had become a "science" and as such had "its own rules, axioms and postulates"[57] marked a watershed in Spanish

55 Pere Molas, *Hombres de leyes, economistas y científicos en la Junta General de Comercio, 1679–1832* (Barcelona: CSIC, 1981), 8–11, and "La Junta General de Comercio y Moneda: la institución y los hombres," *Cuadernos de Historia. Anexo de la Revista Hispania* 9 (1978): 1–36.

56 See Larrère, *L'invention,* ch. 1; Hont, *Jealousy of Trade*, 159–84. Graef felt this principle to be a divine commandment, which implies that he probably read Pufendorf through Barbeyrac, his French translator.

57 DM, no. 4, 191.

Enlightenment thought. These rules were different to those of theology or law, so they could not be accessed through these traditional disciplines: "neither natural law nor the law of nations has created rules to establish manufacturing or navigation."[58] "Trade policy" matters therefore belonged to a different jurisdiction, "other than the state," although always subject to the rule of law and was therefore a partial jurisdiction which had to be anchored between freedom and sovereignty.[59] Merchants should have the right to be consulted about the affairs of this jurisdiction, to administer their own courts or to take matters to the legislator when measures against commerce were established, but always under the umbrella of the general laws and precepts of political authority. Commerce could not usurp the privileges of the legislative authority, which should "be allowed to govern."

Respecting this hierarchy was an obligation, as the interests of private merchants and the state were not necessarily the same. This analysis carries strong echoes of Forbonnais' ideas.[60] Although the interests of commerce and the state were inseparable, they had contradictory objectives, such that commerce could be useful for merchants but disastrous for the state. A need therefore arose to create a "political" science of commerce which defined the two fields clearly and established the hierarchy of the public sphere vis-à-vis the private domain: commerce should receive "protection" from the state,[61] but "true politics" should "steamroll over individual interests."[62] Its function was precisely to match individual interests with the public interests, identifying any activities carried out by private merchant that went against the common good. This implied rejecting the identification of public interests with those of the Royal Treasury: that is, for example, rejecting the possibility of levying new taxes or creating exclusive privileges with the only objective of satisfying the interests of the Treasury or a greedy *arbitrista* of impossible schemes. The culmination of this "true politics" which Graef called for was the inseparability of the interests of the nation, the crown and commerce. Refusal to reform the common idea of trading interests was tantamount to acknowledging the ruin of the state.

58 DM, no. I, *Discurso Preliminar* (1752), paragraph XLVIII.

59 Cfr., for example, with de Rousset de Missy, *Le vrai patriote hollandais*, IV, no. XV, 17 March 1749, 114ff.

60 Forbonnais, *Le négociant*, I, 1.

61 Forbonnais, *Le négociant*, I, IV. This defence included support for tariff protection, an omnipresent idea in the Gee's work; as indicated, it had been translated in Spain in 1753.

62 DM, no. IV, 68.

This is thrown further into relief if it is recalled that Graef published the DM amidst the European debate on how the military and commercial success of the trading republics and Great Britain were challenging absolute monarchies, which implied a radical transformation in the order of these monarchies' traditional civic virtues. The new patriotism of commerce required not only abandoning the anachronous division between the liberal and mechanical arts — including the retail trade — but also accepting the principle of honouring commerce with nobility, with all its consequences. Bestowing noble titles on merchants was what Great Britain and the Netherlands had done; there they were treated like heroes who ensured the country's happiness at their own personal cost. It was therefore necessary to transform the classical virtues that had given rise to the nobility and encourage a new patriotism based on the virtues of commerce; this was all to be found in Gournay and his circle's propaganda path in favour of the *noblesse commerçante*, even before Coyer's well-known text appeared. In addition to its economic advantages, *doux commerce* had helped to generalise a series of virtues that were well-known in Spain before the word "commerce" became "bland and unpleasant," like liberality or charity, which were necessary for strengthening social ties.

However, Graef was highly aware that Spain faced many problems in its attempt to advance towards a "commercial monarchy." Not only was there a mistaken but widespread sense of nobility in the country, which prevented commercial activity from being honoured and decorated, but there was also general lack of interest in the theory of commerce, as well as the difficulties inherent in the Catholic tradition: in Spain it was "almost contradictory to be both a trader and Christian."[63] Despite this, Graef did not hesitate to declare the virtues of the "policy of commerce." In reality, from among those who abided by political laws and were governed by the rules of prudence, it was the merchants who most contributed to the propagation of the Catholic religion and helped to sustain the Crown. That is the reason why Spain was happy when it became a trader.

Graef reproduced the designs of natural law with respect to the "science" of commerce, fusing the universality of its principles in the field of politics with the plurality of laws and customs; his debt to Forbonnais was once again evident here. Although Graef used a language with an intense iusnaturalist character, calling for axioms, postulates and geometric rules, this did not diminish his certainty that the science of commerce should adapt to individual contexts. The title of his *Discurso* included the exact expression "commerce

---

63 DM, no. IV, 26.

in general," which seemed to be an allusion to Cantillon's *Traité sur la nature du commerce en général,* published anonymously in Paris in 1755 on Gournay's initiative,[64] although there is no sign of this in the *Discurso.* This revealing expression referred to a country's overall — rather than sectorial — trade policy, in a similar way to Forbonnais' use.[65] Forbonnais also inspired the rules that organised the theoretical and practical branches of this new science; Graef identified the former with the study of the different means that nations established to govern their trade. Doing so required precise information about the branches, laws and circumstances that affected this governance and the new science was therefore differed little from the study of the "particular details" that Forbonnais called for;[66] however, unlike Forbonnais or Davenant, Graef did not use the quantitative branch of political arithmetic as an essential tool for developing the new science,[67] and thus the acknowledgement of the existence of a theory of trade was not substantiated by a body of abstract and universally applicable laws, as the Physiocrats would do soon after.[68] In any event, Graef followed Forbonnais and maintained that the "new science" of commerce required a new and regulated form of education. Just as merchants needed an education — in 1755 Graef outlined a training plan for the "perfect merchant" inspired by Savary's tradition —, Graef agreed with Forbonnais and Davenant's pioneering recommendation that education in commerce should also be promoted for statesmen and high-ranking civil servants in enlightened Spain, appealing to the authorities to underline the fact that even in exemplary Great Britain, the "science of commerce" still lacked a regulated education system. Graef thus made the transition from Uztáriz to Forbonnais,[69] and wrote a first chapter about the decisive influence exercised by Forbonnais' political economy in Spain in the 1750s and 1760s.[70]

---

64 Richard Cantillon, *Essai sur la nature du commerce en général* (1755; New York: Routledge, 2015).

65 Forbonnais, *Le négociant,* I, 209ff.

66 Forbonnais, *Le négociant,* I, XXVII-XXVIII, 1–2.

67 In *Le négociant,* Forbonnais included a translation of the Davenant's essay *Of the Use of Political Arithmetick* (1698).

68 It should be noted that the publication of the early Physiocratic writings in *L'Encyclopédie,* by Quesnay, coincided with the closing of Graef's periodical.

69 It is worth noting that Uztáriz's *Théorica* had been translated into French in 1753 by Forbonnais himself. In his "Préface du traducteur" he elaborated on ideas which Graef later incorporated into the DM, such as the advantage of commerce for conquests and the idea that during its Golden Age Spain enjoyed the principles of trade: *Théorie et pratique du commerce et de la marine* (Hamburg: Chrétien Herold, 1753), III, VI-VII.

70 Jesús Astigarraga, "Forbonnais and the Discovery of the 'Science of commerce' in Spain (1755–1765)," *History of European Ideas* 40, no. 8 (2014): 1087–107.

The transposition which required accepting commerce as a reason of state in a monarchy led Graef to assess the benefits of different political constitutions, once again seeking to import policies that could be useful for Spain. Graef observed that Spain was an underdeveloped and dependent economy, usurped both at home and in its colonies by the power of Great Britain, France and the Netherlands. The DM was a powerful sounding board for the unstable international political situation in which it was conceived, specifically between the Treaty of Aachen and the beginning of the Seven Years' War. There is no doubt that Graef knew Montesquieu; however, his treatment of the issue was more in keeping with echoes of Rousset's writings.[71] The Treaty of Aachen made it possible for his periodicals to become more than a mere war report, and he transformed them into a powerful sounding board for the diffusion of natural law, particularly for authors such as Grocio, Pufendorf and Barbeyrac, but also Locke and Mably, as well as figures of Dutch political philosophy such as Bayle. Rousset sought to apply these ideas to the new context of European politics, repeatedly addressing problems of civil sovereignty, the division of powers and forms of government in his journals, in which he also defended the Anglo-Dutch alliance, condemned the French monarchy and showed his preference for the Dutch republican system and, to a lesser extent, the British "mixed" system. The DM emphatically criticised France's aspiration to become a universal monarchy, of which Spain was a victim; when Felipe V became King, Spain's manufacturing market began to be dominated by French merchants. The most imminent danger, which Charles Davenant and William Wood had identified, was that France would appropriate Dutch trade,[72] and this led Graef to defend the Anglo-Dutch alliance. Publication of the DM began again after the start of the Seven Years' War in 1755–1756; Graef was highly aware that this was not due to purely military or political reasons but essentially to "trade" reasons.

Graef worked on a different division of the forms of government to Montesquieu's, rejecting despotism and alluding to three other systems in addition to monarchy: democracy, aristocracy and oligarchy. There were certainly no advantages to a monarchy where the ministers and councils' interests ran contrary to the common good, as this not only posed additional difficulties for

71 In this issue Graef always disagreed with Montesquieu, seeming to act dialectically with Rousset; vid. *Le vrai patriote hollandais*, for example, VI, 13 October 1749, 36ff.; 27 October 1749, 59ff.; 10 November 1749, 73ff.

72 DM, no. IV, 55ff., in which the anti-French echoes of Rousset can be heard; vid., for example, *Le vrai patriote holandais*, 1, 4 December 1747, 7ff.

trade and undermined the people's right to be protected by the sovereign, but also diminished the credibility of the ministers and the *arbitristas* who surrounded them and used the pretext of the public good to benefit their own interests. The best system for the development of commerce was a republic, which "through the institution and constitution" should honour and reward trade. Graef praised the British constitution and form of government for introducing the merchant class and debates on commerce into its parliament, as well as for encouraging the publication of writings on this subject. This was part of the Gournay circle's pro-British propaganda, probably via Plumard de Danguel, who maintained that the superiority of English commerce was due to the republican dimension of its constitution and to the fact that the whole nation, including traders, participated in law-making.[73]

The Seven Years' War had brought the colonial issue to the forefront of the international order. Graef identified the management of the empire as one of the principal causes of Spain's economic decline.[74] Although he does not seem to have been familiar with Forbonnais' book about Spanish finance,[75] he followed Forbonnais in referring to the "poor governance" of the Austrias as the main trigger of this decline. He rejected the anachronous regulatory systems for managing the empire, including the Cadiz monopoly, whose outcome had been to hand over real control to foreigners through licit (commerce) and illicit (smuggling) means. However, the DM's most original element was the fact that it provided the first channel for Gournay circle propaganda promoting the British colonial system into Spain. The sources were *Le négociant anglois* and lengthy extracts from *De la Histoire et commerce des colonies angloises* (1755) by Butel Dumont-Forbonnais, which were previewed in the JOE and later commented on at length in the DM.[76] Although Graef argued that the "English colonies are the firmest and most secure supports on which the power and

73 DM, no. IV, 58ff.; Louis-Joseph Plumard de Dangeul, *Remarques sur les avantages et les désavantages de la France et de la Grande Bretagne par rapport au commerce et aux autres sources de la puissance des états* (Leyden: 1754). The book was translated into Spanish in 1771 by Domingo Marcoleta.

74 Graef insisted here on the way open in the 1740s by Uztáriz, Ulloa and, particularly, Campillo on the need to reform the Spanish colonial system.

75 François Véron de Forbonnais, *Considérations sur les finances d'Espagne* (Paris: 1753); on its content, see Niccolò Guasti, "Il 'ragno di Francia' e la 'mosca di Spagna': Forbonnais e la riforma della fiscalità all'epoca di Ensenada e Machault," *CROMOHS* 9 (2004): 1–38.

76 See, particularly, the discourses no. IV, 17 December 1755, 41–61, on Acadia or New Scotland, textual translation of ch. II, 56ff., of *De la Histoire et commerce des colonies angloises dans l'Amerique septentrionale* (London: 1755), and no. XVI, 19 May 1756, 752–71, which comments on a large amount of information from this book on other British colonies of North America. See also other texts on British colonies taken from the JOE, such

grandeur of the British nation rest,"[77] he did not in fact believe that they were a good model for Spain. His criticism began with the diversity of governments in the American-ruled colonies in North America, which led to unequal political and commercial treatment among subjects of the same sovereign. He continued, in agreement with Davenant, by criticising the tyrannical rigidity with which the colonies had been governed by the metropolis, and he ended with a comment on the mother country's poor capacity to force them to abide by the constitutional laws and avoid their foreseeable separation. The alternative to the impossibility of maintaining a friendly union subject to the laws of their homeland was to cut off these "gangrenous and rotten members of the human body." This "poor governance," to which Davenant and Child had referred and which was not recommended for Spain, increased the possibility of losing positions vis-à-vis France in the lead up to the Seven Years' War which, in fact, ended up restoring the colonial balance in a way that clearly favoured Great Britain.

6 Final Remarks

This review of the economic content of Graef's pioneering and forward-looking DM reveals some conclusive results. On the one hand, the publication was a channel for spreading the principals of the secular and traditional *Oeconomie*, for which an intellectual debt was owed to the JOE, undoubtedly the main source of most of the materials that were published during Graef's project. On the other hand, it was also simultaneously a vehicle for the pioneering reflections on the "science of commerce" that were taking shape in France around the Gournay circle, particularly through Forbonnais' writings. For the first time in the Spanish Enlightenment, it was acknowledged that "commerce" had become a "science" and, as such, had "its own rules, axioms and postulates" that were different from those of legal science. These new ideas reflected the transition from the *iusnaturalism* to the new "science" of political economy very well, and Graef used them to stress that commerce had become the main cornerstone of modern politics. Spain therefore had to try to adapt these of the "science of commerce" rules without delay, to become a "commercial monarchy." Graef's definitive message is that the monarchy should be articulated around the new weapon of

as that dedicated to Louisiana. Butel Dumont was the best American scholar on colonial issue in Gournay's group; see Reinert, *Translation*, 155–59.

77 DM, no. XVI, 19 May 1756, p. 765.

modern politics, and that this meant banking on an economic development policy as the best way to guarantee progress, peace and international harmony for the nation. This is why, although never really coming to fruition, the DM holds an eminent place in the history of journalism in Spain as the first publication with economic content.

CHAPTER 3

Political Economy in the *Spectators* Era of the Spanish Press (1758–1771)

1 Introduction

Although press emerged somewhat later in Spain than in te rest of Europe, it is undeniable that there was a boom in the publication of gazettes, letters, miscellanies or mercuries during the 1760's, after the closing og Graef's DM. Although subsisted the strict limits to the freedom of expression and the press was subjected to a double censorship, both civil and inquisitorial,[1] this flourishing phase of the press cannot be understood outside of the context of the cultural liberalisation that came about with the coronation of Carlos III in 1759. The following decade is usually described as the "first golden age" of the press or, more commonly, the *spectators*' era. The reason is that this period was characterised by the long shadow of *El Pensador* (1762–1767), the outstanding newspaper edited by José Clavijo y Fajardo (1726–1806) following the model of Joseph Addison's *The Spectator*.[2] Around forty periodicals, published mainly in Madrid, testify to the flowering of the press in this decade. Therefore, it is not surprising that the analysis of these publications constitutes a significant part of the cultural history studies on the Spanish Enlightenment.[3] This is obvious in matters such as literary ideas or the criticism of society and customs which were predominant in the press at that time. In the hands of the creators of these publications, Nifo, Clavijo or Saura, the professional conscience of the "journalists," "public writers" or "diarists" was forged, forming a community

1 On this issue, see ch. VI above.

2 Guinard, *La presse,* 125–26.

3 Although not exhaustive, some particularly important bibliographical sources are: Sempere, *Ensayo,* IV, 176–98, and Francisco Aguilar Piñal, *La prensa española en el siglo XVIII. Diarios, revistas y pronósticos* (Madrid: CSIC, 1978). With respect to general studies, see Guinard, *La presse*; Sáiz, *Historia del periodismo*; Urzainqui, "Un nuevo instrumento;" and Maud Le Guellec, *Presse et culture dans l'Espagne des Lumières* (Madrid: CV, 2016); on the press and women, Mónica Bolufer, "*Espectadores* y lectoras: representaciones e influencia del público femenino en la prensa del siglo XVIII," *Cuadernos de Estudios del siglo XVIII* 5 (1995): 23–57; and, finally, on the press and the public, Elisabel Larriba, *El público de la prensa en España a finales del siglo XVIII (1781–1808)* (Zaragoza: Prensas Universitarias de Zaragoza, 2013).

 | DOI:10.1163/9789004442894_005

with its own identity inside the Republic of Letters.[4] As time progressed, the volume of journalists became dense enough for "dialogues" between editors to emerge. In these "dialogues," together with the factional game of censorship and accusations or tributes and praise, the value of the press began to emerge as an instrument to civilize the custom and the social habits,[5] as well as of instruction, criticism and the exercise of reason, that is to say, of Enlightenment.[6]

The press also constituted a privileged channel for distributing the new useful knowledge elaborated in the most developed countries: as Israel stated, through the journals, "Europe had, for the first time, amalgamated into a single intelectual arena."[7] This new knowledge included the "science of commerce." The initiatives of Nifo, Barberi and Saura, which will be discussed below, together with that of Graef, constituted an advancement of the Spanish economic press before the first specialised newspaper was established in 1792: *El Correo Mercantil de España y sus Indias*. However, this subject has not been studied systematically.[8] Focusing on the economic press, we seek to analyse the origin of a differentiated genre with respect to two other frontier publishing expressions. The first is the commercial press, which, with secular roots on

4 Regarding the first issue, see Antonio Checa, "La terminología periodística: sus orígenes y su consolidación," *Cuadernos de Ilustración al Romanticismo* 16 (2010): 1–10; with respect to the second, Joaquín Álvarez Barrientos, "El periodista en la España del siglo XVIII y la profesionalidad del escritor," *Estudios de Historia Social* 51–53 (1999): 29–39, and *Los hombres de letras en la España del siglo XVIII. Apóstoles y arribistas* (Madrid: Castalia, 2006), 205–53. The forging of the journalistic identity through the *spectators* has been studied by Inmaculada Urzainqui: "Periodista-*espectador* en la España de las Luces. La conciencia de un género nuevo de escritura periodística," *El argonauta español* 6 (2009), https://argonauta.revues.org/516.

5 On the parallel emergence in Spain of the *spectators* and the literature on good customs, see Mónica Bolufer, *Arte y atificio de la vida en común* (Madrid: Marcial Pons, 2019), 186–93.

6 Inmaculada Urzainqui, "Diálogo entre periodistas (1737–1770)," in *Francisco Mariano Nipho. El nacimiento de la prensa y de la crítica literaria periodística en la España del siglo XVIII*, ed. José María Maestre, Manuel Antonio Díaz and Antonio Romero (Alcañiz-Madrid: CSIC, 2014): 375–418.

7 Israel, *Radical Enlightenment*, 142.

8 Partial studies on the economic press can be found in Luis María Enciso, *Prensa económica del XVIII: El Correo mercantil de España y sus Indias* (Valladolid: Universidad de Valladolid: 1958), and Lucienne Domergue, *Jovellanos à la Société Économique des Amis du Pays de Madrid (1778–1795)* (Toulouse: Université de Toulouse-Le Mirail, 1971): 201–31. A more extensive analysis of the content of this chapter can be seen in Jesús Astigarraga, "Prensa económica de la Ilustración española (1758–1792)." *Studia Historica- Historia Moderna* 40, no. 2 (2018): 199–232. The *corpus* of our analysis comprises the Madrid press due to its predominance — it accounted for 70% of all of the newspapers of the century —; furthermore, the provincial or regional scope mainly extended during the last decade of the century; see Luis Miguel, Enciso, *Compases finales de la cultura ilustrada en la época de Carlos IV* (Madrid: RAH, 2013), 336ff., and Larriba, *El público*, 54–58, 91–100.

a European scale, offered regular information to merchants about prices, interest rates or exchange rates.[9] The second are the journals designed with a clear utilitarian and scientific-technical sense that cultivated useful knowledge and sought to stimulate the improvement of the economic sectors.[10] In Spain, as in its neighbouring countries, information about both of these matters filtered into the general newspapers, including the *Mercurio Histórico y Político* and the *Gaceta de Madrid*, both officials. However, most significantly, after 1760 a press emerged which, without losing its multi-faceted nature, began to incorporate articles on the "science of commerce." In most cases they were simple translations. This requires an analysis of the international circulation of ideas in order to specify the sources that fuelled these first steps of Spanish economic journalism.

2 Nifo and the *Estafeta de Londres* (1762)

Together with Graef, the beginning of Spanish economic journalism in the eighteenth century dates back to Francisco Mariano Nifo (or Nipho) y Cagigal (1719–1803).[11] Born in Aragon into a family of civil servants, he lived in Madrid for most of his life. In 1758 he embarked on his career in the Spanish publishing industry, eventually founding or financing about twenty newspapers. Their titles had enlightening headings including terms such as "buffoon," "thinker" or "murmurer," clearly indicating their multifaceted content. They used an educational and moralising tone and were all aimed at the general public. Nifo's publications were highly innovative in terms of court culture patterns: he introduced many features of the French press into Spain, including the subscription system. His initiatives covered all types of genres: satire, criticism of customs, bibliographic information and literary controversy. Political economy was equally important in his prolific journalistic career. Eight of the newspapers that he published between 1758 and 1771 carried this content. However, the very first of them, the *Diario Noticioso* (1758), was not particularly relevant.

---

9 On this type of press, stimulated by the demand for information that accompanied the profound changes in international trade during the eighteenth century, see J. J. McCusker and C. Gravestein. *The Beginnings of Commercial and Financial Journalism* (Amsterdam: Netherlands Economic History Archives, 1991): 21–41.

10 Mokyr, *The Enlightened Economy*, ch. 3.

11 An overall view on Nifo, in Luis María Enciso, *Nipho y el periodismo español del siglo XVIII* (Valladolid: Universidad de Valladolid, 1956), and José María Maestre, Manuel Antonio and Alberto Romero, eds., *Francisco Mariano Nipho. El nacimiento de la prensa y de la crítica literaria periodística en la España del siglo XVIII* (Alcañiz-Madrid: CSIC, 2015).

It was the first daily newspaper in the history of Spain with "economic" content on its front page. Nevertheless it was imbued with the classical practical philosophy converting "economics" into a mere ethical, political and scholastic section. Its news about "Civil and Economic Commerce" had a very limited scope: it reported purchases, sales and economic geography.[12]

The *Estafeta de Londres* (EL, 1762) was very different indeed. Its two dense volumes, based on letters written supposedly from England, were dedicated to analysing the "course of action in England with respect to its customs, industry, arts, literature, commerce and the navy." Its content was marked by the Seven Years' War (1754–1763). When Nifo began to publish the EL, Spain had already entered the War in defence of Bourbon-ruled France. These circumstances explain the most revealing characteristic of the publication: its profound anglophobia. We do not know exactly which sources were used. They probably came from France, where anglophobia reached its height between 1755 and 1760.[13] Nifo seemed to draw from both the pamphlets which were presented as a *Préservatif contre l'anglomanie*[14] and the French newspaper *État politique actuel de l'Angleterre* (EPA, 1757–1759). This was a government initiative developed by the Secretary of Foreign Affairs, Edme-Jacques Genet, following the guidelines of Antoine-Louis Rouillé, a subordinate of the powerful Secretary of State, Choiseul.[15] The EL had the same purpose as the EPA, that is, to widen the scope of the War to the creation of "opinion:" "*ce sont les gazettes, les journaux et nombre de brochures politiques qui ont servi de champ de bataille.*"[16] In short, it sought to revert the "*English mania*" of the elite Spanish classes, rescuing the country from the "political abduction" of

12 The same was the case of the two pioneering daily newspapers in Catalonia. They were published in Barcelona with the title *Diario curioso* (1762, 1772–1773) by the merchant Pedro Ángel de Tarazona, who followed Nifo's model.

13 Edmond Dziembowski, *Un nouveau patriotisme français, 1750–1770* (Oxford: VF, 1998), 59–110, and, with a wider sense, Josephine Grieder, *Anglomania in France, 1740–1789* (Geneva: Droz, 1985), 7ff.; on anglophobia and political economy, see Reinert, *Translating*, 136–42, 181–85.

14 According to the eloquent title of the satirical publication of Louis-Charles Fougeret de Montbron, *Préservatif contre l'anglomanie* (Minorca: 1757).

15 The newspaper was published until the gradual British victory rendered it obsolete, but it continued in other ephemeral projects (*Papiers anglais*, 1760; *État actuel et politique de l'Angleterre*, 1760). On Genet, see Edmond Dziembowski, "Le peuple français instruit: Edme-Jacques Genet et la traduction des écrits politiques britanniques pendant la Guerre de Sept Ans," in *Cultural Transfers: France and Britain in the Long Eighteenth-Century*, ed. Ann Thomson, Simon Burrows and Edmon Dziembowski (Oxford: VF, 2010), 175–88.

16 EPA, I, V.

England. To do this, Nifo selected some of the central ideas of the EPA defending the superiority of France over Great Britain. Above all, the dire effects of the War on the commercial future of Great Britain were highlighted: if the conflict continued, this country would have to renounce its dominance of the European balance of trade.[17] That said, this imminent decadence was due to deep-seated reasons: it was not only due to the circumstances of the War, it was also a result of the political constitution of Great Britain. The civil liberty of its citizens, that was so admired, was in fact more "misleading" than real; furthermore, it constituted a factor that went against the "public peace" and the "order of subordination."[18] The most harmful freedoms were those of the press, opinion and printing. All of them promoted social turmoil and offended the decorum of religion.

Something similar occurred with the freedoms of a political nature. The British government supposedly enjoyed greater freedom than a republican government, while also reaping the benefits of the monarchy. It was, in fact, a "mixed monarchy, aristocracy and democracy government, in which each part [...] mutually corresponded and counterbalanced the others;" therefore, it was, apparently "the most advantageous of all governments."[19] According to Nifo, this could not have been further from the truth. The parliamentary system was a game of checks and balances. It was based on a false liberty in terms of the election of its representatives. This fostered corruption and a false patriotism based on a factional feeling. The problem resided in that it was not possible to merge three such disparate governments in a "mixed" system. And the main obstacle was not the monarchical component but the republican one: the two parliamentary chambers constituted a source of permanent disputes and, therefore, lacked the legitimacy to force the compliance with the laws. All of this gave rise to a "hermaphrodite" or "amphibian" government, which did not respond to the common good: in short, in Great Britain everything was a "monstrosity."[20] This is how Nifo, amidst the Seven Years' War, laid out the essential arguments that fostered Spanish anglophobia during the decades following the War.

17 Cfr. with the many passages of the EPA in which the War was linked to the future ruin of Great Britain and the heyday of France; for example, I, 111ff.; II, 1–38.

18 EL, I, 41, note. Regarding the recurrent criticism of the British political system in Rouillés newspaper, see, for example, I, letters II (43ff.), IV (96ff.) or VIII (226ff.). As opposed to the advantages of monarchical absolutism, "*un gouvernement mixte est de tous les gouvernements les plus tyrannique*" (57).

19 EL, I, 43–44.

20 EL, I, XIII-XIV.

The countless defects of the British political system cast their shadow over the economic sphere. The problem did not reside in the ethos of its civil society. Nifo praised the spirit of initiative of the British and their love for emulating technical innovations; and all within the framework of a series of virtues such as generosity or the honour related to usefulness which justified the advantages gained by the country in the international trade. An incarnation of theses virtues was the Dublin Society and other similar patriotic institutions. Those dedicated to charity were prominent. However, these examples must be regarded with caution. Spain had to extract a single practice lesson from Britain's economic splendour. The British were the first to identify agriculture as the origin of wealth; therefore, they promoted first their agriculture, then their livestock farming and finally their flax and hemp industry.[21] Their economic power was based on the simple foundations of honouring the workers, promoting the rural industry and fighting idleness through piety. Spain had to emulate these lessons: Britain was rich and fearsome, "an almost absolute lady of the world," due to the solidity, not of its manufacturing sector, but of its agriculture. That said, Nifo's view of Great Britain was very precise: when he praised its agricultural policies he was not referring to the grain trade laws at the end of the seventeenth century or the secular reforms inspired by agricultural individualism. In his *Estafeta,* there was only a small space dedicated to defending these aspects — the elimination of the common land — and other elements of British development policy — navigable canals, roads, fishing or parish charity houses —. It was only the *ethos* of the agricultural world and not the enormous possibilities that commerce offered to increase national and individual wealth which is what really interested Nifo.

All of these proposals were subsumed in *Oeconomie.* Understood in the sense of a correct administration and prudent spending, *Oeconomie* completely characterised the economic and political content of the *Estafeta.* It was also imbued with a highly traditional sense. Nifo presented it perfectly aligned with the virtues of the most refined Catholicism, which were also those of a paternalist manager uncontaminated with the vileness intrinsic of luxury and commerce.[22] In his EL, Nifo did not refer to Graef's DM, however, his principal source was also the JOE. Using its articles, Nifo continually praised the goodness of rural work. There was not doubt about his

21 Rouillé's approach was different: despite his anglophobia, he maintained that Britain's power was based on a well-designed policy of promoting manufacturing and controlling the colonies; he hardly mentioned its agricultural system.

22 On the agriculture as the foundation of both prosperity and civil virtue in the 1750s and 1760s French context, see Shovlin, *The Political Economy*, 72–79.

intense political conservatism. He attributed the dominance of a socio-political organisation conceived as a mere extension of these private virtues to the land owners and the parish priests. Furthermore, he claimed that these virtues should also be the inspiration for the statesman. Land owners and clergymen should also be responsible for directing the longed-for patriotic societies whose only activity should be agriculture as manufacturing and commerce required "other subjects."

In the EL, all of these ideas were presented inseparably united to a profound criticism of the society based on commerce and industry. Great Britain's fate was compromised due to its eminently commercial society. The country should never have implemented such an aggressive and ambitious policy of conquest in order to gain new markets: its natural conditions were conducive for defending itself not for expanding. Its political system did not seem any more promising either. It favoured the hegemony of a new ethos contrary to the virtues of the admirable manager and agronomist. This had all begun with the introduction of splendour and vanity, the ultimate root of idleness. These "idols" were followed by others, also typical of the harmful society of commerce and industry: luxury; the "hateful currency;" its circulation, which multiplied prices "by ten;" and the large cities: London had become the "distress of the whole of England." Nifo associated all of these evils to an economic system based on spending. This was spurred by the artificial changes in individual tastes and by luxury: consumption was identified as the principal origin of all of these disasters.

In his ruthless criticism of the new economy of commerce and luxury, Nifo blamed the Gournay circle, which was characterised by its anglophile affiliation and, to a lesser extent, its admiration of the trading republics. It is undeniable that he knew the original and translated treatises of the members of this circle very well; he used the work of O'Herguety in favour of the Dutch and British fishing policy; he referred to the Englishman Cary, translated into French by Butel Dumont, who defended the goodness of piety; he introduced many chapters on commerce and the colonies from the writings of Gee, translated into Spanish in 1753 and Gournay's precedent; and, finally, he mentioned the political arithmetic texts of Petty and Davenant. However, the principal objects of his criticism were not these authors, but Hume, whom he accused of defending the "genres of vanity," and Plumard de Dangeul, who supported Britain's prosperity despite it aggravating the hardship of other countries. It is no coincidence that the EL began with a reproach of Jean Bernard Le Blanc, who in 1755 translated Hume's *Political Discourses* (1752) into French and was the most anglophile of all the publishers related to Gournay. In short, his accusatory finger pointed to the dazzling "science of commerce." He praised the desire of the British to disseminate their "exquisite theory,"[23] but their principal defect persisted: not only had they not resolved the main problems of the society of vanity and luxury — exhausted treasuries, continual wars, a lack of credit —, but had aggravated them, worsening Great Britain's process of decadence. Challenging head-on the nucleus of economists which, in Spain and a good part of Europe, at the beginning of the 1760s represented the spearhead of the defence of the society of commerce and industry, Nifo expressed his complete opposition to the modernising dynamics implemented by Carlos III, one of whose principal identifying characteristics was precisely his interest in the new treatises on political economy emerging from Paris.

3 Nifo and the *Correo General de Europa* (1763)

The EL, which was discontinued in December 1762, was followed by the *Correo General de Europa* (CGE). Established just one month later, its theme was not just Great Britain, but Europe as a whole. However, its continuity of the EL was undeniable: in the 43 letters of which it was composed, Nifo continued to publish the central topics of *Oeconomie*. To do so he drew from the JOE. It is highly revealing that he republished the discourse of Linneo which identified the natural sciences as the basis of economics, previously published by Graef.[24] He also repeated the programme of the JOE about the necessary balance between agriculture, commerce and the applied arts,[25] although based on the priority of agriculture as it was the natural framework within which wealth was harmonised with the deep-rooted catholic virtues of the prudent manager.[26] However, at the same time, the CGE also had a differentiated character. For the first time in Nifo's writings, it included large extracts of political economy texts that did not correspond to *Oeconomie*. The reason for this resided in the fact that the CGE began to be published after the traumatic defeat suffered by Spain in the War. The Nifo's newspaper reflects very well the change of speed that the Spanish Enlightenment knew after the signing of the Treaty of Paris (February 1763). Spain urgently needed to implement an economic development policy. This necessitated a reconsideration of the worth of texts on political economy which were regarded by the Spanish enlightened elite classes as one of the reasons for the British success and its relentless rise in terms of commerce.

23 EL, I, 376.
24 CGH, I, letter V (129–60).
25 CGH, I, Introducción, XVIIIff.; III, letter VI (345–61).
26 See, particularly, CGH, I, letters IV, V and VI; III, letters IV, V, VI and VII.

Through the texts of Duhamel de Monceau, Nifo opened his newspaper to the "new" Franco-British agronomy that was changing farming methods in the most prosperous regions of Europe.[27] However, the authors who most influenced him were Mirabeau and Bielfeld.[28] Nifo considered "translating and adapting" to his country the famous *L´ami des hommes* (1756–1760) of Mirabeau which was already well-known in Spain.[29] Although this did not happen, the extensive extracts of the text published in his CGE were highly significant. They alluded to the ambitious plan of decentralising the French monarchy through the creation of "provincial states." They originally had an essentially fiscal inspiration but they then expanded to also have an eminently political dimension. From the perspective of post-War, the most relevant aspect of Mirabeau's *Mémoire* was that it instigated a restructuring of the Spanish monarchy on the basis of the legitimacy of representation as an individual right not only for the nobility and clergy, but also for other "municipal" and "civil" orders.[30]

Nifo's use of the *Institutions Politiques* (1761) by the Prussian Cameralist Bielfeld was more exhaustive. In his CGE he inserted long extracts on his project of education, reforming the army and everything related to the Royal Treasury. The latter included the proposal of establishing a body to stimulate economic development — the Higher Council of Commerce —, with full competencies for the promotion of commerce and manufacturing and which, undoubtedly, would inspire a far-reaching reform of the Spanish Board of Trade.[31] This

27 CGH, II, 70–96, from which the Duhamel de Monceau's *Elemens d'agriculture* (1762), a book summarising the "new" agronomy, was extracted. In spite of this, Nifo's preference for classical agronomy prevailed: amidst the strong dissemination in Spain of the new approaches, he published in 1768–1775 a compendium of the treatise of the Castile-born Alonso de Herrera, *Libro de agricultura* (1513).

28 See Enciso, *Nipho*, 105, 116.

29 CGH, II, 315.

30 CGH, II, letters VII-X. La *Mémoire sur les États provinciaux* (1758) appeared in vol. II of Victor Riqueti, Marquis of Mirabeau, *L'Ami des hommes, ou Traité de la Population* (Avignon: 1758–1760). It was published after he became a Physiocrat and with significant changes with respect to a previous *Mémoire* of 1750; vid. Manuela Albertone, "Fondements économiques de la réflexion du XVIIIe siècle autor de l'homme porteur de droits," *Clio@Themis* 3, 2010, http://www.cliothemis.com/Clio-Themis-numero-3.

31 CGH, I, letters III-IV (education plan), Higher Council of Commerce and Manufacturing Policy (I, letters VIII-X), military plan (II, letters IV-VI) and Royal Treasury (IV, letters I-V); vid. Jakob Friedrich von Bielfeld, *Institutions politiques* (The Hague: Pierre Gosse, 1760). This was the first Spanish translation of the Cameralist tradition, given that Bielfeld's extensive text began to be translated in 1767 by Domingo de la Torre Mollinedo; vid. Lluch, *Las Españas vencidas*. Similar ideas about the creation of this new commercial institution that would replace the Board of Commerce will be raised in the later years by authors such as Pérez Valiente, Heros or Cabarrús.

opening up of Nifo to the "science of commerce" highlights the usefulness that Bielfeld offered with his interventionist, regulation-based and monarchic orientation in the remodelling of the two key elements of Spain after it was defeated in the War: the army and the Royal Treasury. With respect to the latter, the Prussian was particularly useful as he proposed a detailed and methodical reform plan inspired by authors close to Gournay, particularly, Melon and Forbonnais. Therefore, through Mirabeau and Bielfeld, Nifo's CGE adhered to the majority opinion among the elite Spanish classes regarding the need to promote socio-economic reforms as a central strategy for reinforcing the battered monarchy. This strategy combined elements of centralization and decentralisation at the same time. This new receptiveness of Nifo led to a greater explicitness of political economy in the *Diario Extranjero*, a newspaper that, in 1763, was published in parallel with his letters of the CGE. It was based on bibliographic criticism and constituted the first in the history of Spain dedicated to the review of texts on political economy. Very eloquently, when alluding to Hume, Nifo transformed into praise what, in his EL, just a year earlier, had been harsh criticism.

At the same time, in 1763, Nifo was engaged in a sour controversy with José Clavijo (1726–1806) regarding a series of articles published by the latter in *El Pensador*. They were the only articles on political economy by this emblematic "spectator."[32] According to Nifo, these articles, far from being original, were a simple translation of the first chapters of the Forbonnais' *Élémens du commerce* (1754).[33] He also considered them to be of a poor quality, leading him to publish his own version of them. The controversy, based on additional translations of new fragments and serious reproaches regarding their quality, was drawn out in the subsequent issues of both newspapers. However, there were other underlying matters in this controversy. The accusations exchanged between Clavijo and Nifo — to which Miguel de la Barrera (1724–1790) also added immediately with his *Aduana Crítica* (1763–1765) — revealed the centrality that the theme of "commerce" had come to occupy in social circles, not only among the elite courtesans, but also among the more general "public:" Clavijo wrote that this subject was "highly useful for the public, which generally hears about commerce in very vague terms without being able to even form fair ideas about such an important sector due to a lack of principles."[34]

32 Astigarraga, "Forbonnais," 1093–095. These articles were published again in around 1780, in the selection of *El Pensador Matritense* (1780) undertaken by the Barcelona-born Pedro Ángel de Tarazona: EPM, III (1780), pensamiento XXXVIII, 247ff.

33 EHJ (1763), no. 1–4, 37–49.

34 EP, III, pensamiento XL, unpaginated.

In this way, "commerce" had become a valuable object of emulation and social promotion, as well as a powerful instrument to create an audience around the politics of the court. Forbonnais' *Élémens* constituted a perfect cover given the good reception that this book was having at the time in Spain among the elite classes that surrounded Carlos III.

There are still two other publishing initiatives of Nifo to consider. In 1769, he gained the support of the Council of Castile and the Board of Trade to compile a statistical record of the monarchy in the form of economic geography, based on a complete questionnaire — about economics, population, policing, etc.[35] —, which was sent to the intendants, magistrates and other local authorities in peninsular Spain. The project sought to address the reiterated complaint regarding the lack of factual information about the Spanish economy (Uztáriz, Ward, Arriquíbar, Campomanes, etc.). At the same time that it was received the British political arithmetic through the work by Davenant — it was translated to the Spanish in 1759 by Campomanes and in 1771 by Arriquíbar, and published in 1779 in his *Recreación política* — [36], the lack of information about the structure of the monarchy emerged as a problem of the first magnitude in order to implement an economic policy which was established from the center of the nation. The objective of Nifo's initiative was effectively to provide a type of "political anatomy" of the monarchy; it was more descriptive than quantitative or political arithmetic in nature. Its results were presented in two periodical publications: the *Correo General de España* (1770) and the *Descripción natural, geográfica, y económica de todos los pueblos de España* (1771). In reality, they were both hybrid newspapers: they combined statistical news sent from the Spanish villages and towns with royal orders, instructions regarding trade and, occasionally, with discourses or theoretical collaborations.[37] However, despite its enormous size, both publications failed. It was due to the most elementary hardships. On the one hand, the Aragonese journalist received very little response from the local authorities and therefore the information that was published had little relevance. On the other hand, there was a lack of political and financial implication by the government, which realised that Nifo's capacity was not sufficient to undertake his ambitious enterprise. In March 1771, after

35 CGE, I, XIXff. The questionnaire had been prepared since 1766 (FUE, AC, bundle 24–18).

36 Davenant's *Of the Use of Politic Arithmetick* (1698). In both cases, the source was the French translation by Véron de Forbonnais, included in *The British Merchant* (I, 159–192); vid. Llombart, *Campomanes*, 81–82, and Jesús Astigarraga and José Manuel Barrenechea, "Estudio preliminar," in Nicolás de Arriquíbar, *Recreación política*, ed. Jesús Astigarraga and José Manuel Barrenechea (Bilbao: Instituto Vasco de Estadística, 1987), 20–22.

37 Guinard, *La presse*, 132–33.

his questionnaire had just been distributed among the local authorities, as it was very costly for them to make copies, the journalist requested the Council of Castile for additional finance. He received silence in response.[38] This decision led to the closure of the two statistical publications of Nifo. This experience gives us cause to question the real autonomy of his journalistic projects. His eloquent journals published during the 1760s, when he was at the forefront of the Spanish press, seemed to respond to precise instructions coming from the power and suggest that his publications were simply a result of official demands. However, the governmental strings that motivated his journalistic projects are still unknown. This makes it difficult to conclusively interpret his sinuous approach to the emerging political economy. However, as we shall see, the conservative and catholic Nifo did not disappear from the Spanish economic journalism scene in the following years, although his influence waned.

4 The *Miscelánea Política* (1763) by Barberi

At the end of August 1763, in the epicentre of the frenetic journalistic activity of Nifo, the first letter of the four that made up the *Miscelánea política* (MP, 1763) by the lawyer Mateo Antonio Barberi (1723-?) was published. Born in Cadiz, he wrote the letters in his native town, immersed in its dense commercial background. As Usoz explained,[39] his MP opened with the most eloquent praise of the whole journalism scene of his era with respect to the "fermentation" of economic texts at the beginning of the reign of Carlos III.[40] Translation particularly contributed to this. Against those who accused translators of plagiarism, Barberi considered it as a "highly important" act of patriotic service to the country. There is no doubt that he sensed that translation had become a powerful lever of social promotion which he wished to try: in 1763, when he began writing his MP, he had already requested the license to publish two translations.[41]

The MP perfectly reflected the double Franco-British affiliation of that Barberi called the "science of commerce" and which, contrary to Nifo, he accepted from the outset. Although his origins were personified in Locke and Newton,[42]

38 AHN, *Consejos*, bundle 5.531–32.

39 Javier Usoz, "Mateo Antonio Barberi: el ideario de la Junta General de Comercio en Aragón," *Cuadernos Aragoneses de Economía* 8, no. 2 (1998): 501–23. The MP was the first of his writings.

40 MP, letter II, 25–26.

41 AHN, *Consejos*, bundle 50.659.

42 MP, letter I, 16; Barberi follows the JC, I, I-XVIII.

Barberi was inspired by Plumard de Dangeul, Forbonnais and different translations carried out within the Gournay circle (King, Child and Culpeper). However, when writing his MP he drew from a privileged source: the *Journal de commerce* (1759–1762, JC). This was a monthly journal published during the Seven Years' War in Brussels, under the shadow of the Austrian power, by the exiled Frenchman Jacques Accarias de Serionne.[43] Its contents covered three topics: the defence of the "patriotism of commerce" and its clearest manifestations such as the proliferation of books and economic societies; its anti-Physiocratic affiliation and its affinity with the Gournay circle; and, finally, its condition as a tool to create anti-British "opinion." It arrived very early to Spain through powerful merchants, such as the Marquis of Iranda or José Antonio de los Heros, as well as Barberi. In fact, in 1763, he had already translated its first volume into Spanish "with several reflections" of his own; however, his version was not published. Before granting him the printing licence, the Council of Castile sent the translation to the Board of Trade which, due to unknown reasons, interrupted its publication.[44]

The MP was a "discourse accommodated to the practical style of commerce,"[45] but it was structured around its socio-economic importance. The central problem of Spain resided precisely in the insignificance of its commerce. This was due to the under-development of its agriculture and manufacturing industry. This gave rise to an inundation of the monarchy with foreign goods, which was lethal for the national economy. Barberi claimed that the solution was not just technical and, in line with the JC, he called for the whole of the apparatus of the political system to be put to the service of the mechanisms of the opulent trading societies. Far removed from the first Nifo, Barberi was in favour of activating the circulation of money; establishing a public general company dedicated to financing commercial activities; and promoting consumption, although regulating it through luxury laws to avoid the excessive import of foreign goods. His advocacy for the social rehabilitation of commerce was based on his defence of the Coyer's *noblesse commerçante* and of education in

43 Hervé Hasquin, "Jacques Accarias de Serionne, économiste et publiciste français au service des Pays-Bas Autrichiens," in *Études sur le XVIIIe siécle*, ed. Roland Mortier and Hervé Hasquin (Brussels: Éditions de l'Université, 1974), 159–70. Barberi made an intensive use of the *Catalogue raisonné* of books on political economy included in the JC (I, 23–51).

44 MP, letter I, 8; AHN, *Consejos*, bundle 50.659. In a series of subsequent letters called *Cartas político-instructivas* (Madrid: Imprenta de Francisco Javier García, 1770), Barberi was inspired by the articles of Serionne in his references to the books by Mirabeau or Patullo, always with an undercurrent of concern for the inactivity of the nobility and the advisability of involving it in commerce and the improvement of agriculture.

45 MP, letter IV, 113.

the "science of commerce" — which should include the "political system of the nations" — among young people, politicians and high-ranking civil servants. In short, the traditional civic virtue should be remodelled in order to allow traders to access the top of the social pyramid. Like the nobility, they exercised a pacific activity that modulated the social customs which was necessary to foster prosperity and the public good; therefore they were "true citizens" who "served the state and the homeland, maintaining many families."[46]

In line with these reflections, another central theme of the MP was established: the legitimacy of the charging of an interest rate in loan operations. There was no religious justification for rejecting this proposal: interest rates were not only a characteristic of the Calvinist and Lutheran cultures but also of Catholicism. This required a reform of the laws in force regarding usury. Although there was some overlapping in his arguments with the business of Cadiz, Barberi wrote about the controversy arising in Madrid regarding the payment of interest for loans granted to the *Cinco Gremios Mayores* — Five Major Guilds —, the powerful institution of Madrid that defended the financial and business interests of the jewellery, retail and textile corporations. The MP was published a little before the Decree of 1764 which finally acknowledged the legality of these payments. This was a Scholastic justification which appealed to the Sacred Scriptures and in which the concepts of *lucrum cessans* and *damnum emergens* intervened. Its reasoning was reminiscent of the *contractus trinus*.[47] However, in addition, Barberi, once again, agreed with the reformism of the Gournay group in defending that the reduction of the legal interest rate was an unavoidable condition to stimulate Spanish economic growth.[48]

However, going beyond his appeals to Catholic orthodoxy, the position of Barberi referred to the pre-eminence that public law and the law of nations had in all societies.[49] Once again, he coincided with the JC, which considered the "science of commerce" as a branch of public law. His starting point was again the idea of the sociability of commerce, founded on the principles of

46 MP, letter IV, 153.

47 Usoz, "Mateo Antonio Barberi," 514.

48 Barberi tacitly quotes the translation of Gournay and Butel Dumont of Josiah Child, *Traités sur le commerce* (Amsterdam-Paris: 1754); it included (441–78) the Thomas Culpeper's *Traité contre l'usure* (1621). In his text, Barberi highlights the advantages of the Dutch economy over the British economy as it operated with low interest rates.

49 MP, letter I, 12. Barberi praised different Spanish publications rooted in this legal tradition, such as those of José Antonio Abreu — Mably's translator — and, in particular, Pedro Pérez Valiente, who "began to lay the first foundations of a building that is not a little difficult to conclude;" however, his sources seem to have been Jean Domat and Francisco Schmier.

safety, protection and mutual help that the civil society offered to individuals, once the social contract was consummated. Commerce was therefore constructed as an essential link of all political societies although their legal systems were different. In turn, the fundamentals of the law of nations established a hierarchy in the political society based on the principle of sovereignty and whose determinations were "obligatory laws." Therefore, given that commercial contracts with interest payments, now of questionable legality, were commonly used, there was no reason to prohibit them. This issue could not be disputed, unless the "general society of men" itself was questioned. This was based on the circulation of money as a basis of commercial activity. The formation of sovereignty was therefore essential for the "science of commerce" whose substance was essentially political. As Graef, in one passage of his letters, Barberi referred again to Forbonnais' argument in which the private interests of the merchant and the public interests did not have to coincide and that the function of the legislator consisted in harmonising them so as to benefit the latter.[50] Through these ideas, Barberi converted his MP into an advocacy of commerce. And there is not doubt that it was well received among the official nuclei. Shortly after being published, its author was promoted to more prominent positions in the Bourbon government. After a few years in the municipal sphere, he joined the Board of Trade, first as the director of the Royal Factory of Saragosse and then, between 1769 and 1772, as the Archivist General of the institution.

5 The Saura's *Semanario Económico* (1765–1767)

The initiatives of Nifo and Barberi were followed by the *Semanario Económico* (SE, 1765–1767). Published under the acronym of Araus, its editor was Juan Pedro de Saura, a journalist of whom we know very little about.[51] In his SE, the news about "commerce" appeared in the form of brief articles or book summaries that usually contained comments from the editor. Most of them were about the applied arts which included agricultural science, although very little space was dedicated to the "new" agronomy. Precisely a traditional text such as Chomel's *Dictionnaire Oeconomique* (1709) was one of the privileged sources of

50 MP, letter II, 25–26.

51 An overall analysis of the SE can be found in Joaquín Ocampo, "El *Semanario Económico* (1765–1767): a la Ilustración por la utilidad," *El Argonauta español* 10 (2013), http://argonauta.revues.org/1926.

the economic news of the SE. In general, the information in this *Dictionnaire* was more related to commercial geography than to the theory of "commerce."[52]

However, this economic news was also drawn from other sources, such as the *Mémoires de Trévoux*, the *Journal des Savants*, the JOE or the JC. The latter was undoubtedly the most consulted by Saura. The JC was first used in the SE in August 1765 in a new section of "Literary and Commercial News." This section mentioned the JC, which, according to Saura, aired "all the principles of the opulence of the nations" and described the principles of "a century that only thinks about taking advantage of all the benefits of commerce."[53] Saura expressed his intention of introducing articles of this "excellent" publication in subsequent issues. In fact, two months later, he extracted the "Introduction" of Serionne for the JC, in which he defended that "politics makes commerce the basis of the states." Saura presented it as a gazette dedicated "solely" to commerce, whose content covered not only "the mechanics of commerce but also its administration, so that it could be contemplated as a manual for merchants and a code for legislators."[54]

In seven instalments, Saura began to compile an extensive commentary of Serionne's work on commerce in Portugal.[55] He chose this particular work as the Portugal's trading pattern was similar to that of Spain; the excess of precious metals from Brazil had devastated the productive sectors of Portugal. His analysis was based on Cantillon's *Essai*. Saura drew from his ideas regarding the inflationary effect of a mine-owning country through the spending mechanism, as well as the incompatibility between the increase in money supply and manufacturing development. He also alluded to the ideas of Serionne, inspired by Forbonnais' *Considérations sur les finances d'Espagne* (1753), regarding the poor public administration of Portugal: the exclusive privilege granted to Great Britain in 1703 in the Treaty of Methuen was the cause of its commercial servitude. The solution resided in opening up Portuguese trade to free international trade. And given its difficulty to compete successfully in the manufactured goods market, it should specialise in the supply of navigation services and agricultural and colonial goods. Similar conclusions were drawn by Serionne in another long report on Spain. Although he was critical with its content, Saura announced its publication.[56] However, it was never published,

52 SE (Saura), II, 14–16, 23–24, 30–32, 39–40, 47–48, 55–56, 64, 71–72.

53 SE (Saura), I, 227.

54 SE (Saura), I, 228; cfr. JC, I, I-XVIII.

55 SE (Saura), I, 227–28, 235–36, 242–44, 251–52, 239–40, 247–48, 256; cfr. JC, from September 1759 to April 1760.

56 SE (Saura), I, 256.

maybe because it had already been "pirated" in 1761 in an extensive *Reflexiones* written by Aragorri.[57]

In other news of the SE, material from the JC and the JOE were combined. In the early months of 1767, it published an extensive summary, in ten instalments, of *Le droit publique de l'Europe* (1746) by Mably.[58] It was justified by the recent end to the Seven Years' War. Like Malby, Saura maintained that each country should create a "fixed political system" in accordance with its geography and government. This system should be respectful of public law, a science engaged in "making the people happy and enriching then with the treasures of peace."[59] Commerce was destined to play a prominent role in all of this: it emerged as a powerful pacifying agent that stimulated the new international equilibriums, to the point where Malby, according to Saura, seemed to have "confused the art of negotiating with the art of making commerce flourish."[60]

This same idea that the balance of "power" was confused with that of "commerce" served as a guide for Saura to claim that the nobility should become involved in commerce. The JC and other well-known publications in Spain, such as the JOE, the *Mémoires de Trévoux* or the *Journal Enciclopédique*, can be found behind the extensive summary that the SE published in 1766, in seven parts, of *La noblesse commerçante* (1755) by Coyer,[61] as was an equally long response from Coyer himself to the rebuttal of his book published by the *Chevalier* d'Arcq.[62] All of this converted the SE into the primary channel for disseminating Coyer's work which was to enjoy enormous success in the Spanish Enlightenment. In his summaries, Saura referred to his central ideas. Given that commerce was the source of national wealth and power, it was essential to open it up to the nobility. This was even more the case when it was the only way to create wealth for their sectors idlers or impoverished. When they prospered, the whole nation would follow. Saura emphasises, undoubtedly with his

57 Astigarraga, "Un nuevo sistema económico," 13–44.

58 SE (Saura), III, 32, 40, 47–48, 55–56, 63–64, 71–72, 79–80, 88, 94–96, 103–04. Mably's *Le droit publique* (1746) had already been translated into Spanish in 1746 by José Antonio de Abreu.

59 SE (Saura), III, 32.

60 SE (Saura), III, 56.

61 SE (Saura), III, 263–64, 271–72, 278–80, 287–88, 203–04, 312, 320. A synthesis on the debate on the *noblesse commerçante*, in Shovlin, *The Political Economy*, 58–65.

62 On the *Développement et défense du système de la noblesse commerçante* (1757) by Coyer, see SE (Saura), III, 251–52, 259–60, 268, 275–76, 283–84. Although the latter was highly influenced by Uztáriz, only Coyer's *La noblesse commerçante* will be translated into Spanish by Jacobo María Espinosa in 1781.

own country in mind, that a significant reason for the underdevelopment of France with respect to Great Britain or the Netherlands was precisely due to the "inaction" of its nobility. All these ideas were omnipresent in the heart of the Gournay circle. The same was the case with calls for a reduction in the legal interest rate which would stimulate the economic growth of France. Saura transmitted this to his readers through an extensive summary of the *Dissertation sur les effets que produit le taux de l'intérêst de l'argent sur le commerce et l'agriculture* (1756) by Clicquot de Blervache.[63]

New topics related to the "science of commerce" reappeared in an extensive "Reflections on the balance of trade" published by the SE in 1765, in four parts. Its principal objective was to illustrate that the customs records were, contrary to the monetary balance, a wrong criterion for quantifying the balance of trade. This was accompanied with an extensive reflection on the way to use the colonies to improve this balance. The most useful model for Spain was that of France. This ratified that the promotion of new agricultural exploitations in the colonies, repopulated with indigents with land and slaves, had resulted in its dominance of the sugar trade; and the same was beginning to happen with tobacco. Government protection was, therefore, a prior condition for successfully operating in international trade. Although he did not allude to it, the undercurrent of this digression seemed to be the new regulation with the colonies approved in 1765 in Spain. Furthermore, it was less original than Saura claimed: it was a simple summary of *The trade and navigation of Great Britain* (1729) of Gee, translated into Spanish in 1753 and reviewed two years later in the JOE.[64] This journal was undoubtedly chosen by Saura in order to introduce a detailed summary of Hume's *Of National Characters* (1748), the first translation of the Scottish in Spain: in 1755, the JOE had published extensive fragments of this text.[65] In short, through his brief articles and book summaries, Saura instructed his readers in some of the most characteristic topics of the "science of commerce," using two highly representative publications, the JOE and the JC, and following influential authors such as Mably, Hume, Blervache, Coyer, Gee or Serionne.

63 SE (Saura), II, 335–36, 343–44, 351–52, 359–60.

64 JOE, April 1755, 168ff.; May 1755, 372ff.; see, furthermore, the Spanish translation of Gee, by Noboa: *Consideraciones*, 199–22, 223ff.

65 SE (Saura), III, 291–92, 347–48; cfr. JOE, from July 1755, 726ff. After three decades of remarkable influence, Hume's *Political Discourses* (1752) will be traslated into Spanish in 1789 by and anonymous autor: *Discursos políticos del señor David Hume* (Madrid: Imprenta de González, 1789).

6 Final Remarks

Saura's initiative and Nifo's subsequent publications with statistical content put an end to the first phase of the Spanish economic press. Between 1758 and 1771, eleven of the approximately forty published newspapers had introduced economic topics into their pages. In spite of this, the overall outcome of this first phase was, in fact, far from brilliant. Like other newspapers published during this period, they were short-lived, experimental and poorly financed projects that depended on patronage or private capital. Furthermore, although there is a lack of accurate information regarding their readership — the subscription system had only just been implemented — , the initiatives still seemed ill-suited to the "public", the "figure of the highest authority" whom, according to Nifo, everyone claimed to serve.[66] Nevertheless, this phase of the Spanish enlightened press was far from irrelevant. Nifo, Barberi and Saura's initiatives seem to have sprung from the same root: political economy had become a focus of interest among the enlightened elites, the audience at whom their newspapers were really aimed. After Graef, the discipline reappeared as a genuine "political science of commerce," essential for the articulation of the state and for creating good public policy, and, viewed in this light, the sources used by the Spanish press take on a different meaning. The disputes between *Oeconomie* and the "science of commerce" were fuelled by the experience of France — and, to a lesser extent, Belgium — and it was in this context that the Spanish economic press took its first steps. It is revealing to note that there is no proof of any influence from the Physiocratic press, with its will to create a *royaume agricole*;[67] instead, Barberi and Saura used the JC to reiterate that the Spanish economy had to take its articulation model from industrialised and trading countries. At the same time, these writers positioned their newspapers in the wake of the "official" Enlightenment. The Gournay circle authors, whose writings were disseminated through their newspapers (Forbonnais, Coyer, Plumard de Dangeul and others) were the chief sources for the economic treatises of the day, which were mainly written by Arriquíbar, Anzano, Romá and Ramos. The prestigious circle of the French Intendant of Commerce represented the mainstream of the Spanish economic Enlightenment during those years. The press thus contributed to the rise of the culture of "commerce,"[68]

66 CGH, I, VI.

67 Mainly, *Éphémérides du citoyen* (1767–1772) and the *Journal de l'agriculture, du commerce et des finances* (1765–1774); see Steiner, "Les grandes revues," 35–78.

68 As Mónica Bolufer has explained, behind all this was also the dispute over the moral consequences of trade and the civilizing role of customs: "Civilizar las costumbres: el papel

creating the background for the two most important economic reforms of the 1760s: the grain trade (1765) and the colonial system (1765).[69]

On the other hand, the soft press boom in the 1760s was one more expression of a wider phenomenon: the gradual forming of the *Habermasian* public sphere in Spain.[70] Enlightened thinkers of the country looked to the model of Britain's experience, shaped in the wake of the Glorious Revolution.[71] In Spain, however, the process followed the path of absolute monarchy; the public sphere did not only emerge late but its institutional *locus* was not parliament, as it was in Britain, but the crown, while its main leitmotif was the struggle for transparency in public affairs, with the aim of ensuring that the *arcanum* ceased to be a principle of government policy. Robertson has given a very good account of the positive role played by political economy in achieving this objective.[72] This discipline and the public sphere began to interact in Spain during the 1740s and 1750s with the arrival of Melon and Forbonnais's writings; however, the issue took centre stage at the end of the 1750s, under the influence of the culture policy developed by Gournay's circle, based on publishing treatises and translations, as well as the promotion of economic societies.[73] However, the long-held *covachuela* tradition of withdrawing into themselves to preserve the essence of the "national interest" found its closest allies at the time in the Seven Years' War and the imminent change of dynasty that led to the enthronement of Carlos III in 1759. These circumstances did not create the ideal scenario for laying bare the mysterious royal and ministerial spheres, especially the

de la prensa periódica dieciochesca," *Bulletin of Spanish Studies* 91, no. 9–10 (2014): 97–113, and *Arte y artificio*, 55ff.

69 Both reforms were rolled out in a context in which many translations of foreign texts were becoming available in Spain (Abeille, Mirabeau, Thomas, Herbert, Accarias de Serionne and Butel Dumont). The first reform established freedom of prices and free trade within Spain and also allowed, under strict conditions, exporting; see Concepción de Castro, *El pan de Madrid* (Madrid: Alianza, 1987), 118ff., and Llombart, *Campomanes*, 155ff. The second ended with Cadiz's trading monopoly, reduced taxes and duties, and allowed participation in trade to the main ports of the Spanish empire, on both sides of the Atlantic; see Stanley Stein and Barbara Stein, *Apogee of Empire: Spain and New Spain in the Age of Charles III, 1759–1808* (Baltimore: John Hopkins University Press, 2003), 83–95, and Delgado, *Dinámicas imperiales*, 235–77.

70 See Jürgen Habermas, *Strukturwandel der Öffentlichkeit. Untersuchungen zu einer Kategorie der bürgerlichen Gesellschaft* (1962). Spanish trans., *Historia y crítica de la opinión pública. La transformación estructural de la vida pública* (Barcelona: Gustavo Gill, 2004), 69–80. In any event, the creation of this public sphere in Spain did not have the bourgeois and strictly anti-absolutist nature attributed to it by Habermas.

71 Habermas, *Strukturwandel der Öffentlichkeit*, 94–103, and Melton, *The Rise*, 35–65.

72 Robertson, "Enlightenment," 15ff.

73 Ives, "Political Publicity," 1–17.

Royal Treasury secrets that maintained trust in the country's potential to win wars against the ever-present enemy beyond its borders. For this reason, some economic treatises from the period — texts by Campomanes, Gándara, Ward and Arriquíbar — were not published in their day. This balancing act eventually tipped in favour of the "new politics" of the "public sphere," partly as a consequence of the outcome of the Seven Years' War, and then of the *motín de Esquilache* — Esquilache riots — in March 1766, a deeply political uprising, started next to the Madrid court and fueled by the liberalising reforms of the grain trade which had been approved in 1765.[74] At the time Spanish elites accepted unhesitatingly that Britain's central role in international trade was due not only to its military power but also to the existence of a vibrant "public sphere," which helped to find solutions to the complexities of the "science of commerce" and apply these by means of suitable reforms. Spanish political economists had been making decisive contributions to this since the 1760s, demanding an active and relatively censorship-free "sphere," producing their own works and promoting the formation of economics institutions.[75] Campomanes endorsed this programme as state policy some years later.[76] The press was destined to play a central role in this "new politics," and at the beginning of the 1780s it rose from the ashes. Its second and definitive "golden age" began.

74 Fernández Albaladejo, *Fragmentos de Monarquía*, 437–52.

75 Javier Usoz, "La 'nueva política' ilustrada y la esfera pública: las introducciones a la economía en el siglo XVIII español." *Revista de estudios políticos* 153 (2011): 11–46, and "Political Economy and the Creation of the Public Sphere During the Spanish Enlightenment," in *The Spanish Enlightenment Revisited*, ed. Jesús Astigarraga (Oxford: VF, 2015), 105–27.

76 Campomanes, "Advertencia a los lectores patriotas," in *Apéndice*, I, III-LII. For a complete analysis, see Niccolò Guasti, "Campomanes' Civil Economy and the Emergence of the Public Sphere in Spanish *Ilustración*," in *L'économie politique et la sphère publique dans le débat des Lumières*, ed. Jesús Astigarraga and Javier Usoz (Madrid: CV, 2013), 229–44.

CHAPTER 4

Decentralising the *Ilustración,* Disseminating the Political Economy

1 Introduction

When in 1746 Fernando VI ascended to the throne of Spain the main responsibilities for economic policy in the monarchy were shared among different central government bodies. Essentially, the Treasury was in charge of tariffs and the main taxes; expenditure on infrastructure was the responsibility of the Secretary of State. Policy for boosting economic growth was mainly divided between the Council of Castile, which dealt with agricultural matters, while the Treasury, which also housed the Board of Trade, was responsible for trade and manufacturing. In 1747 the Board of Trade was thoroughly restructured, becoming the General Board of Trade, Currency, Mines and Foreign Affairs. José Carvajal became president in the same year, and with the support of the Marquis of Ensenada, the powerful Secretary of Finance, War and the Indies, the revamped Board of Trade initiated several courses of action that have been identified with the beginning of a centralised national trade and manufacturing policy.[1] In the 1770s, during the reign of Carlos III, the Board extended its influence in Spain through the founding of new trade consulates and, in parallel, the first economic societies were founded. Both institutions were essentially designed to stimulate economic development and their co-existence was at best uneasy; not only did they form part of different bodies — the Treasury and the Council of Castile, respectively — but they also shared a number of similar powers. In any event, as this chapter will discuss, they were both linchpins in the introduction of the Enlightenment programme throughout Spain and, especially in the case of the economic societies, in the spreading of economic knowledge as well.

1 Guillermo Pérez Sarrión, "La formación de la política manufacturera de la Ilustración española en la primera mitad del siglo XVIII. Una aproximación," in *Más estado y más mercado*, ed. Guillermo Pérez Sarrión (Madrid: Sílex, 2011), 211.

 | DOI:10.1163/9789004442894_006

2 The Trade Consulates and Economic Societies

Under Carvajal's presidency (1746–1754) the newly overhauled Board of Trade mobilised its powers over collecting statistical information, public works — especially ports and roads —, professional training and guild oversight. Meanwhile, it adopted a two-pronged approach to the boosting of manufacturing by granting existing factories tax privileges and exemptions and creating a group of new trading companies and fledgling factories. This second policy was mainly rolled out between 1746 and 1753 and allowed for a new network of factories devoted to the textile manufacture and trading to be set up in most of the country, with the main exception of the Cantabrian area. The aim was to establish the network as a regional development tool,[2] but the project had only limited success; from the 1770s onwards it was subject to relentless criticism from the new government elites, and only the factories in Toledo and Seville survived to the end of the century. However, this was not the case with private trade boards and trade consulates.[3]

These institutions had originated in the late Middle Ages, and the Bourbons inherited a relatively small group of them. They were not only located in coastal trading cities such as Valencia, Barcelona and Bilbao, but also inland — Burgos, Saragossa and Seville —. While primarily operating as trading bodies responsible for commercial registration, regulation and courts,[4] they also had the advantage of opening up a way of participating the world of trade in the structures of the monarchy. Their institutional profile was best expressed by the 1737 Consulate of Bilbao *Ordenanzas* — Ordinances — which were viewed as models throughout the Hispanic world. However, as a result of the growth in trade during the eighteenth century and the strengthening of trading nuclei on the Spanish coastline, the Board of Trade did not only create new consulates, but it also granted them specific powers over every aspect of promoting trade and manufacturing. This took place during the 1760s, when several private boards of trade were founded or re-founded; while the two main initiatives were those in Barcelona (1758) and Valencia (1765), others were also set up in Granada, Seville and Valladolid. While incorporating both merchant registration and the old consulates, they were in fact economic development bodies

2 Delgado, *El proyecto*, 200–22; Pérez Sarrión, "La formación," 209–17.

3 Eugenio Larruga, *Historia de la Real y General Junta de Comercio, Moneda y Minas y Dependencias de Extranjeros* (c. 1788; BCMH, mss. 479A, 479B, 479C), III, sheets 197–200.

4 Robert Sidney Smith, *The Spanish Guild Merchant: a History of the Consulado, 1250–1700* (Durham: Duke University, 1940), and William J. Callahan, "A Note on the Royal y General Junta de Comercio, 1679–1814," *The Economic History Review* XXI, no. 3 (1968): 519–28.

with a regional dimension.[5] The next step in this direction, which was taken in the 1780s, aimed to facilitate the *comercio libre* — free trade — scheme, which in 1778 extended private trading to new ports in Spain and the colonies. If it were to function effectively, consulates in the authorised ports were required, and within this framework new consulates were created both in metropolitan Spain — Seville (1784), La Corunna (1785), Malaga (1785), Santander (1785), La Laguna (1786), Palma de Majorca (1800) and San Lúcar de Barrameda (1806) — and the colonies: between June 1793 and June 1795, these institutions were established in Caracas, Guatemala, Buenos Aires, Chili, Guadalajara, Veracruz and Cartagena de Indias. This overseas expansion was based on a "distinct kind of soft imperialism" in that it assumed that the empire's survival depended essentially on economic growth in the colonies.[6] Therefore, an institutional structure with an imperial dimension orientated towards promoting economic development was not created until the 1790s. The economic societies were also part of it.

The history of these institutions is relatively well-known.[7] Unlike the consulates, their background lay in from the European Enlightenment, specifically, in the movement of institutions for promoting the useful arts, such as the agricultural academies or the economic societies. These began with the Dublin Society (1731) and continued with the societies of Florence (1753), Bretagne (1757) and Berne (1758).[8] All of which these were highly the most influential in the Hispanic context. The first steps in the process of their adaptation to this context were taken in the period 1763–1765. The process was initially both inconsequential and patchy, responding to autonomous local initiatives that were beyond the Council of Castile's political power. Of the three institutions founded during this period, the Agricultural Academy of Lerida (1763) and the Academy of the Kingdom of Galicia (1764) were very short-lived; but the third, the *Real Sociedad Bascongada de los Amigos del País* (1763) — the Royal

5 Roberto Fernández Díaz, "Burguesía y consulados en el Siglo XVIII," in *Mercado y desarrollo económico en la España contemporánea*, ed. Tomás Martínez (Madrid: Siglo XXI, 1986), 32–34.

6 Fidel J. Tavárez, "Colonial Economic Improvement: How Spain Created New Consulates to Preserve and Develop its American Empire, 1778–1795," *Hispanic American Historical Review* 98, no. 4 (2018): 605–634; Paquette, *Enlightenment*, 131ff.

7 The lines that follow briefly summarise Jesús Astigarraga's recent analysis: "Economic Societies and the Politicisation of the Spanish Enlightenment," in *The Spanish Enlightenment Revisited*, ed. Jesús Astigarraga (Oxford: VF, 2015): 63–81.

8 There is a new overview of European economic societies in Koen Stapelbroek and Jani Marjanen, eds., *The Rise of Economic Societies in the Eighteenth Century: Patriotic Reform in Europe and North America* (Basingstoke: Palgrave Macmillan, 2012), but incomprehensibly does not include the study of Spain.

Basque Society of Friends of the Country — was not. This Society was created under the direction of the Javier María de Munibe, Count of Peñaflorida (1729–1785), with a sphere of influence covering the three Basque provinces, and its founding cannot be separated from the important political position held by these provinces, which retained their ancient *fueros* — charters or regional laws — after the War of Succession, at the heart of the Spanish monarchy. The founding of the *Sociedad Bascongada* was in fact the culmination of a long process which began in the 1740s and was undoubtedly rooted in the Enlightenment. The Society was eventually established as a consultative, advisory and coordinating body for the three *Juntas Generales* — the Basque provincial institutions — with the main purpose of reforming the three provinces' economy.[9]

Ten years elapsed between the Society's creation and the emergence of any new initiatives, with the exception of two modest societies that were set up in two cities of Navarre and Andalusia: Tudela (1773) and Jaén (1774). However, in the following decade more than sixty applications to form societies were presented, mainly in response to a project which had been in the making for some time among the political elite surrounding the King; more specifically, it was an initiative of the Count of Campomanes backed by the Council of Castile. His proposal was described in detail in the *Discurso sobre el fomento de la industria popular* (1774).[10] Unusually, the book was distributed through official channels: 30.000 copies were printed and distributed among the main political and government bodies in Spain, and this, together with a royal decree inviting them to apply the principles it contained, provided a strong stimulus for the creation of economic societies. Campomanes' detailed design emphasised that these institutions should strive to mobilise the patriotic zeal of local elites, by which he was referring chiefly to the nobility, the clergy and members of the government and local authorities. The institutions were to address three specific objectives. The first was to form advisory and supporting bodies for the government's economic and social policies. The second was to create a research body to promote the regional economy and carry out factual and statistical studies. The third and final aim was to establish a centre for the cultivation and social dissemination of economic, scientific and technical knowledge

9 Astigarraga, *Los ilustrados vascos*, 23–74.

10 Pedro Rodríguez de Campomanes, Count of Campomanes, *Discurso sobre el fomento de la industria popular* (Madrid: Antonio de Sancha, 1774). Other insights also appeared in his *Discurso sobre la educación popular de los artesanos y su fomento* (Madrid: Antonio de Sancha, 1775) and *Apéndices* (1775–1777).

useful for promoting agriculture, industry, and the arts and trades, as well as combatting poverty and idleness.[11] In short, what Campomanes aspired to was that the societies would represent a kind of "beacon" for political economy and become "a public school for the theory and practice" of this discipline in all Spanish provinces.[12] At the same time, assuming that economics was their primary concern, their activities also had to extend to aspects such as education, book publishing and technical training for the population as a whole, all in accordance with government directives. It was on these centralist criteria that the *Sociedad Económica Matritense* — the Madrid Economic Society — was founded in 1775; its first Director was Campomanes. It was established as the central body for the society movement in Spain and as a model for other societies,[13] as well as an advisory institution for the Council of Castile and Carlos III's governments.

Campomanes' proposal and the Madrid Society were immediately successful. The emergence of economic societies in Spain was basically a phenomenon intrinsic to the final period of the reign of Carlos III and seemed to weaken with the death of the King, although it is true that with the eighty-three initiatives proposed until December 1788 — of which the Council approved more than sixty — it could be deemed a success.[14] Second, between 1775 and 1780, forty initiatives arose including many of the societies which would become the most important and active, some on a regional scale: in addition to the Madrid Society, those of Seville, Granada, Cantabria, Saragossa, Las Palmas, Valencia, Murcia, Segovia, Tenerife, Asturias or Majorca. Lastly, of the forty-three initiatives arising in the period 1781–1788, while some large societies were formed — such as Valladolid, Santiago, La Rioja, Malaga ... —, there were many that corresponded to small towns, which seems to indicate that the local response was greater than expected, and there was a possible emulation effect once the larger scale societies had been created. During the same period, this effect began to extend to the colonies, where, between 1781 and 1810, a dozen economic societies were

---

11 Llombart, *Campomanes*, 277–91; Vicent Llombart and Jesús Astigarraga, "Las primeras antorchas de la economía: las sociedades económicas de amigos del país en el siglo XVIII," in *Economía y economistas españoles. Vol. III. La Ilustración,* ed. Enrique Fuentes Quintana (Barcelona: Galaxia Gutenberg-Círculo de Lectores, 2000): 677–707.

12 Campomanes, *Discurso industria popular*, CLIII.

13 Campomanes, *Apéndices*, II, CCXIV.

14 Gonzalo Anes, "Coyuntura económica e 'Ilustración': Las sociedades de amigos del país," in *Economía e ilustración en la España del siglo XVIII* (Barcelona: Ediciones Ariel, 1969), 11–41.

founded, nine in the period before 1795, which was the most favourable time for their development.[15]

The societies were unevenly distributed around Spain. While large regional-level societies predominated in Asturias, Aragon, Cantabria, Galicia, Majorca, Murcia and Valencia, around thirty societies emerged in Andalusia, more than twenty in New Castile and another handful in Old Castile and Extremadura. In the latter region the societies were mainly founded in small towns with fewer opportunities and resources. The movement was not uniform, firstly because it had two separate models, the Basque Country and Madrid. Despite the differences in their programmes, these societies had an important feature in common: both had been created by political power, the Basque provincial institutions and the Council of Castile. It is therefore no accident that the Basque model was chosen by the Tudela economic society, the only one to be created in the Kingdom of Navarre, which was also a charter area. The Madrid model, meanwhile, was dominant in the rest of the monarchy. However, not all the economic societies accepted the government directives in a disciplined manner. The two best-known cases are those of Seville and Valencia. The Council of Castile had to impose the model of the Madrid Society statutes in Seville when the founders adopted the Basque design and that of the Valencia Board of Trade in the second; in the latter case, this was because the Board of Trade already performed very similar functions to those undertaken by the city's new economic society: in fact it took the Council of Castile nine years to accept the final *Statutes* of the Valencia Economic Society.[16] This conflict of powers was not uncommon and was a symptom of a public administration with no proper hierarchy. The Council of Castile failed to find suitable solutions to conflicts over the control of powers between different government bodies, and this reduced the economic societies' scope for action enormously. Usoz gives a very good account of the trouble the Aragon Society had to fit into an institutional context in which its members had quasi-official status and exercised powers typical of mayors and magistrates.[17] Elsewhere, problems arose from the fact that the economic societies attempted to establish themselves in cities that

15 Robert Jones Schaffer, *The Economic Societies in the Spanish World (1763–1821)* (Syracuse: Syracuse University Press, 1958), ch. 7–12; Paquette, *Enlightenment*, 142ff.

16 Cervera, *El pensamiento*, 466–77.

17 Javier Usoz, "El enfoque regional del pensamiento económico de la Ilustración española y su aplicación elemental a Aragón," in *Nación y Constitución. De la Ilustración al Liberalismo*, ed. Cinta Canterla (Seville: SEESVIII, 2006), 223–42, and "Política y economía en la Ilustración: la Real Sociedad Económica Aragonesa y las instituciones territoriales de la Monarquía borbónica," in *Más estado y más mercado,* ed. Guillermo Pérez Sarrión (Madrid: Sílex, 2011), 261–96.

already had consulates or private boards of trade, as had happened in Valencia. In fact, economic societies were never founded in some of Spain's most important trading centres; in the Basque port cities of Bilbao and San Sebastian this was because high-profile local merchants joined the Basque Society, while in others such as Cadiz, La Corunna and Barcelona there was resistance from nuclei of merchants organised in the local consulates. Barcelona was undoubtedly the most striking case here. Lluch explained that it had no economic society because economic promotion functions were already performed by the Board of Trade of the city. Furthermore, Campomanes' plans did not really match circumstances in Catalonia, whose level of industrialisation was the most advanced in Spain at the time, because the Council of Castile emphasised the development of agriculture and rural industry and was critical of the guilds and the spreading of all non-applied scientific knowledge.[18] It has also been observed that behind these inconsistencies lay the projection of disparate models of growth: while the Board of Trade and the consulates preferred an industrial model, the Council of Castile and the economic societies favoured an agricultural version.[19] However, the accuracy of these interpretations is highly debateable: in the first place, Campomanes was not against all types of manufacturing, and that included factories in urban centres and those producing luxury goods. Secondly, empirical reality shows that the social composition of both the economic societies and the consulates was highly diverse: although the nobility were at the hub of the first and merchants dominated the second, both included sectors of one social spectrum or another, with agricultural and industrial interests that were not always in harmony.[20]

In any event, it is indisputable that the consulates and economic societies moved within a blurred and conflicting framework of powers, resulting in latent but also highly obvious tension between the Board of Trade, on one hand, and the Council of Castile, on the other. The struggle to strip the Board of Trade of its powers intensified with Campomanes' arrival on the Council of Castile at the beginning of the 1760s. There were numerous disputes — control of professional training and statistics programmes — but the issue is best reflected by the struggle over guild power and the reform of their ordinances, which Campomanes tried to pass into the hands of the economic societies. In a bid to resolve the issue, Carlos III granted the Board of Trade express independence from the Council of Castile and the ordinary justice system and attempted to

18 Lluch, *El pensament*, 126–34.

19 Vicent Llombart, "El sorgiment de les societats economiques i llur conflict amb les institucions comerciales," *Recerques* 11 (1981): 181–98.

20 Fernández Díaz, "Burguesía," 9–10.

assign it clearer powers over technical manufacturing issues; however, not only did the problem persist, but it shifted from the upper echelons to local settings. The acrimonious dispute between different local government bodies that was sparked off by the Aragon Society's unsuccessful plan to reform the guilds is well-known.[21] The weakest party in the battle for control of these key elements for stimulating economic growth was undoubtedly the Board of Trade, which not only ranked below the Council of Castile as an institution, but barely participated in communicating its decisions: instead of using the trade consulates, the Council's *ministers* either used the "reserved channel" of the Treasury or the mayors and magistrates. In short, the lack of properly defined powers seriously affected the consulates and economic societies' capacity for act.

Another significant factor was that the full territorial expansion that the economic society movement as a whole had initially sought was only partially achieved. Furthermore, the intensity and quality of the societies' activities was very uneven. Apart from the Basque and Madrid Societies, only those in Aragon, Asturias, Seville, Segovia, Cantabria and Majorca managed to sustain a consistent pace of actions over a significant period of time. The impact of a centralising and homogenising programme that was intended, in short, to structure the monarchy precisely via decentralisation, was thus reduced: the aim had been to engage local elites in state-initiated reforms. This centralising message was especially obvious when the Madrid court attempted to resolve the serious problem of jurisdictional fragmentation with the help of the Basque Society. The most representative episode in this respect occurred during the period from 1778 to 1781, when the Basque provinces and the Kingdom of Navarre examined the court's plans to standardise the local customs system with the rest of Spain, moving the interior customs from the limit with Castile to the coast and the French border. The Basque Society, supported by the Bilbao and San Sebastian trade consulates, pressed all its resources into service in an attempt to find a solution in line with the court's proposal, which was clearly a matter of necessity for economic interests in the Basque Country and Navarre. The provincial Basque *Juntas* and the Parliament of Navarre refused to accept the scheme, leading to a significant loss of influence there on the part of the Basque Society, which was identified as a central government tool for dismantling the *foral* privileges. That was exactly the reason why an economic society was not created in Pamplona, capital of the Kingdom of Navarre, a few years later, in 1793. In general terms, the practical results achieved by the

21 Javier Usoz, *Pensamiento económico y reformismo ilustrado*; Niccolò Guasti, "Introduzione. Nomante e Genovesi: l'economia civile nell *Ilustración* spagnola," in Lorenzo Normante, *Proposiones de economía civil y comercio*, ed. Niccolò Guasti (Florence: Alinea, 2013), 25ff.

economic societies certainly cannot be said to have matched their enormous quantitative output, with the exception of their activities to spread the cultural patterns and ideas of the Enlightenment: numerous translations of political economic texts were made in the shadow of economic societies. In July 1786 the Council of Castile opened an inquiry in order to investigate the causes of their decline.[22] The almost three dozen responses returned by the economic societies referred to an endless series of problems and indicated the need for a fundamental reform of the movement;[23] however the Council of Castile only attempted to resolve only two problems: the lack of funding and the proliferation of societies in small towns. In 1795, the ever clear-sighted Gaspar Melchor de Jovellanos (1744–1811) accepted that, "although they are booed and belittled because of concern and envy," the economic societies had to persevere, reorienting themselves towards training and the spread of useful knowledge, especially in the fields of agriculture and economics, thus banishing "pernicious opinions bred by ignorance of their principles."[24] But, although most of the societies were still active at that time, they gradually became less and less so, in part because of a concealed withdrawal of official support.[25]

3 The *Memorias* of the Economic Societies

The appreciation of Jovellanos really did justice to one of the fundamental task developed by economic societies: unlike the consulates of commerce, they remarkably stimulated the emergence of new publishing formats to disseminate economic and agronomic knowledge that went beyond the classical doctrinal texts. This aspiration was rooted in the heart of the Bascongada.[26] Its creation was triggered by the criticism during the 1750s with the scarce influence that the Bristish utilitarian culture was having in France. Its Director, Peñaflorida, and theirs promoters argued, following authors such as Mirabeau, Plumard de

22 Jorge Demerson and Paula Demerson, *La decadencia de las reales sociedades económicas de amigos del país* (Oviedo: Centro de Estudios del Siglo XVIII, 1978).

23 A good example is the clarifying opinion of Jovellanos, exposed in 1786, in his "Dictamen que dio la Clase de Agricultura de la Sociedad Económica […] sobre las causas de la decadencia de estos cuerpos" (1786), in *Obras completas. Vol. X. Escritos económicos*, ed. Vicent Llombart and Joaquín Ocampo (Gijón: KRK ediciones, 2008), 652–60.

24 Gaspar Melchor de Jovellanos, "Informe de la Sociedad Económica de esta Corte al Real y Supremo Consejo de Castilla en el Expediente de Ley Agraria" (1795), in *Gaspar Melchor de Jovellanos. Escritos económicos*, ed. Vicent Llombart (Madrid: RACMP, 2000): 317–18.

25 Demerson and Demerson, *La decadencia*, 108–09, 114–15.

26 Astigarraga, *Los ilustrados vascos*, 59–64.

Dangeul, Herbert or Patullo, that economics had not penetrated the academic world and, more acutely, that the academies only withdrew useful men from productive activities in exchange for creating an "infinity of writers;" thus, they called for the creation of an academy exclusively dedicated to commerce, the arts and agriculture. The backdrop of these ideas was not only the intense proliferation of societies across the whole of Europe, but also the political support provided by Gournay, through Abeille, for the creation of the *Société de Bretagne*, whose internal structure was copied by the Basque institution. As in the case of the Gournay circle, the "public," that was repeatedly referred to in the early texts of the Bascongada, emerged as an essential player in the design of its activities. One of its four commissions had the precise objective of achieving "the Enlightenment and cultural education of the public."[27] Therefore, the cultural dynamics of the Basque Society understood the Enlightenment as the dissemination of knowledge to the general public. Now the inspiration came from the Dublin Society which, through "instructive papers" and awards, had "made Ireland change its countenance of fate."[28]

The Basque Society chose the expeditious route. Its *Estatutos* — Statutes — defended the freedom of expression, except in matters of religion and good habits.[29] The first voices that presented Great Britain as a model to follow emerged in 1765: for his member Nicolás de Arriquíbar (1714–1775), in this country the books and treatises represented "the crucible where [...] the true national advantages are discovered."[30] It is not surprising, therefore, that from its creation the Basque Society began to disseminate new formats of texts, from simple "useful leaflets" for spreading agricultural or technical innovations to "elementary notebooks" for teaching its students of the Society's Seminar, located in the village of Bergara, for example about the Davenant's political arithmetic. However, the axis of its informative and formative work was its collection of annual *Extractos*, which it continued for 23 years (1771–1793). They were based on the *Corps d'observations* of the Société de Bretagne. This disseminating task was undertaken in a particularly adverse climate: in 1775, the Basque Society complained that its members were contemptuously called *proyectistas* — planners — , a word [...] that suffocates the public spirit in the very beginning.[31] Maybe, this led it to abandon several projects, such as

27 *Estatutos aprobados por S. M. para gobierno de la Real Sociedad Bascongada de Amigos del País* (Vitoria: Robles, 1773): 40–42.

28 The Basque Society copied the *Essais de la Société de Dublin* (Paris: Frères Estienne, 1759): 1–6.

29 *Estatutos aprobados*, 117.

30 Arriquíbar, *Recreación política*, 91.

31 Astigarraga, *Los ilustrados vascos*, 62.

the publication of a gazette that was composed of translated articles chosen from the "foreign magazines," or a periodical publication on sciences, which, based on the *Journal de Physique* (1771–1823) by Rozier, was to disseminate the scientific experiences developed in the Bergara Seminar.

Similar publishing initiatives were developed later by the rest of the Spanish economic societies. The most noteworthy were the Madrid Society, which published five volumes of *Memorias* (1780–1795), and the Segovia Society, which published four (1785–1793); others, such as the Societies of Valencia (1777), Seville (1779), Majorca (1784) or Tudela (1787), published a single one.[32] These publications constituted a model for those that began to proliferate in the final decade of the eighteenth century in the economic societies of the Spanish colonies (Havana, Guatemala, etc.). These volumes, similar to those of the Basque Society, interlaced discourses with news of experiences, innovations and of the internal life of the societies, which reflects their desire to operate within a framework of public transparency. They also often informed of official legislation and news about economic and demographic statistics. The reason for the higher level of publishing activity by the Madrid and Segovia Societies was their closeness to the court. The former was directed by such distinguished men of the Spanish Enlightenment as Campomanes and Jovellanos and, as a consulting body of the Council of Castile for economic and social matters, the principal lines of the official reforms can be traced in its *Memorias*. Meanwhile, in the case of the *Memorias* of the latter, they were used by the Minister of Finance, Pedro de Lerena, to mediate in the public sphere in favour of his fiscal reform (1785–1787), with the support of Vicente Alcalá-Galiano, Diego Gallard and others members of the Society.[33] In the rest of the volumes, the footprint of the ambitions of the different regional Enlightenments can be detected. The Valencia Society's *Instituciones Económicas* (1777) carried information about the problems of the region's major industry, which was silk manufacture, seeking to provide solutions to the decline caused by technical stagnation and the low level of commercialisation.[34] The Seville Society was created on the

32 *Memorias de la Sociedad Económica* (Madrid: Antonio Sancha, 1780–1795, 5 vols.); *Memorias de la Real Sociedad Patriótica de Sevilla* (Seville: Vázquez, Hidalgo y Compañía, 1779); *Memorias de la Real Sociedad Económica Mallorquina de Amigos del País* (Palma de Majorca: Ignacio Sarrá, 1784); *Actas y Memorias de la Real Sociedad Económica de los Amigos del País de la Provincia de Segovia* (Segovia: 1785–1793, 4 vols.); *Memorias de la Real Sociedad Tudelana de los Deseosos del Bien Público* (Madrid: Imprenta Real, 1787).

33 All of the details can be found in José Manuel Valles, *Ciencia, economía política e Ilustración en Vicente Alcalá Galiano* (Madrid: CEPC, 2008), 355–72, 394–415; see, also, Dubet and Solbes, *El rey*, 308–30.

34 Cervera, *El pensamiento económico*, 460–77.

iniciative of Pablo de Olavide (1725–1803), and its *Memorias* (1787) also reported on the stagnation of the Andalusian textile sector. The Majorca Society's *Memorias* (1784) provided information on the agricultural and, particularly, trading problems experienced by the Balearic islands' unique economy. Finally, the Tudela Society was founded and directed by the Marquis of San Adrián (1736–1799), who was very close to the Count of Peñaflorida, and its *Memorias* (1787) presented initiatives for boosting the production and sale of commonly used textiles and various agricultural goods, particularly wine and oil, within the framework of southern Navarre.[35] However, together with this practical programme adapted to each of the regional economics, the core role of the economic societies emerged, which was to spread the enlightened culture to the ends of the monarchy. In his introductory "Discourse" (1783) to the Majorca Society, its second Director, the Magistrate José Antonio Mon (1743–1818), mentioned authors such as Bielfeld, Shaftesbury, Montesquieu, Genovesi, Arriquíbar, Campomanes or Ward.[36] The economic ideas of the founders of the Valencia Society not only referred to well-known Spanish authors, such as Uztáriz, Ulloa or Marcenado, but also to the *Corps* of the *Société de Bretagne*, Mirabeau, Plumard de Dangeul, Serionne, Huet, Savary or Pluche.[37]

4 Going beyond the *Memorias* of the Economic Societies

In addition to their *Memorias*, the economic societies also constituted laboratories for creating new publishing formats in order to ensure a more incisive dissemination of economic and agronomic knowledge. In this process, these disciplines appropriated formats that had already been successfully implemented, such as *re rustica* treatises or merchants' handbooks, with their extremely varied pedagogical proposals (lessons, dialogues, etc.). In some cases, these new formats were created as a result of the emergence of a new public interested in economic matters. As we will see, the creation of the first regulated courses in political or civil economy generated the first manuals of this discipline in Spanish history. The letters was another format which was gaining in popularity. This was the model used by authors such as Nicolás de Arriquíbar or Valentín de Foronda (1751–1821). The latter wrote his principal economic texts — *Cartas sobre los asuntos más exquisitos de la Economía Política* (1789–1794) and *Cartas sobre la Policía* (1801) — under the literary ruse of writing to

35 Astigarraga, "Estudio Preliminar," in *Ilustración y economía en Navarra*, XIII-CXXX.

36 *Memorias de la Real Sociedad Económica Mallorquina*, 1–19.

37 Cervera, *El pensamiento económico*, 472–73.

advise a supposed prince in the government of his country. Dialogues were also used repeatedly. An example of a prelude to this type of publication was *Diálogos familiares* (1741–1748) by the Italian Marcelo Dantini; it was conceived in support of the project of the minister Carvajal in defence of the privileged trading companies.[38] However, this genre really came of age after the publication in 1775 of the Spanish translation of the *Dialogues sur le commerce des blés* (1770) by Ferdinando Galiani, which was promoted by Campomanes.[39] The enormous European success of this book, which was also enjoyed in Spain, was due, among other reasons, to the *finezza* of the pleasant conversations between the Marquis of Roquemaure and the Knight Zanobi. Therefore, it is no coincidence that Fancisco Vidal y Cabasés only took three years to copy this format in his *Conversaciones instructivas* (1778).[40] This beneficiary of the cathedral of Tortosa and member of the Madrid Society, to which his work was dedicated, structured his book around the dialogues of the Count of Monte Mayor with a Knight of Buenos Aires who was in Madrid to "flee from idleness, contrary to the gospel, his own interests and the monarchy."[41] His *Conversaciones* reconstructed the atmosphere of the nocturnal gatherings and used the same narrative techniques as Galiani to visualise the places and times of the dialogues. Vidal justified the choice of this genre as it "further aroused the attention of the public." The conversations enabled the texts to mix "many types as briefly as posible," which was essential when "instructing the public in the most necessary arts."[42] But, with respect to its content, it was far removed from the anti-Physiocrat defence of the freedom of the grain trade supported by Galiani. The work had two central pillars: the *new* agriculture, with an abundance of references to Tull, Duhamel and, most of all, the Swedish agronomist Gyllemborg; and the application of the principles of hydraulics to the construction of canals and irrigation systems, instructed by different scientists and naturalists.[43] But Vidal's work was not unique. It was followed by other very similar texts. In 1785, the priest Pedro de Torres, a member of the Almuñecar Society,

38 See José Miguel Delgado, *Fomento portuario y compañías privilegiadas* (Madrid: CISC, 1998).

39 Ferdinando Galiani, *Diálogos sobre el comercio de los granos, atribuidos al Abate Galiani* (Madrid: Joaquín Ibarra, 1775). The translation was promoted by Campomanes but its author was Juan Antonio de las Casas.

40 Francisco Vidal, *Conversaciones instructivas en que se trata de fomentar la agricultura por medio del riego de las tierras* (Madrid: Antonio de Sancha, 1778).

41 Vidal, *Conversaciones*, CCV.

42 Vidal, *Conversaciones*, Prólogo, 3, 6.

43 However, Vidal also worked with other sources, for example, the Physiocratic article by Quesnay "Fermier" (1756) for l'*Encyclopédie* in his defence of the use of the horse as opposed to the ox in farming tasks (Vidal, *Conversaciones*, VII-IX).

in Andalusia, began to converse with a "curious" reader regarding how to eradicate detrimental rural practices and disseminate instructions throughout the Granada countryside regarding grain and vine growing and the principles of plant nutrition.[44] Finally, in 1798, in Vitoria, an anonymous author constructed a new dialogue defending the freedom of the wine trade. In this case the reader is not given the benefit of the doubt: Oromasis represented the "good side" and Arimanes, the opposite.[45] The dialogues travelled from the south to the north of Spain, but none of them achieved the splendid lucidity of Galiani.

While all of this was happening, at the end of 1795, Jovellanos published his *Informe de Ley Agraria* in the fifth volumen of Matritense's *Memorias*. In his analysis of how to overcome "moral obstacles or those derived from opinion" — that is, those generated by opinions opposing the idea that agriculture was the "first of all the arts"—, the Asturian-born writer had called for the improvement of public instruction. As seen, the text demanded that priority was given to the education of landowners and farm workers through seminars, university chairs or basic schooling. It also sought the stimulation of the dissemination of agricultural knowledge. This was the case of the rural booklets that had to be written in a "plain style which was comfortable for a labourer to understand."[46] It also considered that the economic societies should be involved in this educational undertaking as their primary dedication was agriculture. The *Informe* also called for the rural parishes to become involved, reinforcing a demand characteristic of the eighteenth century in Spain (Campomanes, the Barcelona's Bishop Pedro Díaz Valdés, etc.), which had led the Aragon Society to request its female member Josefa Amar y Borbón (1749–1833) to translate in 1784 a Venetian Francesco Griselini's book on this matter.[47] The relevance of these issues was particularly urgent at the end of this century, when, with the culmination of the agricultural growth cycle through the extension of crops, Spanish agricultural had to generalise without delay these technical and intensive improvements which wide sectors of the Spanish enlightened classes had been calling for since the 1760s.

---

44 Pedro de Torres, *Diversión honesta, en que se forman cinco conversaciones rústico-económicas, para entretenimiento decente* (Granada: Imprenta Real, 1785).

45 *Miscelánea instructiva, curiosa y agradable,* VII (1798), no. XXI, 300–34.

46 Jovellanos, *Informe,* 304–18.

47 Francesco Griselini, *Discurso sobre el problema de si corresponde a los párrocos y curas de las aldeas el instruir a los labradores en los buenos principios de la economía campestre* (Zaragoza: B. Miedes, n. d. [1784]). The translator was a pioneer woman of the Spanish Enlightenment; see María Victoria López-Cordón, *Condición femenina y razón ilustrada: Josefa Amar y Borbón* (Zaragoza: Prensas Universitarias de Zaragoza, 2005).

The appearance of Jovellanos' *Informe* coincided with the publication of the last of the ten volumes making up *Agricultura general*, penned by Spanish agronomist José Antonio Valcárcel (1720–1801).[48] Although he had been a member of the Valencia Economic Society since 1778, this work was a personal task, and the fact that it was finished was largely due to self-financing. A good part of it consisted of an adaptation of Thomas Hale's *A Compleat Body of Husbandry* (1756), following Jean-Baptiste Dupuy-Demportes' French translation (*Le Gentilhomme cultivateur*, 1761–1767); this had in turn taken as a reference the version included by the Marquis de Mirabeau in *L'ami des hommes* (1756, vol. v), enriched with other agronomic texts. However, Valcárcel also adapted numerous texts by European agronomists for his *Agricultura general* (Beguillet, Valmont de Bomare, Home and, of course, Tull and Duhamel de Monceau), inserting many extracts from periodicals (including the JOE and the *Journal de Savants*), "portable" dictionaries and reports from various academies and economic societies around Europe (Dublin, Berne and Bretagne). His work also carried accounts of his experiences in Valencia which were channelled via the Valencia Economic Society and the local trade consulate. Some of these experiences were later published as separate booklets to redouble the dissemination of agricultural knowledge. They specifically referred to growing rice and products such as hemp, esparto grass and flax; these formed the basis for rural industries in the Kingdom of Valencia, of which Valcárcel, following the guidelines in Campomanes' *Discurso sobre la industria popular*, was a firm proponent. The result of Valcárcel's labours was the first work in the Spanish Enlightenment with encyclopaedia format that aimed to disseminate information about the new European agronomy and the new methods, tools and farm machinery that Jovellanos' *Informe* had so longed for.

However, this book had a direct influence in the sphere of popularising knowledge of rural economics. A first key figure at the heart of the Madrid Society was Vicente del Seixo (1742–1802).[49] This Galician-born jurist had held different lower-ranking positions in the Bourbon government before he

48 José Antonio Valcárcel, *Agricultura general, y gobierno de la casa del campo* (Valencia: 1765–1795). On this work see, Cervera, *El pensamiento económico*, 159–93, and "En los orígenes del reformismo: Ilustración y agronomía en Valencia (1765–1812)," *Áreas. Revista Internacional de Ciencias Sociales* 26 (2007): 14–19.

49 For Seixo, see María Luisa Meijide, "Un agrónomo del siglo XVIII: el orensano Vicente del Seixo," *Boletín de la Real Academia Galega* 359 (1977): 183–206, and "Vicente del Seixo y la Sociedad Económica de Amigos del País de Madrid," *Boletín da Real Academia Galega* 360 (1980): 355–72.

formally joined the Society in 1792. Over the following ten years, he developed an intense relationship with its Agricultural Class which was not always harmonious. During these years, a good part of his writings had the hallmark of a vocational disseminator of agronomic knowledge, always of a strong applied nature. This was precisely the orientation of the main text that he presented to the institution: his *Lecciones prácticas de agricultura* (1792–1795).[50] This was an extensive digest of farming instructions whose main value was its compilation format. Seixo included extracts of Spanish treatises and agronomic experiences. He also translated other foreign texts. Occasionally, he strayed from this path to defend the unification of weights and measures.[51] But the five volumes of his *Lecciones* had the objective of comprising a treatise to stimulate the farm workers to improve agricultural methods. To do this, he introduced different formats, such as pedagogical lessons or a narrative in the form of questions and answers.

Seixo ended his *Lecciones* at the precise moment when Jovellanos' *Informe* was published. It is not known whether this was intentional, but Seixo attempted to take advantage of this circumstance in order to engage the Madrid Society in the diffusion of his work. He tried to persuade it that his texts scrupulously responded to the rural booklets recommended in the *Informe*. Therefore, he sought the Society's support in his request to Carlos IV for his *Lecciones* to be sent to the local councils of the Kingdom and to be used in public schools as a complement of elementary education and the Christian doctrine.[52] The failure of his request is better explained if we take into account that it overlapped with a large-scale publishing project being undertaken by another member of the Madrid Society, Juan Álvarez Guerra. In fact, in 1797, the first volume of his translation of *Cours complet d'agriculture* (1781–1800) by the *Abbé* François Rozier was published.[53] This had an alphabetic format and was published in ten volumes between 1781 and 1800. Partially posthumous

50 Vicente del Seixo, *Lecciones prácticas de agricultura y economía que da un padre a su hijo* (Madrid: Pantaleón Aznar, 1792–1795, 5 vols.).

51 Seixo, *Lecciones*, IV.

52 This memorial-type text to Carlos IV had the title *Reflexiones sobre los progresos de agricultura y pastoría* (Madrid: Pantaleón Aznar, 1797), 57–68.

53 François Rozier, Abbé, *Cours complet d'agriculture* [...] *ou Dictionnaire universel d'agriculture* (Paris: 1781–1800, 10 vols.); *Curso completo, o Diccionario universal de agricultura teórica, práctica, económica, y de medicina rural y veterinaria* (Madrid: Imprenta Real, 1797–1803, 16 vols.). For more about Juan Álvarez Guerra and his unique translation, see Jesús Astigarraga and Javier Usoz, "Una alternativa fisiócrata al *Informe de Ley Agraria* de Jovellanos," *RHE* XXV, no. 3 (2007): 427–58, and "Algunas puntualizaciones sobre la fisiocracia en la Ilustración *tardía* española," *RHE* XXVI, no. 3 (2008): 489–97.

and collective in terms of its authors,[54] the *Cours* represented the most complete undertaking of this prolific and influential French naturalist, botanist and agronomist, whose intellectual projection owed a lot to the political support of Turgot. The *Cours* constituted a type of "*summa* of the *new* agriculture," as it systematised the "results of thirty years of experiences and research."[55] Some of the papers that made up this voluminous rural dictionary were complete thematic treatises, which addressed botanical, medical, veterinary or natural history issues. Undoubtedly, the work was one of the best of the whole of the European eighteenth century, not only in terms of its technical or scientific content but because it was also open to the philosophical and social problems.

Juan Álvarez Guerra (1770–1845), the Spanish translator of the *Cours*, was a young man with no public profile when he started his version; so it constituted his first visible contribution to the enlightened cause. In spite of this, he was destined to play a key role, first as a publicist, publisher and writer, and, second, as a politician at the heart of the Spanish liberal currents during the first four decades of the nineteenth century.[56] Born in Zafra and a member of a distinguished landowning family from this little town in Extremadura, he fulfilled, in an almost canonical way, the traditional format of the trajectories of the liberal members of his generation. After graduating in Law from the University of Salamanca in 1795, he moved to Madrid to work as a lawyer. There, he began to become involved in the enlightened institutions. The first was the Madrid Society of which he became a member in its Agricultural Class. This catapulted his dedication to the diffusion of the applied sciences, particularly those related to agricultural matters. His first reflection on this was precisely his translation of Rozier's *Cours*, which he undertook before the age of thirty.

Rozier was an author who was well known within the Madrid Society before being translated. In 1778, when he was already considered as a prestigious scientist throughout Europe, he had already embarked on an ambitious project, under his own initiative, for the foundation in Spain of an agricultural school

---

54 While the first nine volumes are attributed to Rozier himself, Chaptal, Cadet-de-Vaux or Parmentier participated in the tenth and posthumous volume. The work was to be completed in 1805 with two additional volumes, which the Spanish translation, finalised in 1803 did not incorporate. It did not include a "supplement," planned by Álvarez Guerra, which was to include a French-Spanish dictionary of agronomic terminology, given that many terms of the only Spanish lexicographical dictionary with certain attention to the arts and trades, wrote by Esteban Terreros (*Diccionario castellano con las voces de ciencias y artes*, Madrid: Viuda de Ibarra, Hijos y Compañía, 1786–1793, 4 vols.), were "wrong or confused;" Rozier, *Curso*, XVI (1803), 471–74.

55 Bourde, *Agronomie et agronomes*, III, 1590, 1062–063.

56 Astigarraga and Usoz, "Una alternativa," 433–35.

which he offered to direct himself. However, the Madrid Society considered this to be unattainable. Nevertheless, in 1781, after the arrival of the first echoes of the publication of his *Cours*, the Society recommended its translation. This was the project that was undertaken later by Álvarez Guerra, from 1797 to 1803. In any event, his translation was not commissioned by the Madrid Society, although this institution constituted its primary receiving channel. This semi-official nature is highlighted in the inscription of the Primer Minister Manuel de Godoy, whom he thanks for the "influence that he has had in his publication." Another distinctive feature of the version was, as was usual in encyclopaedic works, its collective nature. Álvarez Guerra sought the help of "chemists, botanists, physicists, doctors and veterinary surgeons," although the names of the professionals who worked under his direction are not known, except for his brother. This collective nature even reached an institutional level. The *Curso* included reports and articles of many official enlightened institutions (the Veterinary School of Madrid, economic societies, etc.).

From the point of view of economic ideas, the most notable feature of Álvarez Guerra's translation was its extensive "Introductory Remarks." The translator acknowledged the practical nature of Rozier's work, hence the significance of these "Remarks" in which he summarised his ideas about "agriculture in general."[57] His source of inspiration was Physiocracy, in terms of its economic analysis and policy — *Maximes d'une royaume agricole* —, its philosophical and moral conceptions — natural law — and its political conceptions — legal and China despotism—. In this way, this illustrative text had the distinctive feature of directing the translation of Rozier's work towards Physiocratic economics although the original book was far removed from this field. Given the generic nature of Álvarez Guerra's presentation, it is difficult to determine his exact sources; however, it is clear that he used the volumes on *Économie Politique et Diplomatique* of the *Encyclopédie Méthodique*.[58] On the other hand, it is

57 Rozier, *Curso*, I (1797), IV.

58 This seems to be indicated by the similarity between the information provided by Álvarez Guerra and the extensive entries in the *Diccionario*, such as *"Agricole"* or "Chine," both by the Physiocrat Grivel, who included other many previous texts by Quesnay, Baudeau, Du Pont de Nemours or Turgot. The theory of the territorial tax explained by Álvarez Guerra also seems to be derived from the long summary carried out by Grivel of the ideas of Le Trosne; see Charles-Joseph Panckoucke, ed., *Encyclopédie méthodique. Économie politique et diplomatique* (Paris-Liège: Panckoucke and Plomteux, 1784–1788), I, 57–72, 543–68. However, it should be remembered that an exclusive economic doctrine was not adopted in these volumes — there were also many ideas of Necker or Smith —; see Perrot, *Une histoire intellectuelle*, 127ff., and Catherine Larrère, "L'*Encyclopédie Méthodique*: une économie très politique," in *L'Encyclopédie Méthodique (1782–1832). Des Lumières au Positivisme*, ed. Claude Blanckaert and Michel Porret (Geneva: Droz, 2006), 215–39.

highly probable that the intellectual origin of this Physiocratic piece dates back to the Salamanca University professor, Ramón de Salas, with whom Álvarez Guerra had close contact during his university stage where he began to learn about political economy.[59] But, going beyond the "Introductory Remarks," the translation reveals a significant effort to adapt the content of the original entries to the Spanish context, even, in some cases, being carried away by a nationalist attitude which led him to claim that "in some branches we have made more progress than foreigners." This required "the adaptation to our practices" of the original ideas; extending, modifying or rectifying them; "the invention of new terms as there were not equivalents in Spanish;" or adding "articles that explained unknown terms in French agriculture." All of this was reflected in a version which was clearly marked by the translator's views. Although not in a systematic way, the *Curso* became a channel for diffusing different agricultural experiences and technical inventions undertaken in Spain — and, in some cases, also in its colonies — over the preceding decades and this explains why the ever present French agronomic sources (in addition to Rozier, Daubeton, Parmentier, Duhamel de Monceau, etc.) were complemented with others that were highly representative of Spanish enlightened agronomy: Álvarez Guerra not only recurred to prestigious authors, such as Cavanilles or Bowles, but also to the *Memorias* of the Matritense, the *Extractos* of the Bascongada or the articles of the *Semanario de Agricultura.* He also mentioned, albeit very occasionally, Jovellanos. But the institutional context within which the Rozier's translation was carried out —the Madrid Society — and the dates when it was undertaken — 1797–1803 — suggest that it had to constitute an alternative proposal to Jovellanos' *Informe.* There is no doubt that both texts had an agrarian and liberal content although the discrepancies between them were also very evident: they ranged from Álvarez Guerra's proposal to organise the *royaume agricole* around the principles of property, security and liberty to the consequences of this in the context of economic reforms. Issues such as the unique productivity of agriculture, the free foreign trade of grains or direct taxation through the *impôt unique* established clear differences between the positions of the two authors.

In any event, and returning to the Madrid Society, it is probable that, as well as preventing other similar encyclopaedic projects from being published,[60]

59 Jesús Astigarraga, *Luces y republicanismo* (Madrid: CEPC, 2011), 35–37.

60 During the final decades of the century, Cesáreo Nova Palacio attempted to translate the *Dictionnaire* of the French agronomist Jacques-Christophe Valmont de Bomare; the professor of surgery Joaquín de Villalba sought to create a "Dictionary of rural and veterinarian hygiene and economics;" and, finally, Merino also attempted to create an ambitious

the translation of Álvarez Guerra influenced the fate of Seixo at the heart of this Society. After publishing a treatise on beekeeping in 1797, a year later, the Galician-born author requested support to publish a periodical on agriculture, to no avail. And to cap it all, in 1800, two years before his death, he created a labourer's booklet which did not receive the Society's support either.[61] In reality, the Society had always distanced itself from Seixo. The problem may have resided in the fact that his texts were written within a highly conservative ideological framework. In Seixo's writings, economics was still mostly concerned with the private and domestic domain,[62] and was far removed from the reformist premises being diffused by the Madrid Society, led by Jovellanos' *Informe*. In one of the translations that he carried out during these years of intense reaffirmation as disseminator, the defence of the ecclesiastic celibacy and the volume of clergymen was accompanied by attacks on Bayle, Voltaire and Montesquieu.[63]

The fate of Álvarez Guerra was very different. Not only did he continue his disseminating work in one of Spain's leading scientific gazettes, the *Variedades de Ciencia, Literatura y Artes* (1803–1805), but he also partook in intense political activity which placed him at the forefront of the first Spanish constitutionalism. He could be considered as a type of bridge with the generation of Antonio Sandalio de Arias (1774–1839), José Espinosa (1763–1815) and the brothers Claudio Boutelou (1774–1842) and Esteban Boutelou (1776–1813), the agronomists responsible for keeping the interest in the *new* agriculture alive until the Liberal Triennium (1820–1823).[64] In 1808, one of them, Arias, published, with the help of the Madrid Society, a new agricultural booklet which was of an undoubtedly higher quality than those preceding it as it was perfectly up-to-date with the information about the most recent scientific advances in terms

"Encyclopaedia of Agriculture;" these projects were never carried out (see, respectively, AHN, *Estado*, bundles 2.932–23, 3.182–151, and BNE, mss., 13.455).

61 Vicente del Seixo, *Cartilla de labradores* (Madrid: 1800). A predecessor of the illustrated booklets at the end of the century was the *Cartilla de agricultura de moreras* (Madrid: Gabriel Ramírez, 1761) by Antonio Elgueta; but it is probable that Seixo's initiative was influenced by the prior publication in 1799 of the *Cartilla rústica dispuesta para instrucción de labradores* (Salamanca: Imprenta de Francisco de Tóxar, 1799).

62 Vicente del Seixo, *Compendio de observaciones que forman el plano de un viaje político y filosófico que debe hacerse dentro y fuera del reino en que nacemos* (Madrid: Pantaleón Aznar, 1796), 31–32.

63 Vicente del Seixo, *Reflexiones cristianas y políticas sobre el estado religioso y el celibato, comparado con el del matrimonio* (Madrid: Pantaleón Aznar, 1795).

64 See the collection of texts gathered by Lluis Argemí, ed., *Agricultura e Ilustración* (Madrid: Ministerio de Agricultura, Pesca y Alimentación, 1988).

of agriculture.[65] In any case, the first generation of professional publicists of Spanish history in the field of rural economics was formed by the likes of Seixo, Álvarez Guerra and Arias.

5 Economic Societies and the Promotion of the Economic Press

In addition to their dialogues or booklets, the economic societies were also pioneers in their attempts to promote economic gazettes. They matured in a relatively new context — the Spanish press' "golden age"[66] — and with a specific feature: it was overseen by an "official" Enlightenment which understood its importance as an instrument of instruction and to attract supporters for the reforms being developed. In 1775, Campomanes clearly established what the new pattern should be:

> the trade gazettes, the economic daily newspapers and other periodicals of this type are the writings which have enlightened our neighbours. This same effect will occur in Spain, once their reading and calculation becomes fashionable rather than the trifles that are usually printed in them.[67]

Precisely, the proliferation of these societies generated multiplying effects on the press. The Majorca Society was the promoter of the first newspaper, *Noticia periódica de los precios corrientes de la semana*, a weekly periodical published in Palma de Majorca from September 1779.[68] Its scope was limited to the Balearic archipelago and its format was initially very simple: its first issues only had one page. Its succinct contents described the life of the Society, provided official information and informed about the islands' trade (prices, vessels, etc.). At the same time, originally, the *Noticia* had a brief section on "agriculture, arts and domestic economics;" later, it incorporated another on "economics," although its content was about domestic economics; and, in 1782, another on "politics," although it was dedicated to demography and public health. These

65 Antonio Sandalio Arias, *Cartilla elemental de agricultura acomodada a nuestro suelo y clima* (Madrid: Gómez Fuentenebro y Compañía, 1808).

66 See ch. VII above.

67 Campomanes, *Apéndice*, I, XXII. Sempere raised similar complaints, *Ensayo*, 178.

68 Shortly afterwards its name was changed to *Palma de Mallorca* and, after 1795, when it extended its content and introduced a subscription systems, it was changed again to *Semanario económico, instructivo y comercial de Palma de Mallorca*.

changing strategies responded to an attempt to capture the Balearic public. Its attempt to generate loyalty among the islands' population led to the development of a new way of disseminating all types of useful knowledge: adding the brief instructions published in successive issues, the reader of the *Noticia* could construct short instructive treatises about the bleaching of textiles, grapevines, mulberry trees, beekeeping, etc.

There were essentially three types of sources of the *Noticia*: arts and agronomics treatises (Dupuy, Valcárcel, Reaumur, Chomel, Tull, etc.); several Spanish gazettes, particularly Araus' *Semanario económico* and the Suárez and Núñez's *Memorias instructivas y curiosas*; and, finally, different naturalist and economic authors: together with Buffon, the *Noticia* sporadically referred to the ideas on agriculture of authors such as Goudar, Galiani, Campomanes or Bielfeld. Its pages perfectly reflected the dispute between the *old* and the *new* agronomy. With respect to political economy, the journal did not include a section on "Commerce" with this content until 1782. This decision may have seemed to be a prelude to the step from domestic and rural economics to political economy, but the weekly publication continued to report essentially on the former. The introduction of this new section responded to its condition as a body of the Majorca Economic Society and to the considerable work that this institution had been undertaking to defend commercial activity.[69] A good example of this was the Chair of Commerce and Political Economy, which the Society founded in 1788.[70] This matter clearly reflects that, despite the fact that Majorca Society was peripheral and insular, it had not remained on the sidelines of the circulation flows of economic ideas. The central influences of the founding enlightened circles of the Majorca Society included Genovesi, Galiani and Coyer. *La noblesse commerçante* (1755) written by the latter was translated into Spanish in 1781 by one if its members, José María de Espinosa. Therefore, it is not surprising that the Society used the weekly issues of the *Noticia* to publish summaries of different political economy treatises. In 1784 the *Proyecto Económico* (c. 1762; 1779) by Ward was chosen; in 1787 the *Lezioni* (1765–1767) by Genovesi; and, from the end of 1789 and practically throughout the year 1790, in a comprehensive version, the *Respuesta fiscal sobre abolir la tasa* (1764) by Campomanes. The political intention of this latter was clear: it sought to refute the repeal of the *Pragmática* — Law — (1765) in 1790 referring to the free trade of grains throughout the monarchy, which had been inspired by the Campomanes' *Respuesta*. At the same time, although still

69 *Noticia periódica*, no. I, 3 January 1784.

70 *Noticia periódica*, no. X, 8 March 1788.

a modest publication, throughout the 1780s the *Noticia* began to include other content: economic and demographic statistics on Majorca, other news about commerce and instructions of the bureaucrats and magistrates. All of this did not prevent the slow decline of the publication. In 1796, it sought financial support in order to survive.[71] The acceptance of the subscription system in this year coincided with the opening of the publication to topics such as moral philosophy, education or geography, seeking to reach a wider audience. By this time, political economy had virtually disappeared from its pages.

While this was going on in Majorca, the Madrid Society was continually attempting to create an economic gazette. Its initiatives were virtually official, given that the Council of Castile had granted it the function of undertaking censorship. In June 1777, Juan Bautista Cubié (c. 1743–1782?), official in the Royal Library, announced to the Society his decision to continue publishing Saura's *Semanario.* His initiative did not take long to pass the Society's censorship: the principal precaution of the censor, José Guevara Vasconcelos (1737–1804), was to avoid the excessive fragmentation of articles.[72] Cubié's idea was "to follow Saura's method."[73] This was the case in a formal sense, but not in terms of content. The new *Semanario económico* (1777–1778) did not include informations about commerce, only about arts, trades and rural economics; although the space for the *new* agronomy was broader. For educational purposes, Cubié published different articles on the *new* agricultural instruments (ploughs and seed drills), the rural industry (hemp and flax) and the Tull-Duhamel crop method on which an extensive summary was published in the newspaper in 1777. Nevertheless, a good part of the news was drawn from the JOE and classical texts on rural economics (Liger). Therefore, this new version of the *Semanario* was configured as a further extension of *Oeconomie,* yet outdated: much of its material was more than twenty-five years old. Its principal distinguishing feature was that it possessed communicating vessels with the Madrid Society: its primary audience was, undoubtedly, its Agricultural Class, involved in the diffusion of news on agronomy since its creation in 1776.

In any event, the Cubié's *Semanario* most probably did not fully convince the Madrid Society. Nicolás Fernández de Moratín (1737–1780), the new chief censor, was quick to inform that the Society was not responsible for the veracity of its contents.[74] Its publication was also temporarily interrupted by the Madrid Society itself a few weeks after it began, due to the fact that in October

71 *Noticia periódica*, no. 1, 2 January 1796.

72 AHN, *Consejos*, bundle 5.540–23. His report was from the 20 June 1777.

73 SE (Cubié), IV, 8.

74 AHN, *Consejos*, bundle 5.540–23. His report was dated the 18 October 1777.

1777 the member Miguel Jerónimo Suárez y Núñez had announced his intention of publishing "weekly news about agriculture, industry and commerce," that will soon become his *Memorias instructivas y curiosas* (MIC, 1778–1791). The Council of Castile established that this new request should not cancel the licence held by Cubié, but, undoubtedly, it dealt a deadly blow to his *Semanario*: only twenty-six issues were published between October 1777 and June 1778. Another subsequent proposal by Pedro Dabout, also a member of the Madrid Society, to publish a weekly or monthly economic gazette that would carry on from Cubié's periodical was also aborted.[75]

The first issue of Suárez's MIC was published in 1778.[76] The brilliant profile of its editor surely influenced the rapid approval of the publication by the Madrid Society. Suárez (1733–1791) was endorsed by his membership to prestigious patriotic institutions, such as the Basque Society or the Seville Royal Academy of Literature, and also by a faultless trajectory as a translator of treatises on applied sciences and arts. This trajectory had been acknowledged by the Board of Trade, which in 1772 had appointed him as its archivist, and later by the Madrid Society of which he had been one of the first members of its Arts Class, as well as its Secretary between 1776 and 1781. At the heart of the Society, Suárez had the best support possible: in 1781 Campomanes praised the quality of his translations.[77]

The *Memorias* responded to an initiative that was "ordered by" the Board of Trade, but financed by Suárez himself. It constituted an exemplary initiative due to both the quantity and quality of its contents and its duration over time. Its publication required considerable planning. On many occasions, the MIC published very long treatises, which Suárez had to fragment in order to comply with his weekly instalments. Finally, almost 150 were published in a total of twelve volumes, printed between 1778 and 1791. These papers were translations relating to the fields mentioned in the title of the publication — "Agriculture, Commerce, Industry, Economics, Chemistry, Botany, Natural History, etc." —, with special attention paid to sciences (chemistry) and applied arts (agronomy and textile techniques). Its sources were dictionaries, articles from gazettes and academy records, particularly those of the Academy of Science of Paris and its *Collection des Arts*. Therefore, they constituted a prolongation of the translation of the same collection published by Campomanes in his 1774–1776 *Discursos*.

---

75 Domergue, *Jovellanos*, 203–04.

76 On Suárez, see Francisco Aguilar Piñal, "Un traductor de la ciencia ilustrada: Suárez y Núñez," *Cuadernos Dieciochistas* 7 (2006): 87–112.

77 Aguilar Piñal, "Un traductor," 97–98.

The scope of the MIC extended to political economy. It published the translations of the treatises of Condillac (1778), Necker (1783), Bigot de Saint-Croix (1791), Justi (1791) and Turgot (1791), together with his *Édit* of the abolition of the guilds. This represented a significant step forward in the history of the Spanish economic press: for the first time, complete political economy treatises were published. Furthermore, all of the translations were of an excellent quality, they were hardly subjected to censoring and, with the exception of that of Justi, were complete. Moreover, the texts were written by prominent authors who explained the functioning of the commercial society (Condillac and Turgot) or the development of the official reforms relating to the trade of grain (Necker) or the freedom of labour (Saint-Croix). All in all, Suárez simply followed the general trend of Spanish economic culture of the 1780s, when, thanks to translation, an authentic "explosion" in the dissemination of foreign texts occurred. All of this converted Suárez into one of the most prolific translators of economic texts of the Spanish Enlightenment, although he was most probably not the only material author of these version — in the records of the Madrid Society the occasional help of the member Lorenzo Irisarri was mentioned —. In any event, his MIC had to be published following the precise guidelines of the Madrid Society. The translated texts were not only censored by the Society,[78] but they were well known among its most influential authorities, such as Campomanes and Jovellanos, if not even induced by them. This commitment to political economy was even more logical if we take into account that in 1779, the conservative *Oeconomie* once again gained the support of the ubiquitous Nifo, who took advantage of the new war with Great Britain in 1779 to republish his *Correo General de la Europa*.[79] But the commendable task carried out by Suárez — as well as the *Memorias*, he translated fifteen works by Nollet, Macquer, Duhamel de Monceau and other scientists of the European Enlightenment — is even more valuable if we take into account that his *Memorias* withstood the turbulence caused by the French Revolution. Nobody better than Suárez could reflect the unhappiness of those pioneering journalists who offered their pens and their money to ensure that the press contributed, in the words of Jovellanos, to "accelerating this general trend which is occurring among us towards the study of economics."[80] His death in 1791 coincided with

78 In 1786, the Madrid Society appointed Diego Notario as censor (AHN, *Consejos*, bundle 50.674).

79 It was, in fact, a selection of discourses from this publication. They included the Linneo's emblematic text (II, letter CVII), which was newly republished in 1786.

80 Gaspar Melchor de Jovellanos, "Dictamen sobre la oportunidad de publicar una gaceta económica" (1786), in *Obras completas. Vol. X. Escritos económicos*, ed. Vicent Llombart and Joaquín Ocampo (Gijón: KRK ediciones, 2008), 648.

Floridablanca's Law banning the press in order to prevent the contagion of the effects of the French revolution and amidst times of great hardship.

While all of this was happening, in 1786–1787 the Madrid Society debated about whether to promote an exclusively economic gazette.[81] This intention was underlined by the perception that not only Suárez's MIC but also the large-scale journalistic initiatives of these years — *El Censor* (1781–1787), the *Memorial Literario* (1784–1791), *El Correo de los Ciegos* (1786–1791) or *El Espíritu de los mejores diarios literarios* (1787–1791) — were general and were aimed at too wide an audience. The debate gave rise to three positions. According to Manuel José Marín, the Madrid Society had to use its centrality in the network of economic societies to promote a "national" weekly or bimonthly gazette so as to report the news generated by these societies. Jovellanos, meanwhile, understood that this "national" news would not be enough to fill a gazette with this regularity, so he supported a mixed option which included the translation extracts of foreign works. Finally, Juan Pérez Villamil (1754–1824) proposed a periodical based on theoretical debates. The discrepancies extended to the doctrinal level. Jovellanos' report seemed to come from Condillac: the gazette should be focused on the political relations between the government and the economy "considered relatively one with the other."[82] However, Villamil's proposal seemed, quite certainly, closer to Physiocracy, whose journalistic initiatives aimed at defending the advantages of the *royaume agricole* had not any repercussions in Spain until then. As a consequence of this debate, at the end of 1787, the Madrid Society decided to promote a double publication: a gazette and a monthly economic mercury, the second being a type of leaflet with extracts of discourses.

Through this decision, the Madrid Society also seemed to want to remain unswayed by the "deluge of all types of works that were flooding the literary republic."[83] In fact, while during these years a provincial press was emerging, with a significant presence in Andalusia and the former territories of the Crown of Aragon,[84] between 1786 and 1789 at least five economic gazette projects were also activated. It is highly significant that Nifo was present once again

81 Domergue, *Jovellanos*, 201–31.

82 It is no coincidence that his report was written when Condillac's treatise was being intensely disseminated: it was translated in 1778 in the Gerónimo Suárez's MIC.

83 AHN, *Consejos*, bundle 5.552–8.

84 The most notable and long-lasting was the *Diario de Barcelona*, founded in 1792 by the Neapolitan Pedro Pablo Usson with the support of the city's local government; on the content of its section on "Economics and Commerce," see Lluch, *El pensament*, 79ff. Also very prominent was the *Diario Pinciano*, published in Valladolid in 1787–1788 by José Mariano Beristain, a priest. This weekly magazine was the unofficial channel for information about the activities of the enlightened institutions in this city in Castile, including

at this key moment in the history of the Spanish economic press. In his new initiative, a daily newspaper called the *Año literario*,[85] defended his pioneering role as a translator of "exquisite works" about agriculture and commerce: "in that day people were somewhat inclined to read, much more than when Nifo established the *Diario Universal, Curioso, etc.*" That said, when, months later, the Council requested a sample of his new daily newspaper, he opted to republish, for the third time, his *Correo General de la Europa*.[86] In those years, this pioneering journalist experienced a slow and relentless decline.

The other four promoters included prominent publicists such as Cristóbal Cladera or Tomás Marien y Arróspide.[87] "Commerce" in its theoretical or practical dimension appears in their initiatives interlaced with articles on science, literature and other disciplines. The only exception was the *Biblioteca completa de comercio* proposed by the Bilbao-born trader Marien. However, the strategy of the censors, in general, went against them. Undoubtedly taking into account the experience of the previous phase, their refusal to publish was due to the predictable ambition, inexperience, lack of professionalism and, only marginally, the presence of risks from a point of view of religious orthodoxy.[88] In fact, of all of these initiatives, only one volume of the seven promised by Marien ended up being published.[89] The transcripts of these rejected publications reveal that the press had become both a fertile ground for social promotion and a battlefield for enlightened aspirations. Even more so when, in the words of Larriba, the "journalistic hydra" grew relentlessly with the wind

its economic society; see César Almuiña, "Estudio Preliminar," in *Diario Pinciano, primer periódico de Valladolid (1787–88)*, ed. César Almuiña (Valladolid: 1978): 5–74.

85 AHN, *Consejos*, bundle 50.674.

86 All of this confirms Nifo as one of the central references of the Spanish Enlightenment anchored in the Catholic, absolutist and anti-commerce agrarian current whose sources were authors such as Fleury or Pluche; vid. Rothkrug, *Opposition*, 234–98.

87 The projects were the following: "Biblioteca periódica y elemental de ciencias, artes, literatura y comercio," by Cristóbal Cladera, December 1786 (AHN, *Consejos*, bundle 5.552–8); "Biblioteca completa del comercio," together with a fortnightly paper on universal commerce, by Tomás Antonio Marien Arróspide, Spring 1788 (AHN, *Consejos*, bundle 5.554–42); "Diario enciclopédico de las ciencias, bellas letras, artes y oficios, agricultura, economía y comercio," by an Irish scientist and a French mathematician, November 1788 (AHN, *Consejos*, bundle 3.242–22); "Diario de ciencias, agricultura, comercio, artes y oficios," by two French writers and an Irish scientist, February 1789 (AHN, *Consejos*, bundle 5.555–84). Still in 1804, two individuals proposed a "Biblioteca rural o Diccionario completo del labrador," in the form of a three-weekly "single sheet," to disseminate the articles of the *Semanario de agricultura*; an Order of 1809 banned it (AHN, *Consejos*, bundle 5.567–4).

88 AHN, *Consejos*, bundle 5.552–8.

89 See ch. V above.

behind the government, and the Inquisition, although formally preserving its censoring power, was unable to cut off its head in time merely because it was overwhelmed.[90]

6 Final Remarks

The initiative of the Madrid Society was not implemented. However, the density of the events occurring in 1791–1792 — the death of Suárez; the Order of February 1791 by Floridablanca silencing the press; the discreet repeal of this order a year later by Aranda — gave rise to the emergence, in October 1792, of the first issue of *El Correo mercantil*. Its creation was not isolated from the more than three previous decades of hesitant initiatives of economic gazettes; rather it seemed to be a natural continuation of them. This gradual strengthening of the economic press was not far removed from the growing belief that in the last quarter of the century "commerce" was gaining ground as an unavoidable factor of the "Enlightenment" and the emergence of the economic and agronomic knowledge instigated by the economic societies. All of this confirms their condition of incubators of the public space and opinion.[91] Their relative openness to participation, the equal treatment of different social classes, the regular discussion of topics characteristic of the enlightened culture, the diffusion of new ideas or the relentless publication of memoirs were factors that enabled these institutions to accommodate both new forms of sociability and new cultural dynamics and practices — pre-political in some ways—; this modernizing experience also led to women being included as active members of these institutions, albeit rather timidly.[92] Therefore, these societies became genuine schools of future "citizens," whose status was differentiated from subjects in terms of political criticism, freedom of expression

90 Elisabel Larriba, "Inquisición y prensa periódica en la segunda mitad del siglo XVIII," *Cuadernos de Ilustración y Romanticismo* 13 (2005): 77–92; Lucienne Domergue, *Censure et Lumières dans l'Espagne de Charles III* (Paris: CNRS, 1982), 147–92.

91 See, on this issue, Gloria Franco, "El ejercicio del poder en la España del Siglo XVIII. Entre las prácticas culturales y las prácticas políticas," *Mélanges de la Casa de Velázquez* 35, no. 1 (2005): 51–77, and "Captar súbditos y crear ciudadanos, doble objetivo de los 'Amigos del País' en el siglo XVIII," *Historia social* 64 (2009): 3–23.

92 See, among others, Mónica Bolufer, "Femmes et hommes dans la société idéale. Les sociétés économiques des amis du pays dans l'Espagne des Lumières," *Dix-Huitième Siècle* 43 (2011): 487–504, and Catherine Jaffe and Elizabeth Franklin Lewis, eds., *Eve's Enlightenment: women's experience in Spain and Spanish America, 1726–1839* (Baton Rouge: Lousiana State University Press, 2009).

or ideological plurality. In short, they fostered a high level of participation of the socio-political elite in public life. One of their fundamental functions was to expand the Spanish public sphere by capturing new audiences for their disseminating and popularising publications. Indeed, without their pioneering experience it is impossible to understand the set of political and cultural dynamics that opened the constitutional path for Spain, which culminated in the *Cortes* of Cadiz. In fact, in June 1813, once the Peninsula War was over, these *Cortes* decreed that economic societies should be established in all the main cities of the Kingdom as consultative bodies of the town councils in matters related to economic development and the dissemination of useful knowledge.

CHAPTER 5

Commerce and Political Economy Dictionaries

1 Introduction

In recent decades there has been a gradual increase in interest in the study of dictionaries and encyclopaedias and their role in the processes of developing, adapting and spreading economic ideas. A study of this kind is a response to the encyclopaedic movement's enormous influence on modern European cultural history, particularly after the publication of Moreri's *Grand dictionnaire historique* (1674). This movement not only gave rise to emblematic works such as Bayle's *Dictionnaire historique* (1697), Chambers' *Cyclopaedia* (1728) and Diderot and D'Alembert's *Encyclopédie* (1751–1775), but also led to the creation of smaller alphabetically-ordered specialist works.[1] The proliferation of scientific and technical dictionaries is a relatively unknown aspect of the process of popularising science which took place as Latin was replaced by vernacular languages and scientific developments spread to new fields of knowledge. Other "massive works" such as lexicons or vocabularies, based on the principles of creating an inventory of universal knowledge, presenting it in alphabetical order and the use of "shadow authors,"[2] enjoyed a golden age during the seventeenth and eighteenth centuries. In this way, the old ideal of encyclopaedic compilations held by enlightened scholars was united with Condillac's conviction that "science is nothing but a language *bienfait*;" or, to go a little further, with Condorcet's aspiration to create a *langue universelle* that would go beyond the scientific sphere to reach moral or political dimensions.

This scenario is only partially valid for Spain. It is well-known that the country played a marginal role in eighteenth century encyclopaedic literature. Although her most renowned enlightened writers, such as Campomanes and

1 On lexicons and dictionaries as motors driving the *early* Enlightenment, see Israel, *Radical Enlightenment*, 134–36. Works on arts and crafts or literature on travel also participated of the same encyclopedic spirit; about the latter, see Juan Pimentel: *Testigos del mundo. Ciencia, literatura y viajes en la Ilustración* (Madrid: Marcial Pons, 2003): 215–49. For a previous study of the content of this chapter, see Jesús Astigarraga and Juan Zabalza, "Los diccionarios de comercio y economía en el siglo XVIII español," *Revista de Historia Industrial* 35 (2007): 13–46.

2 The promoting of dictionaries and other works of anonymous collective authorship was also common practice in the Spanish Enlightenment. See María Teresa Nava in the Academy of History sphere: "Ciencia y académicos de la Historia en la Ilustración española: la emergencia del autor colectivo," *Revista Historia Autónoma* 10 (2017): 67–85.

 | DOI:10.1163/9789004442894_007

Jovellanos, promoted and participated in the creation of dictionaries, only Moreri's *Dictionnaire* was even partially translated and no encyclopaedias were ever compiled.[3] However, any definitive assessment requires examining specialist encyclopaedias that were produced in Spain in fields such as "commerce" and "economics." Gómez de Enterría reveals that the emergence of political economy there throughout the eighteenth century led to "the appearance of a new vocabulary which was introduced into the language through the works of economic literature published that century."[4] This *neolexicon* referred to economics and commerce and was fed by the flow of translations from French; it mainly consisted of recent neologisms such as "economists," "competition," and "entrepreneur." It also included traditional terms and throughout the eighteenth century constituted a vocabulary that was still in its early stages but was increasingly becoming accepted and used. Various quantitative studies have argued that despite the explanatory weakness of the term "economics" as opposed to others such as "commerce" and "industry," and the fact that it collates with so many adjectives such as "public," "political" and "civil,"[5] after 1740 a process occurred whereby "economics" emerged in Spanish print culture as a "knowledge with a name."[6] The study of Spain's role in the history of European "commerce" and "economics" dictionaries in the eighteenth century, which has barely been addressed to date, provides a fascinating prism through which to discover new features of the process by which economic science emerged. The backdrop to this chapter is the period from 1723 to 1730, when the *Dictionnaire* compiled by the two brothers Jacques and Louis Philémon Savary des Bruslons

3 The most noteworthy success was in the field of lexicographical dictionaries, thanks to the pioneering *Diccionario de Autoridades* (1726–1739), which was extended into the sciences and arts field in Esteban Terreros' *Diccionario castellano* (1786–1793).

4 Josefa Gómez de Enterría, *Voces de la economía y el comercio en el español del siglo XVIII* (Alcalá de Henares: Universidad de Alcalá de Henares, 1996).

5 Juana Ugarte, *Discurso Historia Informática. La palabra economía en los textos económicos españoles del siglo XVIII* (Oviedo: Universidad de Oviedo, 1996); see also Pedro Álvarez de Miranda, *Palabras e ideas: el léxico de la Ilustración temprana en España (1680–1760)* (Madrid: Real Academia Española, 1992).

6 Jean Vilar coined this expression; see "Des idées, des mots pour 'des choses': l'économie savoir sans nom de l'Espagne classique," in *Les mentalités dans la Péninsule Ibérique et en Amérique Latine aux XVIe et XVIIe siécles* (Tours: Université de Tours, 1978): 55–57. Say's work could represent a decisive step towards the achievement of the new language of political economy, as well as for the acceptance of the innovative theory of the entrepreneur; see, respectively, José Carlos de Hoyos, *Léxico económico en la lengua española de principios del XIX. El 'Epítome' de Jean-Baptiste Say* (San Millán de la Cogolla: Cilengua, 2018), and José Manuel Menudo and Jose María O-Kean, "La recepción de la obra de Jean-Baptiste Say en España: la teoría económica del empresario," *RHE* 23, no. 1 (2005): 117–42.

was published, and 1784–1788 when the last eighteenth century dictionaries covering these disciplines appeared as part of the *Encyclopédie Méthodique*.

2 *Oikonomia* and *Commerce* in the Encyclopaedic Literature of Eighteenth Century Europe

What really characterises the first dictionaries in the history of "economics" is the fact that their content seems to refer to broader fields of knowledge, which is logical if we recall that their most prominent creators, beginning with Quesnay and Smith, understood that political economy was not an independent discipline. Many authors continued to view it according to the Aristotelian concept of *Oikonomia* or *Oeconomie* as the administration of household finance; thus, the management functions typical of a home owner were transferred to the sovereign, and simple analogy could be used to talk about the existence of a political, public or civil economy.[7] This conception predominated in lexicographical dictionaries and also in those for other fields that bordered on political economy, particularly agriculture or *re rustica*, arts and trade. Although such works contain very telling signs of conservatism, from a historical perspective it is important to note that their influence was reinforced by the fact that these types of dictionaries had their own alphabetical texts before the first "commerce" dictionaries were published. France provides a good example, as always: during the period 1666–1750 many encyclopaedic works were created as channels through which to disseminate *Oikonomia* and the useful knowledge associated with it. This was the case with general encyclopaedias such as the works by Moreri and Trevoux, and also with dictionaries in the fields of agriculture, natural history and the arts of the *maison rustique* and the *campagne* written by authors such as Liger d'Auxerre and Pluche. The 1709 publication of Chomel's *Dictionnaire Oeconomique* marked the starting point for the appearance of a large number of *abregés* or *portatives* dictionaries in eighteenth century France.

However, the lexicon of *Oikonomia*, which also dominated eighteenth century encyclopaedic literature in Spain, had little influence on the emergence of the first "commerce" dictionaries. These were underlain by a European trading culture which in the seventeenth century had begun to generate a type of text in which the terms "commerce" or "trade" replaced *Oikonomia*. The merchants'

---

7 Marco E. L. Guidi, "*Economy* and *Political Economy* in Italian Dictionaries and Encyclopaedias (1726–1861)," in *Political Economy and National Realities*, ed. Manuela Albertone and Alberto Masoero (Turin: Fondazione Luigi Einaudi, 1994): 147–75.

handbooks and treatises on trading culture as a whole came under this heading; that is, the fundamentals of wealth creation in a politically organised society. The texts on "commerce," or more precisely, on the "science of commerce" and the "science of commerce in general," to quote Cantillon, aimed to emphasise their theoretical aspirations vis-à-vis merchants' handbooks. They were often conceived in the fields of moral philosophy or public administration sciences as part of the "science" and "art" of government and were thus aimed not only at merchants but also at high-ranking officials in the government of a state economy. In short, what lay behind this lexicographical change was a demand for a scientific systematisation of economic-commercial issues. The most emblematic European works of the period, such as those by Child, Melon, Forbonnais and Genovesi, among many others, were classed as commerce "discourses," "treatises" or "lessons,"[8] and it is thus it is no coincidence that the first dictionaries on the science of economics were in fact on "commerce."

The eighteenth century commerce dictionaries make up a clear subgroup of literature on political economy.[9] Initially conceived almost as a mere extension of merchant's handbooks, they went on to become vehicles for the "general principles" of trade. By the end of the fruitful "Colbert cycle" (1660–1740) of commercial literature,[10] these dictionaries had begun to reflect the intense economic debate that took place in France in the mid-eighteenth century. A cornerstone of the "Colbert cycle" was the pioneering *Dictionnaire universel de commerce* (1723–1730) compiled by Jacques Savary's sons, Jacques and Louis Philémon Savary des Bruslons.[11] This work used the nascent *langue du commerce* to create a *summa* of trade characterised by their pursuit of universality, dignifying commerce — without it, they wrote, "everything in a Kingdom would languish"[12] — while also attributing it a certain degree of autonomy. Even so, theoretical reflection was lacking, and the "facts" and "practice" of commerce prevailed over its "principles." It is therefore not surprising that Ramsay McCulloch complained that the *Dictionnaire* had been designed with

8 William Letwin, *The Origins of Scientific Economics* (London: Methuen, 1963), 214ff.

9 Arthur H. Cole, *The Historical Development of Economic and Business Literature* (Boston: Baker Library, Harvard Graduate School of Business Administration, 1957), 15–16; Christine Théré, "Economic Publishing and Authors, 1566–1789," in *Studies in the History of French Political Economy*, ed. Gilbert Faccarello (London-New York: Routledge, 1998), 26. The alphabetical format was also occasionally used in merchants' handbooks: see Benito Bails, *Aritmética para negociantes* (Madrid: Viuda de Ibarra, 1790), 263–78.

10 Hoock, "Discours comercial," 57–73.

11 Hoock, "Le phénomène Savary," 113–23; Perrot, *Une histoire*, 99–104.

12 Jacques and Philémon-Louis Savary des Brûlons, *Dictionnaire universel de commerce* (Paris: J. Estienne, 1723–1730), I, XII.

the spirit of a *custom officier* — Jacques Savary was a customs inspector in Paris — instead of a true *philosopher.*[13] In any event, this canonical work of the European Enlightenment was based on a format which over time would be come to be a model for future works. It was a type of encyclopaedic *vade mecum* of all the relevant official information produced in France between 1660 and 1715: public company ordinances, legislative orders, *Académie des Sciences* documents and reports by the *intendants*, etc.[14] It also had an unquestionable political intention; officially endorsed and financed, the work's primary objective was to internationalise the protectionist, industrialist and interventionist Colbertist programme, always defending French trading positions. The *Dictionnaire* was successful; translated into German, Russian, Portuguese and Italian, at least partially, many *abregés* and *portatives* editions were also published in France (Lefebvre de Beauvray, Robinet, Lacombe de Prezel, etc.). Five more editions appeared between 1723–1730 and 1759–1765, which updated its content and ensured that it continued to be influential until the end of the eighteenth century,[15] which is clear from the fact that substantial parts were incorporated into the volumes on *Commerce* (1783–1784) in Panckoucke's *Encyclopédie Méthodique.*

The *Dictionnaire* was also a success in Britain. It was the starting point for series of alphabetical works which began with Postlethwayt's *Universal Dictionary of Trade and Commerce* (1751–1755);[16] it was followed by Rolt's *A New Dictionary of Trade and Commerce* (1756) and Mortimer's *A New Complete Dictionary of Trade and Commerce* (1766). The first was relatively well-received in Britain and four editions were published over the twenty years between 1751–1755 and 1774. It was a longer "anglicised" version of the Savary des Brulons' work and introduced many theoretical concepts, which were included in the entries on "*banking*," "*money*," etc. As Stanley Jevons and Henry Higgs noted at the end of the nineteenth century, its content incorporated long extracts from Cantillon's still unpublished *Essai,* which rendered it a plagiarism that was

13 John Ramsay McCulloch, *The Literature of Political Economy* (1845; New York: A. M. Kelley, 1991), XX.

14 According to Charles Coquelin and Gilbert Guillaumin these reports were its most valuable content: *Dictionnaire de l'Économie Politique* (1852–1853; Brussels: Meline, Cans et Compagnie, 1853–1854), II, 648–49.

15 Subsequent editions of the work echoed Melon's *Essai* and the monetary debates between this writer and Law. The fifth edition was the fullest and longest and was published in 1759–1765. So that it could be the Northern European market it incorporated entries taken from the first seven volumes of Diderot and D'Alembert's *Encyclopédie* .

16 Edgar Augustus Jerome Johnson, *Predecessors of Adam Smith* (1937; New York: A. M. Kelley, 1965); Hutchison, *Before Adam Smith*, 241–43.

not yet exempt from enigmas.[17] However, Postlethwayt's sources also included many worthy British authors, from Mun and Petty to Locke and Hume, and his work was the first alphabetically ordered text in the pre-Smith era.[18]

In France, meanwhile, Diderot and D'Alembert's *Encyclopédie* (1751–1775) was the first alphabetically ordered work to include economic principles. This book was a true sounding board for the major economic debates of the time,[19] partly via Quesnay, who wrote various entries including those on "grains," "fermiers," etc. and which identified with the birth of Physiocracy, and partly due to Forbonnais, the author of another series of entries on "agriculture," "commerce," etc., which were far removed from Physiocracy and later appeared in his *Élémens du commerce* (1754). A few years later Morellet's *Prospectus d'un nouveau dictionnaire de commerce* (1769) emerged with support from Ministers Trudaine and Turgot. Although it was intended to be an update of the Savarys' *Dictionnaire*, this project for a future dictionary, which was set to be published in 1770–1775 and whose its theoretical bases are attributed to Turgot,[20] was structured around a meticulous critique of the Savarys' work.[21] Morellet felt that as economic science had reached its maturity, their pioneering work had to be re-written. He believed that establishing a philosophical grammar or universal language of commerce required more organic integration between the "art" (facts) and the "science" (principles) of commerce. However, this apparently promising dictionary was never published, partly for personal reasons and partly because of others beyond Morellet's control.[22] The statistician Peuchet used his material in two dictionaries published in 1800, one on commercial geography and the other on commercial and banking terminology, both of which incorporated an empiricist vision which mitigated the theoretical reflection that Morellet had aimed for.

---

17 The most recent and valuable interpretation is by Richard van den Berg, "Introduction," in Richard Cantillon, *Essai sur la nature du commerce en général*, ed. Richard van den Berg (New York: Routledge, 2015), 1–32.

18 Johnson, *Predecessors*, 405–08. In any case, the most complete analysis of the *Dictionary*'s sources, and certainly not only British, is studied in a recent work by Richard van den Berg: " 'A judicious and industrious compiler': Mapping Postlethwayt's *Dictionary of Commerce*," *The European Journal of the History of Economic Thought* 24, no. 6 (2017): 1167–213.

19 Murphy, "Le développement," 521–41.

20 Hoock, "Le phénomène Savary," 66ff. Turgot wrote his remarkable article "*valeur et monnaie*," based on his subjective theory of value.

21 André Morellet, *Prospectus d'un nouveau dictionnaire de commerce* (Paris: Frères Estienne, 1769): 15–17. The work included a *Catalogue* of political economy, which was one of the first of its kind in Europe; see Théré, "The Publishing," 3–5.

22 See Perrot, *Une histoire*, 102–04.

Morellet's failed attempt was eventually followed by the *Encyclopédie Méthodique* (1782–1832). This was the first encyclopaedic project of the eighteenth century; undertaken as a business venture and with enormous ambition — according to Darnton, it was "*la plus grande enterprise de tous le temps*" —, it came about thanks to Panckoucke, the extraordinary cultural activist.[23] Although the encyclopaedia was originally designed to update Diderot and D'Alembert's *Encyclopédie*, the fact that it was divided up into 26 alphabetically ordered themed dictionaries meant that it acutally bore relatively little resemblance to Diderot and D'Alembert's compilation, which had explicitly ruled out organising its entries on this basis.[24] Three of the sub-encyclopaedias included economic content: *Finances* (1784–1787, 3 vols.), *Commerce* (1783–1784, 3 vols.) and *Économie politique et diplomatique* (1784–1788, 4 vols.). The most important were the two latter, in which the notions of "commerce" and "economics" appeared separately for the first time. Physiocrats Baudeau and Grivel compiled the three volumes on *Commerce* using material from the treatises by Savary, Raynal and Ricard. There were almost two thousand articles on *Économie politique et diplomatique*, the work of Grivel and Smithian economist Démeunier, a fact that highlights the content's doctrinal plurality and topical nature.[25] However, the sub-encyclopaedia did not solely cover political economy, but also included entries for three more disciplines: public administration, diplomacy and political geography;[26] the outcome was a perspective that was close to the cameralist approach to political economy as the core of the sciences of state and public administration.[27] To sum up, in under six decades and via prominent political economists such as Quesnay, Forbonnais, Turgot, Morellet, Grivel and Démeunier, the *langue du commerce* had become institutionalised in the form of an alphabetical vocabulary as something more than a mere expression of the uses and practices of trade.

23 Robert Darnton, *The Business of Enlightenment* (Cambridge-London: Harvard University Press, 1982): 395–459.

24 Denis Diderot and Jean le Rond D'Alembert, eds., *Encyclopédie ou Dictionnaire raisonné des sciences, des arts et des métiers* (Paris: 1751), I, XXXVI. The criterion Panckoucke finally chose led to a huge scientific-editorial puzzle. The work was finally finished in 1832, half a century after Panckoucke began to publish the *Encyclopédie*. Instead of the 42 volumes that Panckoucke had planned, 157 volumes and 53 plates were finally published, thus quintupling the original size.

25 Perrot, *Une histoire*, 127–30.

26 Panckoucke, ed., *Encyclopédie méthodique. Économie politique et diplomatique*.

27 Roberto Martucci, "La *Méthodique* di Panckoucke e il suo dizionario di *Économie politique & diplomatique*," *Storia del pensiero económico* 41 (2001): 213–30.

3 A Commerce Dictionary in Spain: The Project Phase

The first demands for the creation of a commerce dictionary in Spain arose within the framework of the *early* Enlightenment and were voiced by scholars such as Mayans, Feijoo and Martín Sarmiento (1695–1772), who were highly sensitive to the encyclopaedic approach. However, the first encyclopaedia project in Spain was in fact organised by the multi-talented Álvaro Navia, Marquis of Santa Cruz de Marcenado, an Asturian diplomat and soldier (1684–1732).[28] His *Reflexiones militares* (1724–1727) sought to create a vast *Diccionario universal* which also took into account colonial realities and was written in Spanish. Various formats were used, none of which was ultimately successful. Navia's initial intention had been to involve the *Real Academia de la Lengua* (1713) — Royal Academy of the Spanish Language — in the compiling of an ambitious encyclopaedic dictionary which would be ordered both alphabetically and by discipline. His vision went beyond mere lexicography and he sought to include definitions in "sciences, arts and trade," for example, aiming to address the lack of "historical, biblical, geographic, mathematical, economics, chemical, geometric, legal, commercial, marine, music, dictionaries" in Spain.[29] However, Navia subsequently replaced his idea for a single universal dictionary with another work, consisting of eleven specialist dictionaries to which the volumes corresponding to the equivalent entries in different languages would be added. In this encyclopaedic-lexicographical collection, Navia envisaged two dictionaries on economic knowledge, one on "commerce" and another on "economics." Navia's sources were the dictionaries compiled by Savary des Brulons, Chomel and Liger, and to the description of these and the contents, neither work bore much resemblance to a dictionary of the general principles of "commerce."[30] Although this project never came to fruition, Navia was in fact one of the first enlightened scholars in Spain to appreciate the importance of the encyclopaedic works recently appearing in Europe: his future *Diccionario* cited Bayle, Muratori, Moreri and the *Mémoires de Trevoux* as sources. His

28 Pedro Álvarez de Miranda, "Los proyectos enciclopédicos en el siglo XVIII español," in *Europa: proyecciones y percepciones históricas* (Salamanca: Universidad de Salamanca, 1992), 91–96.

29 Álvaro Navia Osorio, Marquis of Santa Cruz de Marcenado, *Reflexiones militares* (Turin: Juan Francisco Mairesse and Alexandro Vimercato, 1724–1727), VIII, 15.

30 While the second was a *re rustica* dictionary, the first resembled a merchants' handbook: it contained information about trading goods, commercial legislation, currencies, weights and measures. Navia (*Reflexiones militares*, IX, 2–4) also intended to incorporate information on economic and demographic statistics into the geography dictionary and information on trade treaties in the history dictionary.

main work on commercial matters a few years later included a novel proposal for Spain: the hiring of "idle men" who were "intelligent in languages" in order to translate *re rustica* dictionaries by Liger, Chomel and Lemery, as well as the Savarys' *Le parfait négociant* and Savary' *Dictionnaire*, meanwhile providing detailed information on their composition and editions.[31]

The fact that the Savarys' *Dictionnaire* was so frequently mentioned was a further sign of the book's success in Spain: the work was in use even before the *Suplement* to its first edition was published in 1730, and prestigious authors such as Feijoo and Mayans also showed interest in it. In fact, the generation of economists during Felipe V's reign, to which Navia belonged, used it so often that it became the main source of economic information in Spain in the early decades of the eighteenth century, together with Moreri's *Dictionnaire*. The fact that contemporary economists such as Uztáriz and Miguel Antonio de la Gándara (1719–17983) supported the creation of lexicographical dictionaries, specifically the Royal Academy's *Diccionario de Autoridades* (1726–1739), did not dispel the demand for dictionaries on "commerce." This shows how necessary it was to adapt commercial practices in more developed trading powers to Spanish commercial culture, and the success of the Savarys' *Dictionnaire* in Spain is inseparable from that of the Colbertist economy as a whole.

Although Uztáriz's *Theórica* (1724) did not explicitly refer to the advisability of producing a Spanish commerce dictionary, the idea was clear from various passages in his work.[32] He included the 1718 *Instrucción* so that "maps of all the provinces in Spain" could be produced in order to improve statistical information about the country, for example, and stressed the advisability of creating a compilation of "navigation and traffic" treaties between Spain and other nations.[33] Uztáriz was also well aware of French and Dutch commercial culture. His main sources for the latter were normally French, such as Huet and Le Moine de l'Espine; particularly *Le parfait négociant*, which, "due to the huge approval that it deserves [...] has been printed seven times," and the Savarys' *Dictionnaire*, from which he copied the entry on the establishment of cloth factories in Sedan and Abbeville in the year following its publication.[34] Uztáriz was followed by Navia. Miguel de Zavala also used the Savarys' *Dictionnaire* to defend the privileged trading companies system,[35]

---

31 Álvaro Navia Osorio, Marquis of Santa Cruz de Marcenado, *Rapsodia económico-política-monárquica* (Madrid: A. Marín, 1732), 183.

32 Fernández Durán, *Jerónimo de Uztáriz*, 328.

33 Uztáriz, *Teórica y práctica*, 119, 410.

34 Uztáriz, *Teórica y práctica*, 54–59, 242–43.

35 Miguel de Zavala y Auñón, *Representación al R. N. Señor D. Phelipe V* (Madrid: 1732): 3rd section.

and Ulloa took information about customs rights and international prices from *Le parfait négociant*.[36] Without a doubt, the contribution made by the Savarys' works partially explains the fact that the Colbertist economy continued to be successful in Spain after it began to lose influence in France, a process that began after the publication of Boisguilbert and Vauban's writings, followed by Melon's *Essai*, more influential work on the international scene than the other two. In 1743 Teodoro Ventura de Argumosa (1711–1774) published a partial plagiarism of the *Essai*, which included a long chapter on privileged trading companies that was entirely copied from the Savarys' *Dictionnaire*.[37] Colbertism's success probably lasted even longer in the trade consulate sphere. The 1737 Bilbao Consulate trade *Ordenanzas*, the most influential in the Hispanic world until 1829, were inspired by Colbert's in 1673 and 1681. In 1759 the Bilbao Consulate commissioned José Francisco Isla (1703–1781), a priest, to translate *Le parfait négociant* into Spanish,[38] a project that was ultimately a failure. A few years later in 1768 Francisco Romà (1727–1784), a Catalan, recommended the manual to the Barcelona Board of Trade as teaching materials.[39] It is therefore clear that Spanish economists considered the Savarys' works canonical texts until the 1760s. They particularly appreciated its teaching method and the fact that it was widely read throughout Europe, either in French or in translation. Similarly to the majority of European countries, in Spain Savary's was the most fortunate of all of the European dictionaries of commerce.[40]

36 Bernardo de Ulloa, *Restablecimiento de fábricas y comercio español* (Madrid: Antonio Marín, 1740): I, 40, 108, 284.

37 It was the longest chapter in his *Erudición política* (Madrid: 1743) and included one of the most extensive historical accounts of European trading companies in eighteenth century Spain; furthermore, Argumosa (23, 216ff.) used the Savarys' work to praise Colbert's trade ordinances and the different privileged public companies promoted under his mandate. In contrast, Melon had already criticised the privileged trading system in his *Essai*; see Astigarraga, "La dérangeante."

38 Teófilo Guiard, *Historia del Consulado y Casa de Contratación de Bilbao y del comercio de la Villa* (Bilbao: José de Astuy, 1913–1914), II, 610.

39 Lluch, *El pensament*, 32. Francisco Romá y Rossell also suggested the Board of Trade produce a work similar to Savary's *Dictionnaire*: *Las señales de la felicidad de España y medios de hacerlas eficaces* (1768; Barcelona: Alta Fulla, 1988): 255–56.

40 Moreri's *Dictionnaire* (1674) was the only great European encyclopaedic work to be partially translated into Spanish, by José Antonio Miravel in 1753. The information on economic geography and the history of commerce and currencies provided by Moreri made the *Dictionnaire* interesting enough from political economy perspective.

4 A Commerce Dictionary in Spain: The Creation Phase

The 1770s marked the beginning of a new stage in the history of commerce dictionaries. In 1774, against the backdrop of enlightened reform, Campomanes made a decisive move to encourage the creation of a work in Spanish. It would be based on the Savarys' *Dictionnaire* but instead of being a simple translation it should cover the whole country, the colonies and Portugal, following the line set by Postlethwayt in the British context. His instructions could not have been more precise:

> what would be desirable is a supplement concerning Spain, including Portugal and the territories of both kingdoms in the Indies, inserting these additions in the corresponding places of the *Dictionnaire* (of the Savarys) and reprinting it, translated with additions in Spanish, as Malachy Postlethwayt did in his English translation of the [...] work of Savary.[41]

Campomanes also recommended Forbonnais, Savary and La Porte's works in various passages,[42] referring to *La science des négociants* (1741), a successful accounting handbook for merchants, for circumstances in France, and Ricard and Hume for Holland and England. His favourite authors were probably the classical Italians — "the first who opened the eyes of the whole of trading Europe," in his own words — and J. Savary and Ricard, whose works explained "the ordinary course of commerce," knowledge of which was "necessary for understanding the trade aspects of law." He also suggested that the future Spanish dictionary would be merged with the work of British-born Wyndham Beawes, which contained information on British commerce and had the advantage that its author had been consul in the Cadiz town of Puerto de Santa María and thus had good knowledge of circumstances in Spain.[43] In any event, such precise information coming from the powerful Council of Castile politician and published in his popular *Discursos* (1774–1776) could only be interpreted as an invitation to act. Through Campomanes the old idea of compiling a Spanish commerce dictionary reached its full political dimension: these events were

---

41 Campomanes, *Discurso industria popular*, LXXXXII.

42 The textual quote from this paragraph can be found in: *Discurso industria popular*, CLXXXII; *Discurso educación popular*, 258; *Apéndice*, IV, LXXXIV-LXXXV.

43 The mention comes from *Lex mercatoria rediviva* (London: Baldwin and Crowder, 1751, 2 vols.). It was a manual for "all businessmen," based on *Le parfait négociant*, particularly noteworthy for its legal content. It was reprinted many times throughout the century, after the fourth edition, which was extended by Thomas Mortimer; see also ch. IX above.

played out against the backdrop of the globalisation of international trade that typified the eighteenth century and which was especially the result of the increasingly important role played by valuable colonial enclaves in Asia and America. High-ranking public officials such as Campomanes were thus forced to promote means through which his country could survive the perennial "jealousy of trade" and above all could protect colonial power. The commerce dictionaries were one of the most essential, no less important than the practical arts and crafts treatises, which Campomanes himself actively promoted and translated. They provided essential information for the exercise of trade in a condensed, centralised and highly accessible form. Their function was twofold: unlike merchants' handbooks, which mainly focused on educating traders, they enabled merchants to manage uncertainty and risk more effectively, as well as to reduce transaction costs related to the lack of information; at the same time, they put information in government hands so that better trade policies could be established. Campomanes' comments in fact led to a great many initiatives to compile a commerce dictionary for Spain.

In 1780 the Aragon Economic Society offered a prize for translating the latest edition of the *Diccionario de comercio del ciudadano*, doubtlessly referring to H. Lacombe de Prezel's *Dictionnaire du citoyen* (1761). The prize was not awarded, and as this was an important matter for "the instruction of our merchants," it was announced a year later, once again without results.[44] After seven years the Society proposed that a treatise on trade with Northern European countries should be written, this time with the collaboration of Saragossa merchants — once again the project failed —. The aim was to give details of goods for import and export in Aragon, together with "the rules relating to the knowledge of their qualities, news of the amendments and accounts of arbitration from Amsterdam."[45] It was suggested that this information should be extracted from Ricard's treatise and the task was assigned to Ignacio de Asso, a talented scientist. The project was clearly linked to the Aragon Society's specific interests — in the 1780s the Society had compiled Aragon's balance of trade as well as searching for new European markets for regional agricultural produce —, but it was also one of the services that the Society provided the Spanish Enlightenment movement, together with maintaining the pioneering

44 ASA, proceeding 8-XII-1780. Prezel's *Dictionnaire* was one of the most important *abregés* dictionaries, compiled in the shadow of Savary's *Dictionnaire*, with relatively substantial theoretical and historical content covering fields such as banking history, the colonies and trading companies. It was widely circulated throughout the whole of the eighteenth century in France and in Italy, where it was translated three times, in 1762 and 1765 (2).

45 ASA, proceeding 9-XI-1787.

Civil Economy and Commerce Chair, which had been founded in 1784. The information issued by the Society was exact in the extreme and even stipulated that extracts from a specific edition of Ricard's treatise must be used: the one "corrected by D. Th. Marien."

This corrector was Tomás Marien y Arróspide, an influential Spanish merchant about whom very little biographical information is available. Born in Bilbao, Marien most probably spent a good part of his life outside Spain, specifically on the Atlantic coast of Europe. He could have been one of the many merchants engaged in consolidating the trading positions of Basque iron or Castilian wool that were shipped to this area from Bilbao, and thus in direct contact with the business culture in Northern Europe. In 1776 he published a text in French classifying the trading rights and treaties established by Denmark in the Sund.[46] This was followed by a more important publication within the overall European Enlightenment context: in 1781, undoubtedly backed up by his knowledge of several languages, Marien was commissioned to supervise a new edition of Ricard's canonical *Traité général du commerce* (1700). As the title itself mentioned, the work was deemed particularly useful for "bankers, merchants, negotiators and, most of all, for the young who wish to learn about commerce and trade." It had been published many times over the course of the century and the original content had been disorted by a series of revisions and extensions, including an accounting section added to the fourth edition in 1721 and information on customs rights and exchange rates that was incorporated into later editions. Marien was responsible for the 1781 edition, which he corrected and modernised, ultimately creating an edition that was "entirely reworked" and "considerably extended." He addressed two major issues: an overall picture of trade between the major European nations and a treatise on currencies, weights and measures, which also included exchange rate operations, trade maxims and different ordinances and uses related to Amsterdam trade insurance.[47] Only two years after the book's reissue, large extracts from it were copied in the volumes on *Commerce* (1783–1784) of Panckoucke's *Encyclopédie Méthodique*.

---

46 Tomás Antonio de Marien y Arróspide, *Tableau des droits et usages de commerce relatifs au passage du Sund* (Copenhagen: M. Moller, 1776); the Spanish version appeared as *Catálogo de los derechos y usos del comercio relativos al paso del Sund* (Madrid: Imprenta Real, 1789). The book's usefulness in Spain was unquestionable. At that time the Baltic markets were essential to the Spanish navy for its supplies of tar, hemp and wood; Torres, *La llave*, 250–58.

47 Samuel Ricard, *Traité général du comerce* (1700; Amsterdam: J. Changuion, 1781), I, Préface. Marien's edition was described by McCulloch (*The Literature*, XX) and Coquelin-Guillaumin (*Dictionnaire*, II, 584) as its greatest quality.

At the end of the 1780s Marien was living between Paris and Madrid, although he had certainly been accepted as a member of Spanish enlightened circles.[48] There is no doubt that he was working in an international trade context and that he was therefore highly aware of the importance to Spanish economic interests of producing a good trade dictionary. In May 1788 he presented his application to publish a fortnightly trade newspaper entitled *El Comercio Universal*, apparently with the help of Juan Pablo Forner, a journalist,[49] and in the same year he sought the Bourbon government's commitment to the creation of a Spanish commerce dictionary.[50] He argued that there had still been no attempt in Spain to "explore the trade part and the mechanisms of it," which was particularly serious taking into account that national prosperity was the result not of new conquests but of the exercise of trade. Without accurate knowledge of the conditions in which commerce was developed the Spanish were condemned to being "victims of other nations' greed." Marien proposed to resolve this problem through translating certain foreign texts, which would be used to create an alphabetically ordered dictionary that was adapted to Spain's trade culture. Although he praised Ricard's *Traité*, he chose the *Guía de las Oficinas de Hamburgo*, a veiled allusion to the successful manual by the German Jurgen Elert Kruse,[51] whose Spanish translation had already been attempted.[52] However, having announced that his translation "was substantially advanced," he then decided to cease work due to problems in adapting information about trading countries and weights, measures and currencies to the Spanish context. Marien stated that if this problem could not be solved, the publication would not be useful in his country, as "we would be engulfed in a vast labyrinth of confusion;" however, he needed government support to finish his work, chiefly because gathering the right information would require assistance from the diplomatic corps and

48 In 1791 he was awarded a prize by the Basque Society for a discourse on "the progress made by the Spanish nation in the reign of Carlos III," whose motto was a text carefully chosen by Basque industrial economist Arriquíbar.

49 AHN, *Consejos*, bundle 5.554–42.

50 AHN, *Estado*, bundle 2.944–429.

51 Jürgen Elert Kruse, *Allgemeiner und besonders hamburgischer contorist* (1753; Hamburg: 1771). Written with Hamburg in mind, this manual provided alphabetically ordered information about the main trading cities in and outside Europe, with their equivalence tables for currencies, measures, weights, etc. Some Spanish sources were used, and its most widely circulated edition was published in 1762.

52 According to Marien's information (*Tratado,* Prefacio) J. M. de Chone y Acha, the bookkeeper for the San Ildeflonso glass factories, had unsuccessfully attempted to publish a translation of Kruse's work "with some news of the North and other parts of Europe" some years previously.

employing someone who would visit the main trading regions and cities. In these conditions he estimated that the translation would be delayed by three or four years, but the overall plan — which he illustrated with an article on Saint Petersburg — was of such grand scale that the delay was justified. What he proposed was a treatise with five sections, beginning with an alphabetical list of the main trading areas and continuing with the each area's location, agricultural products, manufactured goods and institutions (banks, companies, fairs, etc.).

Some of Marien's translation was published, however. In 1789 he brought out the *Tratado general de monedas, pesos, medidas y cambios de todas las naciones*, which can be deemed the first commerce dictionary to appear in eighteenth century Spain. The *Tratado* was only one of the series of five, in which he aimed to summarise "all the trader's science," and contained the following information: a) a description of international trade (3 vols.); b) a treatise on currencies, weights, measures and exchange rates; c) national laws and uses of bills of exchange and contracts; d) ordinances and customs in trading areas; and e) a dictionary of the most common commercial terms. Although Marien attempted to show the close relationship between trade and politics, and thus prove the usefulness of his work for a wider audience, in fact the book was designed like a merchants' dictionary. It contained very detailed information about the history of the European commerce dictionaries and similar works, and specifically mentioned the texts by the Savary brothers, Postlethwayt, Ricard, Morellet and Kruse, although Marien himself stated that it was Kruse's text that had inspired his work.[53] The *Tratado* was published in three books, with the contents organised as follows: a) name and description of the currencies, weights and measures used in the most well-known nations; b) the calculation of exchange rates; and c) logarithm tables. The most interesting economic content was in its Introduction. With occasional nods to Alexis-Jean-Pierre Paucton, Marien covered currencies' historical origin, their national and geographical diversity and the ways in which their metal content could be adulterated. He also criticised the Habsburgs' "fatal policy" of meddling with the value of coins[54] and called for a policy of monetary stability and proposed providing

53 Marien, *Tratado*, Prefacio. It is quite likely that the powerful merchant Simón de Aragorri, Marquis of Iranda, was behind Marien's publications. The Council of Castile commissioned him to undertake the censorship of the *Tratado general*, which he not only approved but also acknowledged that he had known its author for a long time (AHN, *Consejos*, bundle 5.5541–23). A person very close to Aragorri must also have been the prolific translator Domingo Marcoleta.

54 Marien, *Tratado*, Prefacio.

merchants with information about currencies, weights and measures and how monetary operations were carried out in trade.

Marien died in around 1798 and it is highly likely that the real reason his work was never finished was lack of official support. Commerce dictionaries in Europe were generally compiled under the protection of political power and thus the authors had direct access to official statistical and documentary sources. In Spain this was mainly via the Board of Trade and especially the Department of the Balance of Trade, the country's first official statistics agency.[55] Towards the end of the eighteenth century enlightened scholars with links to these institutions, such as Larruga, Virio and Suárez y Núñez, intitiated a major project to create commerce dictionaries in Spanish, while, as we have seen, Álvarez Guerra published at around the same time his translation of Rozier's *Cours* with the backing of the Matritense Society.

In 1788–1789 MIC editor and Board of Trade archivist Miguel Gerónimo Suárez y Núñez published his *Tratado legal teórico y práctico de letras de cambio*. This book was essentially an instruction manual for the use of bills of exchange, designed for merchants and jurisprudence teachers. It was inspired by the work of French jurist R.-J. Pothier and based on other texts from the literature on trading practices, such as the works by Savary, Dupuy de la Serra, Ricard and the *Méthodique*.[56] However, the *Tratado* was not just a technical-legal handbook. The second volume was a dictionary in alphabetical order, with entries on the "uses and customs" of the main Spanish and foreign trade centres regarding bills of exchange, organised by trading area and also providing considerable information about consulates and banking structures.[57]

The monumental *Memorias políticas y económicas sobre los frutos, comercio, fábricas y minas de España* (1787–1800, 45 vols.) by Aragon-born Eugenio Larruga (1747–1803), can certainly not be defined in one simple sentence, and it is not possible to undertake a thorough and analysis of this massive work

55 See ch. 10 above.

56 Gerónimo Suárez y Núñez, *Tratado legal teórico y práctico de letras de cambio* (Madrid: José Doblado, 1788). The translated text was the *Traité du contrat de change* (1763). However, an anonymous translation of the same book had already been published in 1788, although without an alphabetical structure (*Tratado del contrato de cambio*. Madrid: Benito Cano, 1788). Its target audience was the trade consulates, which were required to reform operations involving bills of exchange. It also included a translation of Colbert's 1673 *Ordinances*.

57 Particularly striking was the long description of the Bank of San Carlos and other European banking institutions, as well as the chapters on the consular ordinances regarding bills of exchange; information was also provided about the *vales reales*.

here. For present purposes it must be emphasised that this publication was the most ambitious encyclopaedic work with commercial content in eighteenth century Spain. It was put together at the Board of Trade, to which Larruga was connected as archivist and chronicler from the mid-1780s to 1795. In 1789 he compiled the *Historia* of the institution. The *Memorias* were an extension of this. In terms of their form, the *Memorias* cannot be classified as a commerce dictionary with alphabetically-ordered content; but were a response to the encyclopaedic fervour of the times. They were limited to Spanish trade and manufacturing and were written in a regenerationist spirit which prioritised the publishing of economic writings. Larruga stated that his work did not follow the model of books containing commercial information or those on topical economic literature, but instead consisted of a collection of appropriately ordered reports following a previously established publication plan. The aim was to present "methodically to the nation the status of its commerce, manufacturing and other sectors on which its happiness hangs."[58] The reports selected had to be related to the "science of commerce in general," and limited to subject areas which, although addressed from different disciplines such as chemistry or natural history, were related to trade or could be useful for educating merchants and businessmen. In short, the objective was not to compile an "encyclopaedia" of the fields covered, but a "national trade and manufacturing publication."[59]

To do this Larruga sought to address three central issues: a) "trading and manufacturing establishments," at provincial level, comprising physical, political and economic geography; production statistics; trade structure; currencies; weights and measures; fairs and markets; trading professionals such as merchants and wholesalers, etc., and exchange professionals such as forwarding agents, brokers, etc.; history and ordinances of craftsmen, factories and trading companies; trade institutions and consulates, economic societies, etc.; b) "the materials of trade and different negotiations," throught the country, including: a list of agricultural and manufactured products; taxes; tariff rights, mines and manufacturers; and c) "general administration of commerce and trading jurisprudence," with reference to the whole country, with the following objects: the historical and political status of Spanish trade and manufacturing; international trade agreements; trade and factory institutions — Board of Trade, consulates, arts schools, etc. — ; commercial and tax legislation; commercial practices such as accounts books, bills of exchange, mortgages,

58 Eugenio Larruga, *Memorias políticas y económicas sobre los frutos, comercio, fábricas y minas de España* (Madrid: Benito Cano, 1787–1800), I, XIII, XXI.

59 Larruga, *Memorias*, I, XIII.

insurance, etc.; currencies and exchange rates, weights and measures; fairs and markets; population and demographic laws; luxury and aid policy; taxes, tariffs and customs structure.

Larruga defined his work as being at the heart of the "science of a nation's commerce." In his view this science consisted of "the state's clear knowledge of the political and economic interests of its commerce and of the production of nature and of art of which they are material of exchange." Larruga's *Memorias* were therefore more than a merchants' handbook: he sought to clarify the fundamentals of the "science of commerce," but through a precise methodology which perfectly matched his role as one of the creators of official economic statistics projects at the end of the century. His methodology was based on the detailed presentation of specific events in trade, of which the "general principles" would then be derived from "what belongs to political economy." Larruga mistrusted abstract analytical methods, preferring a relativist and inductive approach, which had to be based on the acknowledgement that "the majority of economic events are relative" and that the "general proposals" in economic issues could only subsequently be drawn from an "in-depth study of all the individual cases."[60] His choice was thus far removed from Morellet-Turgot's alphabetising of the *théorie du commerce en général* and was closer to authors such as Galiani or Necker, who were enormously successful in Spain at the time that Larruga's work was written. His task essentially consisted of copying the mass of material relating to Board of Trade activity and the *Memorias* were so closely linked to the Board's interests that they were actually sponsored by it: in 1788 Larruag received three thousand reels of fleece for each volume published. His work became a type of *container* for relevant information on ordinances, regulations, statistics and other aspects of trade, factories and mines, following the line of the main European commerce dictionaries that he used in his compilation:

> It is well known that Savary, Postlethwayt, Rolt and others works on commerce would had not have been published without the support and protection of their respective monarchies. Savary, in particular, would have not completed his *Dictionary* if the French superintendents and ministries of foreign courts under the instructions of French monarchs had not provided him with the information and instructions that such a project demanded. Savary's brother himself, who published the *Dictionnaire* after Savary's death, admitted that his brother limited himself to transcribing

60 Larruga, *Memorias*, I, IV.

the memoranda submitted by the former to compose the most substantial and useful articles in the *Dictionnaire*.[61]

Unfortunately, the result was an unfinished project, probably due to the fact that the work's gigantic size rendered it unfeasible: over 13 years, 45 volumes were published on the two Castiles, Extremadura and Galicia alone. There were also clear weaknesses in the content. The information was badly-organised and difficult to deal with, and although each volume had indexes, these were scanty and were not truly representative of their content. Always a far cry from the general principles of commerce, the work was also a long way from the highly strategic issue of international trade.

The plans to create a commerce dictionary in Spain were also connected to the administration of customs duties. In 1786, Pedro de Lerena, Minister of the Department of Public Finance (1785–1791), ordered the annual collection of trading information for all Spanish territories and seaports in order to draft the balance of payments for the Spanish economy and to reform the tariff system. Meanwhile, he entrusted his close subordinates Vicente Alcalá-Galiano and Diego María Gallard (¿-1824) with the task of translating a text on French customs duty legislation into Spanish. The enterprise was part of a wider ambitious plan that aimed to create a systematic compilation of existing customs duty legislation in the main nations with which Spain had trade relationships. Two issues seem to have been behind this. First, the implications for Spain of the 1786 Treaty of Eden-Rayneval between France and Great Britain, which was a milestone in European trading history because it established a system by which both countries would gradually reduce their tariffs. Second, the results of the decisive reform of the customs system in Spain carried out by Lerena's predecessor Miguel de Múzquiz in 1778–1782. The reform was broadly protectionist and introduced the *ad valorem* tax; nevertheless, it had the distinguishing feature of being the first in the century to be drawn up with a central unifying criterion, covering the whole of the Spanish empire. In fact it was designed in the context of the 1778 reform to liberalise colonial trade. The trade dictionaries promoted by the Board of Trade at the end of the century tried to maintain and update the tariff discipline achieved by Múzquiz's reform.

The first outcome of this initiative was Alcalá-Galiano and Gallard's *Colección alfabética de los Aranceles de Francia* (1789).[62] The prologue clearly states

61 Larruga, *Memorias*, I, XXIII.

62 Vicente Alcalá-Galiano and Diego María Gallard, *Colección alfabética de los aranceles de Francia* (Madrid: Lorenzo de San Martín, 1789, 3 vols.); on this work, see Valles, *Ciencia*, 431–37.

the authors' goals. Adam Smith's ideas — labour as the basis for wealth, capital as "accumulated wealth" and the skills and "cleverness of the worker" as the origin of "productive" labour — were employed to defeat the arguments of the "philosophers called economists" — the Physiocrats — that tried to identify wealth with agricultural production, to reduce the tax burden to the *impôt unique* and to waive customs duties and other taxes to promote economic development. Paradoxically, Smith's arguments were used to reject free trade, since the authors argued that liberalising trade only benefitted developed countries and so other nations should adopt barriers to prevent industrial dependence on the former. Nevertheless, their defence of protectionism did not mean that Alcalá-Galiano and Gallard adopted the old strong "mercantilist" approach. On the contrary, the policy of commercial prohibitionism and profit balance of trade was harshly criticised for harming consumers, encouraging smuggling and limiting economic growth. The authors proposed a "third way," which in practice meant selective protectionism that avoided excessive customs duties. They considered it necessary to collect information on foreign countries' customs duty structures, in particular France. However, they did not merely translate French custom duty legislation into Spanish, but also incorporated comprehensive alphabetically-ordered information on France's customs and commercial structure, historical information about reforms there — in particular Colbert's 1664 customs reforms — and other general information related to French trade: trading companies, colonial trade, the scope of the trade treaties with the main European countries and the commercial privileges of major towns. Finally, they included information on the French and Spanish equivalences in weights, currencies and measures systems, based on calculations taken from Paucton's *Métrologie* (1780).

The *Colección* actually had the clear political purpose of implementing a centralised standard customs system in Spain that would remove the "inequalities that hinder trade and prevent commerce," setting customs posts at the country's borders and standardising the customs duty system.[63] The authors credited Colbert with introducing the unified customs and trading system in France that they desired for their own country, and their work thus incorporated all the ordinances and regulations he had decreed, as well as any subsequent eighteenth century modifications.[64] The *Colección* therefore seems to have been especially useful to people in the Public Finance

63 Alcalá-Galiano and Gallard, *Colección*, I, 128–29.

64 To do this the comments that René J. Valin and Balthasar M. Émérigon incorporated into the 1760 of edition of Colbert's 1681 *Ordinances* were translated. The translators' complaints about the lack of appropriate vocabulary in Spanish were extremely expressive.

Department Secretariat, who were responsible for reforming the Spanish customs system.[65]

Juan Bautista Virior (1753–1837), or Virio, as he was known in Spain, was a diplomat from the Habsburg territories who was also influential in the history of Spanish commerce dictionaries. A *protégé* of Floridablanca and Godoy, a future liberal and *afrancesado*, he was a talented reformist with close links to the German world.[66] His administrative career included many diplomatic posts, the publication of periodicals such as the *Semanario de agricultura*, and tireless efforts to create the *Departamento de Fomento* — Department of Development —, of which he was the first head for a short time. Virio had excellent knowledge of economic legislation in different European countries, partly because of his successive residencies as part of the Spanish diplomatic corps. At the end of the 1780s he took advantage of his time at the London embassy to compile the lengthy *Colección alfabética de los aranceles de la Gran Bretaña*, which was finished in 1788 but only published four years later. The publication was made possible thanks to both protection and remuneration from the Secretary of State and established him as a true specialist in matters relating to economic development.

His book formed part of the Bourbon government's project to create reports on the tariff structure used in the main European countries: Virio himself left a hand-written document of this type on Austria and Russia.[67] In fact, his *Colección* was, probably, directly commissioned by Floridablanca for the purpose of obtaining a detailed analysis of the new British tariffs following the 1787 *British Consolidation Fund Act*. Virio did not limit himself to simply coping down these tariffs; he partially re-wrote many British texts on trade legislation and promoting the economy, in accordance with an economic conception that sought to show "how powerful England has been in terms of customs and ancillary ordinances to promote agriculture, industry, commerce, navigation and the acquisition of rich vassals."[68] He wished to make this example known in

65 Alcalá-Galiano and Gallard translated Calonne's French Decree on the founding of the Balance of Trade Office (III, 494–96).

66 Jesús Pradells, "Juan Bautista Virio (1753–1837): experiencia europea y reformismo económico en la España ilustrada," *Revista de Historia Moderna* 8–9 (1990): 223–71; Elisabel Larriba and Gérard Dufour, *El Semanario de agricultura y artes dirigido a los párrocos (1797–1808)* (Valladolid: Ámbito, 1997), 19–23.

67 A summary of Virio's report on this country was published in the SAP in 1801.

68 Juan Bautista Virio, *Colección alfabética de los aranceles de la Gran Bretaña, y extractos de las leyes, reglamentos, órdenes y providencias expedidas en aquel reino para el régimen de sus aduanas, y fomento de su comercio* (Madrid: J. Ibarra, 1792), I, VIII.

Spain, especially when the 1786 trade agreement between France and Great Britain consolidated the latter's position at the forefront of international trade.

Virio condensed his publication's overall standpoint in a lengthy *Prólogo*. This contained a handful of general economic ideas and its main principle was very simple: customs duties were not an instrument by which to gain fiscal revenue, but to foster economic growth. Britain's trade hegemony was due to two factors: a suitable tariff arrangement and the tax system, as "it did not oppress the most useful and industrious part of its countrymen." Beyond these ideas the *Colección* was highly pragmatic, and its first aim was to provide a detailed explanation of the Consolidation Act. Although this had meant simplifying and reducing customs tariffs, it also established a fairly complex system: together with export subsidies, which in some cases amounted to dumping, and prohibitionist measures, it entailed the return of tariffs in some cases and at times applied indirect taxes on consumption. These measures all required the creating of a detailed records system in a "State or Tax Office," which would facilitate the design of more appropriate economic policies.[69]

Virio's thoughts went hand-in-hand with abundant praise for Great Britain and the bases of its economy and parliamentary system, to which beneficial and multiplying economic effects were attributed as they favoured the "acceptance of innovations and national promotion."[70] Virio expressed his admiration for the positive balance of payments, public spending policies, debt repayment and other aspects of British economic arrangements, whose tariff principles were particularly relevant for developing the domestic manufacturing sector. He went as far back as the fourteenth century to emphasise Great Britain's unquestionable advantages: "the best linens are English and Irish." These advantages were the result of its protectionist policy, in short, the use of "prohibitions and customs barriers, taxes and other internal measures."[71] The import of raw materials and the export of manufactured goods were boosted by import replacement, an improvement in the quality of domestic manufactured goods and international competitiveness. Although Virio maintained that the development of manufacturing was inseparable from that of agriculture, he argued that the positive effects for the economy as a whole were mostly derived from manufactured goods and their export, considering that they incorporated an added value of "2, 3, 10, 20 and up to 100 times more" than raw material.

---

69 In 1790 Virio called for the creation of a "registration office" that would provide information about the "wealth status of other nations" and would enable more appropriate economic policies to be applied in Spain (AHN, *Estado*, bundle 2.923–476).

70 Virio, *Colección*, I, XVIII-XX.

71 Virio, *Colección*, I, XVI.

The entries in the *Colección* were designed along very broad lines and Virio's main organising criterion was a list of tradable goods; however, there were also articles on economic geography, legislation, weights and measures, colonial trade, trading companies and smuggling. The most important entry was "customs and excises," which took up a large part of the first volume;[72] this not only explained the origins of the Consolidation Act in detail, summarising the content and preamble chapter by chapter, but was also enriched with the laws, forms, instructions and certifications that made the Act operational. The same applied to entries for goods of unquestionable importance in international trade, such as wool, silk and grain: far from simply giving information about prevalent import and export duties and the revenue they raised, Virio added information referring to previous tariffs, excise duty, British trading and manufacturing laws and the instructions, awards and licences that required bureaucratic procedures. He also occasionally included news about parliamentary debates referring to the entries dealt with, particularly those held under William Pitt's mandate. In this way, Virio transformed his work into an important record of legal regulations and economic ordinances, extracted from original sources on the British economy and trade policy. After his work, the Department of the Balance of Trade did not interrupt the translation of texts about tariff structures in foreign countries, such as those on Great Britain in 1803 and France in 1805.[73]

5 Encyclopaedic Literature: The *Encyclopédies* Compiled by Diderot and D'Alembert and Panckoucke

The volumes of Diderot and D'Alembert's and Panckoucke's Encyclopaedias arrived in Spain at the same time as the commercial dictionaries described above appeared. Their circulation was highly conditioned by the fact that they were banned by the Inquisition, yet both works became well known in Spain and were a highly useful way of introducing economic thought into the

72 Virio, *Colección*, I, 5–176.

73 See, *Arancel de la Gran Bretaña del año de 1802* (Madrid: Imprenta Real, 1803), translated by Antonio de Llaguno, and *Arancel de los derechos de aduanas y navegación en Francia, publicado en París en el año de 1800* (Madrid: Antonio Espinosa, 1805), by unknown authors; the latter was a version of the *Code de douanes de la République Français* (Strasbourg: 1802) by Jean-Charles Magnier-Grandprez, although updated to contain the commercial measures decreed between 1800 and 1803. He vindicated the trade reforms undertaken by the Revolution eliminating domestic trade barriers and establishing a single national tariff that was "protective and conservative of the national factories" in 1791.

country. Although consulting the first *Encylopédie* was forbidden by General Inquisitor Edict from 1759 onwards, prestigious enlightened scholars such as Campomanes openly recommended using the work, "taking from [it] what it is useful, and forsaking what justly is harmful," especially articles devoted to arts and crafts.[74] Likewise, there were no insurmountable difficulties to importing the *Encylopédie* and reading it in enlightened institutions such as the economic societies and trade consulates, and prestigious publisher Antonio de Sancha even planned to translate it into Spanish, although the project never came to fruition.[75] Part of the *Encylopédie*'s economic content was already well known in Spain, as French engineer Carlos Le-Maur had translated Forbonnais' *Élémens du commerce* (1754), into Spanish in 1765 and this included the economics entries written for the *Encylopédie.*[76] The Spanish did not seem to realise how unusual the alphabetical ordering of Forbonnais' work was, considering it merely a work on economics that formed part of the first wave of translations undertaken during Carlos III's reign, at the forefront of which was the Gournay circle.

The *Encylopédie Méthodique*, on the other hand, enjoyed some degree of tolerance in Spain.[77] The *Prospectus* announcing the plan for the book was translated into Spanish in 1782 by jurist José Covarrubias and the publisher Antonio de Sancha. At the same time, subscriptions to the first French edition began; the 330 subscribers included the Head of the Spanish Inquisition himself. Likewise, the Council of Castile sanctioned the introduction of the volumes of the French edition into Spain. However, Nicolas Masson de Morvilliers' article "Espagne" in the volume *Geographie* (1782) criticising Spanish socio-cultural reality and the nation's scant contribution to enlightened culture ("What did Europe owe Spain in the eighteenth century?") naturally increased the Spanish authorities' suspicions. The Council of Castile in particular changed its

74 Campomanes, *Apéndice*, II, CLXIII.

75 Gonzalo Anes, "*L'Encyclopédie ou Dictionnaire raisonné des sciences, des arts et des métiers* en España," in *Homenaje a Xavier Zubiri* (Madrid: Moneda y Crédito, 1970), 123–30. The fact that there is no Spanish translation of the *Encylopédie* must be properly interpreted in the European context. In Russia more than five hundred articles from the work were translated, but there were no more consistent attempts at other versions in different languages except in Italy and Great Britain: Frank A. Kafker, "Les traductions de *l'Encyclopédie* au XVIIIe siècle: quelle fut leur influence?" *Recherches sur Diderot et sur l'Encyclopédie* 12 (1992): 165–73.

76 *Elementos de comercio* (Madrid: Imprenta de Francisco Xavier García, 1765, 2 vols.).

77 Gonzalo Anes, "La *Encyclopédie Méthodique* en España," in *Ciencia social y análisis económico,* ed. José Luis García Delgado and Julio Segura (Madrid: Tecnos, 1978), 105–52; Luis María Enciso, "La recepción de la *Enciclopedia* en España," in *Las Enciclopedias en España antes de l'Encyclopédie*, ed. Alfredo Alvar (Madrid: CSIC, 2009), 501–45.

indulgent attitude towards the Encyclopaedia and proposed to "drain" the work before it was launched onto the domestic market, which delayed the distribution of the volumes previously ordered by subscribers. Floridablanca commissioned clergyman Francisco Villalpando (1740–1797) to produce a censorship report, which was favourable towards publishing the *Encylopédie* but did suggest introducing an explanatory comment on the controversial "Espagne" entry. Censorship extended far beyond clerical circles though, and Campomanes assigned distinguished members of the Spanish Enlightenment such as Antonio de Capmany, Manuel de Lardizábal, Manuel de Aguirre and Jovellanos to censor certain specialist dictionaries included in the *Méthodique*: Grammar and Literature; Jurisprudence; Military Art; and Public Finance, Political Economy and Diplomacy. In line with a pragmatic policy, Campomanes undoubtedly aimed to satisfy the Inquisition in order to safeguard the work's distribution, a goal that was not achieved due to ensuing events.

In 1788, when the Council of Castile had taken a more moderate attitude and promoted subscriptions to the Encyclopaedia, the Inquisition tightened up its "siege" of the *Méthodique*. It compelled the Council of Castile to prevent any increase in subscriptions through actions such as prohibiting the distribution of the Encyclopaedia in Spain and checking the religious and political content of the first volumes, which had already been translated into Spanish under Sancha's supervision. As a result there were only seventeen deliveries of the French version of *Encyclopédie Méthodique* in Spain and Sancha's plan was cut short a few years later after just eleven volumes had been translated and published. Discontinuing the publication probably led to a halt in the translating of the volumes *Commerce* and *Économie politique et diplomatique*, which had already been approved in two favourable reports written by Villalpando and Jovellanos, both of whom recommended its distribution in Spain. Villalpando considered the volume on *Commerce* "extremely excellent" and he praised the simplified introductory dissertation: "such a difficult science [...] to simple notions." Jovellanos sent his report on the first volume of *Économie politique et diplomatique* to the Council of Castile in June 1785. He pointed out that the volume had been inspired by "the spirit of freedom which was usual amongst politicians;" however, in his opinion, there were no grounds for suggesting that publication of the book should cease, although he did recommend rectifying the content of the "*auto de fe*" — act of faith — entry.[78] The Council

78 Gonzalo Anes, "La Inquisición en la *Encyclopédie*: una censura inédita de Jovellanos," in *El siglo que llaman ilustrado*, ed. Joaquín Álvarez Barrientos and José Checa (Madrid: CSIC, 1996), 87–97.

of Castile approved Jovellanos' report a few days later and gave its consent to the distribution of the volume.

In the end, *Manufactures, Arts et Métiers* was the only volume of the *Encyclopédie Méthodique* with economic content to be translated into Spanish. The task was undertaken in 1794 by Antonio Carbonell, librarian and professor at the Seminary of Nobles of Madrid. Publication was delayed due to the difficulty of properly defining economic terms;[79] in fact, Carbonell acknowledged that he had visited "factories and offices" seeking advice from manufacturers and experts to name the "utensils" correctly, just as the foreign authors of the original entries had done. Two further factors delayed publication: the scant response that he received from public Spanish textile manufacturers — only the Guadalajara manufacturer provided information on this — and the need to create new terms especially for specifically Spanish professions. In fact, the translation was never completed and the second volume ended with the entry on "silk." The work was divided in two sections, the first on textile manufacture and the second on leather, dye, oil and soap. The entries had a similar structure and covered occupation, typology of raw materials and derived products as well as detailing guild ordinances. The dictionary entries were generally adapted to circumstances in Spain and Carbonell sometimes included limited information related to the state of the affairs in specific manufactures and professions in Spain, normally those based in Madrid. It is worth noting that Carbonell was the first to introduce the term "*empresario*," or entrepreneur, into Spanish dictionaries, differentiating it from terms like "merchant" or "manufacturer," and he did something similar with terms such as "factories" and "manufactures."[80]

6 Final Remarks

The commerce dictionaries of the eighteenth century were undeniably a component of the intense "dialogue on political economy" that took place during the European Enlightenment. However, as outlined above, their history in Spain had more downs than ups. It is true that most European dictionaries with this type of content, including Morellet's *Prospectus*, were well-known in Spain, and that some of them, particularly the Savarys' *Dictionnaire*, were lynchpins in the creation of Spain's economic literature in the eighteenth century, from Uztáriz to Jovellanos. It is no less true that there was a generalised

79 *Enciclopedia metódica. Fábricas, artes y oficios, traducido del francés al castellano por Don Antonio Carbonell y Borja* (Madrid: Sancha, 1794), I, Anuncio del editor.

80 *Enciclopedia Metódica*, I, 144–59, 241–45.

awareness of the need for a Spanish commerce dictionary throughout the eighteenth century, yet none of the main European commerce dictionaries were ever translated into Spanish. On the other hand, countries in Europe such as Great Britain, France, Germany, Italy and Portugal produced successful whole or partial translations of different versions, and usually managed to adapt them to the domestic context.

The efforts made to create a Spanish dictionary of Commerce were more successful. This can be seen in the works of Marien, Larruga, Virio, Suárez or Alcalá-Galiano and Gallard. The conditions in which their dictionaries were conceived are certainly very revealing. All of them were civil servants and their works were promoted and financed by the Board of Trade or the Balance of Payments Department. This highlighted that, as it had happened in France and Great Britain, the only possible way to create a work with the technical difficulties of a dictionary — the complaints of the Spanish authors about the lack of information and the difficulties of terminological and linguistic nature were continuous — was under the shadow of the political power. Therefore, in the case of Spain, these dictionaries were delayed until the time when the public administration began to have centralised and specialised agencies that, among other issues, were able to accumulate and create official statistics. This is precisely what happened at the end of the century with the two institutions aforementioned. In any case, even if the results obtained by these pioneers were not particularly brilliant, their works should not be underestimated, and even less so in a more long-term perspective: the relationship between the encyclopaedic efforts of the Spanish enlightened scholars and the canonical dictionaries on Finance compiled in the 1820s and 1830s by the Liberal Minister José Canga Argüelles (1771–1842) has not yet been studied in depth.

CHAPTER 6

In support of the Enligthened Reforms

The Memorial Literario (*1784–1808*)

1 Introduction: The Press in the "Golden Age"

In 1781, Luis García del Cañuelo (1744–1802), a journalist, began to publish one of the most emblematic periodicals in eighteenth-century Spain: *El Censor* (1781–1787) This marked the beginning of the "golden age" of the Spanish press, which lasted until 1808, albeit with some ups and downs.[1] During this period, the exponential growth in the number of newspapers was matched by an improvement in their quality and duration. The press flourished in Madrid and also in the provinces during the final decades of the century, the period in which the main newspapers of the eighteenth century were founded: *El Censor* and also the *Correo literario de la Europa* (1781–1782, 1786–1787), the *Memorial literario* (1784–1808), the *Correo de los ciegos* (1786–1791), the *Espíritu de los mejores diarios literarios* (1787–1791), *El Observador* (1787) and the *Semanario erudito* (1787–1791). In 1786, Jovellanos, who was witnessed this boom at first hand, wrote that the press had brought about "the silence of ignorance and the beginning of our Enlightenment."[2]

This stage of expansion can be explained by external factors and also by factors intrinsic to the press. On the one hand, it was a result of the population growth, the increase in literacy and the fact that more sectors of society were becoming aware of enlightened ideas, which taken together increased the press' potential readership.[3] On the other hand, the boom was also brought about by improvements in circulation, due to advances in publishing techniques and a reduction in postage costs. The press was a fast and low-cost channel for shaping public opinion, specialising knowledge and disseminating it among large audiences: as José Guevara Vasconcelos, a member of the Matritense, pointed out, it was a "compendium" of useful things, which awakened "curiosity, the novelty and taste" and which was used to "try out certain

1 Guinard, *La presse*, 219–20.

2 Quoted by Inmaculada Urzainqui, "Libertad de imprenta y prensa crítica a fines del siglo XVIII," in *El nacimiento de la libertad de imprenta*, ed. Elisabel Larriba and Fernando Durán (Madrid: Sílex, 2012), 43.

3 Le Guellec, *Presse el culture,* 24–26.

 | DOI:10.1163/9789004442894_008

ideas before putting them into practice;"[4] and, according to Juan Sempere y Guarinos (1754–1830), "to extend the Enlightenment more quickly and generally to all classes of citizens."[5] Cultural agents from many professional sectors participated in the vibrant atmosphere of the eighties, including booksellers, publicists, editors and university teachers. Meanwhile, those who were part of newspaper companies began to find that this provided a steady income: as one editor, Juan José López de Sedano (1729–1796), confirmed, "writing has become a business and a way to make a living."[6] In general, the *papelistas* or "public writers" were still men from the provinces, with limited financial resources, but with an education: they were members of religious orders or worked as teachers or civil servants.[7] However, during the 1780s, they began to be identified socially as "journalists" in the true sense of the word, emerging as a new figures in the Republic of Letters.[8] In their hands, the press began to exercise its more genuine functions: criticism, instruction and public opinion creation. It should also be noted that the "golden age" of the press coincided with the development of the most emblematic Bourbon economic reforms: the liberalisation of the grain trade (1765) and colonial trade (1765, 1778, 1789), guild reform (1775), the creation of the economic societies (1775) and the reform of the customs duties (1778) and the fiscal system (1785–1787).

However, the new phase begun by *El Censor* benefited from an even more decisive factor: a shift from private financing or patronage to the subscription system. Although this system had existed since Nifo's *Cajón de sastre* (1760–1761),

4 AHN, *Consejos*, bundle 5.540–23.

5 Sempere, *Ensayo*, IV, 176.

6 Álvarez Barrientos, "El periodista," 31–2. This was also due to the fact that, as in all of Europe, in Spain there was a notable advance in the acceptance of the copyright, specifically since 1764. In 1813 the *Cortes* of Cadiz recognized the right of literary property. On Europe, see Roger Chartier, *Les origines culturelles de la Révolution française* (Paris: Le Seuil, 1990). Spanish trans., *Espacio público, crítica y desacralización en el siglo XVIII: los orígenes culturales de la Revolución francesa* (Barcelona: Gedisa, 1995), 66–76; Melton, *The rise*, 174–86; Munck, *The Enlightenment*, 120–25. On Spain, Álvarez Barrientos, *Los hombres*, 246–50. On the Republic of Letters as an example of a transnational phenomenon that contributed to the spread of a certain enlightened public spiritedness, see Marc Fumaroli, *La República de las Letras* (Barcelona: Acantilado, 2013). On the impact of faith-based conflicts on the development of the Republic of Letters, see Herbert Jaumann, ed., *Die Europaische Gelehrtenrepublik Im Zeitalter Des Konfessionalismus. European Republic of Letters in the Age of Confessionalism* (Weisbaden: Harrassowitz Verlag, 2001). And, finally, on the press and the Republic of letters, Dena Goodman, *The Republic of Letters. A Cultural History of the French Enlightenment* (Ithaca-London: Cornell University Press, 1994), 165–75.

7 Guinard, *La presse*, 91–2.

8 Álvarez Barrientos, "El periodista," 29, 38.

it became more widespread after 1781.[9] The outcome was a shift in the relationship between the editors and the public, as there was a certain active emulation among the editors. The press comprised an element of distinction and social progress, at least in the political sphere and the world of letters. Furthermore, as Larriba explained, the subscription system enabled the "audience" at whom this press was aimed to be more accurately defined, leading to new editing formats. This "new public" was able to access the rapidly circulated, multi-faceted and low cost cultural product more easily, breaking the relationship between culture and the elite classes. Press readership became broader, increasingly anonymous, professionally more diverse and urban. Data from men of the Spanish Enlightenment indicate that newspapers and journals were read in a number of different places, especially in cities: salons, social gatherings, coffee shops and semi public libraries, such as those belonging to the economic societies. However, not only did more people read, but they also read differently. The press in Spain played a fundamental role in the "reading mania" of the eighteenth century which favored the transition towards individual, silent and extensive reading.[10] This is applicable to the creation of a "new public" that was interested in these unique "economic papers," which, as Jovellanos observed, were read "in cafés, at dressing tables or literary gatherings" and whose contents should therefore combine the meticulousness of "good writing" and rigour.[11] However, as Fuentes warned, an essential problem lurked in whether there really was a large enough audience to warrant the creation and continuity of an independent press.[12] The truth is that print runs and the readerships were still fairly meagre: the *Correo de Madrid* or the *Mercurio Histórico y Político* had a print run of ten thousand copies, while the commercial press' was barely five hundred; only five or six thousand people purchased newspapers in Madrid between 1786 and 1788.[13]

The flourishing 1780s also provided a more favourable climate for the press. A campaign was begun to foster the freedom of expression,[14] initiated in 1780

9 Larriba, *El público*, 22–24. In France, this system existed from 1716: Goodman, *The Republic*, 175–82.

10 Roger Chartier, *The Cultural Uses of Print in Early Modern France* (Princeton, NJ: Princeton University Press, 1987), 183–219, and *Les origines culturelles*, 81–106; Munck, *The Enlightenment*, 76–83, 100–09, 115–53. On Spain, Álvarez Barrientos, *Los hombres*, 79–89, 128–32.

11 Jovellanos, "Dictamen sobre la oportunidad," 649.

12 Juan Francisco Fuentes, "El Censor y el público," *Estudios de Historia Social* 52–53 (1990): 223.

13 Guinard, *La presse*, 85.

14 For the contemporary campaign mentioned, vid. Elisabel Larriba, "Las aspiraciones a la libertad de imprenta en la segunda mitad del siglo XVIII," in *El nacimiento de la libertad*

by Valentín de Foronda (1751–1821), who brought the climate prevailing in the Bascongada Society, of which he was an active member, into the public sphere. Comparing ideas was healthy, as it "eliminated the fetters and chains" that oppressed the truth. Furthermore, press freedom was nedded to prevent a generalisation of "the most barbaric uses, the most detestable actions and the interests that go most against us and the society in which we live."[15] The campaign had the enthusiastic supported of the most eminent enlightened scholars of this period, from Miguel de la Gándara and León Arroyal to Manuel de Aguirre and Francisco Cabarrús, all of whom understood that freedom of the press and freedom of opinion were inseparable principles. The press itself mediated in the campaign, driven by leading figures in the sector such as Luis García del Cañuelo at *El Censor*, Manuel Rubín de Celis (1743–1809) at *El Corresponsal de El Censor* (1786–1788) or José Marchena (1768–1821) at *El Observador* (1787). Their demands not only included civil freedom but also political freedom.[16] Towards the end of the century, Cristóbal Cladera (1760–1816) used his *Espíritu de los mejores diarios* to complement the recurring allusions to the beneficial British system with the first positive echoes of the constitutional experience in North America, including its healthy system of the press freedom. This exhuberant context explains Floridablanca's famous reform of press legislation of 19 May 1785, followed by another on 19 August 1788. These were the first official regulations established to both boost and protect the press; while not eliminating censorship or political tutelage of the press, they manifestly increased the press' room for manoeuvre.[17]

---

de imprenta, ed. Elisabel Larriba and Fernando Durán (Madrid: Sílex, 2012): 19–41. A new approach, in Javier Fernández Sebastián, "Toleration and Freedom of Expression in the Hispanic World Between Enlightenment and Liberalism," *Past and present* 211 (2011): 166–76. In general, the fight against censorship was slower in the countries where "moderate" Enlightenment dominated: Israel, *Radical Enlightenment*, 116–18.

15 Valentín de Foronda, "Disertación sobre la libertad de escribir," in *Miscelánea o colección de varios discursos*, ed. Valentín de Foronda (Madrid: Imprenta de Manuel González, 1793), 176–98. It had been written in 1780, presented in the Valladolid History and Geography Academy in 1786 and published in 1791 in the EMD; vid. Ignacio Fernádez Sarasola, "Estudio Preliminar," in Valentín de Foronda, *Escritos políticos y constitucionales*, ed. Ignacio Fernández Sarasola (Bilbao: Universidad del País Vasco, 2002), 44–50.

16 Urzainqui, "Libertad de imprenta," 43–78.

17 The printing licenses of publications that did not exceed 4 to 6 books, which were the majority, remained under the competence of the printing judge, while the latter were analysed by the Council of Castile; vid., Elisabel Larriba, "Inquisición y prensa periódica en la segunda mitad del siglo XVIII," *Cuadernos de Ilustración y Romanticismo* 13 (2005): 78, and Le Guellec, *Presse et culture*, 21–24.

Censorship was an additional factor that accounted the enthusiasm of the "golden age" of the press. Like other publications, newspapers were subjected to "double ideological screening:" the Council of Castile did a preliminary civil check, which was usually carried out by the Print Judge, followed by a religious check by the Inquisition.[18] However, the balance between these two powers underwent a shift particularly during the second half of the century. In 1763 and 1768 two regalist regulations were decreed increasing the Council`s power vis-à-vis the Holy Office, while, after 1769, the Council's strategy of centralising control over the publication of Spanish books, on one hand, and the importing of foreign books, on the other, intensified, which struck a further blow at the Inquisition's ubiquitous presence. Finally, there also seems to be some indication that those favouring a liberal approach to the granting of licences were slowly succeedding in their quest.

Entrusting the task of civil censorship to certain literary groups, as was the norm elsewhere in Europe, also had a positive influence, although these groups only ever played an advisory role and the final decision remained in the Council's hands. After 1769 institutions such as the History Academy, Language Academy and the Bar Association began to take on regular censorship responsibilities, and when the Madrid Economic Society was founded in 1775 it too formed part of this group. However, contrary to Juan Sempere's claims that the latter monopolised the books on "politics, economics, commerce [or] arts,"[19] many publications about these matters also went to the History Academy. In fact, Velasco's studies on this Academy and Lorenzo's work on the Language Academy reveal that these institutions had no consistent selection criteria,[20]

18 Lucienne Domergue, "La prensa periódica y la censura en la segunda mitad del siglo XVIII," *Estudios de Historia Social* 52–53 (1990): 141–49. The matter has drawn growing interest, based on the classical studies of Domergue (*Censure et Lumières dans l'Espagne de Charles III*. Paris: CNRS, 1982) and Marcelin Defourneaux (*Inquisición y censura de libros en la España del siglo XVIII*. Madrid: Taurus, 1973). Particularly recommendable are: María Luisa López-Vidriero, "Censura civil e integración nacional: el censor ilustrado," in *El mundo hispánico en el Siglo de las Luces* (Madrid: SEESXVIII, 1996), II, 855–67; María Teresa Nava, *Reformismo ilustrado y americanismo: la Real Academia de la Historia, 1735–1792* (Madrid: Universidad Complutense de Madrid, 1989), 301–86; and, finally, Eva Velasco, *La Real Academia de la Historia en el siglo XVIII* (Madrid: CEPC, 2000), 217–75, and "Las censuras de la Real Academia de la Historia (1746–1772)," in *Instituciones censoras*, ed. Fernando Durán (Madrid: CSIC, 2016), 113–58.

19 Sempere, *Ensayo*, I, 70. On the censoring activity of the Madrid Society, vid. Domergue, *Censure et Lumières*, 81–85.

20 Velasco, *La Real Academia*, 255–75, and "Las censuras," 117–24; Elena de Lorenzo, "Notas sobre la actividad censora de la Real Academia Española en el siglo XVIII," in *Instituciones censoras*, ed. Fernando Durán (Madrid: CSIC, 2016), 202–05.

a conclusion that was confirmed by Pampliega and López Vidriera's studies of the "dark and wretched use" of the censors.[21]

If civil licenses were to be liberalised, which also benefited the press, it was fundamental for the heads of these institutions to make decisions regarding the censors and the outcome of the censorship, as on the whole these were later accepted by the Council of Castile. This is undoubtedly what happened at the History Academy, the most active of these institutions, during Campomanes' long mandate (1764–1791). Progress was also enhanced by the gradual selecting of secular censors, which diluted religious orders' traditional dominance, and the inclusion in this group of enlightened movement heavyweights such as Jovellanos, José Vargas y Ponce, José Guevara Vasconcelos and Casimiro Gómez Ortega at the History Academy, and Benito Bails and José Abreu at the Language Academy. Although it is difficult to generalise, Jovellanos' censorship was more concerned with achieving press freedom than controlling and purging publications.[22] All these factors combined to give rise to the emergence of more enlightened censors who, rather then adhering to the classic triad of criteria that characterised civil censorship — privileges, good customs and dogma — ,[23] complemented them with others related to honouring the nation and, most of all, a publication's educational value and social use. The previous censorship system was better able to adapt to the discursive aims of power; in Velasco's words, it was used to "mould the discourse, discipline and warn authors or translators and to create a literary space which [...] would facilitate or hinder the diffusion of other principles and ideas."[24] This proto-liberal environment also gave rise to the inefficiency of the system of controlling reading via the book supply, a type of barrage against supposedly dangerous publications, which, as Defourneaux stated, "ended up allowing a large wave of all kinds of works."[25]

As mentioned previously, the "golden age" of the Spanish press was characterised by ups and downs, and the most important event was certainly the French Revolution. In an attempt to avoid contagion from the revolutionary

---

21 López-Vidriero, "Censura civil," 855–67, and Víctor Pampliega, "*Empleo oscuro y penoso.* El trabajo del censor," in *Instituciones censoras*, ed. Fernando Durán (Madrid: CSIC, 2016), 31–38.

22 Elena de Lorenzo, "Jovellanos: desde la censura dieciochesca hacia la libertad de imprenta," *Hacia 1812, desde el siglo ilustrado*, ed. Fernando Durán (Gijón: Trea, 2013), 991–1007.

23 On the role of the press to modulate social customs, see Bolufer, "Civilizar las costumbres," 97–113, and *Arte y artificio*, 186–93.

24 Velasco, "Las censuras," 144.

25 Defourneaux, *Inquisición*, 45–53.

climate, Spain's borders were closed, censorship was tightened and the crown and the Inquisition embarked on a "newspaper hunt."[26] On 24 February 1791 Floridablanca decreed that all newspapers were to be suppressed except for the *Gaceta de Madrid* and the *Mercurio Histórico y Político*, which were under the direct control of the Secretary of State. However, Aranda discreetly revoked this decision in 1792 and with Manuel Godoy as the new Secretary of State (1792–1798) both the press and the Bourbon reforms entered a new period of splendour.[27] In the lead up to the War of Independence, there was a new boom in the creation of newspaper, at the same time as a strictly "political" press emerged, largely due to the fact that there was no legal framework for this regulation until November 1810. The press gained its freedom, although with limitations, that year, and this right was constitutionalised by the Cadiz *Cortes* in 1812.[28]

2 Political Economy in the Press: Diverse Channels

At this stage of maturity the press's sphere of influence reached all disciplines, and political economy also found a space in the multi-faceted cultural press. Its introduction was uneven, however, and many gazettes carried no related content whatsoever. This was the case with the *Gabinete de lectura española* (1787–1793), the last *spectators* such as *El apologista universal* (1786–1788), *El Duende de Madrid* (1787) and *El filósofo a la moda o el maestro universal* (1788), the culmination of this brilliant and moralising phase of Spanish journalism, with its focus on social criticism.[29] It was also true of Marchena's *El Observador* (1787), although this paper was very close to European political economy. In the short-lived compendium of Enlightenment philosophy, with its snippets of social and theatre criticism,[30] Marchena praised the works of Mably, Condillac, Montesquieu, Mirabeau and, particularly, Mercier de la Rivière because he had taught him more about the order of societies than Pufendorf or Heineccio.[31]

26 On the Floridablanca's "panic," see Herr, *The Eighteenth-Century Revolution*, 197–221, 245–60; Domergue, *Censure et Lumières*, 147–92, and Defourneaux, *Inquisición y censura de libros*.

27 Emilio La Parra, *Manuel Godoy. La aventura del poder* (Barcelona: Tusquets, 2002): 174–86.

28 Larriba, *El público*, 21–22.

29 Urzainqui, "Libertad de imprenta," 44–45; *El Corresponsal del Censor* (1786–1788): I, 22.

30 José Francisco Fuentes, *José Marchena. Biografía política e intelectual* (Barcelona: Crítica, 1989), 4.

31 *El Observador* (1787), discurso I, 9–10; discurso VI, 90.

Other newspapers, however, did incorporate news about political economy, but this was of little and marginal value. Under the leadership of French bookseller Jacques Thevin, the *Diario curioso, erudito, económico y comercial* (1786–1787) — later called the *Diario de Madrid* — continued Nifo's focus on historical news and daily and business life in Madrid, only occasionally publishing texts with economic content.[32] A similar situation existed at Manuel Rubín de Celis' *El corresponsal de El Censor* (1786–1788); this radical publication, which formed part of the critical press, carried a plethora of criticisms of primogeniture, the excessive number of ecclesiastics and complaints about Spain's underdevelopment in the arts and trade and the fiscal system, identifying these as the causes of depopulation.[33] Meanwhile, at the other end of the ideological spectrum, *La Espigadera* (1790–1791), which was printed in Madrid by Alfonso Bravo, a professor at the University of Valladolid, carried only one economic discourse in its entire run of 17 issues.[34] However, the text was a highly significant piece of writing, which lashed out against the majority view held by the official Spanish Enlightenment (Ward, Campomanes, Jovellanos, etc.) that Spain's excessive number of clergymen was one reason for its prostration. The anonymous author maintained that neither the number, the wealth nor the celibacy of members of religious orders was harmful to the nation, and that as a Catholic country Spain should increase their numbers. This all translated into a critique of political arithmetic — data provided by De Paw and the Spaniard Vicente Pérez Vizcaíno (1729–1799) were mentioned — and the texts by the *señores proyectistas* — political economists — who were described as "anti-Catholic philosophers and anti-Spanish."

In contrast to the somewhat timid incorporation of economics in the press, two more effective channels opened up, the first of which was the publication of whole texts on political economy. As seen above, this model was used in Suárez and Núñez's *Memorias instructivas y curiosas* (1778–1791) and a later it was adopted by Antonio Valladares de Sotomayor (1737–1820) for his *Semanario erudito* (SEV, 1787–1791). Although the publication focused on unpublished

32 It exceptionally included long extracts of the discourse on Finance by Diego Gallard, published by the Segovia Economic Society, defending the reforms of the minister Lerena: *Diario, curioso, erudito, económico y comercial* (1786–1787), V, 274–75, 278–79, 284–83.

33 See *El Corresponsal de El Censor* (1786–1788), especially, vol. IV.

34 "Reflexiones filosóficas y políticas sobre si el estado eclesiástico que tiene la nación española puede perjudicar a su población, a sus artes, a su milicia," in *La Espigadera* (1790–1791): no. II, 41–54; no. III, 81–92; no. IV, 113–21; no. V, 145–56; no. VI, 177–90. It received both favourable and opposing replies: no. VIII, 249–56; no. XII, 387–99.

literary works from the Spanish Golden Age, it also printed economics texts. Some of these had an undeniable political sense and referred to important documents from the reigns of Fernando VI and Carlos III.[35] These included a pioneering defence of the free grain trade written by the Flemish merchant Craywinkel in 1760,[36] and economics texts by Galician-born Sarmiento, as well as others on finance and industrial regulations during the early years of Carlos III's reign, written by two high-ranking civil servants, Joaquín de Aguirre and Joaquín Adame. The SEV also published different writings by political authorities under Fernando VI, such as Melchor Rafael de Macanaz (1670–1760) and Ensenada's famous 1751 *Representation* to the King outlining the political priorities of his reign.[37] Valladares' resurrection task uncovered several unpublished texts written in the shadow of a powerful financial and commercial institution, the *Cinco Gremios Mayores de Madrid* — Five Major Guilds of Madrid — including some by the head, Juan Antonio de los Heros (c. 1725–1780). His works followed in Coyer's footsteps and constituted a vigorous defence of the dignification of commerce and the *noblesse commerçante*.[38] However, unlike the writings mentioned above, the SEV did not always align itself with official positions. In an extensive "political and economic discourse" on the guilds,[39] the Catalan Antonio de Capmany (1742–1813) discussed the traditional justifications favouring the guilds and criticised the liberal line taken by Campomanes in 1775 amidst the debate on the possibility of adopting Turgot's abolitionist path. In any event, Valladares' publication model was successful and 34 volumes of the SEV were published before it was suppressed on Floridablanca's orders in February 1791. The SEV functioned as a mirror for subsequent initiatives. The *Almacén de frutos literarios inéditos de los mejores autores* (1804) can also be attributed to Valladares. This carried an unfinished version of Gándara's previously unpublished *Apuntes sobre el bien y el mal de España*. Written in in Naples around 1759, the text sought to transfer the anti-curial and regalist content of Tanucci's reforms to Spain;[40] and was highly original in its day, but seemed far less innovative when it finally appeared in print by which time the

35 Guinard, *La presse*, 281ff.

36 SEV (1787–1791), XXXIV, 131–50.

37 SEV (1787–1791), XII, 260–82; XI, 36–80, 81–161.

38 The Heros' *Discursos sobre el comercio* were published in the SEV, vols. XXVI, XXVII and XXVII; on its content, see José Manuel Barrenechea, "Prólogo," in Juan Francisco de los Heros, *Discurso sobre el comercio* (c. 1775), ed. José Manuel Barrenechea (Madrid: Banco Bilbao Vizcaya, 1989), XV-LXXXV. The latter volumen also published two texts of the Five Guilds defending their positions favouring usury.

39 SEV (1787–1791), X, 172–224.

40 *Almacén de frutos literarios inéditos de los mejores autores* (1804), 5–156.

works of Galiani, Genovesi, Filangieri and other Neapolitans had already been published there.

Echos of Valladares' SEV can also be found in Valencian Juan Sempere y Guarinos' *Biblioteca española económico-política* (1801–1821), at least at formal level. With Floridablanca's consent, the newspaper had begun to take shape in 1786, and its content was fully aligned with Campomanes' ideas. Sempere understood that one of the causes of Spain's decline was its limited cultivating of the new science of political economy, the origins of which dated back to the seventeenth century.[41] Also like Campomanes, he understood that this would encourage the creation of a political history of Spain similar to Hume's, and a systematic collection of works by Spanish authors to support the teaching of political economy.[42] However, Sempere's project also reactivated other lines: his *Biblioteca* began with a paper aimed at boosting the creation of "an exact physical and economic description of Spain," following different initiatives of the official statistics of the reigns of Felipe V and Fernando VI, including the latter's famous single contribution.[43] In short, Sempere continued what Campomanes had started in his *Apéndice a la Educación Popular* (1775–1777) by reissueing works by Sancho de Moncada (1580–1638), Francisco Martínez de Mata (¿-1665) and other Spanish *proyectistas* — political economists — whose "errors" were due to lack of education, opinion and criticism. In any event he extended the chronological spectrum of authors selected from the sixteenth and seventeenth centuries.

The second means of inserting political economy into the press was by publishing discourses, articles, translations and reviews with this content in multifaceted publications, whether literary, cultural or on customs. This was the clearest sign that the discipline was beginning to enjoy social recognition, and as a result economics became the object of systematic information among the general public; in fact, after 1780 political economy emerged as a true touchstone of newspaper quality. While the least significant publication in this respect was *El Censor*,[44] three of the most prominent gazettes of the "golden age" were key: the *Memorial Literario, instructivo y curioso de la Corte de Madrid, El Correo de Madrid o de los Ciegos* and the *Espíritu de los mejores diarios literarios*

41 *Biblioteca española económico-política* (1801–1821), the quote in I, 2; on this Sempere's work, vid Cervera, *El pensamiento económico*, 339–61.

42 *Biblioteca española* (1801–1821), III, V-VI.

43 *Biblioteca española* (1801–1821), I, 1–36.

44 On the economic content of *El Censor*, vid. Jesús Astigarraga and Juan Zabalza, "La fortuna del *Essai sur la nature du commerce en général* (1755), de Richard Cantillon, en la España del siglo XVIII," *Investigaciones de Historia Económica* 7, no. 3 (2007): 9–36.

que se publican en Europa. The newspaper that pioneered the introduction of regular information about political economy was the *Memorial Literario* (ML, 1784–1808).

3 The *Memorial Literario*

The ML was a monthly periodical which had a style that was entirely new in Spain at the time.[45] Contrary to the two official newspapers, the *Gaceta de Madrid* and the *Mercurio Histórico y Político*, which were focused on current political affairs and Spanish life, it was a multifaceted publication providing literary, scientific and cultural information. It published official legislation, news about art and literature criticism and information about the main scientific disciplines (chemistry, botany, medicine, natural sciences), applied arts (particularly, agriculture) and the emerging social sciences of the Enlightenment, especially, public law and political economy. It also specialised in the publication of the statutes and study plans of the principal Spanish education centres and the dissemination of bibliographical information through the publication of reviews.

The ML was founded by Joaquín Ezquerra (1750–1820) and Pedro Pablo Trullenc (or Trullero) who were Aragonese-born and based in the court. However, the principal editor was the former. Trullenc had no academic training (he was the doorman of the Chamber of Castile), and died early, in December 1789 or January 1790. Ezquerra, meanwhile, was one of the most distinguished journalists of the latter part of the eighteenth century in Spain. A bachelor in Philosophy and Canon Law, in his youth he had studied in Paris and Rome. Upon his return to Spain, in 1771, he began studying at the Royal Studies of San Isidro, one of the most prestigious educational centres of the court, which had switched from Jesuit management in 1766 to fall under the royal jurisdiction. There, he obtained a professorship in Latin, although he also taught other

45 The first volumen was published as follows: *Memorial Literario, instructivo y curioso de la Corte de Madrid, correspondiente al mes de Enero de 1784*, Imprenta Real. Our references to ML include, month, year, part I or II (from September 1787 it doubled its monthly issues) and pages. For the first phase of the periodical, the most studied, see Guinard, *La presse*, 252–65; Sempere, *Ensayo*, III, 11–17; and, in particular, Inmaculada Urzainqui, "Los redactores del *Memorial literario* (1784–1808)," *Estudios de Historia Social* 52–53 (1990): 501–16, and "Crítica teatral y secularización: el *Memorial Literario* (1784–1797)," *Bulletin Hispanique* 94 (1992): 203–43. The lines that follow briefly summarise Jesús Astigarraga's recent analysis: "Spreading the Official Economic Enlightenment in Spain: the *Memorial Literario* (17684–1808)," *Bulletin of Spanish Studies* 96, no. 10 (2019): 1607–625.

classical and humanistic disciplines. He combined all of this with his journalist career. He collaborated in a number of different initiatives, but the most important of these was the ML.

Although the ML was an initiative of Ezquerra and Trullenc, it undoubtedly had political support. It had the backing of the Secretary of State, the Count of Floridablanca, and enjoyed a special censorship arrangement.[46] This explains why it was a privileged channel of diffusion for the key official institutions of the day: the economic societies, the fine arts or jurisprudence academies and other scientific institutions (the Cabinet of Natural History or the Botanical Garden, both in Madrid). Floridablanca urged them to send their unpublished discourses to the periodical.[47] However, the memorials were not always original. In many cases, the ML simply reproduced previously published news or discourses (for example, those appearing in the minutes of the economic societies). The multidisciplinary nature of the periodical meant that Ezquerra received outside help, although the names of his external collaborators are not known.

The journal's varied focus was part of a strategy aimed at reaching a diverse readership. It is obvious that the ML sought to count the enlightened ecclesiastical sector among its readership — it published texts from a range of religious —; but editors also courted the elite including high-ranking officials, doctors and, particularly, lawyers. At the same time, it did not ignore the general public, rather it intentionally incorporated anecdotes and a number of articles of "pure curiosity."[48] The result was that, although based in Madrid, the ML gained popularity across many Spanish provinces. It grew subscribers, particularly among urban readers. Its specialization in literary criticism meant it was also popular among booksellers.[49]

In effect, bibliographical dissemination was one of the driving forces of the ML. It was a pioneering publication in this respect at the time. All of its issues contained bibliographical reviews, grouped in a section under three headings: printed books, re-printed books and translations. Another section was dedicated to "foreign literary texts." The reviews were created according to highly rigorous bibliographical criteria, and were carefully planned. They only referred to books previously mentioned in the *Gaceta de Madrid*, which is

46 The ML should have only held the licence from the Print Judge upon the approval of Manuel de Lardizábal (1739–1820) and José Miguel de Flores (1724–1790), Secretaries of the Spanish and History Academies, respectively (Sempere, *Ensayo*, III, 16–17).

47 Urzainqui, "Los redactores," 506.

48 Sempere, *Ensayo*, III, 16.

49 Larriba, *El público*, 85–88, 144–45.

another sign of the semi-official nature of the ML. On the whole, they were not translations copied from foreign journals, but were written by the ML, according to homogeneous criteria. All of this was also the case, without exception, for the texts on political economy. Save for a few isolated previous cases, the first reviews of this discipline in the history of Spain appeared in the ML. They included national publications, translations and, exceptionally, texts unpublished in Spain. This was down to Ezquerra's personal efforts: his academic background and solid humanistic training are evident. In fact, the section on book criticism remained as a permanent feature in the first two phases of the periodical when he was editor, it virtually disappearing when it was transferred to other hands.

In order to reinforce the impact of the reviews of the ML, during the period 1784–1791, Ezquerra published the *Biblioteca periódica anual para utilidad de los libreros y literatos*.[50] This was a catalogue of the annual bibliographical novelties, many of which were reviewed in the ML. Its objective was to address the lack of catalogues of these types of published works in Spain so that texts may be "disseminated more easily" and reach different audiences other than the reader interested in cultural novelties to whom the ML was directed. In fact, the principal target audience of the *Biblioteca* were the literary scholars and, primarly, booksellers.[51]

The semi-official nature of the publication explains its moderate tone. The ML had an intense utilitarian, scientific and patriotic prupose: in 1786–1788 and in 1808 it actively joined those critics who had railed against the provocative article "Espagne" witten in 1782 by Nicolas Masson de Morvilliers for the *Encyclopédie Méthodique*. Its secularising mark was also evident. In this respect, it was particularly informative in terms of theatrical criticism and its perspective on religion and was demystifying and militant with regard to the most traditional Scholasticism.[52] These characteristics can be seen in the three periods of its publications. Its first phase was between 1 January 1784 and 31 December 1790, when it was forced to close by Floridablanca's Resolution of 21 February 1791 to isolate Spain from the contagion of the French Revolution. However, it was the only periodical of the 1780s that resumed publication in the 1790s, thanks to the hidden support of Godoy, the prime minister under Carlos IV. It first re-emerged between July 1793 and December 1797 as the *Continuación del Memorial literario, instructivo y curioso de la Corte de Madrid* and later, without Ezquerra as editor, between 1801 and 1808, as the *Memorial literario o Biblioteca*

50 *Biblioteca periódica anual para utilidad de los libreros y literatos* (1784–1791).

51 *Biblioteca periódica* (1784–1791), I, no. II, unpaginated.

52 Urzainqui, "Crítica teatral," 203–43.

periódica de ciencias, literatura y artes.[53] In this way, in discontinuous periods, it covered a quarter of a century, becoming the periodical with the longest publishing history of the Spanish Enlightenment.

3.1 *The* Memorial Literario *in Spain's Territorial Pluralism*

Political economy had a relevant space in the ML throughout its three phases. However, it was mainly concentrated in the first two phases, when Ezquerra was editor. It was he who established the economic content of the publication. This content was characterised by the diversity of formats: information about official institutions (the Bank of San Carlos), economic charters and decrees and, occasionally, news about trade (exchange rates or prices). News about agricultural experiences and industrial techniques, particularly, in the textile sector, was especially frequent. As previously mentioned, many of the discourses presented in the economic societies and official academies were published, particularly those on law — the *Academia Teórica-Práctica de Jurisprudencia* —. All of this conditioned the editorial line of the publication. Contrary to other leading journals of the time, its economic content remained in general within the limits of the Spanish official Enlightenment.

Ezquerra's plan for the ML was a deliberate strategy to integrate Spain's territorial pluralism. The fact that he was from Aragon could have been a key factor in this respect. Another decisive factor was that the ML was created during the decentralisation period of the Spanish Enlightenment. Thanks to the creation of the network of economic societies and that of trade consulates, the local elite classes became increasingly committed to the enlightened programme.[54] Therefore, the ML was not simply a periodical of the court of Madrid. The texts contributed by the economic societies covered an extensive part of the Spanish peninsula (Madrid, the Basque Country, Segovia, Jaén, Granada, Santiago de Compostela, Vera, Valencia, Majorca, Aragon and Cantabria). This enabled the impact of these writings, normally confined to a local context, to be extended to a national scale. At the same time, the ML reported on strategic projects that were emerging in the regional enlightenment movements, such as the

53 Its closure was also caused by a delicate economic situation. Before Ezquerra transferred the editing rights of ML in 1805, from 1801 a Murcia-born journalist, Pedro María Olive (1768–1843), acted as the principal memorialist. It has a long final period in its third phase comprising five issues published at the end of 1808; see Elisabel Larriba, "La última salida al ruedo del *Memorial Literario* (10 Octubre-20 Noviembre 1808)," *Cuadernos de Ilustración y Romanticismo* 16 (2010): 1–88.

54 See a highly favourable discourse on theses societies, "Discurso sobre la utilidad de las sociedades patrióticas," by Nicolás Martínez de la Torre, in ML, IV-1789, 531–43.

fisheries for the region of Cantabria by the Galician-born Juan José Caamaño (1716–1819), the navigable canals of Aragon and Urgell, and the geographical research conducted by the Aragon-born Isidoro de Antillón (1778–1814). Influential discourses on fiscal reforms by Vicente Alcalá-Galiano from Segovia, ordered by the Minister of Public Finance Pedro de Lerena, were also published, as were eminent observations on natural history by Antonio José Cavanilles (1745–1804) from Valencia.[55] This territorial pluralism was limited to the Spanish peninsula: only in the second phase, and in a very tentative way, did the ML publish information drawn from periodicals from Havana and Guatemala.

Of all of the Spanish regions, the Principality of Catalonia left the most significant mark on the ML, especially during its second period. This was particularly notable in the scientific content — members of the Academy of Sciences of Barcelona collaborated with the publication, including the applied science inventor Francisco Salvá y Campillo (1751–1828) — , as well as in the economic subject matter included. In this later field, particularly noteworthy were Jaume Amat, José Castellnou and, most importantly, the enigmatic Abate Asbert. The person behind this pseudonym, whose identity is unknown, was an enlightened scholar based in Barcelona. He was highly knowledgeable about the economic reality of Catalonia. He was also well connected — one of his letters to the ML was addressed to Francisco Armanyà (1718–1803), Bishop of Tarragona — and, he was, most probably, a member of the Barcelona Board of Trade, about which he wrote one of his discourses. Asbert sent a dozen collaborations to the ML, always on economic content. Although they began in August 1790, they were mainly written in the period 1793–1797.

The writings of Abate Asbert reveal the unique features of the economic Enlightenment of Catalonia. By this time, it had become a powerful source for generating economic ideas. As seen, its principal advocate was the Barcelona Board of Trade. This organisation was leading the exuberant industrialisation process of the textile sector, based on disciplined guilds, protectionist tariffs and access to the internal and, particularly, the colonial market, which the monarchy had opened to the Principality as part of its liberalising programme of 1765, 1778 and 1789.[56] Asbert used the ML to disseminate projects supported

55 On Alcalá-Galiano, see Valles, *Ciencia*, 222–67; on Cavanilles, see Cervera, *El pensamiento económico*, 222–68, and "En los orígenes del reformismo," 21–24. Only two volumes of his *Observaciones sobre la historia natural, geografía, agricultura, población y frutos del Reino de Valencia* (1795–1797) saw the light of day. They were devoted to statistics and observations on botany relating to the Kingdom of Valencia (with substantial debts to the works of French agronomists such as Tessier, Bernard and Rozier).

56 See Lluch, *El pensament;* on the programme of liberalising the colonial trade, see Stein and Stein, *El apogeo del imperio*, 83–95, and Delgado, *Dinámicas imperiales*, 235–77.

by the enlightened sectors of Catalonia, such as the afore-mentioned canal of Urgell.[57] Nevertheless, he also subsumed them in official reform programmes. His favourable position with the guilds was in line with the moderately liberalising plans launched in 1775 by the Council of Castile that were inspired by Campomanes. Asbert dedicated a paper to defending the commitment of the parish priests to rural industry and teaching of the arts; another described the enormous economic possibilities for the monarchy of trading with the colonies; and a third was focused on arguing that the problem of Spanish depopulation could be resolved with the development of the productive arts.[58]

However, the paper that best reflected his alignment with the official positions was the one dedicated to lamenting the lack of an economic society in Barcelona and to calling for its creation, reopening a twenty-year old debate in Catalonia.[59] According to Asbert, this Society should follow the official guidelines defined by the parent society, the Matritense, and be implemented throughout the whole Principality. His main justification resided in the advantages for regional industrial development. The textile industry in Catalonia, although more robust than that in the rest of the peninsula, had still not reached the same level as other countries. As examples, Abate referred to China (in one of his texts he studied the envied industriousness of its inhabitants);[60] but his role models were the French, Flemish and British manufacturing industries. While he regarded them with envy, Asbert pointed out the advantages that the monarchy as a whole would obtain from projecting the Catalan model across the different regions. With a previously planned design, in the ML he presented four consecutive papers on "favouring the public happiness" of Aragon, Majorca, Valencia and Murcia.[61] They were short essays on regional economics. Together with the unique economic possibilities that could be exploited in them, all four of these regions shared the underlying principle of the priority of industry in economic development. In this sense, the Catalan model, with its powerful textile industry, its exemplary guilds and its expanding trade, emerged as a true model of emulation and progress for these regions. In order to incite the development of "factories," Asbert enriched his papers with an abundance of very specific examples of the economic reality of Barcelona and Catalonia as a whole. In this way, the ML exploited a type of unique economic

---

57 ML, XII-1793, I, 322–29.

58 See, respectively, ML, VIII-1790, II, 513–19; IV-1795, II, 225–36; III-1795, I, 72–80.

59 ML, IX-1795, I, 335–50; vid. Lluch, *El pensament*, 119–34.

60 ML, III-1794, II, 472–79.

61 Vid. ML, XI-1795, I, 178–202 (Aragon); II-1796, I, 168–85 (Majorca); I-1797, I, 3–33 (Valencia); IV-1797, II, 81–117 (Murcia).

patriotism: it was not necessary to look beyond the borders of the monarchy, to the envied Great Britain or France, to find models which could inspire Spanish economic progress. In placing the spotlight on Catalonia and other Spanish regions, the ML became the periodical that best captured the economic pluralism of the Spanish Enlightenment. This could be the reason why it was influential among readers who were remote from the court.

3.2 *The Journalism Power of Controversies*

Ezquerra used his role as editor skilfully to plan the publication of an array of controversial topics in the ML which would help to grow an "informed public." Political economy proved to be a particularly fertile ground for doing this. During its first two phases, the ML addressed three controversies exploiting this content.

The first referred to the problem of usury, in other words, the legitimacy of charging interest rates for loan operations. Economic, moral and religious issues were all intertwined within this topic: in a secular way, the most conservative Catholicism refused to accept the legitimacy of usury. For this reason, it was frequently addressed in the Spanish press of the day. In the case of the ML, a paper was printed in 1790 that defended the interest rate: it claimed that not only did interest rate charges respect natural laws and the gospel, but that it was an unavoidable necessity in order to sustain trade. It was unlikely that trade could earn capital without the interest rate premium. Only one month after this paper appeared, the ML published a profoundly conservative article that constituted a forceful response. It gave a detailed account of the arguments of the most reactionary sector.[62] A third contribution to the argument defended not only the payment of an interest rate, but also held that such a rate should be enshrined in law. This paper could be said to represent the position the ML itself took on the subject, and was strategically published last and without a rebuttal article.[63] The objective of this last contribution was to defend not only the payment of an interest rate, but also that it should be established by law. Outside the confines of Scholastic rigidity and referring to the series of laws enacted by Carlos III in defence of the payment of the interest rate, the paper cited the authority of Antonio Genovesi, his Spanish translator, Victorián de Villava, and Locke, who campaigned agaisnt government regulation of interest rates. In opposition to the criterion of Locke, the ML defended the legal establishment of a lower interest rate at a lower rate with the aim of

62 ML, XI-1790, I, 333–37; XII-1790, II, 578–88.

63 "Discurso sobre el establecimiento de una ley que fije el interés, rédito o premio del tanto por ciento en el préstamo," in ML, XI-1794, I, 141–78.

stimulating economic growth as in Great Britain or the Netherlands. In this way, the Ezquerra's periodical also contributed to deconsecrating economic life and to defending the reformism of Carlos III.

Another example of the debates circulated through the ML can be seen in two opposing papers published in 1788 and 1790. Written by two eminent merchants, Francisco Cabarrús (1752–1810) from Bayonne and Jaume Amat from Catalonia, they had both been published prior to appearing in Ezquerra's periodical.[64] This controversy referred to the tariff level necessary for the development of national industry. In his tribute to the ex-finance minister Miguel de Múzquiz, Cabarrús argued that international competition constituted the principal incentive for the development of the arts. At the other extreme, Amat responded with the theory of prohibition or high tariff protection. Underlying this position was, once again, the defence of Catalonia's booming industrial model: tariff protection was vital in the Principality given that its factories were still in their "infancy." However, Amat used his response to dispute two topics rooted in the Spanish Enlightenment. Firstly, he argued that the success of the much-envied British model was not due to its political constitution and regime of individual freedoms; on the contrary, the real reason for its success resided in the regulatory framework of the economic laws in which Britain operated, together with its ability to raise capital, its marine supremacy, the low interest rate and the high tariff barriers. Secondly, Amat questioned Cabarrús' Neckerian conviction regarding the capacity of public opinion to modify the legislation: this public "tribunal," although vigorous, could not deny the importance of the tariffs in underpinning textile industrialisation process in Catalonia. However, going beyond the Catalan context, Amat ended his paper with praise for the economic societies and for Campomanes, for arousing favourable public opinion with respect to national industry through his writings. In this way, Ezquerra deftly closed the debate between Cabarrús and Amat by aligning the ML with the official lines of the enlightened reforms outlined in the *Arancel* — Customs duty — in 1778–1782.

The third economic controversy of the ML was related to a problem that was repeatedly addressed in it: depopulation in Spain. In 1787, after lamenting the non-existence in Spain of a treatise similar to *L'ami des hommes* (1756–1760)

64 Extracts from the *Elogio del Exmo. Sr. Conde Gausa* (Madrid: Viuda e hijos de Ibarra, 1785), presented by Cabarrús in the Matritense Society, can be found in the ML, VIII-1788, I, 680–93; the Amat's *Observaciones de un comerciante sobre la nota XVII del Elogio del Excelentísimo Señor Conde de Gausa* (Barcelona: Pla, 1789) were published in their entirely: ML, I-1790, I, 104–26; II-1790, I, 161–87. For a detailed account see Lluch, *El pensament*, 170–77.

by the Marquis of Mirabeau, an anonymous author outlined in the ML the structure of a future book which described the political, physical and moral causes of low population.[65] Two years later, the official Alfonso Tabares used the calculations and reasoning of Spanish authors such as Miguel Álvarez de Osorio, Ward and Campomanes to estimate the potential population of Spain, but his exercise of political arithmetic was dubious and unreliable, although it must have been eye-catching for a reader who was not used to these types of quantifications.[66]

In between these two articles, the ML had published another two opposing papers on this issue. The first was written by Ramón de Salas (1753–1837), one of the most audacious professors at the University of Salamanca. He attributed the problem of depopulation to ecclesiastical celibacy and the corruption of traditions, while, at the same time, he defended the economic and social utility of luxury.[67] It is not surprising that, althought relatively radical, his tirade was brief and published in Latin — meaning it largely escaped notice with the result that it did not receive an inmediate response—. The author of the response was Manuel Romero del Álamo, about whom little is known except that he exchanged correspondence with Campomanes.[68] During the year 1789 he sent eight long letters to the ML. They constituted the most remarkable economic discourse of the publication. Starting as an analysis of the depopulation in Spain, from the second letter onwards the subject of the "pernicious effects of luxury" dominated.

At first sight, Álamo's discourse seemed to be just another compendium that expounded the usual arguments against luxury, that it causes idleness, apathy, usury, depopulation, etc., eventually leading to "the complete ruin of the state." However, the lengthy political arithmetic calculations increased the quality of the paper. These calculations were understood as an essential guide to economic policy. Although Romero mentioned the founder of this economic current as the British-born William Petty, his estimates were based on the economic quantativism of the Spanish Enlightenment, through authors such as Nicolás de Arriquíbar and, particularly, Francisco Joaquín de Villarreal (1691–1769). In fact, his letters were far from original. They constituted a compact

65 "Elementos para la historia de la despoblación de España," in ML, VII-1787, II, 325–36.

66 ML, X-1789, I, 166–84; X-1789, II, 241–53; XI-1789, I, 321–30.

67 ML, II-1789, 304–06.

68 ML, IV-1789, II, 623–38; V-1789, I, 5–20, and II, 92–103; VI-1789, I, 173–89 and II, 241–57; VII-1789, I, 353–70 and II, 425–41; VIII-1789, I, 483–98 and II, 563–77; the paper was republished in 1985 by Elvira Martínez: *Efectos perniciosos del lujo* (Oviedo: Universidad de Oviedo, 1985).

summary of extensive fragments of Villarreal's *Elementos políticos,* which had remained in manuscript form since they were written, between 1748 and 1754, although we do not know how Romero got hold of this text.[69]

Like Villarreal, Romero based his letters on the concept of "competent, rational and proportionate" maintenance. This guaranteed the highest volume possible of population and, therefore, he argued, should guide political decisions. Romero conducted a historical review in which he showed that the cost of maintenance had increased, particularly from the beginning of the sixteenth century due to "the idol of profusion and vanity."[70] In his case, the emphasis was placed on the consequences of introducing luxury goods in the real wage. This had caused family expenditure to grow gradually further away from the necessary "rational" minimum and, at the same time, had altered the hierarchical order of the different social strata. "Fine politics" was advocated to help to reverse this trend. Romero aligned himself with the Scholastic approach of Villarreal, with his commitment to abundance, low prices and a tight control of expenditure until it reached moderate levels, for economic and moral reasons.

Romero's similarity with Villarreal can also be observed in the use of numerical calculations. This was the case when he estimated the potential population depending on the fertility of the land, its capacity to maintain the population and, most strikingly, the multiplying effect of the increase in income and population generated by the expenditure process. Trace of the Pierre de Boisguilbert's work can be seen in Romero's own studies, and the Frenchman had also proved an inspiration to Villarreal's *Elementos Políticos,* instead of the Physiocrats, who were the privileged source of the Arriquíbar's *Recreación política* (1779). It was based on the idea that agriculture and the arts were productive and mutually dependent sectors. The exchange of income between the two gave rise to an economy in which the factor of land was underemployed and in which the production of agricultural goods increased by a value of twenty million. Given that the wage level was estimated at one thousand *reales,* this increase generated a rise in agricultural employment of twenty thousand

69 See Jesús Astigarraga and José Manuel Barrenechea, "Estudio Preliminar" to *Recreación Política,* and José Manuel Barrenechea and Jesús Astigarraga, *"Estudio Preliminar,"* in Francisco Joaquín de Villarreal y Ecenarro, *Elementos políticos,* ed. José Manuel Barrenechea and Jesús Astigarraga (Vitoria: Gobierno Vasco, 1997): XIII-CX. The latter referred to the existence of different manuscripts by Villarreal, which may have circulated in different points of Spain. On these issues, the Cantillon's *Essai* (1755) was also fundamental; it was well known in Spain for that time: Astigarraga and Zabalza, "La fortuna del *Essai,*" 9–36.

70 ML, VII-1789, I, 535–70.

people. But this was not all. Through the circular flow, this activated an intense exchange of income and expenditures between the two sectors. Through consumption and trade, the exchanges between labourers and craftsmen generated multiplying effects on production and the population, and the higher the consumption, the more widely distributed the final income: in the end, Romero estimated that the population would have increased by one hundred and twenty thousand people. However, this would only be the case if there was no personal consumption within each class, if all of the income was turned into expenditure and, most of all, if this expenditure was not used for the purchase of luxury goods. The reason resided in the fact that in an economy with a low level of industrial development, such as Spain, these goods mainly came from abroad. Therefore, this would not only be detrimental to national industry but would also cut domestic spending, thereby interrupting the above-described multiplying effects. Romero illustrated this point through another of his calculations: the harmful effect on the national population caused by the import of foreign-manufactured goods.

For these reasons, the effects of luxury were different in France and Spain: the former was a producer of luxury goods; therefore the money spent remained in the domestic economy. The opposite was the case in Spain. Hence, the alternative would require an extensive set of public policies. In short, everything was focused on restoring "comfortable and decent" maintenance.[71] It was not a question of fostering an autarchy but of establishing trade regulations which, through prohibitionist or highly protectionist policies, prioritised internal national trade and made the sale of foreign-manufactured goods more difficult. These policies were also designed to slow the export of basic necessities and raw materials until Spain had developed its manufacturing skills. While there was no risk of internal trade endangering the power of the state, this was not true for external trade. Therefore, while domestic trade allowed, according to natural law, the freedom of trade — which included price fixing — foreign trade required protectionist policies. Only this method guaranteed both abundance and the low prices on which the external competitiveness of the national economy depended. So, together with the control of expenditure on luxuries, which increased real wages, the *rentas provinciales* — *alcabalas, cientos* and other taxes — which were established on goods of basic necessity had to be transferred to luxury products. The moderate approach of the ML was supported by Romero's paper which opposed luxury. However, the relevance of his article went beyond its content. Through the three controversies described

71 ML, VIII-1789, II, 570.

above, Ezquerra sought to build a well-informed and secularised public, familiarising readers with topics that formed a central part of the enlightened discussions of the day.

3.3 *Agriculture, Industry and Trade*

The economic content of the ML was expanded to include all sectors. News on trade and the industrial arts were spread through discourses aimed at training merchants on topics such as bills of exchange, insurance and the right to confiscate goods. In addition, two further relevant topics were addressed. The first was clearly oficial in origin and referred to the desirability of designing a Code of Commerce.[72] The second referred to the guilds. The most significant paper on this issue, published amidst the debate triggered by the arrival in Spain of Turgot's abolitionist theories, was aligned with Campomanes: it rejected the unlimited freedom of trade and work and defended the gradual reform of the urban guilds and the freedom of work in rural industry.[73]

Agriculture overwhelmingly dominated the content of the ML. Interest in it was manifested through many reports on practical agriculture and, exceptionally, translations.[74] However, there was a theme which ran transversally through the first two phases of the ML, namely the official agricultural reforms. The series began with an article published in 1786 defending an aspiration that had been repeated since 1766 in the Spanish Enlightenment: the creation of a *Ley Agraria*.[75] Its content was restricted to issues arising during the period between the texts by Pablo de Olavide (1766) and Manuel Sisternes (1783): property reform, distribution of communal lands and the type of leases and their duration.[76] A year later, another paper was published which defended the

---

72 See ch. IX above.

73 Juan Antonio Angli, "Disertación sobre las utilidades o perjuicios de los gremios," in ML, X-1787, I, 209–19. On the reception of Turgot's abolitionist theories in Spain, see Jesús Astigarraga, "Turgot et le débat sur la liberté du travail dans l'Espagne des Lumières (1776–1813)," *Mediterranea. Richerche Storiche* 40 (2017): 343–72.

74 With respect to the agricultural translations, see "Plan de las experiencias e indagaciones que deben hacerse para formar el cuadro razonado de la agricultura de un reino", by Henri-Alexandre Tessier, in ML, II-1789, 337ff.

75 A complete overview in Gonzalo Anes, *La Ley Agraria* (Madrid: Alianza, 1995).

76 Daniel Sanza, "Disertación sobre una ley agraria," in ML, VII-1786, 323–37; "Legislación agraria," in ML, X-1786, 160–68. On Olavide, see Luis Perdices, *Pablo de Olavide (1725–1803). El ilustrado* (Madrid: Editorial Complutense, 1992), 304–21; on Sisternes, Vicent Llombart, "Estudio Preliminar," in Manuel Sisternes, *Idea de una Ley Agraria española*, ed. Vicent Llombart (Barcelona: Alta Fulla, 1993), 5–39.

Pragmática — Decree — of the free trade of grain of 1765.[77] In 1793, during the periodical's second phase, an article was printed that highlighted the relevance of parish priests in economic development and education, in line with the views of the Venetian-born Francesco Griselini — whose text, as seen, was translated in 1784 —, even proposing the creation of chairs of political economy and agriculture.[78]

The interest in agriculture intensified after 1796, due the presentation of the *Informe de Ley Agraria* (1795) by Jovellanos to the Matritense Society. The ML published a number of contributions related to the contents of this seminal book. It drew heavely on the *Memoires* of the *Société Oeconomique* de Berne, publishing five articles from this work between 1796 and 1797, including one on practical agriculture.[79]

Publication on this subject began with the translation of a four-part paper written by Gabriel Seigneux de Correvon in 1796.[80] Seigneux de Correvon is of note because he was the recipient of an award from the afore-mentioned Berne Society, of which he was a member. The award shared the same subject matter as Jovellanos' *Informe*: "What should be the spirit of legislation that favours agriculture?"[81] For Correvon, the first response to this question was to be found in Montesquieu: the "spirit of the laws" should

77 ML, VIII-1787, II, 423–26. On the history of this *Pagmática*, from 1765 to 1790, see Llombart, *Campomanes*, 155–90.

78 "Sobre las sociedades económicas," in ML, XI-1793, I, 218–25.

79 This information has not been taken into account until now regarding the *Informe* of Jovellanos. The most complete interpretation was conducted by Vicent Llombart: "Estudio Preliminar," in Gaspar Melchor de Jovellanos, *Escritos económicos*, ed. Vicent Llombart (Madrid: RACMP, 2000): 45–110, and "El *Informe de Ley Agraria* de Jovellanos: núcleo analítico, programa de reformas y fuentes intelectuales," in *Economía y economistas españoles. Vol. III. La Ilustración*, ed. Enrique Fuentes Quintana (Barcelona: Galaxia Gutenberg-Círculo de Lectores, 2000): 421–46.

80 Gabriel Seigneux de Correvon, *Essais sur l'esprit de la législation, favorable à l'agriculture, à la population, au commerce, aux arts, aux métiers* (Paris: Dessaint, 1766), cfr. ML, VII-1796, II, 112–42; VIII-1796, I, 173–86 and II, 263–87; IX-1796, I, 323–57. A member of the Economic Society of Berne and President of one of its affiliate bodies, that of Lausanne, Coverron was a translator and jurist who specialised in natural law (he edited the work by Burlamaqui). He had participated in 1759 in the competition of this Society which awarded a *Mémoire* by Mirabeau of Physiocratic content. He later included it in *L'Ami des hommes* (1756–1760). The *Mémoire* had already been translated into Spanish in 1764 by Serafín Trigueros.

81 Coverron's article was published in the *Mémoires et observations recueillies par la Société Oeconomique de Berne*, I, part III, and one year later in a volume that compiled the four winning papers of the afore-mentioned competition: *Essais sur l'esprit de la législation*, 380–474. This volume was translated into English in 1772.

address a diverse range of factors (including climate and customs); with the result that agricultural law could not be considered universal, but had to be adapted to the circumstances of each nation. The paper followed a pattern that was familiar during the Spanish Enlightenment. It was based on the idea that agriculture formed the basis of political edification and described the relationships of this sector with the population, the arts, manufacturing companies and trade. The text perfectly reflected the time in which it had been written, three decades before it was published in the ML. Its content referred to the open debate in France during the 1750s between the Vicent de Gournay and François Quesnay circles which was then transferred to the heart of the *Société Oeconomique* de Berne. Coverron was aligned with the Gournay circle. This was evident in his sources: he mentioned two members of this circle: Plumard de Dangeul and Thomas. The writings of these economists had major influence in the 1750's and 1760's. His hand was evident in Coverron´s programme for revitalizing agriculture.

This programme included a rejection of public granaries and communal land, and a defence of agricultural individualism, agricultural training and "freedom with no strings attached" which bore no signs of the Physiocrats. Furthermore, the author renounced small crops, the *bon prix* and absolute laws: in line with Montesquieu, he affirmed that different forms of government imposed different economic codes. In keeping with the anti-Colbertist tradition, opposed to privileges, monopolies, guilds and luxury, Correvon favoured protectionism and a programme to stimulate the population. In short, his paper defended a pre-Physiocratic populationist agrarian reform which was highly liberal and in keeping with the main current of the economic Enlightenment and the Jovellanos' *Informe*, with the only exception being that it seemed to support the free export of grain.

The contribution of the ML to the controversy over the Agrarian Law also took into account perspectives that were critical of Jovellanos. An extensive text written by the agronomist José Castellnou tacitly raised significant discrepancies with him.[82] First, Castellnou argued that the process of preparing this Law was as essential as its content. According tho him, a pyramid-shaped institutional structure should be organised on three levels taking into account village, capital and nation. The information should circulate in one direction and another. He proposed that local boards were established at the base, which in turn would be governed by economic societies

82 "Disertación sobre agricultura experimental," in ML, VI-1797, I, 327–57 and II, 420–31; VIII-1797, I, 167–75.

based in the provincial capitals. Topping the pyramid should be a body of "experts" on a national level, made up of three or four hundred academics. Their functions would be to direct the pyramid's organization and co-ordinate the teaching of agricultural sciences at each level. Castellnou believed that this structure should be imbued with a patriotic spirit similar to that of the economic societies and that the Agrarian Law should be the fruit of this structure and emerge from the bottom and grow upwards, that is, in the opposite direction to how it was being created at the time. Castellnou's concern throughout was similar to that of the Valencian Manuel Sisternes (1728–1788) in that he was in favour of a decentralised Agrarian Law that integrated Spain's regional diversity.[83] Castellnou also justified his position by saying the Law should have an experimental basis. To find this basis, he called for the existence of a physical and economic science which depended on the development of auxiliary sciences, such as physics or chemistry. He suggested that a body of "experts" should then stimulate the teaching of these sciences. However, the Agrarian Law also had to take into account the experiences of the local boards, given that agriculture was an experimental science. Throughout his paper, Castellnou expressed the fear that this Law would be speculative and not address the farmer's real problems.

The ML returned to the agricultural theme before the publication of Castellnou's text. In July 1797, a new paper was published in the journal which insisted on the idea of agriculture as a principal source of wealth and, therefore, on the advisability of protecting it with public policies and the publicising of these policies through a series of seminal books.[84] A short time later, the periodical returned to a topic that was much-loved by agricultural economists: the rejection of luxury. It did so through a diatribe extracted from the *Mémoires* of the Berne Society: luxury was presented in it as an intolerable abuse, contrary to religion and a source of social disorder, whatever the form of government.[85] All of this culminated in two more, particularly significant and Physiocratic, texts. Both were both drawn from the *Journal d'agriculture, du commerce et des finances* (1765–1783), one of the periodicals edited by the *économistes*, with those particular texts arriving into the laps of the editors of the ML through the mediation of the *Mémoires* of the Berne Society.

---

83 See Llombart, "Estudio Preliminar," in Sisternes, *Idea de una Ley Agraria*, 31ff.

84 "Reflexiones sobre la agricultura de un presbítero residente en Madrid," in ML, VIII-1797, II, 239–55.

85 "Examen de la definición del lujo," in ML, IX-1797, II, 416–23; cfr. "Sur le luxe," *Mémoires et observations* 9, no. 1 (1768), 99–108.

The first text was a book commentary by Louis-Paul Abeille.[86] His paper examines different "immutable" principles derived from the "order that was evidently more avantageous for the public cause." It began with the inviolability of private property and its security insofar as these constituted the rights of society. Then it criticised the concession of exclusive privileges in agriculture and trade, as they were detrimental to property rights and destroyed employment and industry. It ended by analysing the dependency that existed between national wealth and the extension of domestic and foreign trade. This is where the Physiocratic economic analysis was conducted: the priority of agriculture, agricultural goods as a source of wealth and the population, the *bon prix* and free domestic and foreign trade which should be "as far reaching as posible." All of this was perfectly complemented by the second text. It was a brief extract, probably written by the director of the *Journal d'agriculture*, Pierre-Samuel Du Pont de Nemours.[87] Its objective was to highlight how monopolies and others with exclusive privileges, including the guilds, could have a detrimental effect on wealth and social order. To illustrate his point he cited *Philosophie rurale* (1763) by Mirabeau and referred to the "Tableau économique." Anyway, the purpose of these two texts was none other than to contribute to the debate about "opinion" raised by Jovellanos' *Informe*. Given that this book had no Physiocratic influence, the ML seemed to invite authors to radicalise the doctrinal and reformist proposal expounded therein following the *économistes*. This was not an isolated case: it was the same channel chosen by the liberal Juan Álvarez Guerra a year later. All of this confirms that, contrary to what has been normally assumed, Physiocracy was not absent from the debate raised by the *Informe*, but contributed to devising an alternative to it.[88]

Furthermore, these two texts virtually concluded the substantial economic content of the ML. In its languid third phase (1801–1808), now without Ezquerra as editor-in-chief, it became a mere channel for disseminating treatises and translations. Texts on political economy were very marginal.[89] The new editors

86 ML., X-1797, I, 3–24. Louis-Paul Abeille, *Effets d'un privilège exclusif.* The comment had been originally published in the *Journal d'agriculture, du commerce et des finances*, September 1765, 36–141, and later in the *Mémoires et observations* 9, no. 1 (1768), 109–40. In 1797 the first project to disentailment of the lands of the Church was begun in Spain and this can explain this radical defense of the right to private property.

87 ML, X-1797, I, 25–31; vid. *Journal d'agriculture*, November 1765, 189ff., and *Mémoire et observations* 9, no. 1 (1768), 132–40.

88 See Astigarraga and Usoz, "Una alternativa fisiócrata," 427–58, and "Algunas puntualizaciones," 489–97.

89 The only content worth highlighting is a translation of Arthur Young and a text by Justo José Banqueri (1772–1847); base on authors such as Bernardo Ward and Adam Smith, he identified the priority of domestic trade over foreign trade: *Discurso sobre la*

were keen for the ML to specialise in researchs on economic statistics and history, following the model used by Cavanilles in Valencia.[90] This outcome was not at all representative of what the ML had once been.

4 Final Remarks

The ML was a pioneer in the introduction of information about political economy in the multidisciplinary press during the "golden age" of the Spanish Enlightenment. It clearly signified that in the 1780s this discipline already enjoyed substantial social recognition, and was ready for public consumption. Introducing this economic content was not guided by an exclusionary doctrinal criteria. Rather, it had to be defined in relation to the readership. In the 1780s most European governments began to use the press as a necessary complement to contemporary politics.[91] By these dates, also the Spanish enlightened scholars were fully aware that the press was a powerful instrument for creating "opinion" and, therefore, was most useful for helping shape public opinion about officil reforms. In fact, this was the driver that best explains the economic content of the ML. With very few exceptions, this publication was a channel for publicising the reforms programme that the Bourbon governments had been implementing since the 1760s. It sought to persuade the general public of its usefulness and appropriateness. But the ML must also be highlighted for other reasons. It was a newspaper with a national dimension that played a fundamental role in strengthening the relationship between the centre and the peripheries through circulating information in both directions: in the same way that it spread information from the court (for example, the Royal Academies' discourses) to all the regions in Spain, it also transmitted the intellectual products originating there (for example, the economic societies' discourses and memories) at national level. At the same time the ML managed to integrate the regional diversity characterising Spain into a national framework, including Catalonia. The figure of Ezquerra, tutored by Floridablanca, was decisive in establishing this position and in introducing economic content into the periodical in such a way that this content virtually disappeared in the third phase of the ML when he gave up his rights as editor.

---

libertad, facilidad y utilidad del comercio interior (c. 1801), RAH, mss. 9/4729; cfr. ML, XLVI (1804), 81–87.

90 ML, 10-I-1808, 9; 30-V-1808, 363. For the scarce economic content of the last five issues of the ML, see Larriba, "La última."

91 Munck, *The Enlightenment*, 184.

CHAPTER 7

The Critical Press and Public Opinion

El Correo de Madrid *(1786–1791) and the* Espíritu de los Mejores Diarios *(1787–1791)*

1 Introduction

In July 1789, while France was being shaken by revolutionary events, the press in neighbouring Spain was showing unmistakable signs of enjoying tremendous vitality. That month the *Memorial Literario* offered its readers various dissertations on topics such as the law of nations, the usefulness of criticism and the pernicious effects of luxury; *El Correo de Madrid* carried a new extract from a literary work by Cadalso and a tribute to trade with echoes of Hume; and, finally, the *Espíritu de los Mejores Diarios* carried that issue's instalment of a lengthy work by Foronda on with Physiocratic overtones, which that month dealt with domestic trade political economy. Although it would not be long before news from Paris dealt a body blow to the Spanish Enlightenment, the press continued to cultivate the fertile exuberance that it displayed during its "golden age." In the late 1780s its importance could be measured in both quantitative and qualitative terms: not only had newspapers and journals multiplied at court and in the provinces but, as Habermas noted, they had become a key piece in the new domain of the public sphere.[1] During these years some of them not only supported the language and ideas that had preceded the revolutionary events in France, but they also emerged as a new form of political communication in which political economy continued to take pride of place. From a position that was reasonably far away from power, these periodicals became a crucial factor for shaping public opinion in Spain; that is, a system with implicit authority, relatively independent from political power that emerged as a type of "invisible, impersonal and anonymous tribunal," as described by Ozouf and Baker.[2] In Enlightenment Spain the two main symbols of this new critical

1 Habermas, *Strukturwandel der Öffentlichkeit*, 79ff.

2 Mona Ozouf, "L'opinion publique," in *The Political Culture of the Old Regime*, ed. Keith Michael Baker (Oxford: Pergamon Press, 1987), I, 419–34, and Keith Michael Baker, "Politics and Public Opinion under the Old Regime: Some Reflections," in *Press and Politics in Pre-Revolutionary France*, ed. Jack R. Censer and Jeremy D. Popkin (Berkeley-Los Angeles: University of California Press, 1987), 204–46. In the same line, Goodman, *The Republic*, 235–42. On the concept's appearance in its historical context, see Edoardo Tortarolo, "Opinion publique tra Antico

 DOI:10.1163/9789004442894_009

journalism, bursting with economic content and protagonists in the opening up of a new channel for intervening in political life with the aim of shaping "the tribunal of public opinion," were *El Correo de Madrid o de los ciegos* and the *Espíritu de los mejores diarios literarios*.[3]

2 *El Correo de Madrid o de los ciegos* (1786–1791)

El Correo de Madrid o de los ciegos (CMC) first came off the press on October 10th, 1786. Although its name originally included a reference to the blind ("los ciegos") because it was to be sold in the street, it was also available on subscription,[4] and from April 1787 until publication ceased in February 1791 was called simply *El Correo de Madrid*. First issued on a fortnightly basis, in 1790 it began to be printed every week. It was edited by José Antonio de Manegat, a clergyman, under the penname of Abate Matanegui. It aimed to "spread the love of reading" and "encourage the public" to write to the press;[5] in fact, it was the journal of its day that most welcomed external contributions and was full of articles, discourses and readers' letters, which frequently produced replies that crossed. Its most loyal contributors were Cayetano Cabo, Manuel Casal (1751–1837) and

---

Regime e rivoluzione francese. Contributo a un vocabolario storico della política settecentesca," *Rivista Storica italiana* CII, no. 1 (1999): 5–23; on its modern historiography and on the relationship between political economy and public opinion in the intellectual context of the European Enlightenment, see John Robertson, *The case*, pp. 35ff., and "Enlightenment, Public Sphere and Political Economy," in *L'économie politique et la sphère publique dans le débat des Lumières*, ed. Jesús Astigarraga and Javier Usoz (Madrid: CV, 2013), 15–32. On the meaning of the concept of "opinion" in eighteenth century Spain, see Pedro Álvarez de Miranda, *Palabras e ideas*, 227–34; on the other forms of libel and pamphlet-based political opposition, see Teófanes Egido, *Opinión pública y oposición al poder en la España del siglo XVIII (1713–1759)* (Valladolid: Universidad de Valladolid, 1971); and, finally, on the history of public opinion in this country: Ignacio Fernández Sarasola, "Opinión pública y 'libertades de expresión' en el constitucionalismo español (1726–1845)," *Historia Constitucional* 7 (2006): 159–86, and Javier Fernández Sebastián, "From the 'voice of the people' to the freedom of the press: the birth of public opinion," in *The Spanish Enlightenment revisited*, ed. Jesús Astigarraga (Oxford: VF, 2015): 213–25.

3 Another journal with the same characteristics was *El Censor*, but it was less important in terms of economic ideas. On its content, see Elorza, *La ideología*, 208–34, and Sánchez Blanco, *El absolutismo*, 303–48.

4 Nieves Iglesias and Ana María Mañá (*Correo de Madrid o de los Ciegos, 1786–1791*. Madrid: Hemeroteca Municipal, 1968) created an index of the publication and described its history (I-XIX); on its general content, see Elorza, *La ideología*, 263–92, and Guinard, *La presse*, 231–38.

5 CMC, I (1787), unpaginated.

Manuel de Aguirre, but it also carried pieces by Juan Pablo Forner (1756–1797), Tomás de Iriarte (1750–1791), Juan Meléndez Valdés (1754–1817) and José Cadalso (1741–1782), whose *Cartas Marruecas* (1789) and *Noches lúgubres* (1790) were published there. This broad participation was fostered by the multidisciplinary content: news about literature, science and technology rubbed shoulders with items on politics, economics and law. In spite of its broad ideological spectrum, the CMC was one of the symbols of critical journalism of its day, waiting just three months to publish a terse letter against the reactionary clergy and in defence of Lorenzo Normante, the holder of the Economics Chair at Saragossa University, who had been accused by the court of the Inquisition.[6] This was soon followed by an article on "The freedom that must reign in writers."[7] Until the triumph of the Revolution in France, the paper was impregnated with a lucid, combative and visionary ideology: "This century, which we call enlightened, will be held in contempt by those who come after when they see that we lacked the resolve to break the chains binding the majority of society to the most deplorable lot."[8]

The author of this sentence was Manuel María de Aguirre.[9] His plentiful contributions to the CMC, published under the penname "*el militar ingenuo*" (the naive soldier), set the paper's editorial line for the first three years and made it the most radical of its day. A native of Biscay, Aguirre (1748–1800) was a soldier; he joined the Cavalry Regiment in 1761 and spent a good part of his military career there, attaining the rank of marshal. He taught at the military schools in Avila and Ocaña and became head of the latter. He joined the Academy of the History in 1783, but his publishing activities began at a very young age in the Bascongada Society. He maintained especially close links with this Society from 1770, so much so that he was invited to run the Seminary of Bergara in the early 1790s, although the proposal came to nothing. As well as the Bascongada he frequented the Aragon, Madrid and Antequera Societies before he began contributing to the CMC in late 1786. Required by law to sign his articles in September 1788, he chose to fall silent instead.

Aguirre's contributions enhanced the CMC's inherent ideological diversity. Where economic content was concerned, the Catholic view of the *Oikonimia*

6 CMC, I (1787), no. 34, 135–36; no. 35, 137–39; see also ch. VIII above.

7 CMC, I (1787), no. 52, 209–10.

8 CMC, I (1787), no. 75, 318.

9 On Aguirre, an author who deserves a wider readership, see Antonio Elorza, "Estudio Preliminar," in Manuel de Aguirre, *Cartas y Discursos del Militar Ingenuo al Correo de los Ciegos de Madrid*, ed. Antonio Elorza (San Sebastián: Izarra, 1974): 11–68. Aguirre's main articles in the CMC are reissued in this work.

predominated in early issues. Later on it received many contributions in support of the government reform programme led by Campomanes,[10] as well as others expressing different opinions rooted in Physiocracy: in a translation of the Margrave of Baden's work praising the suppression of serfdom, it was argued that property and freedom were the real pillars of all agrarian societies and that *bon prix* would be achieved through free trade.[11] However, Aguirre's articles took a different starting point from these contributions. In the first place, the origin and foundations of civil society needed to be addressed if it were then to be accepted that its survival depended on trade. Classical virtue, presented through numerous examples from Lacedaemonia, Rome and Greece, was insufficient to maintain harmony in a society marked by riches and luxury. The debate between "ancient" and "modern" peoples, between virtue and law and wealth and corruption, surfaced in all its rawness in the writings of the "naive soldier." The fundamental problem was how to make the crumbling Spain referred to in his articles more civilised and moral, in a context in which the classical virtues of heroism, military spirit and altruism not only failed to explain human behaviour but no longer justified the social recognition of glory and privilege either. In the face of all these virtues, actions in support of the public good now emerged, inspired by the new commercial patriotism activated by the balance between pleasure and pain; in short, by self- interest. Aguirre's articles reverberated with the ideas of authors such as Hume, Helvetius, Montesquieu, Rousseau, Necker, Filangieri, Genovesi and Beccaria, along with the great themes that had been given an airing by American Independence.

The article by Aguirre that best reflected these issues was the "Discurso sobre la legislación," which was published in October and November 1787. The text was originally written for a competition organised by the Sociedad Matritense on the topic of the proper spirit of a legislature, taking into account diversity in terms of climate, natural products and "its inhabitants' national character." Clearly echoing Montesquieu, the competition enabled Aguirre to publish in the CMC the Spanish Enlightenment's first proposal for a political constitution.[12] The press thus joined in a debate that was gathering pace

10 The defence of Campomanes' programme, underscoring the priority of domestic trade, is very well reflected in the CMC, III (1788), no. 156, 871–72; no. 158, 888; no. 159, 895; no. 160, 904; no. 166, 948–49; the main agrarians in the programme appears in III (1788), no. 200, 1226–227; the defence of the creation of agricultural colonies for idlers appears in I (1787), no. 100, 450–51; and, finally, "commerce" as a civilising factor that was contrary to the "spirit of conquest" appears in IV (1789), no. 312, pp. 2508–509.

11 CMC, III (1788), no. 158, 887–88.

12 See Ignacio Fernández Sarasola, "Constitution Projects During the Spanish Enlightenment," in *The Spanish Enlightenment Revisited*, ed. Jesús Astigarraga (Oxford: VF, 2015), 129–47.

during the 1780s and to which the names of León de Arroyal (1755–1813), José Marchena, Manuel Rubín de Celis, Valentín de Foronda and other fathers of *early* Spanish constitutionalism would soon be added.[13]

Unlike Arroyal's contemporary document, the proposal that Aguirre named "constitutional laws" or "constitutional code" did not hark back to a historical constitution. It was instead based on the recognition that ancient civilisations' legal codes were useless: "It is ridiculous for modern writers to talk about the constitutions of the past and propose them as models," wrote an anonymous CMC contributor, going on to add: "What would Licurgo say if he found himself at court [in Madrid]?"[14] Aguirre was undoubtedly encouraged in his beliefs by the United States' constitutional experience, details of which he received via Jacques-Pierre Brissot de Warville. However, as Fernández Sarasola emphasises, his "Discurso" was remarkable because it was so early — the Constitution of the United States had not yet been published — for its simplicity — it contained only fifteen articles — and for its unmistakably rational-normative approach. Aguirre was sympathetic to Hobbes' contractualism, although he was actually inspired by Rousseau: according to Elorza, the content of his "Discurso" was a response to a Rousseauian critique of the social order.[15] Aguirre reaffirmed the concept of the division of powers and a political system underpinned by elected bodies with representative functions, which, however, was far from radical: "It seems that Aguirre was designing a limited monarchy in which the supreme head of society restricted his functions through governing bodies — central and provincial — which he formed himself."[16] Distributing legislative power among different bodies invoked a type of constitutional balance along the lines of the British constitutional pattern, which was very well-known in Spain at that time.[17] However, the most radical element of Aguirre's code was his defining of individual rights and freedoms: he was among the first to invoke the "rights of man" as the basis for a constitution. The right to own

---

13 See Fernández Sarasola, ed., *Proyectos constitucionales en España (1786–1824)* (Madrid: CEPC, 2004). On constitutional culture's first steps in Spain, see, among others, José María Portillo, *Revolución de nación* (Madrid: CEPC, 2000), and Javier Fernández Sebastián, "Estudio introductorio: Ibáñez de la Rentería y el pensamiento político de la Ilustración," in *La Ilustración política*, ed. Javier Fernández Sebastián (Bilbao: Universidad del País Vasco, 1994), 17–151, 205–42.

14 CMC, I (1787), no 100, 450.

15 Elorza, "Estudio Preliminar," 38ff.

16 Fernández Sarasola, "Constitution Projects," 138.

17 However, in the CMC itself criticism was levelled at the proliferation of legislative bodies: unlike France, which was divided into provincial parliaments, Great Britain fortunately had a single centralised body: III (1788), no. 188, 1123–126.

property was the hub, although it was not conceived in absolute terms. Aguirre also called for religious tolerance and, like Beccaria, procedural rights and the application of humanism to criminal justice. Further articles published in the CMC after the Discurso continued to draw on a similar rationalist argument in support of the idea of the social contract as the origin of civil society: Aguirre sternly rebuked Cristóbal Cladera in his theory that the contract's conjectural nature annulled its explanatory nature.[18]

The defence of the "rights of man" invoked in Aguirre's "Discurso" was in keeping with his other contributions to the CMC. His critical opinion of the Spain of the time led him to attack the feudal system and the clergy, as well as the "political errors from barbaric centuries" that had survived to his day. He also lambasted the tax exemption enjoyed by the privileged classes, the bad distribution of agricultural property, state monopolies, idleness and religious power's control over the public sphere. The Italian cleric Salvador Roselly inspired him to write some of the Spanish Enlightenment's most brilliant pages against Scholastic philosophy and its epigones, in the shape of civil and religious intolerance. All Aguirre's writings were infused with a moralising tone, which in the end infected the entire CMC. His purpose was to inspire principles that were far removed from "barbarous feudal law." Influenced by Helvetius, he realised that education had an essential role to play in achieving this end, as did his bold programme for extending the *Lumières*, inspired by the principle that they "can never be harmful."[19] Aguirre also wrote one of the eighteenth century's most articulate texts in defence of economic societies — *Sistema de sociedades patrióticas* (1785) — and called for new forms of expression for enlightened social activity, such as the press, cafes and "civilising debates and meetings," with the aim of discussing "public roles." He also demanded the acceptance of the principle of transparency in public life, which he extended to the issue of public finance and the economy: "there are no secret companies now" one anonymous contributor to the CMC commented.[20]

Articles by the *militar ingenuo* did not only reveal the new demands on political power made by the *fin de siècle* enlightened generation, but also served to unveil its opponents. In December 1787 Aguirre published his "Discurso sobre el lujo" in the CMC. It was in fact a text that he had presented at the Sociedad Bascongada in 1776 and was nothing more than a bowdlerised version of Hume's "Of Luxury,"[21] a far from trivial topic as it had immediately attracted

---

18 CMC, III (1788), no. 186, 1107–109; no. 187, 1115ff.

19 CMC, IV (1789), 1356.

20 CMC, I (1787), no. 100, 450.

21 Astigarraga, *Los ilustrados vascos*, 126–31. On the broad debate about luxury, see Shovlin, *The Political Economy*; as Anoush Fraser Terjania explains (*Commerce and its Discontents*

the attention of the Inquisition. The "Discurso" was promptly criticised in the CMC by two of its contributors, Lucas Alemán and Antonio Cocea, the pen-names of Manuel Casal, a doctor, and Cayetano Cano.[22] Throughout 1788 they took it upon themselves to remind readers in great detail that luxury not only subverted the traditional virtues but also confounded the hierarchy of social orders, destroying the very foundations of society. The tone of their writings was so scathing and contemptuous that they made Aguirre and his ideas appears almost ridiculous; the fact is that although the controversy was played out under the cover of pennames, the individuals involved knew each other well and were fighting an ideological battle that went far beyond the boundaries of a terse exchange about luxury.

An anonymous contributor came to Aguirre's defence, quite possibly Ramón de Salas, the teacher at the University of Salamanca. The main purpose of his two contributions to the CMC was to attempt to remove the dispute from the sphere of morality, in which Casal and Cocea were particularly convincing, and reposition it in the sphere of politics and economics: to the two "impertinent and ridiculous" writers, politics may have been a "secret of the confessional," but where economics was concerned Aguirre's defender wondered how the multi-faceted topic of luxury could possibly be addressed by individuals that "are ignorant of the principles of civil economy."[23] Furthermore, he accused them of unfamiliarity with Genovesi, Serionne, Cary, Filangieri, Forbonnais and many Spanish authors, from Campomanes and Romà to Ward and Arriquíbar, closing the matter in his second contribution by once again presenting a brief summary of Hume's discourse.[24] This would suggest that the contributor, who went by the name of "Etcetera Sparrowhawk," could have decided on his strategy with Aguirre himself. In any event, the debate showed how difficult it was for enlightened groups to remove what were essentially political issues from the domain of traditional moralism. There can be no doubt that Aguirre was sincere: in spite of the Inquisition accusation hanging over him, he went back to pushing genuine questions into the public sphere: "Who frees us from ignorance or the errors of those who stand up in

---

in Eighteenth-Century French Political Thought. Cambridge: CUP, 2013, 26–27), luxury emerged as one of the best options for those who were displeased with trade. This dissemination of Hume's ideas coincided chronologically with the publication in 1789 of the Spanish translation of his *Political Discourses* (1752).

22 The most important was an article by Cocea: CMC, III (1788), no. 152, 832–35; no. 153, 842–43; no. 154, 750–852; no. 155, 858–59.

23 CMC, III (1788), no. 184, 1096–098.

24 CMC, III (1788), no. 191, 1153–154.

pulpits and are looked on as oracles of truth?"[25] However, Aguirre was fighting a losing battle, with the Inquisition on the other side. In 1790 he was punished again; a further case file was opened against him and the CMC was ordered to withdraw its copies.

When the row over luxury had abated, an argument about the status of the nobility became a new cause for controversy in the journal. Aguirre's oft-repeated criticisms of aristocratic privilege and the factors that made it possible — primogeniture, tax exemption and the exclusive code of honour — were highly influential. Not a single one remained unanswered. A very meaningful reply was developed in a "Discourse" on the "origin of inequality among men,"[26] which argued that natural differences in strength and intelligence were the main causes of sociality. However, as the mutual aid that society provided its weakest members could only make sense in a political community that was ordered into classes, the existence of the nobility and honour as essential components of all well-organised societies was justified. Meanwhile, the nobility's traditional commitment to agriculture and its central role in rural life comprised a bundle of virtues that immunised society against social disorder. Similar ideas were expressed a few weeks later in a "Discurso sobre la nobleza;"[27] based on the ideas of Montesquieu and Boulainvilliers, it argued that as equality of wealth and social class was an illusion, a distinguished nobility was essential for the monarchical system.

A "Discurso sobre la nobleza de las profesiones," published in 1789, appeared to have been written in response to both these articles.[28] Although published anonymously, it was actually the work of Foronda and was a copy of an article he had presented at the Sociedad Bascongada twelve years previously under the significant title "Lo honrosa que es la profesión del comercio." Its chief source was "Of Commerce," the opening essay in Hume's "Political Discourses" (1752).[29] Foronda used Hume's arguments to point the finger at the traditional nobility, those "braggarts, a disgrace to the nation, unworthy descendants of the distinguished ancestors of whom they boast so much." According to the author, far from contributing to the public good, they

25 CMC, I (1787), no. 35, 139.

26 CMC, III (1788), no. 183, 1088; no. 184, 1092; no. 185, 1105–106; no. 187, 1112–113; no. 188, 1119–120.

27 CMC, III (1788), no. 198, 1207–210; no. 201, 1230–232.

28 CMC, IV (1789), no. 274, 2201–206; no. 275, 2210–213.

29 José Manuel Barrenechea, *Valentín de Foronda, reformador y economista ilustrado* (Vitoria: Diputación Foral de Álava, 1984), 112–19; Astigarraga, *Los ilustrados vascos*, 144–46.

undermined it; driven by false pride, these nobles despised their participation in an activity that was as essential for the common good as trade. The discourse presented in the CMC was marked by Foronda's stark utterances: it was unacceptable that those who used their capital to speculate and made "the price of grain exorbitant" dared to disparage those whose incomes came from "setting up factories."

Parallel to the dispute over the nobility, in 1789 the CMC introduced an observation on the implications of advances in art and science, in which the journal itself took on the task of refuting Rousseau.[30] Defending modern science had inspired Aguirre to write an exquisite treatise on geography — *Indagación y reflexiones sobre la geografía* (1782) — several extracts from which were published in the CMC. However, the journal chose to use more subtle means, which consisted of presenting fifty modern philosophers over a period running from October 1789 to April 1790. The series was a Spanish version of Alexandre Savérien's *Histoire des philosophes modernes* (1762–1773) translated by Juan Pons, editor of the *Correo* since 1790 (Manegat had resigned for health reasons).[31] The aim of using Savérien's work was to highlight the current century's superiority over ancient times, while also presenting the general history of philosophy as a combination of the different academic disciplines. The series therefore began with Erasmus and Hobbes and ended with the French naturalists, botanists and chemists of the eighteenth century. A connection was thus established with literature on the progress of the human spirit, a topic that Savérien addressed in another book, partially translated in 1775 by Manuel Rubín de Celis under Campomanes' supervision. However, by this stage the CMC's original boldness was flagging somewhat. There were many reasons for this: in August 1788 it was forced to withdraw an issue containing a satire that mocked the government bureaucrats popularly known as *covachuelistas*; a month later Aguirre left, and as if this were not enough, it was particularly affected by the impact of the French Revolution. A thorough-going internal restructuring was carried out the following month, after which the journal's main concerns became education, history and poetry, all of which were approached in very moderate terms. In April 1790 Savérien's series on modern thinkers was replaced with the basics of good taste in literature. Political economy had now become a nuisance: "if this itch for *arbitrista* writers carries on,

30 CMC, V (1789), no. 271, 2179–180.

31 Iglesias and Mañá, *Correo de Madrid*, 43–46. This may not be the original translation. In 1770 Francisco Pérez Pastor had translated Savérien's work and attempted to have it published, but the Academy of the History censor's report demanded corrections were made; see Velasco, "Las censuras," 151–53.

I'm going to burst with laughter or fury," commented the anonymous writer of a letter to the journal.[32]

3 The *Espíritu de los Mejores Diarios* (1787–1791)

In July 1787, a year after *El Correo de los ciegos* was founded, the *Espíritu de los Mejores Diarios* (EMD) began publication;[33] initially produced every three weeks, in May 1788 it began to appear every week. What was set it apart from the rest was its content, which was mainly articles about books, including reviews. The Academy of the History was probably influential in its founding, as there was no other journal of this type in Spain.[34] Floridablanca could also have been behind the choice of its only editor, Majorcan clergyman Cristóbal Cladera (1760–1816). Educated at the Literary University in Palma de Majorca, Cladera then studied Theology at the Murcia and Orihuela Seminaries, obtaining a degree in Civil Law and a doctorate in Theology. After sojourns in Seville and Cadiz he settled in Madrid in 1785, where he became a member of the Sociedad Matritense and, on the basis of his training in languages, tried unsuccessfully to join the Language Interpreting Secretariat. His life bears witness to his membership of the enlightened and reforming ecclesiastical sector in Spain. In his twilight years he aligned himself with the pro-France *afrancesados* group and signed the Bayonne Constitution in 1808. When the regime in Spain fell, he emigrated to France; in 1814 he pledged allegiance to Fernando VII and returned to Spain, where he was granted the canonry of the cathedral in Palma de Majorca, the city in which he died. His extensive work was a true record of his unwavering commitment to the ideals of the Enlightenment; translator (Addison and Fénelon, among others), historian and jurist, he was involved in various press enterprises, the most important of which was his work at the head of the EMD.

---

32 CMC, VII (1790), no. 329, 2643–47.

33 On the journal's general content, see Guinard, *La presse*, 265–72, and Elorza, *La ideología*, 119–38. There are two indexes: Eulogio Varela, *Espíritu de los mejores diarios literarios que se publican en Europa, Madrid 1787–1791* (Madrid: Sección de cultura "Nora," 1966), and Siegfried Jüttner, *Espíritu de los mejores diarios literarios que se publican en Europa (1787–1791). Indices (onomástico y de fuentes, de obras y toponímico)* (Frankfurt am Main: Peter Lang, 2009); the second is the most comprehensive.

34 In 1787 Cladera attempted to have journal approved that was entitled *Biblioteca periódica y elemental de ciencias, artes, literatura*. The Academy of the History censor's report was not favourable to the project, but it did defend the usefulness of publishing a "journal of the works that come out inside and outside Spain;" see Varela, *Espíritu*, 65.

The EMD rapidly took shape as a superb cultural journal. While aimed at literate elites with an interest in topical ideas, it also included curious news items for those who were not interested in "things that were too abstract." It also carried reports on legislation, official institutions and enlightened societies in Spain and the rest of Europe (discourses and awards), although little space was devoted to them. Its undeniable success was partly the result of a subscription system, while its print runs of around 1.400 copies were unusually large for the day and it circulated not only at court but also in the provinces and the colonies.[35] Its subscribers included the main Enlightenment figures of the day,[36] for the simple reason that it was a vital tool for keeping up with current affairs. In fact, the EMD's main content was "reproductions and compilations" and it carried translations of new works that had appeared in the foreign press, mainly in France. By this means it became a cosmopolitan and pan-European loudspeaker for the intellectual activity of European Enlightenment figures and contributed to enhancing their impact in Spain. As well as its excellent work disseminating the great names of the *late* Enlightenment period in Europe, from Smith and Condorcet to Raynal and Filangieri, it was responsible for spreading information relating to the most defining issues during the fertile period between American Independence and the French Revolution,[37] which it did widely and impartially. The struggle against religious intolerance, despotism and economic monopolies, the defence of a humanitarian approach to criminal justice and pacifism were all recurring topics; so were anti-slavery positions, the defence of the "rights of man" and the American constitutional experience, towards which the EMD adopted an approach that was nothing less than pioneering in the context of the Spanish Enlightenment. Nonetheless, it had some red lines; religious and colonial questions were dealt with carefully and extreme positions were balanced.

The EMD included debates as well and from time to time requested pieces from Cladera and other contributors such as J. de Ugartiria, Valentín de Foronda and Isidoro Morales (1758–1818). Ugartiria was actually a penname, which undoubtedly concealed the identity of an author with links to enlightened Basque circles. His EMD articles recreated the gatherings held at the house of Joaquín María de Eguía, Marquis of Narros (1733–1803), in Bergara, the village where the headquarters of the Bascogada Society was located; the Marquis was its secretary and the names of Vauban, Raynal, Linguet, Necker, Mercier

35 Larriba, *El público*, 88–89.

36 Jüttner, *Espíritu*, XI.

37 Vincenzo Ferrone, *La società giusta ed equa. Repubblicanesimo e diritti dell'uomo in Gaetano Filangieri* (Roma-Bari: Laterza, 2003), 22–48.

and Mirabeau "rang out" at such occasions.[38] The journal's critical stance vis-à-vis official reforms emerged in these articles. Ugartiria called for an end to *vales reales*, which were the cause of price rises in Spain, as well as to *rentas provinciales*, the taxes levied on staple goods and thus affecting the working classes — demands which tied in with criticisms of the moderate fiscal reform enacted by the government minister Lerena (1785–1787) —. Ugartiria's ideas appeared to be rooted in Physiocracy: he demanded respect for "sacred and primitive" principles of property, freedom and security, the foundations of the *économistes*' natural order. Agriculture, trade and industry should be organised to provide the "greatest possible freedom" in the exercise of individual interest, until it became possible to "sow, benefit, collect, work and sell freely and with no taxation at all, whatever and however one wishes in Spain and our American colonies." He argued that the inhabitants of the latter should enjoy the same rights as they would in Spain; as a result of these comments, the EMD temporarily lost its publishing licence in 1789.

While Ugartiria is virtually unknown, Valentín de Foronda (1761–1821) has received the attention merited by his status as one of the great figures of the Spanish Enlightenment.[39] Traveller, debater and unrepentant writer, a type of "philosopher trader," as he described himself, he was Spanish consul general in Philadelphia (1801–1809), where he formed a friendship with Thomas Jefferson, ending his life as a genuine agitator in support of a democratic and liberal Constitution for Spain. Barrenechea, who has done the most research into Foronda's life, rightly comments that this "could never be called lukewarm." Foronda was born in Vitoria and joined the Sociedad Bascongada in 1776, contributing to some of its most important reforms in his youth, such as the campaigns for smallpox inoculation. He founded the Vitoria Alms House in 1776 along the lines of the charitable model used by Necker in in the parish of Saint Sulpice in Paris. Following Society guidelines, he actively intervened in the unsuccessful and controversial attempt between 1778 and 1781 to have the provincial Basque-Navarre internal customs moved to the French border. During the same period, he edited *Recreación política* (1779), written by his

38 Ugartiria's articles were rescued from oblivion by Elorza, *La ideología*, 186–89.

39 The best guide to the Foronda's work is Barrenechea, *Valentín de Foronda*; on his life, 7–58; see also, by the same author: "Estudio Preliminar," in Valentín de Foronda, *Cartas sobre los asuntos más exquisitos de la Economía Política y sobre las leyes criminales*, ed. José Manuel Barrenechea (Vitoria: Gobierno Vasco, 1994), XVII-CXX. His personal and intellectual relationship with the Sociedad Bascongada is analysed in Astigarraga, *Los ilustrados vascos*, 224–47. On his political thought, see Ignacio Fernández Sarasola, "Estudio Preliminar," 9–94.

deceased fellow member Arriquíbar, to which he added Davenant's essay on political arithmetic. He became increasingly involved with the Bascongada after 1782 when he went to live in Bergara with the "sages and philosophers" at the Society Seminary, which at that time was one of the Spanish Enlightenment's pioneering centres of teaching and science. Foronda already had some experience as a published author, sending his first writings to the Bascongada between 1778 and 1784; these were far from uncontroversial as they levelled harsh criticism at the parasitic nobility, the "foetid" Inquisition and the reactionary clergy. He had also edited a partial translation of Condillac's *Logique* (1780) and of Bielfeld's *Institutions politiques* (1768–1774) — limited to the chapters on Portugal and Spain —, and a subtle politico-economic description of the Basque Country and Navarre based on the German geographer Friedrich Büsching's non-quantitative statistics.[40] He sent contributions — on chemistry, logic, literary criticism and, of course, politics — to the Valladolid Academy of Law, Aragon Economic Society and the Barcelona Natural Sciences Society, and also expressed support for the Bank of San Carlos (1782) and the Company of Philippines (1785).[41] However, Foronda's intellectual maturity was actually the result of his work with the EMD; the fact that he chose the journal as a vehicle for his writings bears witness to the enormous importance that the press had acquired among the enlightened thinkers of his generation. Between May 1788 and November 1789 he sent the journal twenty letters, which he later published in a single volume that comprised his main work: *Cartas sobre los asuntos más exquisitos de la Economía Política y sobre las leyes criminales* (1789–1794).[42]

Foronda's submissions to the EMD contained the results — albeit somewhat disorganised — of his richly varied reading on economics, which was made possible thanks to the Bascongada's excellent library at the Bergara Seminary. His letters showed a wide knowledge of European writings on economics from the middle of the previous century: Cameralism; Gournay's Circle; Hume and other Scottish authors; Physiocracy and some of its proponents such as Condillac or Turgot; anti-Physiocrats like Necker, Galiani, Graslin or Serionne; and the

40 See, respectively, *Instituciones políticas* (Bordeaux: Francisco Mor, 1791) and *Cartas escritas por Mr. De Fer al autor del Correo de Europa* (Bordeaux: Louis Boudrie, 1783).

41 Publications from this period appeared together in *Miscelánea o colección de varios discursos* (Madrid: Benito Cano, 1787).

42 A third edition of the work was published in 1821 with numerous additional notes in which Foronda did not so much alter the substance of his ideas as reinforce them through the authoritative writings of post-Smith British and French economists; see Barrenechea, *Valentín de Foronda*, 278–81.

great social philosophers such as Rousseau, Filangieri, Brissot de Warville or Beccaria. However, what really gave his letters coherence was the Physiocratic premises regarding the natural order.[43] According to Foronda, the three well-springs of the happiness of states were the rights to property, liberty and security; in later years, he was inspired by Rousseau to add a fourth: equality. These rights took their inspiration from Mercier de la Rivière and, in the words of the Physiocrats, were "clear" and "indivisible." They were also universal, as they fulfilled criteria that were "fixed and eternal, like those governing surveyors,"[44] and could only be fully exercised within the framework of a free market economy. Foronda placed these rights and freedoms in central position: if they were respected, economic legislation in all countries, including his own, would be radically transformed and only in this way — also in line with Physiocracy — could economic and moral optimums be guaranteed at the same time. The Physiocratic philosophy of natural order was therefore placed at the service of a programme of radical economic liberalism. Free competition in the domestic market was the guiding principle, and this had to function without impediments, taxes and licences, taking on the role of the "impartial judge that made sovereign decisions" over prices and production. Foronda also rejected exclusive privileges, state-owned companies and price intervention and was the first Spanish author to support suppressing the guilds.[45] He was also one of the first to back free foreign trade, eliminating trade tariffs and all policies to increase or restrict imports and exports, while at the same time repudiating the usefulness of measures aimed at obtaining favourable balance of trade figures. These principles should be extended to cover grain, which should cease to be a "subsistence" item and become a "trade" item.[46] In short, the state sector should not use regulations and policies to interfere in the principles of the natural

43 This is what Barrenechea called Foronda's "Liberal-Physiocratic shift;"; see, by this author, *Valentín de Foronda*, 128–45; "Estudio Preliminar," LXXXVIIIl-C. The intellectual climate in France at that time reached Spain via Foronda. Physiocracy reappeared with the French Revolution, extending the principles of natural rights to political representation theory through Sièyes; see Larrère, *L'invention*, ch. VIII. However, the approach of Foronda was absolutely singular. It should be emphasized that the Physiocratic thoght was a minority in the Spanish Enlightenment (see Lluch and Argemí, *Agronomía y fisiocracia*), as well as in the "economic turn" that led to the appearance of the political economy in Europe during the fifties and sixties: Kaplan and Reinert, "The economic turn," 11–14; additional arguments in Reinert, *Translating empire*.

44 Valentín de Foronda, *Cartas sobre los asuntos más exquisitos de la economía* política, *y sobre las leyes criminales* (1789–1794; Vitoria: Gobierno Vasco, 1994), 443; on his connection with rationalist iusnaturalism, see Fernández Sarasola, "Estudio Preliminar," 23ff.

45 Foronda, *Cartas sobre los asuntos*, 39–65.

46 Foronda, *Cartas sobre los asuntos*, 379–420.

order but should limit itself to creating the institutional framework to enable economic agents to use their productive resources freely without constraining private economic activity. The linchpin was extending "property rights" and supporting the justice system that protected them — part of Foronda's work dealt with criminal laws —, then, as "fire makes the air expand in a pile of gunpowder," with these rights and the exercise of emulation, agriculture, the arts and trade would flourish spontaneously.[47] Barrenechea showed that Foronda was inspired by Baudeau, Le Trosne, Mirabeau, Quesnay, Grivel and, especially, Mercier de la Rivière, with whom he had maintained an acerbic exchange of views about the Bank of San Carlos in the mid-1780s.

Although Foronda's letters were anchored in the Physiocrats' natural order, this was less relevant at the level of economic analysis. Foronda did not use the conceptual categories that were most characteristic of Quesnay and his disciples, nor did he accept thoroughly their views on political economy. This was chiefly because he rejected the principle that agriculture was the only productive sector: although it was "true wealth," "nations also need factories."[48] This led him to reject the *bon prix*, precisely on the basis that it did not guarantee the simultaneous development of industry. He did not accept the *grande culture* or the *impôt unique* either: it was one of those "lovely systems with magnificent elegant facades, but mean and miserable inside."[49] In short, he accepted Physiocracy only selectively, and this was closely related to the ultimate aim of his letters, which were steeped in a strong Enlightenment spirit. Foronda appealed to his readers to "examine [...] my ideas, compare them and rub them against their own, so that the clash of one against the other will create a spark [that facilitates] the drawing up of a government plan that delights the human race."[50] With his unique radical liberalism Foronda attempted to expose the weaknesses of official reforms of his day, rejecting that British policy would be adopted as a model of economic stimulus.

To return now to the EMD, the publication there of Foronda's letters containing accounts of these principles and the contributions from Ugartiria marked the journal's identity, especially in 1790, and even distorted its original profile somewhat. Erudite and containing lengthy notes, these two authors' academic articles were aimed at a specialist readership and ended up limiting the journal to "boundaries that were too narrow." In January 1791, with the aim of regaining its readers' interest, the EMD was reorganised into

47 Foronda, *Cartas sobre los asuntos*, 270.
48 Foronda, *Cartas sobre los asuntos*, 373, 402.
49 Foronda, *Cartas sobre los asuntos*, 240.
50 Foronda, *Cartas sobre los asuntos*, VI.

two sections: it retained its "Art and Science" section and created a new one for "Literature, Trade, Agriculture and Political Economy." It was thus able to reinforce the original content: the presentation of new publications through book reviews. The EMD published over six dozen of reviews of books on political economy by British (Millar, Priestley, Playfair or Smith), as well as French (Clicquot de Blervache, Du Pont de Nemours, Mirabeau or Necker) and Italian writers (Fabbroni, Filangieri, Galanti or Pagano). Unlike those in the ML, these reviews were not original pieces but translations of articles taken from foreign newspapers. The EMD's model and chief source was *L'esprit des journaux français et étrangers* (EDJ, 1772–1818), the popular monthly title published in Liège by Jean-Louis Coster and Jean-Jacques Tutot.[51] Where economic content was concerned, there were two similar publications: the *Journal encyclopédique* (JEC, 1755–1794), another international press digest that was also published in Liège by the cultural entrepreneur Pierre Rousseau, and Simon-Nicholas-Henri Linguet's *Annales politiques, civiles et littéraires du Dix-huitième Siècle* (APC, 1777–1792, Vol. XIX). These three journals acted as intermediaries with others from Italy, Great Britain, Germany and Flanders, imbuing the EMD with a cosmopolitan feel and converting it into the most important "reproductions and compilations" periodical of the Spanish Enlightenment.

Linguet's *Annales* proved a particularly rich source for Cladera and this successful — and very profitable — bimonthly publication fertilised the entire EMD. After presenting the APC to his readers in December 1787, Cladera wanted to reproduce it with the articles in the original order;[52] in the end, the EMD carried twenty extracts, normally in the form of summaries of articles originating in its Paris, London and Brussels phases, always from the pre-revolutionary period. Cladera did not turn his back on the most controversial articles by the caustic Linguet and his contributors, which included Brissot de Warville, and the extracts selected revealed the APC's eminently political identity as well as its pervasive openness to the economic situation: of its seven sections, one was devoted to finance and another to trade. All this was made eminently clear in

51 Guinard, *La presse*, 265; Jüttner, *Espíritu*, XI.

52 EMD, no. 73 (12-XII-1787), 681. The first of Linguet's articles to be published in the EMD matched this volume down to the last detail, with the exception of the opening extract (APC, I, 16–35). On Linguet, see Darline Gay Levy, *The Ideas and Careers of Simon-Nicolas-Henri Linguet: A Study in Eighteenth-Century French Politics* (Urbana: University of Illinois Press, 1980). His journal gave a voice to those who were discontented with *commerce odieux* (Terjanian, *Commerce*, 23) and was the best reflection of the great vitality of political journalism in the Ancien Régime, above and beyond censorship and other restrictions; see Censer and Popkin (eds.), *Press and Politics*.

the first article published in the EMD, which revolved around religious tolerance and reflected Linguet's doubts about the possibility that different forms of worship could coexist in the same state.[53] This was followed by others on the disposal of Church assets, the state of incomes in Spain, war in "modern" civilisations and public trust. The articles covered the main topics discussed in the APC, with the exception of the colonial question. Although some submissions were devoted to analysing current international political developments (eliminating customs in the Low Countries) and to examining the commonly-held view on the despotism of Arab countries (through an analysis of the political system in Morocco), most of the main articles focussed on European politics. The first of these condemned legislative systems as not fit for purpose when specifying how rights should be distributed between the sovereign and the people. As the legal system's collusion could always be relied on, this encouraged abuse on the part of the first while condemning the second to "poverty, ignominy and begging."

Another series of articles in the EMD echoed Linguet's acid observations on trade, which took issue with its supposed civilising abilities. The *Annales* presented trade as one of the greatest revolutions of its time, to the point of being the cause of the anarchic balance that existed between "modern" peoples. It all began with the discovery of America and the subsequent struggle for control of the colonies. The conflict had created a monster with two purportedly incompatible heads: war and trade.[54] Despite the perennial expansion of trade, Europe was still subject to the power of militarised states and the international balance was simply that existing between the military might of the great powers. Far from being a humanising and peace-promoting factor, trade had decisively encouraged armed conflicts, and with them a type of militarised despotism in the form of the "wretched modern military system" that assailed Europe. The art of politics, which had always been conditioned by the intrigues and private interests of merchants and industrialists, was now simply at the service of war.[55] Linguet pointed his finger at the "traders' republics" that dominated both hemispheres and capriciously ruined kings. Furthermore, he had no doubt that Spain was one of the main victims of this system. Cladera did not omit the harsh criticism levelled at his country in the APC. Its underdevelopment was the consequence of an imperial power in decline, while its weak international position was still conditioned by the millstone of the American colonies and the

53 EMD, no. 130 (26-V-1788), 136–41; no. 131 (2-VI-1788), 20–22.

54 EMD, no. 134 (23-VI-1788), 136–41.

55 EMD, no. 163 (12-I-1789), 779–83.

wrongheaded policy of hoarding precious metals: far from being a source of prosperity, these had become the underlying reasons for its subordination and hardship.[56]

The struggle for control of international markets naturally cast a shadow over the economic system. The thread linking military spending, the national debt and tax increases was sharply depicted in another passage chosen by Cladera. The "fatal leprosy" of the national debt was especially oppressive as it was passed on from one generation to the next and created international disorder by encouraging smuggling and luxury. Linguet believed it to be one of the most serious problems faced by France, Great Britain and other "modern" states. The conflict between these two nations was repeatedly evoked in articles written for the APC that were published in the EMD, and they provide an excellent reflection of the unclassifiable Linguet. In spite of his contempt for the British parliamentary system, he did slip in favourable comments relating to its policy of budgetary transparency. However, none of this prevented Britain from showing its economic weakness, which had been exacerbated by the dreadful consequences to the English textile industry of the 1786 free trade agreement between Britain and France. This pessimistic diagnosis was refuted in some quarters and the EMD began to accept articles criticising Linguet. An anonymous British writer used Davenant, Young and the Physiocrat Le Trosne's calculations to argue that the British economy was more buoyant than the APC claimed,[57] while another commented on the balancing act performed by Cladera in order to keep his journal alive. Harsh criticisms directed at the Church on account of its enormous economic power mingled with a comprehensive argument (in the form of a letter sent to the APC) against the confiscation of Church assets on the basis that this was a type of usurping of royal sovereignty.[58]

The EMD also echoed Linguet's positions on economics, accurately reflecting his critical stance on manufacturing: its existence was not only "precarious" but was always "a tributary of all whims."[59] However, this did not give way to a dogmatic defence of agriculture; quite the reverse. The EMD reverberated with rejections of Physiocracy and Turgot, as well as Linguet's sympathy towards

56 EMD, no. 163 (12-I-1789), 779–83. Linguet wrote: "L'Espagne en'offrant qu'un grand nom et une ombre de son ancien pouvoir; ombre qui couvre encore plus de terrein que n'en a jamais occupé l'empire des *Césars*, mais qui cédera bientôt à l''éclat de la liberté, si elle reste aux américains" (APC, I, 7–8).

57 EMD, no. 210 (7-XII-1789), 343–47.

58 EMD, no. 161 (29-XII-1789), 721–26.

59 EMD, no. 149 (6-X-1788), 452–56.

the humanitarian paternalism characteristic of Necker. So, in his tacit repudiation of the *économistes* he roundly condemned "all the scientific treatises with which we have been inundated for the last twenty years."[60] Instead of placing itself at the service of property owners, society's first duty was to guarantee the livelihood of the populace and protect consumers, who lived under the constant threat of shortages and hunger. For this reason, Linguet opposed indirect taxes on consumption and the Physiocratic policy of high prices: "this scarcity is murder and no economic-political subterfuge will make it unlawful to deplore it nor very important to destroy it." To sum up, although Cladera failed in his desire to publish the complete APC series, the passages he chose from Linguet's prestigious publication were an excellent reflection of the hallmarks of this emblematic and successful periodical in pre-revolutionary France, and they became its gateway into Spain.

4 Final Remarks

The closure of the CMC and EMD in February 1791, motivated by the Bourbon government's "terror" of the revolutionary winds blowing from France, put an end to a fertile period in the history of the Spanish press, including publications covering economics; indeed, the experience of the 1780s was a real turning point. A substantial change had come about in the field of cultural mediators: writers and men of letters from across the entire ideological spectrum saw the press as a powerful tool for spreading opinions and information and channelled their writings towards it; journalists broadened their social base, taking in outsiders that were relatively distant from political and cultural power, and publishers at last opened their publication to their readership and encouraged debate and criticism; booksellers, magistrates, university teachers and enlightened individuals from different social backgrounds also took part in this battle. It was the public that benefitted most from all this: they began to have access to a more diverse range of material that was less conditioned by political power and was also equipped with new rhetorical skills and innovative literary forms. During these years, led by titles such as the CMC and EMD, the press emerged as a powerful communication channel in society, as a separate form of political activity: it became, in short, a key element in the shaping of public opinion. Indeed, during the 1780s and 1790s, thinkers such as Foronda, Cabarrús, Almodóvar, Jovellanos and Arroyal were fully aware that they were ushering in the new

60 EMD, no. 178 (27-IV-1789), 1149–50.

social force of the "public tribunal,"[61] as well as the fact that its functioning was enhanced in proportion to the number of individuals that helped to shape it.[62]

However, the press was only one part in the complex machinery that fostered the emergence of public opinion during the Spanish Enlightenment. The way in which periodicals such as the CMC and EMD helped to multiply the effect on society of specific ideas that had been circulating among small groups of individuals since the 1770s has already been detailed. This was also possible due the slow maturing process of a public sphere that gained independence vis-à-vis political power during the 1780s; to the spread of Enlightenment institutions, with their innovative forms of socialising; to the appearance of a more radical generation of late Enlightenment thinkers (Aguirre, Foronda, Salas, Arroyal, Marchena, etc.) and, finally, to the circulating in Spain of works by authors such as Necker, Filangieri, Turgot, Raynal and Condorcet, whose writings are considered decisive in the creating of public opinion. Latent echoes of Great Britain were always present in the gradual process of changing ideas about political power; this was a country where the existence of "politicised" public opinion was essential for the functioning of its parliamentary system. In Spain, however, the main influence came from France, whose experience of the 1750s and 1760s showed that it was possible for the critical press and political absolutism to co-exist;[63] the explosion of political economy literature was "one phase in the rise of an educated reading claiming for itself the right to pass judgment on public affairs."[64] It is therefore not at all surprising that in Spain, as in France, Necker's work should instigate the definitive transition from the classical concept of "opinion," in the works of Feijoo and other *early* Enlightenment authors, to the innovative concept of "public opinion,"[65] as well as its shift from the traditional sphere of morality to the political arena. As a result of Necker's hegemony the "the tribunal of public opinion" came into being in the economic sphere before the political: as Baker has emphasised with respect to France,[66] although this "tribunal" matured in Spain in the context of

61 Fernández Sebastián, "From the 'voice of the people'," 215–23.

62 Baker, *Au tribunal de l'opinion*, 219–65.

63 Jack R. Censer, *The French Press in the Age of Enlightenment* (New York: Routledge, 1994), 15–54. Italy was also ahead of Spain, due to the Verri brothers, Beccaria and the *Il Caffè* reformers; see Edoardo Tortarolo, "Public opinion and the Italian Enlightenment. Approaches to a historical vocabulary," in *Concepts and symboles du Dix-Huitième Siècle europèen: Opinion*, ed. Peter-Eckhard Knabe (Berlin: Arno Spitz, 2000), 34–44.

64 Shovlin, *The Political Economy*, 4.

65 Jesús Astigarraga, "La traduction au service de la politique. Le succès de Jacques Necker dans les Lumières espagnoles," *Annales Historiques de la Révolution Française* 364 (2011), 3–27.

66 Baker, "Politics and public opinion," 204–46.

debates on the grain trade — from Campomanes (1764) to Jovellanos (1795) —, the government's arbitrary procedures and Treasury reforms — especially that adopted by Lerena from 1785 to 1787—, disputes over luxury and the nature of "commerce" also played their part, as mentioned above. The critical stances presented in the CMC and EMD, together with those of other newspapers such as García del Cañuelo's *El Censor*, Marchena's *El Observador* or Rubín de Celis' *El corresponsal de El Censor*, not only caused clashes between their own contributors but also with a range of journals that represented more conservative ideological positions. Once the existence of a diverse "public" to which the crown had to appeal to achieve its objectives had been recognised, political power was forced to reinvent the mechanisms through which it participated in the public sphere, with the aim of preventing the latter from becoming a factor that could dilute the reform programme and the political expression of the state. This was a further reason for the emergence of institutions towards the end of the century, including the press and professionals linked to the creation of "opinion." Political economy, which enlightened Spaniards now viewed as a coherent body of systematic principles, unfolded its full potential during this process.[67] As Robertson explained, this intellectual credibility was decisive for the growth of social credibility and made it a powerful nutrient for public opinion.[68] In the face of pragmatic reformers that had monopolised the Enlightenment stage in Spain until that time, the ideas of the new "prophets" of the movement could be heard loud and clear in the CMC and EMD, and the new language of the "rights of man" emerged, coined between the American and French Revolutions.[69]

---

67 Usoz, "La 'nueva política' ilustrada," 11–46, and "Political Economy and the Creation," 105–27.

68 Robertson, "Enlightenment, Public Sphere," 24ff.

69 Ferrone, *La societá giusta*, ch. 2.

CHAPTER 8

Training the New Bureaucrats

The Political Economy Chairs (1784–1808)

1 Introduction

On 24 October 1784 the Aragon Economic Society founded the Civil Economy and Commerce Chair in Saragossa. The first of its kind in Spain and one of the first in the whole of Europe, the Chair was not only an unmistakable sign of the remarkable development of economic culture in the country during the eighteenth century, but it also gave a definitive boost to the reforming positions held by the enlightened sectors. The Chair was founded amidst a thorny battle between reformers and reactionaries in Spain over the modernisation of university teaching, a battle that began in 1766–1767 when the Count of Aranda was Prime Minister and the expulsion of the Society of Jesus gave the reform of the Spanish education system more room for manoeuvre. While Bourbon policies did not bring about any radical changes in the methods, contents and structures of the university education of the day, some progress was made in the last thirty years of the eighteenth century thanks to impetus from the court and reforming groups.[1] Their first step was to advance their aim of dispensing with the Scholastic bias of the more classical university disciplines and modernising their educational programmes. Secondly, they promoted centralisation and a certain standardisation in university education. Thirdly, they made progress with respect to the institutionalising of new "useful" subjects designed for training craftsmen, merchants and farmers (draughtsmanship, seamanship and agriculture), and other more university-rooted fields which represented a true sign of progress in social sciences during the Enlightenment era, including political economy, commerce, public law and moral philosophy. These new fields of study were normally introduced outside conventional university structures, in new-style institutions such as trade consulates and economic societies. The Saragossa chair was fully immersed in this general modernisation

1 A general outline can be found in the classic study by Mariano Peset and José Luis Peset, *La Universidad española (siglos XVIII y XIX)* (Madrid: Taurus, 1974), 86–116, and Lafuente and Peset, "Las actividades," 29–79. On reforms at the University of Salamanca, where most of the upper echelons of royal bureaucrats were educated, see Georges M. Addy, *The Enlightenment in the University of Salamanca* (Durham: Duke University Press, 1966).

 | DOI:10.1163/9789004442894_010

process and was the best reflection of the new style of education and the fact that the enlightened elites acknowledged political economy as an increasingly independent academic field, particularly with respect to law, moral philosophy and politics, the disciplines with which it had always maintained a close secular association.

The founding of the Saragossa chair was not independent of the progress that was being made in political economy teaching in Enlightenment Europe. This discipline was already widely taught on moral philosophy degrees in Britain and in departments of the principles of government and economic policies in Germany. However, in 1727 a decisive step was taken in a different direction with the founding of the *Oeconomie, Polizei* and *Kammer-Sachen* Chair at the University of Halle, which was immediately followed by similar experiences in the Protestant region of northern Germany.[2] This university culture expanded considerably between 1760 and 1790, with support from the Prussian monarchs and influenced by canonical textbooks written by Justi (1755) and Sonnenfels (1765–1766); around eighty chairs of *Polizei* and *Kameralwissenschaft* were created in central and northern Europe during this period. Those at the University of Uppsala (1740) and Vienna (1763) played very prominent roles, and, instigated by Beccaria, the phenomenon then spread to Austrian Lombardy with the founding of the Milan Chair of *Scienze camerali* (1768) and the creation of another chair in the Duchy of Modena (1772).

Meanwhile, in Bourbon Europe, the institutionalisation of political economy in France had to wait until 1793, when a chair at the *École Normale* of Paris led by Alexandre Vandermonde was created.[3] Naples had played an undeniable leading role outside France and three chairs had already been founded in the *Regno delle Due Sicilie* before that date.[4] The process started with the *Cattedra di Commercio e Economia Civile* in Naples, founded in 1754 under the auspices of Carlo di Borbone and run by Antonio Genovesi, to be followed in 1779 with the creation of two chairs in Palermo and Catania. Meanwhile, this phenomenon was spreading beyond national borders and soon reached Spain. Echoes of the Uppsala and Vienna experiences arrived with others from three of the five Italian chairs, those in Milan, Modena and Naples. However, it was the Naples chair that provided the model for all the initiatives to introduce

2 Keith Tribe, *Governing Economy. The Reformation of German Economic Discourse, 1750–1840* (Cambridge: CUP, 1998), 36ff., 91ff.

3 Perrot, *Une histoire*, 79, 371.

4 See Massimo Augello, Marco Bianchini, Gabriella Gioli and Piero Roggi, eds., *Le cattedre di economia politica in Italia* (Milan: F. Angeli, 1988), 31–46, 47–92, 93–138.

economic studies in Spain during the last twenty five years of the eighteenth century, including the Saragossa chair. Once again, Spanish enlightened elites sought to adapt foreign experiences to their country, and they kept a close watch on events in the Kingdom of Naples.

2 Maturing the Projects, Shaping "Opinion"

The creation of the Saragossa chair was the culmination of a project which had been coming to fruition in the heart of the Spanish public sphere over many years. The chair represented a specific institutional response to a state of "opinion" which had emerged in enlightened circles from the 1760s onwards in favour of promoting economic studies. These circles had thus paved the way for the development of this innovative project, which was otherwise viewed as "suspicious." The "opinion" had been formed through contact with experiences elsewhere in Europe. There was no tradition of economic studies in Spain prior to this.[5] They were completely ignored by Gregorio Mayans' more mature modernisation plans for higher education (1767) and Pablo de Olavide (1768) also omitted all mention of the issue. However, these plans did support the introduction of natural law, and the most advanced project, designed by Olavide for the University of Seville, supported introducing political science using Bielfeld's *Institutions politiques*.[6] When news of the founding of the Naples chair first arrived in Spain, the situation began to change. Gándara's *Apuntes*, written in 1759 in the *Regno* itself, recommended founding agriculture, manufacturing and commerce chairs in Spain.[7] The situation was comparable to the impact on Graef, Barberi and Saura when Gournay and Quesnay's economic debates reached Spain from Paris. During the 1760s authors such as Davenant, Forbonnais and Serionne were decisive in forming the idea that "commerce" was an independent science and that, to quote the title of a sharp discourse

5 The Spanish enlightened class usually referred to Spanish *proyectista* Sancho de Moncada's 1619 demand to improve the education of the ruling classes through creating chairs on politics: Manuel Martín, "Estudio preliminar. La institucionalización de los estudios de economía política en la universidad española (1784–1857)," in Marqués de Valle Santoro, *Elementos de Economía Política con aplicación particular a España*, ed. Manuel Martín (Madrid: IEF, 1989), XVI.

6 Mariano Peset and José Luis Peset, *Gregorio Mayans y la reforma universitaria* (Valencia: 1975); Perdices, *Pablo de Olavide*, 292–95.

7 Miguel Antonio de la Gándara, *Apuntes sobre el bien y el mal de España* (1804; Madrid: IEF, 1988), 106, 184. His proposal for reforming higher education studies was broader; see 176–86.

by Forbonnais, the "incorporation of the study of trade and finance in politics" was thus obligatory.[8]

From then on the emerging public sphere in Spain was flooded with arguments supporting the idea. In 1765 the Basque merchant Arriquíbar proposed that two new institutions should be founded to promote "economic studies" in Spain: a board which would compile and publish economic data and promote "writings, plans, inventions or perfections;" and a study seminary, which, within the "great science of the State," would observe the "economic and political laws of the Kingdom, its culture, industry and trade."[9] Jovellanos reinforced these demands some years later in 1776 when he presented political economy as an essential science of political action in support of public happiness, and therefore indispensable for training law students.[10] Jovellanos included new arguments supporting economic studies in a 1781 "Discurso" that he presented to the Asturias Economic Society, which included a proposal for the founding of a seminary similar to that created in Bergara by the Basque Society to teach the new sciences.[11] In the 1780s other authors such as Foronda, Alcala-Galiano and Aguirre argued in favour of similar options; however, the work which most influenced the process of shaping "opinion" in favour of economic studies was Campomanes' widely circulated *Discursos* in 1774–1776. The Council of Castile *Fiscal* believed that the positive experiences in "teaching the true rules of general trade" in Naples and Milan were good examples to follow for Spanish economic societies, which had to operate as "public schools" for the "theory and practice of political economy in all the provinces of Spain."[12]

As usual, Campomanes' advice was interpreted by enlightened elites in Spain as guidelines for practical action. In fact, during the two-year period from 1775–1776, the two leading economic societies in Spain, the Basque Society and the Madrid Society, mobilised their resources in an attempt to create

8 On Carlos Le-Maur's 1765 Spanish translation of Forbonnais' work, see Astigarraga, "Forbonnais;" on Serionne, *Historia y descripción general de los intereses de comercio de todas las naciones de Europa en las cuatro partes del mundo* (Madrid: Miguel Escribano, 1772–1774): I, 11ff. Its author was Domingo de Marcoleta (1717–1796), the most prolific translator of political economy texts during the Spanish Enlightenment.

9 Arriquíbar, *Recreación política*, 93–94.

10 Gaspar Melchor de Jovellanos, "Introducción a un discurso sobre el estudio de la economía civil" (1776), in *Obras de Don Gaspar Melchor de Jovellanos* (BAE, vol. LXXXVII), ed. Miguel Artola (Madrid: 1956): 7–17.

11 Gaspar Melchor de Jovellanos, "Discurso económico sobre los medios de promover la felicidad de Asturias dirigido a su Real Sociedad" (1781), in *Obras completas. Vol. X. Escritos económicos*, ed. Vicent Llombart and Joaquín Ocampo (Gijón: KRK ediciones, 2008): 267–304.

12 Campomanes, *Discurso industria popular*, 111–12.

economics chairs. In 1775 Count of Peñaflorida, the head of the Basque Society proposed creating seven chairs at the Bergara Seminary, which had a suitable practical and professional orientation. One was intended for the study of the "science of government" for future civil servants and included instruction in political science, public administration, public law and political arithmetic; however, the project ultimately foundered due to lack of finance.[13]

In April 1776 an initiative was proposed by José del Río, member of the Madrid Society and Spanish consul in Lisbon, which reflected Campomanes' resolute opinions.[14] He suggested establishing a wide network of "patriotic business schools" under royal approval, which would be attached to a central school at the Madrid court. However, the project was subsequently severely criticised in a lengthy unsigned "Memoria," which was written shortly afterwards in 1776 or 1777 and presented to the Madrid Society.[15] It was based on a defence of a type of teaching that went beyond business training and provided an education in the "general principles of commerce." In support of his argument the author quoted the Basque Society and several seventeenth and eighteenth century Spanish authors: Fernández Navarrete, Martínez de Mata, Sancho de Moncada, Ulloa and Campomanes. However, the most significant aspect of the "Memoria" was its selective mention of foreign authors whose works had not always been translated into Spanish at that time. First, there was reference to a group of four well-known French Gournay circle economists (Herbert, Butel Dumont, Coyer and Forbonnais). Second, Cantillon's *Essai*, which was also well-known at the time was mentioned, albeit anonymously. Third, three British authors appeared: Petty, Davenant and Cary; the first two were cited, as usual, as pioneers in the use of political arithmetic, which had been introduced into Spain as a result of Forbonnais' mediation. Cary's *Brief History of Trade in England* (1695) had never been translated into Spanish but was known there through the Italian version, which brothers Antonio and Pietro Genovesi had translated in 1757 from Butel Dumont's 1755 French version.[16] This text strongly supported the idea of the disciplinary independence of the emerging science of political economy and the advisability of teaching it as a subject in its own right: in the words of its Italian translators, the *practica della*

13 Astigarraga, *Los ilustrados vascos*, 136–37.

14 His manuscript can be found in the ASM, bundle 4–13. It was published in *Memorias de la Sociedad Económica*. II, 107–20. On Del Río's project, see also ch. IX above.

15 On this report, see Jesús Astigarraga, "André Morellet y la enseñanza de la Economía en la Ilustración española: la *Memoria sobre la utilidad del establecimiento de una escuela de Comercio*," *Cuadernos de Historia Moderna* 35 (2010): 143–73.

16 On Cary's book's long journey across Europe, see Reinert, *Translating Empire*.

mercatura and the *scienza politica del commercio* were separate disciplines that required their own fields in education.[17]

The *Prospectus d'un nouveau dictionnaire de commerce* (1769) by French author Morellet was also influential and underpinned the thread that ran though the "Memoria" in favour of teaching the theory of political economy. In the *Prospectus* Morellet established the central line of what should have been a future commerce dictionary that was different to the Savary brothers' *Dictionnaire*.[18] Morellet believed that economic science had reached maturity, which meant that this canonical work needed to be entirely re-written so as to achieve a better integration between the "art" — concrete facts — and the "science" — general principles — of commerce, with the aim of establishing a universal language of commerce.[19] The plan was based around three different lexicons: a) commercial geography; b) "all commercial goods;" and c) "the general and abstract terms of the public economy." Morellet's highly innovative proposal was clear for all to see in the Madrid Society "Memoria." The most significant aspect was the argument that the principles of the "general theory" of commerce could only be acquired through education, as no art could be perfected without first studying the rules that "form part of the theory." Studies of this type were thus as essential as translations or "public rules" to overcome the "prejudices that drag a nation down" and to find proper solutions to its "political problems." This all serves to highlight the distinct economic culture of individuals who, from within the Madrid Society, were striving for Spain to internalise the progress made by the European "science of commerce." The shadow cast by Campomanes, the Madrid Society head, is clear throughout: not only was he the most quoted author in the "Memoria," but he was also probably its real instigator.

3 The Saragossa Chair: An Official and Experimental Experience

There is no doubt that the idea put forward in the "Memoria" was subsequently developed during the last stage of the Spanish Enlightenment. However, at

17 John Cary, *Storia del commercio della Gran Bretagna scritta da John Cary* (1758; Naples: Istituto Italiano per gli Studi Filosofici, 1984): I, 126–27.

18 Morellet, *Prospectus*. The project, which was never finished, was carried out with Turgot's help and official support from Minister Trudaine: see Perrot, *Une histoire*, 102–04; André Morellet, *Mémoires inédits de l'Abbé Morellet, sur le Dix-huitième siècle et sur la Révolution* (Geneva: Slatkine Reprints 1967): I, 181–91.

19 Morellet, *Prospectus*, 350.

the beginning of the 1780s the Madrid Society passed the initiative to promote this field of study over to the Aragon Society, maybe out of a sense of caution vis-à-vis the problems that teaching the "suspicious" science of political economy may create at court. Together with the Basque Society, the Aragon Society was in the best position to develop an enlightened educational programme in Spain.[20] The events preceding the creation of its Civil Economy and Commerce Chair reveal that the Aragon Society may have been providing studies in trade practices of some kind since 1782.[21] However, the Society's proposal to the Council of Castile two years later was to establish a specific chair along the lines of "the one which, under the auspices of our sovereign, the renowned Antonio Genovesi directed."[22] Although it received some support from the Aragon Society, the proposal's main backers were Juan Antonio Hernández Pérez de Larrea (1730–1811), an Aragonese priest, and Arias Antonio Mon y Velarde (1740–1811), an Asturian magistrate. It may have been Pérez de Larrea that was responsible for transferring the idea of promoting economic studies from the Madrid Society to the Aragon Society, as he had been a member of the former since its establishment in 1775. Appointed Dean of Saragossa Cathedral in the same year, this future Bishop of Valladolid was also part of the founding nucleus of the Aragon Society, where he was not only one of the main ideologists behind its ambitions educational programme, but also censor.[23] The president of the Aragon Society between 1784 and 1790, Mon y Velarde, played a decisive role in overcoming the political and institutional obstacles that surrounded the establishing of the chair, as he was also a magistrate at the Saragossa Court from 1773. Both men proposed appointing Lorenzo Normante y Carcaviella (1759–1813) as the chair's first head. Normante had been a member of the Aragon Society since 1781 and may have been chosen for his training and teaching vocation. He had studied Philosophy and Law at the Universities of Huesca and Saragossa and had been awarded doctorates in Civil and Canon Law by the age of twenty two, before being appointed secretary of the Royal Academy of Legal Practice in Saragossa in 1779, around the time that he began teaching Law at the University of Saragossa. Normante was only twenty five when he

20 The Society created chairs of mathematics, agriculture, public law, moral philosophy and civil economics and commerce. It also promoted draughtsmanship schools and others for teaching trades; see Usoz, *Pensamiento económico*.

21 ASA proceedings 11-1-1782, 1-2-1782, 8-2-1782, 7-XI-1783.

22 ASA, proceeding 28–11-1784.

23 José Benito Cistué, *Elogio del Ilustrísimo Señor D. Juan Antonio Hernández Pérez de Larrea, Obispo de Valladolid y Director de la Real Sociedad Aragonesa* (Zaragoza: 1803). He was named Director of the Aragon Society in 1798.

was selected, and was responsible for developing the chair's innovative teaching methods: lectures were accompanied by practical themed sessions for the students. The chair was far from inward-looking and had a clear public dimension, holding annual events with dissertations and exams and awarding public prizes to the most distinguished students.

The court in Madrid immediately gave its blessing to the appointment and a series of well-orchestrated events then took place which led to the Council of Castile approving the Civil Economy and Commerce Chair in 1784, under the very specific conditions detailed by Usoz.[24] On the one hand, it would have a distinct "official" nature, not only in in the sense of being managed by the Aragon Society, but also in terms of Secretary of State Floridablanca's control over naming the chair, appointing the professor — he accepted Normante immediately — and devising the course syllabi. On the other hand, it was clearly an experimental project. From the outset, the enlightened government valued the "use" that could be made of the experience "throughout the rest of the country," leaving open the possibility of its implementation elsewhere via the network of economic societies. It is no coincidence that the final push to create the chair was preceded by a Council of Castile Order in 1783 which required law students to be "examined in political economy."[25] This reinforces the idea that the chair was an institutional creation, prompted and managed by the government and essentially aimed at recruiting future civil servants and statesmen and using new educational material that could be standardised.

Taking into account the infinite network of ties that connected Spain and Naples during the Enlightenment,[26] it is not surprising that the model chosen was the chair created in 1754 under the private patronage of Bartolomeo Intieri in the Naples of Carlo di Borbone and Tanucci.[27] Although Intieri's initial proposal had a distinctly technical and applied dimension — "mechanics applied

24 Usoz, *Pensamiento económico*, 373–411. Other useful studies are: Juan Francisco Forniés, "La Cátedra de Economía Civil y Comercio de la ciudad de Zaragoza en el período de la Ilustración (1784–1808)," *Información Comercial Española* 512 (1976): 108–18; Alfonso Sánchez, José Luis Malo and Luis Blanco, *La cátedra de Economía Civil y Comercio de la Real Sociedad Económica Aragonesa de Amigos del País (1784–1846)* (Zaragoza: Ibercaja and Real Sociedad Económica Aragonesa de Amigos del País, 2003); Guasti, "Introduzione," 49ff.

25 ASA, proceeding 14-V-1784.

26 See, among others, Franco Venturi, "Economisti e riformatore," 532–61; Jesús Astigarraga, "Diálogo económico en la 'otra' Europa. Las traducciones españolas de los economistas de la Ilustración napolitana (A. Genovesi, F. Galiani y G. Filangieri)," *CROMOHS* 9 (2004), http://www.fupress.net/index.php/cromohs/article/view/15645/14511.

27 On the history of this chair see Francesco Di Battista, "Per la storia de la prima cátedra universitaria d'economia. Napoli, 1754–1866," in *Le cattedre di economia politica*, 31–46.

to agriculture" — , its first professor, Antonio Genovesi, implemented a more ambitious design, broadening the chair's scope to include his research field in civil economy as a true "science of trade" which held that a state achieves its greatest possible wealth and population within a politically organised society.[28] At the same time, Genovesi was able to include the chair in the reform programme that Carlo di Borbone had been implementing since he arrived in the *Regno delle Due Sicilie* in 1739. During the fifteen years of the chair's history — Genovesi was its head until his death in 1769 —, he transformed it into a benchmark institution that concurred with the emergence and development of political economy, which had begun to appear in the *Regno* in the 1740s. Two similar chairs were founded in Palermo and Catania in 1779, partially following his example, and the Naples chair became a decisive part of the future history of enlightened culture in the *Mezzogiorno* in intellectual and reforming fields.[29]

Given these precedents, it is only natural that the Aragon Society should have requested Carlos III's permission to implement what had successfully been developed thirty years earlier in Naples: in others words, once the Madrid Society had paved the way for opening of "commerce theory schools," the Aragon initiative's main aim was to adapt the Naples institutional experience to Spain. The Saragossa chair was in fact based on Genovesi's model, from which it also took its name. A free public school, it was privately funded, effectively by the Aragon Society. Although independent from the University of Saragossa, activity at the chair was synchronised to facilitate student attendance. Three courses were taught, all in Spanish; although especially aimed at law students and future civil servants, they were open to the entire social spectrum, from noblemen, artisans and merchants to businessmen. The chair's founding was thus a clear institutional manifestation of the spreading of the republican principles of commerce through education: the chair wished to imbue future public servants with respect for all economic activities, including commerce, and noblemen were therefore educated in the same conditions as students from other social classes. This was all made abundantly clear in the *Discurso* (1784) that Normante prepared for the public opening of the chair, in which he cited

28 Antonio Genovesi, *Delle Lezioni di comercio o sia di economia civile* (1765–1767; Naples: Istituto Italiano per gli Studi Filosofici, 2005), I, 271.

29 A list of examples, though incomplete, is: Franco Venturi, *Settecento riformatore* (Turin: 1969–1784), I, 523ff., and "Il movimiento riformatore degli illuministi meridionale," *Rivista Storica Italiana* 74 (1962): 5–26; Vincenzo Ferrone, *Scienza Natura Religione. Mondo newtoniano e cultura italiana nel primo Settecento* (Naples: Jovene Editore, 1982); Robertson, *The case*, 350ff.

authors such as Campomanes, Serionne, Cary, Hume, Forbonnais, Muratori, Bolingbrocke, Mirabeau and, most of all, Genovesi, defending political economy as a science of government and the "public good" which should therefore be studied methodically.[30]

Although based on the Naples model, the Saragossa chair had several of its own distinguishing features. First, its educational programme was coordinated those of the moral philosophy and public law chairs. Second, the original project defined the civil economy and commerce chair as an important centre for creating and spreading economic knowledge through the establishing of a "great library of economics writers" and the development of an ambitious programme of economics translations instigated by Pérez de Larrea. Between 1784 and 1789 Society members translated texts by Mun, Carli, Condillac, Casaux, Griselini, Melon, Filangieri, Forbonnais, Genovesi and probably Serionne, mainly book reviews, summaries and extracts which could then be adapted for teaching puposes.[31]

The main result of all this effort was the impact it had on Genovesi's work. In October 1784, just a few months after Normante began classes with 23 students, Floridablanca asked the Aragon Society to choose a textbook from among "the best Italian, French and English writers" on which to base his classes.[32] It is no coincidence that the text chosen was Genovesi's *Lezioni di commercio* (1765–1767), and that in 1785–1786 Victorián de Villava (1747–1802) published a methodical and accurate Spanish translation of this successful textbook.[33] Unlike Normante, Villava was a mature jurist when he undertook the task, and this was clear from the high quality of his translation. He had been born into an Aragonese family of high-ranking civil servants and graduated in Law from the University of Huesca. In 1777 he was appointed to the chair of Code, which

30 Lorenzo Normante, *Discurso sobre la utilidad de los conocimientos económico-políticos, y la necesidad de su estudio metódico* (Zaragoza: Blas de Miedes, 1784).

31 Jesús Astigarraga, "La prima versione spagnola della *Scienza della legislazione*," in *Diritti e Costituzione. L'opera di Gaetano Filangieri e la sua fortuna europea*, ed. Antonio Trampus (Bologna: Il Mulino, 2005), 61–84.

32 ASA, proceeding 17-8-1784.

33 Antonio Genovesi, *Lecciones de comercio, o bien de economía civil* (Madrid: Viuda de Ibarra, 1785–1786). The "Discurso Preliminar" written by Villava to justify his translation was published independently: *Discurso preliminar del traductor de las Lecciones de comercio del Genovesi, en que se da razón de la obra y se la califica con imparcialidad* (Huesca: Viuda de Miguel de Larumbe, n. d.). On this Spanish translation, see Jesús Astigarraga and Javier Usoz, "From the Neapolitan A. Genovesi of Carlo di Borbone to the Spanish A. Genovesi of Carlo III: V. de Villava's Spanish translation of *Lezioni di Commercio*," in *Genovesi economista*, ed. Bruno Jossa, Rosario Patalano and Eugenio Zagari (Naples: Istituto Italiano per gli studi filosofici, 2007): 193–220.

he held for twelve years and combined with his position as vice-chancellor in 1785 and 1786 as well as his activities in the Aragon Society. Villava's translation was favourably received by Pérez de Larrea and Mon y Velarde and was immediately adopted by the Society as a teaching tool for the chair, although it was not the only book used there. During the two-year period between 1784 and 1786, before Villava's translation was finished, the text in use was Bernardo Danvila's *Lecciones de Economía Civil* (1778), which will be referred to again later. Works by other Spanish authors such as Uztáriz, Ulloa, Ward and Campomanes were also frequently used in the early years, as well as books by various foreign authors. At the same time, Normante created different *cuadernos,* or notebooks, for teaching purposes, originally planning to write one a year. In 1785, he published a brief compact summary of Genovesi's *Lezioni*, which included a chapter on *police* taken from Bielfeld, and a year later he created another from Melon's *Essai sur le commerce* (1734).[34] A subsequent notebook was deemed "superficial" and "lacking originality," however; it was a simple plagiarism of *The British Merchant*, Forbonnais and Ward and was never published.[35] Some chapters from Serionne's manuscript *Les intêrest des nations* (1766) were also circulated. Lectures covered some of the main topics relating to Enlightenment economic and political culture, ranging from free trade, luxury and the celibacy of the clergy to forms of government, and it was common for students to apply this knowledge to the individual circumstances of Aragon, Spain and its colonies. In later years the chair displayed a remarkable ability to modernise its programmes and adapted, if somewhat slowly, to the changes that were occurring in European political economy.

4 The Forgotten Natural Law and Moral Philosophy Chairs

In December 1785, fifteen months after the Civil Economy and Commerce Chair was set up, the Aragon Society opened two new chairs to the public, one in natural or public law and the other in moral philosophy.[36] The University of

---

34 Lorenzo Normante, *Proposiciones de economía civil y comercio* (Zaragoza: Blas de Miedes, 1785), and *Espíritu del Señor Melon en su Ensayo político sobre el Comercio* (Zaragoza: Blas de Miedes, 1786).

35 Sánchez, Malo and Blanco, *La cátedra.*

36 A detailed study of the history of both chairs can be found in Jesús Astigarraga and Javier Usoz, "El pensamiento político y económico ilustrado y las cátedras de la Sociedad Económica Aragonesa," *Anuario de Historia del Derecho Español* 78–79 (2008–2009): 423–48.

Saragossa's first reaction to the project had been so negative that immediate attempts were made to prevent the plans from being put into practice. This seemed a natural reaction; the Society's new initiative directly overlapped with the University's activities, as the two proposed chairs were mainly aimed at students studying law and, to a lesser extent, philosophy. The Society's objective was to complement students' university education with subjects that were not taught on the normal courses. Teaching activities were in fact designed and organised so as not to be dependent on or overlap with the university teaching programme. The courses were free of charge and were taught three evenings a week over two years during the eight months of the academic year. They were taught by a tenured professor, once again appointed by Floridablanca.

The University of Saragossa's adverse reaction to the project was not only part of a territorial dispute, but was in fact another chapter in the conflict between the reformist and reactionary university sectors. One area of dispute was precisely the reformists' intention to establish chairs similar to those set up by the Aragon Society, especially after 1770 when a Natural Law Chair was created in the Seminary for the Nobility in Madrid, and similar initiatives emerged in other Spanish universities.[37] The Council of Castile quickly announced that it would not prevent the Aragon Society from carrying out its proposals, a reaction that effectively neutralised the University of Saragossa's resistence. The speed with which the Society made its announcement was undoubtedly influenced by the enormous success enjoyed by the Economics Chair during its first year and a half.

By setting up the Public Law and Moral Philosophy Chairs and appointing the first two professors in December 1785, José Broto (1742–1806) and M. Latorre, the Aragon Society launched a pioneering teaching experience in Spain. The three disciplines at the forefront of the renewal of thought in the social sciences during the European Enlightenment were introduced into lecture halls; furthermore, they were taught as independent subjects, which served to set this experience apart from other teaching establishments such as the Seminary for the Nobility, where political economy was taught as part of public law and moral philosophy. The fact that the teaching undertaken in the two

37 Sánchez-Blanco, *El Absolutismo,* 194–22; Antonio Álvarez Morales, "La difusión del Derecho Natural y de Gentes europeo en la Universidad española de los siglos XVIII y XIX," in *Doctores y escolares. II Congreso Internacional de Historia de las Universidades hispánicas* (Valencia: Universidad de València, 1995), I, 49–60. For an updated analysis, see María Victoria López-Cordón, "El bien público y el *sistema político de la Europa,*" in *Bajo el velo del bien público*, ed. Jesús Astigarraga and Javier Usoz (Zaragoza: IFC, 2020), 249–78.

newly-created chairs would turn out to be less prominent than it was in the economics chair, and more limited time-wise, was another matter.

These two chairs did not have an easy existence, even in their early years. The fact that both of them, particularly the Public Law Chair, almost closed down several times cannot be uncoupled from the hostile socio-political climate of the time. University of Saragossa teaching staff caused further problems and in March 1787 Latorre informed the Aragon Society that there were very few students in his classes as a result of the teachers' rejection of "these patriotic establishments." The situation was so serious that it was proposed that the Society should either "discontinue the teaching or continue it for this year only."[38] The crisis was eventually resolved, however, without having to suspend the teaching, and the chairs gradually returned to their normal routine. A further problem arose from their policy of accepting students from a very wide geographical area outside Aragon, mainly Navarre, the Basque Country, La Rioja, Santander and Catalonia, which proved so unpopular, particularly after these years of crisis, that in October 1792 the Public Law was closed down, albeit temporarily.[39] This was also due to a lack of educational incentives for the students, as the Aragon Society was unable to ensure, as it had intended, that its courses could be validated as a year of Law or Philosophy.

The supply of teachers was also probably an influential factor. The teaching staff were on the whole graduates and doctors in law who had studied at the University of Saragossa. However, the Aragon Society's initial aim of including professors on its teaching staff could not be maintained over time. On the other hand, the lack of an educational circuit specialising in teaching materials was addressed, although only partially, through moving the teachers between the chairs, including the economics chair. A similar situation arose with the students, as law and philosophy students at the University of Saragossa were usually enrolled in all three specialisations. The chairs thus enjoyed few periods of stability and the main underlying reason was finance; since there was relatively little activity, the Aragon Society could not make teaching there a full time occupation and it was thus always understood to be a supplement to a main occupation, such as a practicing law or lecturing at the University of Saragossa, or even simply as starting point from which various public positions could be accessed. In some cases, the frequent changes in the chairs were due to the fact that their incumbents were "highly involved in the affairs of their profession;"[40] in others, they rose to positions such as mayors, canons or other

38 ASA, proceeding 2-III-1787.

39 ASA, proceedings 27-IX-1792, 26-X-1792.

40 ASA, proceeding 6-II-1789.

posts and thus quickly abandoned their chairs. The Public Law Chair, for instance, had three heads and a substitute in less than ten years, while the Moral Philosophy Chair had ten or eleven professors from 1785 to 1798, most of whom had theological training.

The teaching content was fairly moderate and did not seem to change during the fifteen years that this educational experience lasted. The Moral Philosophy Chair used *Philosophia moral* (1755), by Aragon doctor and philosopher Andrés Piquer (1711–1772), as its main text. This book had several advantages: it was Spanish and had a university textbook format, and while philosophically eclectic, it was politically and religiously moderate and seamlessly defended the principles of Catholicism. For these reasons it enjoyed remarkable success in Spain throughout the eighteenth century and was republished twice, in 1775 and 1787. The only attempt to introduce a different textbook was made by Joaquín Traggia (1748–1802). He had translated *La Morale* (Paris, 1755), by French philosopher and teacher Jean B. Cochet who was a member of the moderate current in the French Catholic Enlightenment. Traggia sent his translation to the Society for use as a moral philosophy textbook; however, after studying the version in detail, the Society decided to stand by Piquer's text.[41]

However, it is highly likely that moral philosophy students also studied *Elementa Juris naturae et gentium* (1758) of Johann Gottlieb Heinecio, a disciple of Christian Wolff, which was the work chosen for the Public Law Chair.[42] This text had the advantage of being designed to be used primarily for teaching, which explains why it was more successful in a strictly educational context than other *iusnaturalist* texts that were also well-known in Spain, particularly Barbeyrac's widely-circulated French translation of Pufendorf's work. In spite of the fact that it was on the list of banned books in 1756 and 1779, Heinecio's *Elementa* was read widely in Spain. Eminently educational, it was well-received by the influential Mayans, who recommended it as a text for future chairs of natural law in 1767, and then by his disciple Joaquín Marín y Mendoza (1727–1782). Between 1771 and 1780 Marín y Mendoza was the first professor of this specialisation at the Royal Studies of San Isidro, and was also the author of the first Latin edition of the *Elementa* to be published in Spain, duly corrected in aspects that revealed the fact that its author was a Protestant. This edition was probably used in Saragossa; it was reissued a few years later in Valencia

41 The Society considered the translation to be "somewhat muddled" and unsuitable for teaching (ASA, proceeding 27-X-1786). There is an unpublished handwritten copy in the RAH archives.

42 ASA, proceeding 23-XII-1788.

and used in the early years of the teaching of public law in Spain, as well as enjoying great success in the reformed jurisprudence academies.[43]

The *Elementa* was a suitable work because it could easily be adapted to an educational context, but the fact that it was used so widely to train Spanish jurists during the Enlightenment is directly related to its content. Its view of natural law set in a legal culture rooted in positivism — and therefore a far cry from the rationalism characterising more typical authors in this academic tradition — combined with the absolutist and conservative nuances which revealed its political ideology made it particularly useful for a cultural context such as Spain.[44] Introduced as a textbook immediately after the Saragossa chair was founded, it remained in use even after the chair disappeared in 1794, and a good part of what was taught there was probably transferred to the still active of Moral Philosophy Chair in any case.[45] However, as usual, it is difficult to be sure of the real scope of the lessons taught in the Aragon Society lecture halls, which could in fact have been more progressive, as specific passages in Society meeting records allude to the teaching of "other greater authors" than Heinecio. It has been shown that there was a relationship between the Moral Philosophy and Public Law Chairs and authors that were far removed from the absolutist conservative Catholicism that characterised Heinecio. These authors, which were also used elsewhere in Spain, included Giambattista Almici, François Jacquier, Manuel de Aguirre and Bernardo María de la Calzada (1751–1825); while de Aguirre contributed various discourses, de la Calzada sent his translation of Condillac's *Lógica* and his literary texts, as did Juan Meléndez Valdés and Valentín de Foronda. Despite this, the general atmosphere in the chair's environs could not have been particularly reformist, and in 1794 the most brilliant students were awarded a text by Clemente Peñalosa y Zúñiga (1751–1804), *La Monarquía* (1793), which was not exactly characterised by its criticism of absolutism.[46]

---

43 See, respectively, Antonio Mestre, *Mayans y la España de la Ilustración* (Madrid: Instituto de Espasa Calpe, 1999): 171–74; Peset and Peset, *Mayans*, 244–45; Álvarez Morales, "La difusión," 49–60; Salvador Rus, "Una versión del 'estado de naturaleza' en la España del siglo XVIII: el texto de Joaquín Marín y Mendoza," *Cuadernos Dieciochistas* 1 (2000): 257–82. However, these teachings must have had much broader sources, as is evident from the fact that in 1774 the University of Salamanca librarian finished a translation of Vattel's manual, which was not granted permission for publication.

44 Sánchez-Blanco, *El Absolutismo*, 197–98.

45 However, there is no indication that Heinecio's text was replaced at the beginning of the 1790s by one by the Italian Catholic jurist G. Almici, as it was in other chairs of this kind in Spain.

46 Portillo, *Revolución de nación*, 85ff.

5 Beyond Saragossa: Madrid, Majorca and Salamanca

Genovesi's influence was not limited to the Saragossa chair; as previously mentioned, he inspired other economics teaching experiences in Spain at the end of the eighteenth century.[47] The first involved the Seminary for the Nobility of Madrid, an institution that was in the vanguard of the modernising of pre-university teaching during the Spanish Enlightenment. Genovesian economics was introduced into the Seminary by one of its most distinguished professors: Bernardo Joaquín Danvila y Villarrasa (c. 1740-c. 1787). Born into a family that had settled in Valencia after the War of Succession, Danvila completed a doctorate in Jurisprudence and Canon Law at the University of Valencia in 1767. Three years later he moved to Madrid, where he worked as a lawyer, becoming the holder of the Chair of Moral Philosophy and Public Law at the Seminary for the Nobility in 1775 and later joining the Academy of History (1778) and the Madrid Society (1780). However, his main occupation was his teaching at the Seminary for the Nobility. The *Lecciones de Economía Civil o de el Comercio* (1779) was written for his courses. The book is the most palpable sign in the entire Spanish Enlightenment of the importance that economic content was acquiring in moral philosophy and public law studies; in fact, in the opinion of Danvila's contemporaries, it was the first Spanish political economy teaching manual. Danvila was inspired by the usual Spanish sources such as Uztáriz and Campomanes, but the seven chapters of his *Lecciones* were also influenced by a range of foreign writers such as Hume, Melon, Plumard Dangeul and Bielfeld. His book's main hallmarks — an agricultural orientation and moderately liberal tone — were mainly due, however, to Cantillon, Condillac and especially Genovesi.[48] In fact, Pérez de Larrea, the individual behind the founding of the Saragossa chair, even viewed it as a "tiny extract" from the *Lezioni*,[49] and for this reason it was widely used and was reissued in Saragossa in 1800.

Meanwhile, in the spring of 1788, the almost unknown Academy of Political Economy was forming in Majorca.[50] This initiative was the clearest evidence that the enlightened government did not want the Saragossa experience to be an isolated case: the Academy was created thanks to a "fund" granted

47 On this matter, see Jesús Astigarraga and Javier Usoz, "The Enlightenment in Translation. Antonio Genovesi's Political Economy in Spain, 1778–1800," *Mediterranenan Historical Review* 28, no. 1 (2013): 24–45; Guasti, "Introduzione," 69ff.

48 Cervera, *El pensamiento*, 105–22.

49 Sánchez, Malo and Blanco, *La cátedra*, 132–33.

50 Our information is taken from a Majorca Society publication, the *Diario de Palma de Mallorca*, no. X, 8-III-1788, no. XI, 15-III-1788, both unpaginated.

by the sovereign to the Majorca Economic Society, which was the institution responsible for its establishment. In this context it is not surprising that the Majorca Society chose to use the Aragon Society's model. The two institutions were linked in the person of José Antonio Arias Mon y Vearde (1743–1818), the younger brother of the president of the Aragon Society, who belonged to the enlightened sector of the Spanish magistracy, like his brother. A Majorca court judge from 1777, a year later he became a founder member of the Majorca Society, of which he was appointed vice-president. Under his responsibility the Academy of Political Economy became a "public school of theory and practice of commerce." The opening ceremony in March 1788 contained many echoes of Normante's ideas: the Academy aspired to "banish the deep-rooted concerns that denigrated commerce."[51] Its internal system was similar to that of the Aragon chair, with evening classes, regular public exams and awards for distinguished students. While its teaching was quite certainly inspired by Genovesi,[52] the Academy also had its own distinguishing features, teaching the "history of commerce, the balance of payments, trade treaties, law and tariffs, commerce in all parts of the world," interwoven with commercial techniques and practices, which were not included in the material used at Saragossa. The Academy seems to have aspired to instruct both local bureaucrats and Majorcan merchants.

While this was happening in Madrid and Majorca, Salamanca was emerging as another centre of economics teaching, under the tutelage of Aragon-born Ramón de Salas y Cortés (1753–1837), one of the most distinguished jurists and professors of the turn of the century generation. Educated in Guatemala under the supervision of his uncle, an archbishop, Salas ended up at the University of Salamanca, where he was destined to have a brilliant teaching career. He finished his doctorate in Law in 1776 and became vice-chancellor three years later. Salas belonged to a group of reforming teachers who maintained a controversial dispute with powerful reactionary sectors at the University of Salamanca throughout the 1780s and 1790s.[53] In 1787 he founded an Academy of Spanish Law with support from Juan Meléndez Valdés, Toribio Núñez (1766–1834), Diego Muñoz Torrero (1761–1821), Mariano Luis de Urquijo (1768–1817) and other future fathers of early Spanish constitutionalism. The Academy's innovative nature was reflected in its teaching methods, which were similar to those of modern seminars and therefore at the opposite end of the scale to

51 *Diario de Palma*, no. XI, 15-III-1788, unpaginated.

52 The *Diario de Palma* published a summary of Genovesi's *Lezioni* throughout 1787.

53 The references to Salas are taken from Jesús Astigarraga, *Luces y republicanismo* (Madrid: CEPC, 2011).

Scholasticism, which still predominated. Salas aimed to replace anachronistic jurisprudence and theology courses with other "useful" disciplines that were not covered by the university curriculum. He gave pride of place to political economy, thus creating the first economics teaching experience at a major Spanish university, which was aided by the fact that teachers and students participated enthusiastically in *tertulias* — gatherings — held at his home. With their help he produced handwritten translations of many works in the public law, moral philosophy and political economy fields by authors such as Bodino, Voltaire, Rousseau and Schmid d'Avenstein, to which access was restricted in Spain at that time. The manuscripts were copied and secretly circulated among intellectual circles in Salamanca and neighbouring towns; the reforming activities undertaken by Salas and his circle were clearly a far cry from those of the official Spanish Enlightenment, which were channelled through economic societies and similar institutions. The structure, forms of sociability and contents were far more in keeping with a radical current of the Spanish Enlightenment that was virtually unknown as yet.

This was the environment in which Salas devised his highly unique translation of Genovesi's *Lezioni*. It was a heavily annotated manuscript covering the first twenty-one chapters of the book and was written during the second half of the 1780s for the Academy of Spanish Law, where Salas' teaching was based on Genovesi's book. It is clear from the title — *Apuntaciones al Genovesi y extracto de las Lecciones de Comercio y Economía Civil; Annotations to Genovesi and Extracts from the Lessons on Commerce and Civil Economics* — that the author intended to discuss Genovesi's ideas. The *Annotations* are actually a refutation of his economic and political ideas and constitute a "book within a book." Salas' work is thus an interesting document, flanked by the *Lezioni*, on one side, and Villava's balanced Spanish translation, on the other. Salas' lengthy comments actively used ideas drawn from three traditions of political thought: modern *iusnaturalism* from Locke's tradition, the republicanism of the *peuples anciens* based on Rousseau and Mably's writings and the empirical and historical-genetic approach typical of Montesquieu. His defence of criminal and civil liberties was also inspired by Beccaria and Filangieri. Genovesi's moderate reformism in terms of economic ideas had been criticised by a group of authors that occupied a wide ideological spectrum, from the Gournay circle and the Physiocrats to Condillac, Hume and Necker. The end result of Sala's labours had little in common with either Genovesi's original ideas or Villava's moderate translation of his book. Salas defended free trade in grain, the abolition of privileges and monopolies, freedom of labour and other similar measures that were far removed from official economic reforms. Given his political orientation this is not surprising; when he taught in the Academy of Public

Law, he was a republican and a liberal whose ideology and forms of sociability were in line with radical currents in the *late* Spanish Enlightenment. In any event, his experiences, and those of Normante, Mon and Danvila, show that by 1790 promoting economics teaching had become one of the distinguishing features of enlightened sectors in Spain. It is also no surprise that while political propaganda favouring economics teaching intensified in the public sphere, the enlightened government was inundated with new proposals from Cadiz, Valencia, Barcelona and Madrid to found new "theoretical schools" of commerce; but without producing any positive results.[54]

6 The Counter-Enlightenment Reaction

While Spanish enlightened sectors received the promotion of economics teaching with enthusiasm, it was met with immediate and profound suspicion from more reactionary sectors, who soon began to express their hostility towards the Saragossa Civil Economy Chair, leading to a well known episode.[55] In 1786, before the end of the first year, the city was inundated with anonymous posters and pamphlets attacking Normante and political economy, the "science of the day." Against this backdrop, the most famous preacher of the time arrived in Saragossa: *Beato* — Beatus — and Capuchin monk, Diego José de Cádiz (1743–1801), who was known for his fiery sermons. In December that year he denounced Normante to the Inquisition because of four ideas contained in his "notebooks:" the drawbacks of clerical celibacy; the non-admission of men under twenty-four to the priesthood, luxury and support for usury. This was undoubtedly a political action: Cádiz was invited to Saragossa by the Archbishop when the Moral Philosophy and Public Law Chairs were about to be inaugurated and the Civil Economy Chair was attempting to consolidate the success of its first year. Over and above Normante and the question as to whether the denounced contents had any orthodox religious meaning, the inquisitorial proceedings were a head-on attack on the Aragon Society's educational reform strategy, which was of course backed by the enlightened government.

54 Astigarraga, "André Morellet."

55 The best documented study is by Guillermo García Pérez, *La economía y los reaccionarios al surgir la España contemporánea* (Madrid: Cuadernos para el Diálogo, 1974); see also Sarrailh, *L'Espagne*, 278–89; Herr, *The Eighteenth-Century*, 272–75, and Astigarraga and Usoz, "The Enlightenment in Translation," 33–34. On the Counter-Enlightenment in Spain, see Herr, *The Eighteenth-Century*, 166–94, and Sánchez Blanco, *Europa*, 264–304, and *El absolutismo*, 222–49.

When Cádiz's onslaught began, another Capuchin monk from Cordova opened fire on a different front. Jerónimo José de Cabra was a former theology teacher who in 1787 had published a detailed justification of Cádiz's denunciation in which he refuted Normante's "notebooks."[56] Although thorough and meticulously detailed, Cabra's refutation lacked theoretical interest, consisting simply as it did of his confirmed "anti-economics" standpoint. His arguments were based on a strict interpretation of the Holy Scriptures and insisted on the Catholic religion's absolute authority over political and economic issues. In actual fact, Cabra's main target was political economy itself. He made disparaging references to Dutot, Montesquieu, Cantillon, Mirabeau, Forbonnais and other innumerable "unholy politicians" as propagators of ideas that are "outlandish, foreign and unheard of in this Spain of ours."[57] His "theological arguments" were especially critical of Melon and Genovesi and contained a detailed repudiation of the latter's enthusiastic support for population growth, the restriction of celibacy, the lawfulness of luxury and his educational proposals.

Cádiz and Cabra's offensives were immediately reinforced by three members of the Oratory of Saint Philip Neri, the most vocal of whom was Eduardo Corriols.[58] In July 1788 Cádiz and Cabra denounced three economic texts to the Inquisition for expressing support for usury: the authors were a Spanish priest, José María de Uría Nafarrondo (1750–1791), Accarias de Serionne and Genovesi. The denunciation was yet another confrontation in a conflict that raged throughout the entire eighteenth century: the legitimacy or otherwise of applying interest rates pitted eminent churchmen such as Jesuit Pedro Antonio de Calatayud (1689–1773) and Dominican Antonio Garcés against reputed commercial institutions of the Crown, including Madrid's Five Major Guilds and the Bilbao and Barcelona trade consulates. Corriols' accusations against Genovesi and Villava were equally serious: "they do everything within their power to convince the faithful of their lies that commerce cannot survive without moderate usury." In the end the three Oratory members requested a ban on the "*Delle usure*" chapter in the *Lezioni*: Corriols pursued the matter untiringly between 1788 and 1791, gradually raising the tone of his accusations, but achieving nothing. The real significance of this episode is that it illustrates the enormous difficulties encountered by the Spanish Enlightenment. Cádiz, Cabra and Corriols created a reactionary movement that put political economy in the dock and identified Genovesi as one of the chief offenders.

---

56 Jerónimo José de Cabra, *Pruebas del Espíritu del Sr. Melon y de las Proposiciones de economía civil y comercio del Sr. Normante* (Madrid: 1787, 2 vols.).

57 Cabra, *Pruebas*, I, 15, 17, 27.

58 AHN, *Inquisition*, bundles 4.482–11, 4.463–10.

That this was a very serious crisis for the Saragossa chair is clear from the fact that its activity was practically paralysed as a result. However, Public Law and Moral Philosophy Chairs were also affected, and teachers attempted to resign from their posts for different reasons and with no apparent justification. It was only thanks to decisive action from the Aragon Society that both chairs continued to function; the Society not only refused to accept the professors' resignation, but it obliged them to look into how to "make these studies permanent, popular and well-used."[59] At the same time, the attack on the Saragossa chair divided public opinion and new initiatives from Enlightenment supporters were required to rescue the pioneering experiment. The Aragon Society itself was the first to apply defensive measures: it embraced Normante's cause as its own and Pérez Larrea wrote a detailed report defending Normante and his ideas. The institution also successfully requested support from numerous economic societies. At the same time, distinguished members of the Spanish Enlightenment such as Valentín de Foronda and Manuel de Aguirre transferred their support for the chair to the press. However, these actions were of little avail. The situation became even more complicated when the Archbishop forced the Saragossa court to find against Normante, a "proud" young man, "imbued with a republican spirit," preventing Arias Antonio Mon y Velarde, a magistrate and president of the Aragon Society, from intervening in the drafting of the final report. In the end, the anonymous but effective assistance of the court in Madrid succeeded in snuffing out the fuse lit by the devout Cádiz. A decree on 10 September 1788 defended Normante's arguments and guaranteed the chair's continuity, but obliged both parties to remain silent on the matter "*de palabra y por escrito*" — "in speech and in writing" —. The fine balance between opposing forces in the conflict is epitomised by how much Cádiz eventually achieved: public exams were resumed in 1789–1790 but there were only six students; Normante never published again; the Aragon Society abandoned its "library of economics writers" project; the possible modernisation of Moral Philosophy and Public Law studies was interrupted and no more economics chairs were founded in economic societies, except the Majorca Society. All in all, the possibility of institutionalising innovative educational models for training future bureaucrats and the high political classes went up in smoke.

While this was happening in Saragossa, the Inquisition was relentlessly persecuting Professor Ramón de Salas in Salamanca. The process began in 1786 and continued until 1795, ending with a summary trial, one of the most severe of the Spanish Enlightenment, which condemned Salas for "propositions,

59 ASA, proceeding 31-VIII-1787.

reading forbidden books and because he was suspected of being the author of several anonymous manuscripts and papers that were harmful to the religion and the state." He was imprisoned, his assets, books and private "papers" were seized and he was stripped of his university professorship. Salas' trial and imprisonment took place during a new phase in the modernisation process that was slowly taking place on the university scene in Spain. The new political climate that now prevailed as a result of the French Revolution brought about the closing of cultural borders, the repression of the critical press and the public law chairs, the activating of censorship and what effectively amounted to an intense counter-offensive from reactionary sectors; it also contributed to paralysing the modernisation process. The events had profound impact on the university reformers' most representative achievements, including Salas' Spanish Law Academy, which was dissolved in a way that reflected the new times very well. Salas stopped teaching there after only five years in 1792. In February 1793, the reactionary sectors at the University of Salamanca asked him to stop teaching political economy, a "dangerous and inconsistent knowledge." Their request had immediate results and was followed by an exhaustive and meticulous censorship of Salas' teaching methods and all political economy teaching at university level, which they claimed had also been going on in the Vienna, Naples and Milan chairs. At Salamanca the time used for teaching this science should simply be spent on "the knowledge of our own laws," in particular, the "law of the Romans." The main focus of their criticism was, of course, Genovesi, whose work they severely refuted.[60]

After Salas' academy closed the only related institution with a bright future was the Saragossa chair. When the conflict with the Inquisition was resolved, the chair enjoyed a period of splendour which lasted until 1808. Removed from the sights of Cádiz and his followers, the Aragon Society did not temper its ambitions in the slightest; on the contrary, it reinforced them, discreetly yet no less effectively. From 1790 onwards the chair's courses were extended from three to four years. Although student numbers did not reach the levels of the first year until 1795, it subsequently maintained a sizeable enrolment, with more than fifty students in some years.[61] Reopened in 1815 after the War of Independence, the chair remained active, although with some interruptions, until 1846, when it was absorbed by the University of Saragossa. As a result of this development it had a slightly longer lease of life than its sisters in public law and moral philosophy; the former closed in August 1794, in a political context of the fear of

60 Astigarraga, *Luces*, 181–82. Salas' main opponent was the priest José María de Pando.
61 Sánchez, Malo and Blanco, *La cátedra*, 533–34.

contagion from revolutionary ideas,[62] and the latter probably in summer 1798. This asymmetry reflects the fact that political economy had become an active channel for spreading ideas that went beyond strictly economics, clearly replacing the contents of what was offered by the other two chairs.

Normante headed the Economics Chair for 17 years until 1801, when he moved to Madrid to work in the Treasury secretariat. He was followed by three of his students, Juan Polo y Catalina (1801–1803), José Benito Cistué (1803–1806) and finally Benito José de Ribera (1806–1808). In their hands the chair gradually modernised its course contents; in 1798, not only the major Spanish economists of the seventeenth and eighteenth centuries were taught there, but many French (Quesnay, Melon, Dutot, Dangeul, Forbonnais, Condillac and Necker), British (Davenant, Mun, Child, Cary, Hume and Smith) or Italians authors (Muratori, Genovesi and Verri).[63] By 1804 works by Herrenschwand, Garnier, Canard and Say had been added. The exact moment when Smith's *Wealth of Nations* was introduced is not well known. It is possible that Normante had already done this in his teaching and had influenced his disciple Cistué who spoke highly of the Scottish economist when he took over as director of the Chair in 1801. The book was well-known in Spain by then. It had arrived very shortly after publication in London in 1776, on Campomanes' personal initiative; however, the cycle of versions and translations of the book did not really begin to take off until the early nineties.[64] In 1792 Carlos Martínez de Irujo (1763–1824) published a translation of the Marquis of Condorcet's succinct compendium, and a year later Alcalá-Galiano followed suit with a summary of Smith's ideas on Public Finance, which appear in book v of *The Wealth of Nations.* The first full translation was finally produced in 1794 by José Alonso Ortiz (1755–1815)[65]. However, there is nothing to prove that this was used at the Chair of Saragossa. Condorcet's translation was in fact more suitable for an

62 The chairs in natural law subsisted in other cities, but replaced Almici's book with a work by the Frenchman Jacquier; La Parra, *Manuel Godoy*, 176–77.

63 ASA, proceeding 22-VI-1798.

64 All details are in Robert Sidney Smith, "The *Wealth of Nations* in Spain and Hispanic America, 1780–1830," *Journal of Political Economy* 4 (1957): 104–25; Llombart, *Campomanes*, 296–305; Ernest Lluch and Salvador Almenar, "Difusión e influencia de los economistas clásicos en España (1776–1870)," in *Economía y economistas españoles. Vol. IV. La economía clásica*, ed. Enrique Fuentes Quintana (Barcelona: Galaxia Gütenberg-Círculo de Lectores, 2000), 98–104; and Salvador Almenar, "El desarrollo del pensamiento económico clásico en España," in *Economía y economistas españoles. Vol. IV. La economía clásica*, ed. Enrique Fuentes Quintana (Barcelona: Galaxia Gütenberg-Círculo de Lectores, 2000), 12–20.

65 *Investigación de la naturaleza y causas de la riqueza de las naciones* (Valladolid: Viuda e Hijos de Santander, 1794, 4 vols.).

educational context because of its size and the fact that it was a compendium. The teaching of more liberally-inspired political economy was consolidated in 1807 when the chair, then headed by Rivera, adopted a new cycle of educational texts focussing on Jean-Baptiste Say's work. That year Say's *Traité d'Economie Politique* (1803) began to be used as a manual; its Spanish translation had just been finished and it made a decisive contribution to consolidating the teaching of political economy at university.[66]

7 Final Remarks

The progress made in studies on political economy during the Spanish Enlightenment may seem insignificant but in actual fact this was not the case. It cannot be denied that the counter-Enlightenment forces effectively won some important battles in the short term. However, this assessment would change if we consider the difficulties encountered by the first steps of the institutionalisation of political Economy in most of Europe in the educational field, including Genovesi's chair.[67] Furthermore, we should also evaluate the result of the dispute between reformists and reactionaries in this field in the light of the *long* Enlightenment. This issue is particularly relevant in the case of the chair of Saragossa. The number of students educated in its lecture theatres was, as well as abundant, highly notable; in addition to those already mentioned — Juan Polo y Catalina (1777–1813), José Benito Cistué (1772–1812) and Benito José de Ribera — , they included José Canga Arguelles, Tadeo Calomarde (1773–1843), José Duaso (1775–1849), Isidoro Antillón (1778–1814) or Francisco Escolar. They were all destined to play highly relevant roles in the turbulent first decades of the nineteenth century in Spain. The chair of the Aragon Society not only created the first stable platform in the history of Spain for teaching political economy, but it also activated the modern mechanisms of professional specialisation. Its mark was particularly noticeable in the Secretariat for the Balance of Trade, the first official Statistical Agency in the history of Spain: together with Larruga, also from Aragon, Normante, Polo and Escolar successively worked there. Secondly, it also had a presence in the parliamentary scene during the *Cortes* of Cadiz, through parlamentaries such as Antillón, Canga Argüelles or

66 José Manuel Menudo and Jose María O'Kean, "Ediciones, reimpresiones y traducciones en español del *Tratado de economía política* de Jean-Baptiste Say," *RHE* 37, no. 1 (2019): 169–192.

67 The series of interruptions caused by the difficulty of finding a suitable replacement for Genovesi are outlined in Di Battista, "Per la storia."

Duaso; the latter two were most key figures in the debates on the Treasury issue. Finally, in the political arena, its students covered the whole ideological spectrum. They included conservative figures, such as Calomarde, but the majority of the core group, led by Normante, Duaso, Cistué or Canga Argüelles, identified more with the *frenchified* and Liberal currents. The great splendour of this generation is reflected in the figure of Canga Argüelles, Minister of Finance in 1811 and 1820. But the idea that relates the slow progress of modernity in Spain with the previous experience in terms of the teaching of economics is further reinforced if we take into account that the figure of Ramón de Salas and some of his students in his Academy of Spanish Law (Toribio Núñez, Mariano Luis Urquijo or Juan Álvarez Guerra) are inseparable from the early steps of Spanish constitutionalism. Furthermore, it should be remembered the colossal task that the Salas' disciples undertook in disseminating the ideas of the Enlightenment in the early decades of the nineteenth century through treatises, dictionaries or translations (Bentham, Canard, Rozier, Say, etc.); a venture that also reached the Spanish colonies to where Victorián de Villava or Manuel Belgrano (1770–1820) — student of Salas in Salamanca — implanted the language of political economy. Undoubtedly, one result of all of these previous efforts was the *Plan* designed by the Minister José Antonio Caballero (1754–1821), enacted in June 1807, which committed, for the first time, to introducing political economy in the faculties of law and paved the way for its slow and definitive insertion in the university structure.[68]

68 Martín, "La institucionalización."

CHAPTER 9

Merchants' Handbooks (1760–1808)

From Office Desks to Chairs of Commerce

1 Introduction: An Overview (1699–1808)

Carlos III's arrival on the Spanish throne in 1759 was a turning point in the production of merchants' handbooks.[1] The previous stage, during which thirty-eight new-style handbooks were issued, began with the publication of Corachán's *Aritmética* in 1699, but seventy-seven more handbooks appeared over the fifty years between 1759 and the outbreak of the Peninsular War in 1808. The second stage thus accounted for around two thirds of the new style of handbook published between 1699 and 1808 (see Appendix IV). While production during the first phase peaked in the 1730s, coinciding with the monetary reforms of 1726–1737, from 1760 to 1808 it traced an ever-rising curve which reached its height during the last decade of the old century and the first of the new one, when thirty-one and forty-six new handbooks were published respectively. This was to a large extent a consequence of the monetary measures enacted from 1772 to 1779, the proliferation of compendiums of *vales reales* (twenty-seven copies between 1780 and 1808) and the publication of the *Almanak Mercantil* (fourteen volumes from 1795 to 1808). The period from 1790–1808 saw an increase in the reissuing of texts for merchants if those written for sixteenth, seventeenth and eighteenth century that reappeared from 1699 to 1808 are included: the seventy-eight published between 1699 and 1760 represent less than a third of the total. Of the remaining 174, just over half (51%)

1 See Appendix IV. The content of this section is based on an analysis of a database created by the author, which includes 252 entries of Castilian Spanish and Catalan texts for merchants published in the period 1699–1808. The set includes new-style handbooks, *vales reales* compilations and reissues of handbooks from the sixteenth, seventeenth and eighteenth centuries. The exact date of two of the handbooks is unknown. The database includes the references in the Biblioteca Nacional de España, the Biblioteca del Palacio Real, the Biblioteca Nacional de Cataluña, the Catálogo Colectivo del Patrimonio Bibliográfico Español, the HathiTrust Digital Library, the Bibliothèque Nationale de France and the Francisco Aguilar Piñal's exhaustive work: *Bibliografía de autores españoles del siglo XVIII* (Madrid: CSIC, 1981–2001, 10 vols). The complete references for sources cited in this chapter appear in Section III of the bibliography. I would like to thank Prof. Elena Ausejo for her thoughtful comments regarding chapters 1 and 9 of this book.

 | DOI:10.1163/9789004442894_011

were published between 1790 and 1808, and three out of four (74%) from 1780 to 1808. In short, the period from 1699 to 1808 witnessed a growth in handbook production; as with all the writing and print culture during the Spanish Enlightenment,[2] the movement was most vibrant during the three last decades, when more than half of all the handbooks published appeared.

A striking feature of these texts was their geographical diversity, and early evidence of this is provided by their authors' birthplaces.[3] The largest group came from the Crown of Aragon and were mainly Catalan and Valencian: together with the Aragonese, they account for half the handbooks produced. The other half was almost equally split between Castile, Andalusia and the Basque Country-Navarre area. More evidence of this diversity is provided by the places where the handbooks were published, although this was not always representative of either the setting in which they were written or the target readership (see Appendix I, II and III). Naturally, Madrid is over-represented, accounting for around half the total places of publication during the two periods in question (1699–1759: 14/35; 1760–1808: 57/108). The remainder reflects the continuity of urban-based economic regions, especially around the country's peripheries.[4] The Crown of Aragon regions emerged once again as an important production centre: during the earlier period, Valencia, Catalonia and Aragon, in that order, accounted for forty per cent of the handbooks, although geographic dispersion was more marked in the later period, during which production increased. Fewer were published in the old Aragonese kingdoms, which produced less than a third of the total. Andalusia (Cadiz and Seville) continued to show a significant level of activity (10%), while the remainder came from Guipúzcoa, Navarre, Murcia and Castile. The most significant trend vis-à-vis previous centuries was Castile's relative decline in importance.

Professional diversity was a further factor. As in previous centuries, the handbooks' authors hailed from a myriad of trades and professional backgrounds (see Appendix V). However, the largest group tended to be mathematics teachers, which endorses the books as commercial literacy tools. During the first period (1699–1749), almost 40% of the handbooks were written by school and university teachers (12/31), followed by mint assayers, with just under a quarter (7/31) and churchmen, with around a tenth (4/31). The rest were merchants, booksellers, printers, lawyers, private accountants, master builders and

2 Álvarez Barrientos, *Los hombres*, 203–05.

3 The data is mainly limited to editions from the sixteenth and seventeenth centuries and the first half of the eighteenth, when this information was normally included in handbook paratexts.

4 See ch. I.

senior government employees, all of which reflects, on one hand, the fact that publishing the handbooks was a sign of social distinction and, on the other, that it required no specialised training; moreover, as there was no copyright control, plagiarism and pirating were rife. However, a slight tendency towards specialisation is perceptible during the second period, resulting from the early experiences of chairs of commerce (see Appendix VI), and in line with this teachers became the largest group of authors, accounting for half the new handbooks published. The other half was shared among government employees, private accountants, merchants and churchmen, who produced between 10 and 15%, while a handful were written by farmers and soldiers. It is interesting to note that churchmen continue to be under-represented in these figures, and also that the emergence of a group of senior public servants — Bails, Gallard, Gómez Ortega and Marcoleta — reflected the impact of translated texts and the strategic importance that was ascribed to books of this type by those in positions of power.

2 The Strengthening of Local Genealogies (1760–1790)

Several factors facilitated the increasing production of handbooks between 1760 and 1808. The most important was the long period of economic growth between 1730 and 1790; while tentative and lacking modern features, it had a positive impact on all productive activities including domestic and foreign trade. Various government reforms played positive roles in the process: the monetary reforms adopted by Carlos III did not disrupt the fragile inheritance system, but instead contributed to stabilising it. The most important reforms were enacted during the 1770s: monetary law was changed in 1772, which caused a covert devaluation of gold and silver, but in 1779 gold recovered its old value with respect to the dual silver. The possible scarcity of silver in the domestic market remained the main monetary problem, and the circulation of old coins, which was the core obstacle to commerce, persisted in spite of repeated measures to withdraw them.[5] For their part, the liberalisation of grain trade (1765), acts establishing free trade with the colonies, (1765, 1778, 1789) and the *Arancel*, involving tariffs (1778–1782), all essentially broadened private merchants' scope for action, which in turn stimulated the demand for knowledge about trade. Alongside this, the 1765 suppression of Cadiz's monopoly and the gradual authorisation for various ports in Spain and the colonies to trade

5 Hamilton, *War*, 62–72; Bernal, *España*, 322–23; Pérez Sarrión, *La península*, 288–90.

directly from one side of the Atlantic to the other fostered the consolidation of these regional trading centres, where handbooks were already being produced (Cadiz and Barcelona, for example). The local handbook production genealogies were thus established throughout the final third of the eighteenth century, and timid progress was made towards modernising the content. As Cole remarks,[6] this was linked to changes in the sphere of ideas: the importance of quantification, which came from political arithmetic, and the recognition of trade as a state science, all of which encouraged the proliferation of treatises and translations at a pace that matched handbook publication.[7]

In the old Aragonese kingdoms the books continued to be published in different formats. As seen, in 1784 the Aragon Society created in Saragossa a Chair on Civil Economy, drawing on local commercial arithmetic teaching. While its aim was to provide education in the theoretical principles of "trade," studying Savary, La Porte and Larue was also recommended.[8] Naturally, the Chair did not squeeze out the private teaching of commercial arithmetic; in 1789 José Biel, a Jesuit, published a simplified handbook in Saragossa to make this accessible to young people and merchants.[9] Meanwhile, in Valencia the silk sector continued to be the specialist, while the diversity of formats in Catalonia was enriched by the fact that two languages were in use there, as shown by Francisco Guerra's accounting book in Catalan, published in 1779.[10]

The most active centres in Andalusia were Seville and Cadiz. While Seville merchant Martínez Gómez's *Manual* (1795) was well-informed about affairs relating to currency and government bond legislation, it particularly focussed on the standard coin, weights and measures equivalences in Spanish cities (Seville, Malaga, Bilbao, etc.).[11] Cadiz was the nerve centre of trade with America and silver dealing and had a long-established tradition of commercial arithmetic teaching. In 1763 Rendón y Fuentes created a compendium of common foreign exchange transactions there.[12] It was followed in 1777 by a basic commercial arithmetic handbook written by González Cañaveras "for use in his private

6 Cole, *The Historical*, 24ff.

7 Llombart, "Traducciones," table IV.2.

8 Normante, *Discurso*, 34.

9 José Biel y Aznar, *Aritmética especulativa, y práctica para lo mercantil* (1762; Zaragoza: Medardo Heras, 1789).

10 Francisco Guerra, *Valor y reduccio de la moneda de or y de plata a altres especies de moneda* (Gerona: Narcis Oliva, 1779).

11 Vicente Martínez Gómez, *Manual de comercio, en que se halla la descripción de las monedas, pesas y medidas que se usan en los reinos de España* (Madrid: Benito Cano, 1795).

12 Francisco Rendón y Fuentes, *Prontuario aritmético o breve reducción de unas monedas a otras* (Cadiz: Espinosa de los Monteros, 1763).

school."[13] However, the most significant example was provided by Jerez printer Luque y Leyva (1741–1800), who in 1780 published the best adapted handbook for commercial uses in Cadiz.[14] The title, the *Arte de la partida doble* (1774), also refers to the sources of texts on accountancy published in eighteenth century Spain. The book marked the end of a period lasting over 150 years during which no works on Luca Pacioli's tradition were produced.[15] This stagnation was influenced by the long shadow cast by the *Libro de caja* (1590), whose author Bartolomé Salvador de Solórzano pioneered the introduction of double-entry bookkeeping (*doble partida*) in Spain.[16] Foreign handbooks also played their part, both the generalist works by Savary and Ricard — the 1721 fourth edition incorporated accountancy, contributed by H. Desaguliers — and some of the popularisers of double-entry bookkeeping in France such as Mathieu La Porte (1685), Pierre Gobain (1702) and Miteau de Blainville (1784). The latter's book was translated into Castilian Spanish in 1800 by José de Cabredo as a short handbook in the form of lessons with examples tailored for Spanish trade.[17] The Spanish version by Accarias de Serionne (1772–1774) was in the same vein: in spite of being a general economics treatise, the last volume also dealt with accountancy and business economy.[18] Luque de Leyva's book, however,

13 Juan Antonio González Cañaveras, *Aritmética especulativa y práctica* (Cadiz: Manuel Espinosa de los Monteros, 1777).

14 Luis de Luque y Leyva, *Aritmética de escritorios de comercio* (Cadiz: Imprenta del autor, 1780). On accounting techniques in the Spanish Treasury during the 18th century, see Dubet and Solbes, *El rey*, 123ff., 397ff.

15 Esteban Hernández, "A Spanish Treatise of 1706 on Double Entry Bookkepping: *Norte Mercantil y Crisol de Cuentas* by Gabriel de Souza Brito," *Accounting and Business Research* 15 (1985): 292, and "Origins and development of Accounting in Spain (from the 13th to the 19th century)," in *Accounting in Spain*, ed. José A. Gonzalo (Madrid, Asociación Española de Contabilidad, 1992); Rafael Donoso, *Una contribución a la historia de la contabilidad* (Sevilla: Universidad de Sevilla, 1996).

16 Solórzano's *Libro* inspired the chapters on Accountancy in Gabriel de Souza Brito's treatise, which was written in Spanish. The author was a Portuguese Jew that had settled in Amsterdam, where he taught mathematics and accountancy: *Norte mercantil y crisol de cuentas, dividido en tres libros* (1706; Amsterdam: Casa de Juan ten Houten, 1770); for information about another Jewish author who wrote about local trading concepts in Spanish, Jacob de Metz, see Hernández, "A Spanish," 291–96.

17 Miteau de Blainville, *Instrucción para la teneduría de libros en partida doble, que contiene los principios de esta ciencia* [...] *Escrita en francés, por M. Miseau Blamville, y traducida al castellano, por D. José de Cabredo* (Madrid: Viuda de Ibarra, 1800). There were also attempts to translate texts from the Portuguese tradition *das partidas dobradas*; see AHN, *Consejos*, bundle 5552–59.

18 Accarias de Serionne, *Historia*, IV, ch. XXVIII, XXXIX, 47–68 (accountancy concepts); however, the content of the book was closer to that of political economy chairs.

was a very simplified version of Lyon merchant Jean Larue's *Bibliothèque des jeunes négociants* (1747–1758).[19] While the work can be credited with reintroducing the double-entry bookkeeping into enlightened Spanish circles, it was very basic — it can also be levelled this criticism at the extended and corrected 1783 second edition — , even with regard to the accountancy techniques used in different Spanish companies and institutions of the day.[20]

Jócano y Madaria also took up arms in the cause of double-entry bookkeeping in 1793. An accountant in the Indies Secretariat, his *Disertación crítica* reflected the impact of political economy books on business economy. In fact, the book was written as a reply to Accarias de Serionne and Bielfeld, whose translated works were in circulation. Jócano accused both authors, but especially Bielfeld, of favouring the duplication of accountancy systems: double-entry in commerce and single-entry — *cuenta y data* — in the government. Encouraged by his superiors in the Indies Accountancy Division,[21] Jócano presented double-entry as a route towards the modernisation of public accountancy, defending quantification as an unavoidable public policy. While somewhat scornful at times — "there seem to be as many *calculistas* as there are wigs" today[22] —, he recovered Bielfeld's brilliant chapter on the science of political arithmetic:[23] although he wrongly ascribed this to John Graunt, a disciple of William Petty, it was nonetheless "indispensable for governing."[24] Choosing the right public accountancy method was thus not a trivial issue and, contrary to Bielfeld's view, this could only be double-entry bookkeeping, to whose development Spain had contributed in no small measure.

In fact, the state of public finances was one of the driving factors behind the production of texts for merchants, although not for the causes mentioned above. The actual reason was the issue of *vales reales* created in 1780, partly on the basis of a proposal from Bayonne merchant Francisco Cabarrús.[25]

---

19 Luis de Luque y Leyva, *Arte de la partida doble* (1774; Cadiz: Imprenta del autor, 1783), part II.

20 José María González Ferrando, "El sevillano Luis de Luque y Leyva, *reintroductor* de la partida doble en la bibliografía española," *Cuadernos de investigación contable* 4, no. 1–2 (1992): 81–148; Donoso, *Una contribución*, 146ff.

21 Donoso, *Una contribución*, 147.

22 Sebastián de Jócano y Madaria, *Disertación crítica y apologética del arte de llevar cuenta y razón contra la opinión del Barón de Bielfeld, acerca del arte en general y del método llamado partidas dobles en particular* (Madrid: Gerónimo Ortega y Herederos de Ibarra, 1793), 85.

23 Bielfeld, *Instituciones políticas*, IV, ch. IV.

24 Jócano, *Disertación*, 85.

25 The best interpretation is in Torres, *El precio*, 360–408; see, likewise, Hamilton, *War*, 77–85, and Pedro Tedde de Lorca, *El Banco de San Carlos (1782–1829)* (Madrid: Banco de España-Alianza Editorial, 1988), 31–55.

The aim was to fund the government deficit, which had been exacerbated by the new war with Britain (1779–1783). As Torres has shown, they were used in moderation during Carlos III's reign;[26] however, the slowdown in economic growth, the stagnation of tax revenue and the new armed conflicts that broke out towards the end of the century all combined to turn them into a resource that was in permanent use. This led to a loss of confidence in the Spanish financial system and in the recently-created Bank of San Carlos (1782), one of whose main functions was to guarantee the *vales*' conversion rate and prevent their depreciation.[27] In 1798 the *Hacienda* established a *Caja de Amortización* that was separate from the Royal Treasury, but this failed to prevent a highly significant part of the accumulated public debt being caused by the issuing of ever more depreciated *vales*. This situation was reflected in the books for merchants. The *vales*' reputation and state solvency both relied on having guaranteed conversion rates. The books aimed to reinforce public confidence in a system that increasingly lacked it and thus became information vehicles; during the 1780s many began to include *vales* conversion tables, to which the value of the securities issued to finance the building of the Imperial Canal was added. However, the *vales* also generated their own specific literature: in 1802 Juan Reguera collated all the legislation concerning these debt certificates, and compendiums and value tables proliferated between 1780 and 1808. Although normally published anonymously and mainly produced in Madrid and Barcelona, they also appeared in Cadiz, Seville, Valencia and Palma de Majorca, which confirms that the circulation of these titles took hold in Spain's trading cities; the high price for the period (300 or 600 *reales*) implies that they were popular among wealthy citizens.[28] This was also logical, as the *vales* involved wholesale trading, operating like paper currency, albeit with limited functions.

The Spanish handbooks began to use more diverse sources in terms of nationality as the century advanced. According to the brief information they provided, the Italian tradition declined and was superseded by the Dutch and French. As already noted, the French dominated the scenario in terms of accounting books (Barrême), accountancy (La Porte, Gobain and Blainville) and merchants' handbooks (Savary, Larue and Ruelle). This was also true of the mineral testing sphere: Casimiro Gómez Ortega's (1741–1818) 1785 translation of the methods of treating precious metals used by Balthazar Georges Sage in the Chair at the Paris Mint — founded by Necker in 1777 — reflected the

26 Torres, *El precio*, 403–07.
27 Tedde, *El Banco*, 57–78.
28 Torres, *El precio*, 377–78.

stagnant state of Spain's technical tradition.[29] France's influence was only logical, given that Spain's domestic market was dominated by French trading networks.[30] Meanwhile, with the important exception of Wyndham Beawes, British commercial treatises played only a marginal role. Campomanes recommended his successful *Lex mercatoria redivida* (1751), inspired by Savary des Brulons' *Dictionnaire*, as it contained important information about Spain.[31] Beawes was British consul in Cadiz and Seville for some thirty years, and four decades later he published *A Civil, Commercial, Political, and Literary History of Spain and Portugal* (1793), a wide-ranging study of the geographical, administrative and legislative structure of the two countries. Three chapters focussed on the Spanish economy, specifically its taxation system, its weights, measures and coins and its production sectors. However, its usefulness from the Spanish perspective was questionable; as well as authors such as Dutot, Davenant and Locke, Beawes used out-of-date Spanish sources such as Uztáriz's *Théorica*, and his statistical information stopped at the 1760s: in short, the text was aimed at a British readership. Its most useful aspect was conversion tables for coins and weights and measures, but even these were based on out-dated sources — Davenant and Defoe, for example —. Beawes thus failed to salvage Spanish commercial literature, whose tentative modernisation of its contents had merely begun between 1760 and 1790.

3 Bails and Enlightened Reformism Handbooks

In 1790 Catalan mathematician Benito Bails (1730–1797) published the *Aritmética para negociantes*, an exceptional piece in the vast universe of Spanish handbooks. Its creation was an initiative of the Bourbon government, behind which was the Secretary of State, the Count of Floridablanca, to whom it was dedicated. Bails acknowledged that Floridablanca had not only granted permission for the printing, but had offered him "any other aid" that was needed. At the height of the merchants' handbook boom, this Bourbon government operation implied a double purpose: firstly, to put the growing social use of this type of literature at the service of its reforms, and secondly, to move from

29 Balthazar Georges Sage, *Arte de ensayar oro y plata* (Madrid: Joaquín Ibarra, 1785).

30 Pérez Sarrión, *La península*, 175–229.

31 Campomanes, *Discurso industria popular*, CLXXXII. In fact, during the last decade of the eighteenth century Minister of Finance Diego Gardoqui (1735–1798) commissioned a Spanish translation of Beawes' text from Adam Smith's Spanish translator José Alonso Ortiz, but the project was not successful; see AHN, *Consejos*, bundle 5552–59.

regional to national handbooks; a real sign that the increase in trade was contributing to the structuring of the domestic market. The content of Bails' handbook reflected both aspects. The choice of author was no accident. Bails was acknowledged to be one of the most brilliant mathematicians of his generation, as well as being close to Bourbon power.[32] He is known to have been educated in Perpignan and Paris, and then to have settled in Madrid in 1763, where he was a *habitué* of the highest authorities in Carlos III's governments. His handbook was written almost three decades after he was appointed to the Chair of Mathematics at the *Academia de Bellas Artes de San Fernando*. By then, thanks to guidance from the scientist Jorge Juan, he had not only created his main works of theory, *Elementos de Matemáticas* (1772–1783) and its simplified version, *Principios de Matemáticas* (1776), but had also gained a reputation for his subtle treatises on mathematics applied to architecture and music.

The Bails' *Aritmética* was far more than another simple commercial arithmetic treatise: in fact, this was only covered in one part of the book. Underlying the work was the desire to propose more inclusive models in Spain, probably in line with Ricard and the Dutch tradition — hence its concise and precise title — . It also included a chapter in the form of a dictionary of trading cities, perhaps taken from Kruse. The work was in fact a collection of short treatises and was structured as follows: a) simple arithmetic (with integers and fractions); b) simple arithmetic (with decimals); c) metals (properties, classification, alloying and separation); d) currency (production, usages and typology); e) trade geography; f) coins (national and international equivalences, and banks); g) exchange rates; h) weights and measures equivalences. To maintain the fine balance between theory and practice, Bails used a set of very comprehensive and visually clear tables, a marked improvement on the charts and graphics that usually appeared in Spanish handbooks. Bails' ambitious approach extended to the handbook's prospective readership; it was written not only for merchants and exchangers but also for those who worked with accounts of different kinds.[33] It is worth noting that it was also aimed at future chairs of commerce, whose knowledge went far beyond basic arithmetic. In short, with

---

32 On Bails and the development of mathematics in eighteenth century Spain, see Mariano Hormigón, "Las matemáticas en la Ilustración española. Su desarrollo en el reinado de Carlos III," in *Ciencia, técnica y Estado en la España ilustrada*, ed. Joaquín Fernández Pérez and Ignacio González (Zaragoza: Ministerio de Educación y Ciencia, 1990, 2 vols.), 265–78, and Elena Ausejo, "Las matemáticas en la Ilustración hispana: estado de la cuestión," in *Ilustración, ilustraciones*, ed. Jesús Astigarraga, María Victoria López-Cordón and José María Urkia (San Sebastián: 2009), II, 693–713.

33 Benito Bails, *Aritmética para negociantes* (Madrid: Viuda de Ibarra, 1790), Prólogo.

Bails, trade handbooks ceased to be simple treatises on mathematics applied to the commercial sphere, and a phase of relative sophistication began.

From the mathematics perspective the handbook's aim was clear: to introduce calculation with decimals into Spain once and for all.[34] Bails believed this to be the quickest and most useful system for merchants and accountants, and to achieve his goal he duplicated what he explained in simple arithmetic by means of fractions. This had actually been an objective since the times of Corachán, and one of the reasons was that Spanish merchants found it difficult to understand foreign trade handbooks because they used the decimal system. In any event, Bails' excellent training was clear throughout the *Aritmética*. While algebra was not covered, insurance was, which meant that the book included pioneering references to the importance of insurance in creating probability statistics applied to demography.[35] A further feature was its connection with various developing reforms. When dealing with metals, Bails gave an account of recent experiments recently carried out by French scientists (Macquer, Baumé and Morveau) on platinum, an important metal for the Spanish economy as it was only found in the country's dominions in the Americas.[36] His treatment of interest rates was equally illustrative.[37] This issue invoked the controversial matter of usury, which other handbooks avoided; however, Bails managed to tackle it without questioning the legitimacy of charging interest, even among "self-interested and grasping" men. He favoured its reduction and the preventing of monopolies in the capital market as a way to stimulate economic growth. He also criticised the recent trend for using capital to purchase housing instead of for productive activities. In spite of being in line with official reforms, all these ideas turned out to contain an element of risk, and it should not be forgotten that just a year after publishing *Aritmética*, Bails was tried by the Inquisition for spreading suspicious ideas, sent to prison and exiled.

A further factor behind the writing of *Aritmética* was Bails' mistrust of the calculation equivalences in Spanish handbooks. His concern reflected the greater weight that foreign demand had acquired in the Spanish economy, a factor that was related to the recovery of colonial trade and the profitable international trade in silver managed from Madrid and Cadiz. Setting exchange

---

34 A later and informative example of the application of decimals in basic arithmetic was provided by Gaspar Fernández, *Compendio para hacer todos los cambios y descuentos por el nuevo cálculo decimal, en que se facilitan las operaciones que exige este ramo* (Madrid: Imprenta Real, 1804).

35 Bails, *Arismética*, 224–25.

36 Bails, *Arismética*, VI, 249ff.

37 Bails, *Arismética*, 141–45.

values was not "a task for one man," and Bails therefore opted to publicise figures from Ricard's *Traité*. It should be recalled that the 1781 edition, one of the century's best, had been put together by Bilbao merchant Marien Arróspide and had been popularised in the *Encyclopédie Méthodique*. This was a common way of updating Spanish handbooks from the end of the century; in fact Castelar, another pioneer in the use of decimal numbers, had done this a few years before Bails in a work on exchange rates in Madrid and Cadiz.[38] The handbooks' inclusion of exchange values also indisputably contributed to their modernisation during these years, and they provided the contents for two others written by Madrid accountant Ignacio Bes. The first was produced in 1765 and contained exchange rates between Spain and France and the second, written in 1775 and extended in 1804, included three more European cities.[39] It was completed by Molledo the following year with information about Hamburg.[40] Iturburu made more significant progress in this area by establishing an algorithmic multiplier for estimating exchange rates that was independent of the face and actual value of coins.[41] However, the publication of Bails' handbook was the symbol of a new age, and the last decade of the century witnessed the beginning of a phase of engagement in support of creating a modernised unified trading culture of imperial scale. A key element in this was the *Correo Mercantil*.

4 The *Correo Mercantil* and the Modernisation of Trading Culture

The first issue of the *Correo Mercantil* (CM, 1792–1808) appeared in 1792, two years after the publication of Bails' handbook. Edited by Diego María Gallard, it was Spain's first trader-orientated newspaper.[42] Its founding highlighted the press's importance as a powerful communication tool in society, and its considerable number of subscribers guaranteed greater penetration for commercial information. Its circulation was also mainly in urban contexts, where there was a greater flow of information, and it was in this scenario that the "reading

38 Emilio Castelar, *Cambios sobre las más principales plazas de Europa* (Madrid: Andrés de Soto, 1785).

39 Ignacio Bes y Lavet, *Tratado útil, y provechoso para los comerciantes* (Madrid: Gabriel Ramírez, 1768), and *Manual de comerciantes* (Madrid: Joaquín Ibarra, 1775).

40 Jerónimo Molledo y Martín, *Nuevo manual de comerciantes* (Madrid: José del Collado, 1805).

41 Joaquín de Iturburu, *Nuevo método para las operaciones de cambios de España con las principales plazas extranjeras de comercio* (Madrid: José del Collado, 1805–1806).

42 See ch. X above.

mania" that characterised the eighteenth century was played out.[43] As a biweekly publication, the CM rendered merchants' handbooks obsolete in terms of transmitting up-to-date news about issues such as prices and exchange rates. It was also the first publication in the history of commercial literature to have an imperial dimension: it aimed to bring together trading structures on both sides of the Atlantic. To help achieve this objective, Gallard published the *Almanak mercantil* (1795–1808, 14 vols.) for fourteen years as a complement to the CM. The *Almanak* was an annual guide for merchants and functioned as a channel for information — more qualitative than quantitative — contributed by trade consulates in Spain and the colonies. Its content varied little over the years and included news about currency equivalences and *vales reales*, but the bulk of the volumes contained information about trading cities abroad, in Spain and in the colonies (registration, insurance, etc.), government institutions and economic legislation such as the 1778–1782 *Arancel* and the 1778 fair trade decrees, which were published there.

One of the CM's main tasks was information provision. As well as carrying weekly news on prices, exchange rates, etc., it published numerous commercial geography reports to promote the expansion of markets. Quantitative information focused on the use of official statistics, which merchants were invited to consult as the most reliable available. It also published budget and balance of payment figures and, from 1802 onwards, regular reports on statistical yearbooks produced in France and other countries such as Holland, which provided up-to-date versions of the same economic information as trade newspapers.[44] In 1805 it also carried a review of a book on statistical science by August Ludwig von Schlözer, a German. However, at the heart of the CM there was not only information but also merchant education. In January 1793, just a few months after its first issue was published, there was an article devoted to explaining the system for calculating exchange rates, in view of the evidence that "there are many readers who do not understand it."[45] In 1800 similar explanations on bills of exchange and the balance of trade were provided.[46] By that time the paper had undertaken a pioneering defence of the metric system approved by the French National Assembly in 1791. This system was presented as the fastest route to the definitive standardisation of Spanish weights and measures. In 1794 the CM published a paper in its defence that had been read

43 Roger Chartier, *Libros, lecturas y lectores en la Edad Moderna* (Madrid: Alianza, 1993), 153–58; Melton, *The rise*, 116–19.

44 CM, no. 6 (2-VIII-1802), 481–82.

45 CM, no. 9 (7-II-1800), 67–71.

46 CM, no. 45 (5-III-1800), 355–57.

at the Academy of Sciences in Paris.[47] Four years later the CM summarised Tillet and Abeille's observations in this respect and then presented the correlations with Spanish units, calling for similar measures to those adopted in France, including the establishing of a public weighing apparatus linked to the system and a teacher to show how it worked.[48] Its positions led up to the 1800 publication of the first dissertation in defence of the metric system in Spain, written by Valencia scientist Gabriel Ciscar,[49] according to whom the new system's advantages — consistency, the simplification of arithmetical operations, uniformity and exact matches — could easily be extended to trade, as the CM had argued.[50] In 1801 Carlos IV finally issued an order requiring the official equivalences of normal weights and measures used in the Spain to be established as a preparatory step towards introducing the metric system. However, as was frequently in other countries, this was to prove a lengthy process.[51]

As its main path to modernisation the CM chose to publish long reviews of merchants' handbooks, specialising in information of this type after 1799. Its preferred source was France and the journals there that collected news about literature and politics — especially the *Journal de Paris*, which the CM limited itself to translating —. These journals also functioned as intermediaries for handbooks in other countries, mainly Germany. The selection chosen by the CM must have been overseen by a specialist, as the reviews appeared almost immediately after a book came out. A substantial series was published, once again reflecting the great diversity of the literature aimed at merchants.[52] At times the CM highlighted the usefulness of lexicons of commercial terms,[53] as well as almanacs, correspondence books and compilations; these were pamphlets put together "to carry around in your pocket" and were useful for many

47 CM, no. 9 (31-I-1794), 91ff.

48 CM, no. 31 (14-III-1799), 242–44.

49 Emilio La Parra, *El Regente Gabriel Ciscar. Ciencia y revolución en la España romántica* (Madrid: Compañía literaria, 1995).

50 Gabriel Ciscar y Ciscar, *Memoria elemental sobre los nuevos pesos y medidas decimales fundados en la naturaleza* (Madrid: Imprenta Real, 1800), 28–34.

51 Ciscar himself defended the usefulness of the metric system in the *Trienio liberal*, but it was not finally established until 1849, twelve years later than in France.

52 While not exhaustive, as the information supplied by the CM was neither complete nor exact, the series included Spanish authors such as Gerard (1799, 1800, 1801) and Iturburu (1806), but most were foreigners: J. E. Kruse (1799); S. Ricard (1799); P. Le Clercq (1799); J. Peuchet (1799, 1800); F. Reishammer (1800); P.-J. Migneret (1800); P. Piet (1801); Ch.-L. Aubry (1801); Blondel (1802); D.-V. Ramel de Nogaret (1806); P.-F. Bonneville (1806); Le Page d'Arbigny (1806); P.-B. Boucher (1807); L'Abbé M. (1807); J. Bertrand de Greuille (1807), J.-F. Guiton (1808) and M. Maugeret (1808).

53 CM, no. 60 (27-VII-1807), 473–84.

professionals such as teachers and surveyors. At others these treatises' desire for brevity was highlighted. Migneret's successful handbook was presented as a compendium of French classics such as Larue and Laporte. At the same time the paper published literature on merchants' functions in international arbitration. It also covered works of theory, taking the lead regarding the use of logarithms in commercial exchanges and recommending a book by Carl I. Gerhardt, a German: "there is nothing easier to understand in a short time, as long as you can do ordinary arithmetic." The original handbooks were also reviewed regularly. Ricard's work was the "most highly-esteemed of its genre," and the 1798 edition was recommended as it covered all the continents.[54] The volumes of Peuchet's *Dictionnaire universel* (1799) were presented as definitively superior to Savary's treatise and also as irrefutable evidence that commerce was a science.[55] Finally, the CM also publicised the first handbooks written in France under the 1808 Code of Commerce, such as J.-F. Guiton's.

5 The Purpose of Drafting a Code of Commerce

The CM was also an active spokesperson in support of drawing up a Spanish Code of Commerce, which would include the regulation of maritime laws. This opened a new front in the process of unifying and centralising regulation of trade, as for the first time the need for a single legislative code operating throughout Spain and its colonies was raised openly. The issue gathered force during the 1790s, undoubtedly receiving a boost from the triumph of the Revolution in France. If the aim of establishing a European space of republican trade ultimately led to the War of the Convention between Spain and France, it was the loss of traditional diplomacy based on family alliances that was behind the collapse of the third *Pacto de Familia* — Family Compact — between Spain and France in 1793, and the establishing of an Act of Navigation as a tool for trade defence.[56] Released from the ties that had bound it to France for three decades, at least in a formal sense, Spain was forced to rebuild its political and trade alliances. At the same time, its colonial system was being completely restructured under the free trade scheme, a key element of which

54 CM, no. 50 (24-VI-1799), 396.

55 CM, no. 56 (15-VII-1799), 442–44; no. 57 (18-VII-1799), 451–53; no. 67 (21-VIII-1800), 531–32.

56 Marc Belissa, "What Trade for a Republican People? French Revolutionary Debates About Commercial Treatises (1792–1799)," in *The Politics of Commerce Treaties in the Eighteenth Century. Balance of Power, Balance of Trade*, ed. Antonella Alimento and Koen Stapelbroek (Cham: Palgrave MacMillan, 2017), 421–38.

was the founding of new consulates in both Spain and the colonies, creating a new front of legislative fragmentation.

It seems to have been the latter issue that inspired the Catalan Antonio Capmany to create a Castilian Spanish edition of the Catalan *Llibre del Consolat del mar*[57] — *The Book of the Consulate of the Sea* — in 1793 under the auspices of the Barcelona Board of Trade. His starting point was the "dire need" for a code of Spanish maritime law to address the serious problem of "every port and consulate" being governed by its own local code. If the issue were to be dealt with successfully, a correct translation of the *Llibre* was needed. The book dated from the second half of the thirteenth century and Capmany's fine work of historical archaeology acknowledged that in the text the traditional practices used in trade and shipping among Mediterranean nations had become fossilised: the *Llibre* was a type of code of customs whose authority lay in "reason, practice and need;" it had been elevated to the condition of common law by these nations' "voluntary convention."[58] There was thus a compelling need for an accurate translation to replace the flawed versions in circulation — which included the two Spanish edited in Valencia and Barcelona — to ensure that it was not misunderstood. However, the practicality of using this old text to create a maritime code of positive laws backed by state power was another issue altogether. Capmany's thorough investigations led him to the same conclusions with regard to other emblematic treatises in the Spanish legal tradition. The 1737 Bilbao consular Ordinances were the most representative, but according to Capmany they were of little use because they were chiefly devoted to local traditions: "of the volume's two hundred bulky wide printed pages, only eighty can serve as norms for general cases of trade and shipping."[59] Other works such as those by Bartolomé de Solórzano, Juan de Hevia Bolaños (1570–1623), José Veitia (1620–1688) and José Antonio Abreu (1683–1756) were valuable for understanding the history of trading with the Indies, but were otherwise not much use either: not only were they out of date, but they failed to constitute a "body of maritime law" that was applicable to

57 See Antonio de Capmany *Código de las costumbres marítimas de Barcelona, hasta aquí vulgarmente llamado Libro del Consulado* (Madrid: Antonio de Sancha, 1791), I, I-LXXII, Discurso del editor. On Capmany, see Lluch, *El pensament*, 35–55, and Fernández, *Cataluña*, 49–85.

58 Capmany, *Código*, VI.

59 Capmany, *Código*, LXVI. However, it should be remembered that, when Capmany was writing, the ordinances of Spanish consulates, starting with the Barcelona *Junta*, varied from those of Bilbao insofar as they contained broad powers for economic promotion together with classical mediaeval content of a corporative nature; see Fernández, "Burguesía."

the proper administration of justice.[60] The only way forward was thus to set about compiling a new code, which required both better knowledge of foreign treatises and their translations. In Capmany's analysis, the impact of treatises favouring codification was clear, especially those by French authors (Cleirac, Valin, Pastoret, Emerigon, etc.). The fact that his comments were made on the basis of in-depth knowledge was clear from his detailed bibliographical list of trade and maritime case law in Europe.[61]

Capmany was undoubtedly acting as spokesperson for broader-based opinion. In the year that the *Llibre* was published, Cesáreo de Nava Palacio edited a collection of translations in Madrid that included two highly successful texts with roots in the Grotian legal tradition.[62] The first was a version of Charles Molloy's *De Jure Maritimo et Navali* (1682): in spite of being over a century old, it was still one of the best compilations of the maritime customs of Britain's prosperous trade reality.[63] The second was *Del commercio dei popoli in tempo di guerra* (1786) by Giovanni Lampredi, Professor of Public Law at the University of Pisa. This book formed part of a wide-ranging but little-known debate at the time involving writers at the forefront of the European Enlightenment (Vattel, Galiani, Peuchet, etc.). The discussion revolved around the question of neutral states' rights to trade with other countries, including the warring parties, in times of war — of particular interest to Spain because it appeared at the start of the War of the Convention[64] — . The most likely hypothesis is that behind Nava's translations lay the desire, originating with the political authorities, to create a compilation of works that could make a positive contribution to the drafting of a unified Code of Commerce at a time of deep uncertainty: he was very close to Jovellanos.

The fact is that these developments overlapped with lectures on the same content given by a lawyer, Ramón María de Zuazo, at the Madrid Academy of International Law in 1795.[65] They were based on the standardising and

60 Capmany, *Código*, 222.

61 Capmany, *Código*, 217–23.

62 Charles Molloy, *Derecho marítimo y naval, o Tratado de los negocios marítimos y del comercio: obra escrita en inglés por el señor Carlos Moloy; y traducida al castellano por D. Cesáreo de Nava Palacio, con varias adiciones* (Madrid: Imprenta Real, 1793).

63 McCulloch, *The Literature*, 118.

64 The importance of this forgotten topic, which was central to the European Enlightenment, re-emerged recently in Koen Stapelbroek, ed., *Trade and War. The Neutrality of Commerce in the Inter-State System* (Helsinki: Collegium for Advanced Studies, 2011).

65 An extract from his lecture was published in the ML, IV-1795, I, 5–24, 172–89. The longer version is entitled *Memoria económica sobre el comercio y la navegación, origen de los juzgados consulares, su organización, y reformas de que son susceptibles* (c. 1796; BNE, mss.

codifying legal principles of the Enlightenment; having demonstrated that anti-trade prejudice amounted to "ridiculous opinions from the centuries of the barbarians,"[66] Zuazo argued that commerce was an independent science, using the example of Neapolitan Genovesi's Chair. This reinforced the possibility of establishing a body of commercial law that was separate from private common law and whose implementation would be overseen by courts, trials and judges that were also distinct from ordinary ones. Far from being a privilege similar to the guilds', this was the consequence of commerce's usefulness to society and the fact that it had "its axioms, its rules, its system, in short, its special nature."[67] However, unlike Capmany, Zuazo put forward a commercial codification based on the revision and unification of consular ordinances; that is to say, his proposal was closer to a general trade and marine ordinance than a new trading code.[68] It should be recalled that his lectures were written when the new consulates were being founded and in an intellectual context which could be qualified as Neo-Colbertiste, to use Hont's expression.[69] The figure of Louis XIV's minister was an inspiration for Spain's consular ordinances, and Zuazo himself invoked Colbert's famous trade and marine regulations of 1673 and 1681 as a possible model: "it is the most comprehensive trading code known," better than any of the Spanish ordinances, including Bilbao's.[70] Taking this context into account, it is not surprising that a translation of these Colbertiste regulations should be published in 1801.[71]

9515), along the same lines, see the *Tratado de comercio y de la jurisdicción consular* (c. 1796; BUS, mss. 32–218), which was awarded a prize by the Spanish Law Academy in 1796.

66 Zuazo, *Memoria*, f. 20v.

67 Zuazo, *Memoria*, f. 57v.

68 Juan Francisco Lasso Gaite, *Crónica de la codificación española –6–. Codificación mercantil* (Madrid: Ministerio de Justicia, 1998): 28–50; Dionisio A. Perona, *Notas sobre el proceso de la codificación mercantil en la España del siglo XIX* (Madrid: Dykinson, 2015).

69 Hont, *Jealousy of trade*. For a recent view that reformulates the idea of an "ultra-protectionist" Colbert, see Moritz Isenmann, "*Égalité, Réciprocité, Souveraineté*: the Role of Comercial Treaties in Colbert's Economic Policy," in *The Politics of Commerce Treaties in the Eighteenth Century. Balance of Power, Balance of Trade*, ed. Antonella Alimento and Koen Stapelbroek (Cham: Palgrave MacMillan, 2017), 93–95, 102.

70 The Colbertiste stamp on these Ordinances is analysed in Carlos Petit, *La Compañía mercantil bajo el régimen de las Ordenanzas del Consulado de Bilbao 1737–1829* (Seville: Universidad Hispalense, 1980).

71 *Proyecto de Mr. Colbert al rey Luis XIV de Francia sobre el comercio* (Madrid: Imprenta Real, 1801). The translator, Alejandro de Silva y Ayanz, was the Royal Armies' Commissioner for War. The edition of Colbert's *Ordinances* mentioned by Valin was well-known in Spain. Therefore, the fortune of *Colbertism* in Spain was not less than in France; see Philippe Minard, *La fortune du Colbertisme* (Paris: Fayard, 1998).

Zuazo was a member of the managing board of the Sociedad Matritense, and it is highly likely that the Society was involved in these actions, and also that the set of circumstances influenced Carlos IV's decision to order the Board of Trade to create a commercial code for Spain, which in fact came to nothing. Four years later Zuazo asked the King to appoint him commissioner to resume the task. Subsequent years produced further demands along these lines from the Council of Finance, by Virio, and the Council of the Indies, none of which prospered either.[72] The course of this tentative path was ultimately decided by Napoleon's codifying process, under which the civil, commercial and penal codes were created between 1804 and 1810. The CM undeniably played a central role in disseminating the 1807 commercial code: in fact, from 1799 onwards its readers were kept abreast of key events in its drafting, ranging from the pioneering report ordered by French Interior Minister Chaptal to observations from French chambers of commerce.[73] From October 1807 onwards, during its last year of publication, the CM focussed on lectures given by state advisors explaining the content of the *Code de commerce*. When the *Code* entered into force on 1 January 1808, the numerous versions endorsed the Emperor's proposal to turn it into the "Code of Commerce of Europe."[74]

The Spanish translation of the *Code de commerce* was a type of postscript to the CM's work in disseminating news and knowledge. It was published at the end of 1808.[75] It was inserted in the first wave of European versions of the *Code*. Gallard and his contributors must have been behind this, as the paper contained numerous extracts that had already been published elsewhere. The translation was impeccable. Its anonymous author was a specialist in Spanish commercial legislation and in his innumerable original notes he tried to "Spanishize" the French *Code*, illustrating the content with Spanish legislative measures taken from the *Novísima Recopilación*, the Five Guilds' regulations and, especially, the Consulate of Bilbao Ordinances. This once again pointed to consular jurisdiction as a possible source of a Code of Commerce and also reasserted the continuing central role played by the Ordinances in commercial legislation in Spain, as well as their familiarity with Colbert's Ordinances. Speeches by French state advisors had insisted on the precursory nature of

72 Perona, *Notas*, 15–17.

73 CM, no. 2 (7-I-1802), 11–12; no. 66 (18-VIII-1803), 522–24; no. 67 (22-VIII-1803), 530–32.

74 *Código de comercio de Francia con los discursos de los oradores del Consejo de Estado y del Tribunado* (Madrid: Imprenta de la Calle de la Greda, 1808), 6.

75 The translation was published late: it was expected for January 1808. It was reissued in Valencia (1812) and Madrid (1825). It was a very faithful version of the *Code de Commerce* (Paris: 1807), massively reissued in 1807 and 1808.

the 1673 and 1681 commercial Ordinances, but also that they were now inadequate for articulating an international trade that had undergone a profound change in the century and a half since they were drafted.[76] In fact, the new *Code*'s purpose was not to reform the Ordinances but to recast the case law of parliaments, municipalities and all kinds of specific ordinances in a code built on new principles; when a new Civil Code was passed in 1804, this became inevitable. Where the Spanish translation of the *Code* was concerned, the *Colbertiste* nature of the Bilbao Ordinances made it easy to compare it with the French code. It was also an expeditious way of showing that, just like in France, surrendering the Ordinances opened up the possibility of proposing a Spanish code. However, despite Joseph Bonaparte's new proposals for a code during the French occupation of Spain, the first Spanish Code of Commerce was to prove a lengthy process.[77]

6 The Chairs of Commerce and Their Handbooks

The CM carried constant pleas for regulated commerce teaching. In 1800 it published a full teaching programme in order for merchants to be able distinguish themselves from "simple traders,"[78] following this two years later by the educational plans of the Bordeaux and Cadiz schools of commerce.[79] Some months before the publication closed down, it alluded to failed teaching attempts in Cadiz, La Corunna and Madrid and publicised a new programme to give trainee merchants the same support as other professionals.[80] By means of such reports the paper also echoed the repeated attempts to found chairs of commerce, as had been done for draughtsmanship and seamanship. There had already been isolated initiatives in this direction in Cadiz and Barcelona in 1771 and 1775 respectively. In 1776 the Sociedad Bascongada attempted to establish a chair in its Bergara Seminary, only to be prevented by lack of funding.[81] A year later Campomanes raised the issue to official level, arguing in favour of founding schools of commerce in Madrid and the main trading ports in Spain

76 *Código de comercio*, 2–3.

77 Ángel Rojo, "José Bonaparte (1808–1813) y la legislación mercantil e industrial española," *Revista de Derecho mercantil* 143–144 (1977), 121–82. The attempts to put together a commercial code continued in the Cadiz and Trienio Courts, culminating with Cadiz native Pedro Sáinz de Andino (1786–1863), father of the 1829 Code; see Lasso, *Crónica*, 56–62.

78 CM, no. 169 (17-III-1800), 172ff.

79 CM, no. 92 (2-XII-1802) 762–65; no. 78 (29-IX-1803), 637–38.

80 CM, no. 13 (15-II-1808), 98–100.

81 Astigarraga, *Los ilustrados vascos*, 137.

and the colonies.[82] As seen, José del Río, the Spanish Consul in Lisbon, had already submitted a proposal to the Sociedad Matritense to take advantage of the dense network of economic societies with the aim of promoting schools that taught "the solid, methodical and unchanging" principles of trade.[83] What his proposal did was to publicise in Spain the *Estatutos* of the *Aula do Comércio*, founded in Lisbon in 1759 by the *Junta do Comércio* — Board of Trade — through the initiative of the Marquis de Pombal. This was a pioneering experiment in Europe in the official teaching of commercial subjects free of charge.[84] In line with this model, Del Río's training proposal for the Madrid school did rather more than institutionalise the knowledge in trade handbooks. Commercial arithmetic opened a training programme which included accountancy, consular ordinances, customs management, commerce agreements, insurance and economic geography. In short, Del Rio aimed to consolidate a new way of gaining access to the mercantile profession. Once these studies were certified by economic societies, their beneficiaries were to be free to begin trading and to be given preference in public company and customs office management. Although the initiative was very well put together, it never came to fruition; the reasons why are unknown.

The problems may have arisen from a lack of human ability or funding, but they were also undoubtedly due to the fact that economic societies were not the right channel for the project. Informal commerce teaching was carried out under the aegis of the consulates, so it is not surprising that it was these institutions that ended up taking on more formal teaching, particularly when the José de Gálvez's *Reglamento* (1778) stipulated that all ports that had been authorised for free trade should have consulates. From the 1780s onwards, a collection of ordinances and laws (1785, 1797 and 1803) established the obligation to found schools of commerce in the consulates.

The period from 1787 to 1808 was therefore the first stage in the history of the teaching of commerce.[85] Its framework was a series of ports where there was traditionally a consulate and handbooks were produced (Barcelona, Cadiz, Seville, Bilbao and Malaga), although schools were also set up in cities with new

82 Campomanes, *Apéndice*, IV, XI-XII.

83 There is a sizable extract from the report in the Sociedad Matritense, *Memorias*, II, 107–20.

84 Cfr. *Estatutos da Aula do Commercio ordenados por el Rey* (Lisbon: Miguel Rodrigues, 1759); see António Almodovar and Jose Luis Cardoso, "Textbooks and the Teaching of Political Economy in Portugal 1759–1910," in *The Economic Reader. Textbooks, Manuals and the Dissemination of the Economic Sciences During the 19th and Early 20th Centuries*, ed. Massimo Augello and Marco E. L. Guidi (London-New York: Routledge, 2012), 189ff.

85 There is an overview in Agustín Escolano, *Educación y economía en la España ilustrada* (Madrid: Ministerio de Educación y ciencia, 1988), 129–50.

consulates (Santander).[86] The first commerce teachers in the history of Spain were appointed, Joaquín Riquelme in Cadiz, and Francisco Alsina in Barcelona. The first programmes for this institutionalised teaching were also established, the most noteworthy being at the *Colegio de San Telmo* in Seville (1786), which was intended to be the model for schools created in free trade ports.[87] The curriculum was aimed at two hundred maritime pilots and focused on mathematics and commercial arithmetic. The programmes in Malaga (1802) and Bilbao (1804) were broader and covered accountancy and a set of subjects that included insurance, law, consular ordinances, commercial geography and trade agreements; the history of trade was also taught in Bilbao, to demonstrate its "usefulness."[88] The Santander school added trade policy and business ethics. In Cadiz, meanwhile, training was organised into three chairs: commercial arithmetic, commercial geography and history, and trade theory with mercantile law.[89] In spite of being very well thought-out, not one of these courses of study was continued. The problems were not only tangible (lack of qualified teachers, funding and premises); the influence of established merchants' corporate resistance to an access route into their profession over which they had no control must also have been a factor.

The handbooks created by these emerging schools did not differ greatly from earlier publications. Carratalá, a mathematics teacher, devised his book (1799) in Cadiz in a context of "huge growth" in enrolments in arithmetic and geometry.[90] Characterised by its highly practical nature, it was suitable for local trading usages and included a useful book devoted to foreign exchange rates. Another, written by Narciso Herranz (1790), a literacy teacher in Madrid, also concerned basic mathematics and was even more specialised on

86 There was a further group of failed initiatives, which highlight the effervescent spirit that typified these years: for example, in 1785 a private citizen from Cadiz made an application to Ministro Lerena to promote "board for political and commercial lectures" there, which would draw up a treatise on commerce or a supplement to the Savary's *Dictionnaire*, among other things (ASM, bundle 73–7); the request from a member of the *Matritense* a year later to print a text entitled *Escuela de comerciantes* (ASM, bundle 83–5); the 1786 application to create a school devoted to the "main elements of trade" in Valencia (AHN, *Estado*, bundle 3.188–377); and another similar application to Floridablanca from Barcelona a year later (AHN, *Estado*, bundle 2.927–302). In 1787 the *Matritense* stopped a project aimed at founding an "academic school for commerce and language" (ASM, bundle 91–3).

87 *Ordenanzas para el Real Colegio de San Telmo de Sevilla* (Madrid: Viuda de Ibarra, 1786), 2.

88 Guiard, *Historia*, II, 866–71.

89 CM, no. 78 (29-IX-1803), 637–38.

90 Esteban Carratalá, *Aplicación de la aritmética a las operaciones más usuales del comercio, según la práctica y uso de esta plaza de Cádiz* (Cadiz: Juan Jiménez, 1799).

foreign currency equivalences.[91] Although the 1798 book by presbyter and ex-mathematics teacher in Paris Juan Gerard was the simplest,[92] it was repeatedly chosen by the CM to be reviewed on the basis of its excellent didactic qualities. At the same time, it was disseminated throughout the Spanish geography and could thus become an instrument to homogenize the teaching of commercial arithmetic.

The most interesting handbooks were undoubtedly those produced in Catalonia. The main figure in this sphere was Manuel Poy y Comes,[93] and his experience provides a good account of a process that was repeated elsewhere. A latin and literacy teacher, he was authorised to open a free public school by Barcelona Council. With the support of a high court judge, he began to teach commercial arithmetic and in 1787–1788 the court opened a young people's school for him, which eventually held public examinations: "I saw myself with over 200 listeners [...] most of them were merchants and craftsmen and there were also several philosophy and theology students." In 1790 he presented the Council with a plan for regulating elementary education in Catalonia, thus supporting a process of modernisation which connected with the aspirations of enlightened bishop José Climent. His three commercial arithmetic handbooks were devised together with the Barcelona Board of Trade for use in teaching; he was also assisted by one of the city's merchants, Antonio Buenaventura Gassó. In the first, *Elementos de aritmética* (1786), Poy presented a basic course on trade in which there was a better balance between theory and practice than in user handbooks: some contain "dazzling speculation and few practical examples" and in others "the north of speculative science is lacking."[94] The *Llave aritmética y algebraica* (1790) was written in the form of a dialogue and aimed to reinvent teaching texts to some extent. Together with the usual concepts and applications of arithmetic, Poy included long extracts on the monetary history and legislation of eighteenth century Spain. In several chapters he proposed popularised economic ideas that fitted perfectly with Board of Trade ideology.[95] In his discussion of "Exchange, balance and bills," Poy defended protectionism: he

---

91 Diego Narciso Herranz y Quirós, *Aritmética pura y comercial* (Madrid: Benito Cano, 1790).

92 Juan Gerard, *Tratado completo de aritmética, o método para aprender a contar por principios* (Madrid: Imprenta de Vega y Compañía, 1798).

93 Jaume Carrera, *La enseñanza profesional en Barcelona en los siglos XVIII y XIX* (Barcelona: Bosch, 1958), 79–83.

94 Manuel Poy y Comes, *Elementos de aritmética y álgebra, para la instrucción de la juventud* (Barcelona: Francisco Suriá y Burgada, 1786), Advertencia, unpaginated.

95 Manuel Poy y Comes, *Llave aritmética y algebraica* (Barcelona: Francisco Suriá y Burgada, 1790), 140ff., 197ff., 206ff.

advocated using not exchange policy but tariffs instead taxing imports and subsidising exports. The "Balance of Payments" chapter echoed Hume in the sense that the state of the balance and the flow of money depended on a country's level of industry. Finally, in a chapter on "bankers," Hume's ideas regarding *doux commerce* and his analysis of the effects of increases in currency on the real economy emerged once again. Poy's handbooks were not an isolated case, however; Gassó's book on "exchanges, balance, bankers and bills," which circulated unpublished in teaching environments in Barcelona, had a similar profile.[96] Another handbook that was undoubtedly very close in spirit was written by Miguel Solá. A numeracy teacher and headmaster of a private school, Sola's work was written in the form of a dialogue and included a chapter devoted to accountancy, although, the real reason for its unique nature lay in the last chapter. Within the framework of Barcelona's intense trading experience, Solá defended the social legitimacy of all types of trade,[97] and recommended reading Serionne; Coyer's *noblesse commerçante* also left a clear mark on his book. In short, the emergence of a first generation of professional commerce teachers and the publication of handbooks with more diverse contents can be seen more clearly in Barcelona than in any other city in Spain; logically, since it was one of the most important Spanish's commercial port. However, any assessment of these changes needs to take into account the arrival in Spain of news of experiences of teaching commerce, not only from France and Portugal, but also from the successful experiment in Flemish schools, specifically in Ghent.[98]

7 Final Remarks

When the Peninsula War broke out in 1808, the only city where schools of commerce remained active was Barcelona; all other such activities in the country having ceased. Nonetheless, their value should not be underestimated as they laid the foundations for a new stage. It began in 1815 and was linked to the first in many ways by Jovellanos and Quintana. In 1798 and 1808 Jovellanos advocated including the teaching of subjects related to the "mercantile profession" in parallel with Political or Civil Economy during intermediate and university

96 Poy, *Llave*, 240ff.

97 Miguel Solá, *Aritmética teórico-práctica mercantil dispuesta en forma de diálogo* (Barcelona: Compañía Jordi, Roca y Gaspar, 1801), 290, 399–406.

98 Vid. "Plan de una escuela de comercio," in *Código de comercio*, I-XXVII. His author was the merchant of Lyon Vital-Roux.

education.[99] However, it was the Liberal Manuel José Quintana who finally gave the legacy of the Enlightenment legislative shape. His *Proyecto sobre el arreglo de la enseñanza pública* (1813) argued that the teaching of commerce should be undertaken, like all "noble" subjects, in colleges especially set up for that purpose.[100] The *Reglamento General de la Instrucción Pública* (1821), passed by the *Cortes* of the *Trienio Liberal* (1820–1823), finally established Special Schools of commerce in places that had spearheaded the provision of handbooks and teaching for merchants in previous decades (Madrid, Cadiz, Malaga, Alicante, Barcelona, La Corunna, Bilbao and Santander, together with fourteen more overseas). This benchmark was initially erased by Fernando VII's absolutist policies, but was later recovered by Liberal sectors, in whose hands chairs of commerce generally flourished. Trade was no longer considered a lesser art, the object of discrimination and suspicion, but had been raised to the same level as the "noble" arts. From traders' desks and private schools led by humble teachers it had gone on to nourish public chairs at university level.

99 Gaspar Melchor de Jovellanos, "Plan para la educación de la nobleza y las clases pudientes" (1798), in *Obras de Don Gaspar Melchor de Jovellanos* (BAE, vol. LXXXVII), ed. Miguel Artola (Madrid: 1956), ch. XIV, and "Bases para la formación de un plan de educación pública" (1808), in *Obras publicadas e inéditas de G. M. Jovellanos* (BAE, vol. XLVI), ed. Cándido Nocedal (Madrid: Rivadeneyra, 1858), 272–73.

100 Manuel José Quintana, "Informe de la Junta creada por la Regencia para proponer los medios de proceder al arreglo de los diversos ramos de la instrucción pública" (1813), in *Obras completas del Excmo. Sr. D. Manuel José Quintana* (Madrid: M. Rivadeneyra, 1852), 175–91.

CHAPTER 10

The Specialised Economics Press

The Correo Mercantil (*1792–1808*) *and the* Semanario de Agricultura (*1797–1808*)

1 Introduction: Board of Trade and the Official Statistics Agency

Criticism of the Board of Trade intensified during the last thirty or so years of the eighteenth century. Ward's *Proyecto Económico*, written in 1762 and published in 1779, bemoaned the fact that after decades of activity the Board was a mere dispute settlement court.[1] However, it was also clear that the Board urgently needed to become a centralised agency for economic growth, which could be established in different cities via the trade consulates. This was proved by the example of more developed countries, not only England and Holland, but also other absolute monarchies like France, whose network of mayors and inspectors had been a powerful machine for the growth of trade and manufacturing since the beginning of the century.[2] Criticism of the Board probably had a significant impact: Ward, an Irishman, was a renowned expert on economic issues who had been recruited by Fernando VI and had served as secretary of the Board of Trade. Demands for the Board to be granted its own powers continued. In 1768 Romá y Rosell proposed grouping together the powers of the bodies responsible for the Indies, the Navy, trade and taxes related to trade diplomacy, customs management and international treaty drafting, economic statistics and trade translations and dictionaries into a single organisation.[3] As these suggestions came from someone with close links to the Barcelona Board of Trade, established as an institution only five years previously, they carried a good deal of weight.

Requests for the Board of Trade to be elevated to a higher level within the Bourbon government structure could not be ignored either. Pedro Pérez Valiente, a prestigious Board member, had clashed with the Council of Castile in 1766 over his arguments in support of forming a new Supreme Board of Trade,[4] an idea that was finally given shape a few years later by Juan Antonio de los

1 Ward, *Proyecto económico*, 149–52.
2 Minard, *La fortune*, 212–24.
3 Romá, *Las señales*, 244–59.
4 Barrenechea, "Prólogo," LX-LXI.

 | DOI:10.1163/9789004442894_012

Heros (1725–1780) and his nephew Juan Francisco de los Heros (1749–1812). Natives of Biscay, both men had risen to management positions in the Five Major Guilds of Madrid, overseeing manufacturing, financial and wholesale trade interests. Juan Antonio was in fact the architect of the new direction taken by the institution in the decisive phase after 1752 during which the different guild branches were unified. Meanwhile, with his uncle's support, Juan Francisco successfully combined his work at the Five Guilds with a brilliant career in the government, holding several posts including Board of Trade prosecutor from 1784–1795. In 1775 the two men wrote the *Discursos sobre el comercio* in defence of the Five Guilds, which was published in 1790. This lengthy work revolved around the idea that trade required exclusive treatment within the national government. Their arguments referred back to 1625, when the first Board of Trade was created in Spain.[5] However, the reforms undertaken since then had failed to produce a real specialised body for trade management, and consequently the country desperately needed a new institution: the Supreme Council of Trade, Agriculture, Population, Factories and Arts.[6] Once again Spain looked to countries like Great Britain and France for an example, evoking authors such as Savary, Serionne and especially Bielfeld, whose extensive recommendations in this respect had been circulating in the Spanish Enlightenment since their translation by the journalist Nifo in 1763 and certainly influenced *Discursos sobre el comercio*. Juan Francisco de los Heros also provided a detailed programme for the long-awaited Supreme Council. This institution should both centralise statistical information and be at the forefront of promoting all national economic sectors, including foreign trade. In De los Heros' words, the aim was to prevent "the cruel and capital epidemic of the powers with which the court is continually oppressed, more interesting to the true happiness of the state and the nation [the Board of Trade]."[7] But, at the same time, resolve complaints raised by enlightened individuals such as Tomás de Iriarte and Eugenio Larruga about the fact that the Board *ministers* came from the Councils instead of the world of trade; as a result they lacked proper training and did not give their work the priority it deserved. De los Heros proposed granting the Supreme Council exclusive jurisdiction and organising it into two sections, one devoted to justice and the other to economic growth. The number of members should be increased, with the aim of embedding the creators of economic growth into the management of the new body: directors of royal

5 Juan Francisco de los Heros, *Discursos sobre el comercio* (1790; Madrid: Banco Bilbao Vizcaya, 1989), 233.

6 Heros, *Discursos sobre el comercio*, 172–252.

7 Cited by Barrenechea, "Prólogo," LXI; in the same vein, see Larruga, *Historia*, I, sheets 3, 285.

factories, members of the Five Guilds and representatives of trade consulates, including those in Mexico and Lima. In this way the Supreme Council would become the trade professionals' gateway into central government. The *Discursos* evoked authors who supported activating changes in the political management of trade — albeit with patchy criteria — such as Forbonnais, Davenant and Coyer, whose defence of the *nobleza comerciante* was one of the work's cross-cutting themes.

It may be no coincidence that the *Discursos* were published in 1790 when Juan Francisco de los Heros was Board of Trade prosecutor, and that criticisms of the Board intensified rather than falling away. In 1783 Cabarrús, the French financier and founder of the Bank of San Carlos, attacked the Board for being unrepresentative and over-zealous where regulation was concerned. Probably inspired by De los Heros, Cabarrús revived the idea of forming a Supreme Council for Trade, managed by 16 merchants and oriented to honouring mercantile activity by means of "stimulating interest and honour," simplifying legal procedures and centralising statistical information.[8] Campomanes took a still more devastating approach: in keeping with his relentless radical opposition to the Board of Trade, he wrote a report in 1790 that was not only full of reproaches but maintained that it was not a "suitable tribunal" as its members paid "accidental" attention to trade, trespassed in disputes that belonged in the sphere of ordinary justice and were incapable of bringing together the information necessary to lead Spanish trade.[9] Far from being rhetorical, the demands for promoting fundamental changes in the Board were a reflection of the serious problems facing Spain at the end of the century. The irreversible deterioration of public finances had coincided with the end of a long, mainly agricultural, growth cycle based on crop expansion, low levels of mechanisation and certain ancestral uses of agricultural land; the outcome was a pressing need for an intensive system of agriculture to be implemented and for economic growth in Spain to be taken over by industry and commerce.

However, the criticism from these notable representatives of the Spanish Enlightenment had no decisive effects: the Board of Trade was never reformed. This was a symptom of the routines of power preventing a change in the Spanish government that responded without reservation to the challenge that trade was acting de facto as one of the essential forces in politics. Nonetheless, a certain pragmatism eventually imposed itself, as it tended to during

8 AHN, *Estado*, bundle 2.944–434.

9 FUE, AC, 20–11.

the Spanish Enlightenment, and from the 1780s changes — hidden at first but more manifest later on — were gradually wrought in the Board of Trade's structure and representativeness, resulting in a substantial overhaul of its profile. This was partly due to the appointment of eminent scientists as *ministers*, as well as members of the Sociedad Matritense — Jovellanos, Sixto de Espinosa, Iriarte and Guevara Vasconcelos — and publishers who were familiar with political economy — Barberi, Larruga and Suárez y Núñez —. However, the really decisive changes emerged when Lerena was Treasury Minister, and in 1786 the Balance of Trade Office, the first official statistics agency in Spain, was created. It was based on French models established a few years earlier by Necker and Calonne and finally took shape between 1792 and 1795, largely owing to pressure from Juan Francisco de los Heros and Juan Bautista Virio for a foreign trade registration agency that would facilitate the creation of balance of payments records.[10] In fact, the new Office's function was twofold. Firstly, it solved the problem of the lack of an official statistics agency, an issue that was influenced not only by the Bourbon reform programmes that began in 1718 with the aim of gathering information about the country's economic and demographic structure, but also by the positive reception in Spain to political arithmetic since the 1760s. As the century went by with no conclusive results, the lack of a statistics agency was perceived as an impediment to Spanish development, as it prevented the design of more efficient economic policies.[11] Secondly, the Office bolstered another oft-repeated demand from enlightened sectors: the establishing of a transparency policy for economic and financial issues. In fact, the first public budgets in Spanish history were published while Lerena was minister, following Necker's *Compte rendu* (1781).[12]

The Balance of Trade Office was very soon incorporated into more ambitious government agencies.[13] In 1797 the little-known *Junta de Comercio y Navegación* — Board of Trade and Shipping — was formed, some of whose members also sat on the Board of Trade. In the same year, informed by a committee that included Cabarrús, Iriarte and Iranda,[14] Secretary of State Godoy created the *Dirección de Fomento o Departamento de Fomento General del Reino* — Development Authority or the Department of General Development for the Country —, which initially came under the authority of the Secretary of

10 AHN, *Estado*, bundle 2.923–476.
11 See Sempere's *Biblioteca española*, I, 1–36.
12 Astigarraga, "La traduction au service de la Politique."
13 Molas, "Hombres de leyes," 18ff.
14 La Parra, *Manuel Godoy*, 180.

State and then of the Treasury.[15] The new agency, whose first head was Juan Bautista Virio, was aimed at correcting the Board of Trade's traditional failings. Its purpose was to collect information obtained by diplomatic representatives and mayors, with a view to orienting economic policy. From 1795 all these changes were transferred to the Board of Trade, which in the same year began to recruit staff from the Balance Office, the Mines Directorate, the Mint and the Machines Office, who acquired more weight among the seventeen *ministers*. Finally, in 1802 the Balance Office and the *Dirección de Fomento* merged into a new agency, which was divided into two sections — foreign trade statistics and population and domestic production — headed by Board of Trade members.

The outcome of this circuitous process was that Spain was finally equipped with a centralised agency for statistics and economic growth albeit rather late in the day. Moreover, it had a relatively professionalised profile: as mentioned previously, Lorenzo Normante and other teachers at the Chair of Civil Economy of Saragossa were employed there. A range of official economics studies were immediately activated within its framework, not only related to budgets and trade balances but also population censuses (1797), art and manufacturing censuses (1799), international foreign trade treaties and reference works on the Treasury, the Spanish government and trade, including the series of dictionaries already discussed.[16] In addition, the agency instigated the rebirth of the Spanish press after the closure of its leading titles in 1791 as a result of Floridablanca's "terror" of the revolutionary events in France. The *Correo Mercantil* (CM) and the *Semanario de Agricultura* (SAP) were published from 1792 and 1797, respectively, under its aegis; these two publications are regarded as being among the most brilliant of the "golden age" of Spanish press for various reasons. The first is their consistency and the fact that, like *Memorial literario,* they had relatively long lifespans, which only ended in 1808. The second is that together they were the most important means in Spain of spreading news about the useful arts of the Enlightenment, of which the European press provided essential coverage.[17] Finally, the special commitment to topics related to trade and agriculture means that they can be identified with the first steps of professional journalists specialising in economics issues in the country.

15 AHN, *Estado*, bundle 3.436–12.

16 See ch. V.

17 Mokyr, *The Enlightened Economy*, 40ff.

2 The *Correo Mercantil de España y sus Indias* (1792–1808)

The CM was founded in 1792 on the initiative of lawyer and publisher Diego Gallard, who was assisted during the first year by Eugenio Larruga.[18] The publication's history can be divided into three main stages: during the first it was under Ministry of Finance auspices and supervision (1792–1795), after which it was linked to the Balance of Payments Office and official tutelage increased (1795–1799), before it finally returned to Gallard's hands (1799–1808). The CM retained its official character throughout these three phases, and although initially open to readers' contributions it mainly carried Ministry of Finance, consular and Board of Trade news, while also covering economic societies to a lesser extent.[19] These institutions all helped to increase its circulation and subscribers. First sold only in Madrid, it soon began to arrive in the main provincial capitals as well as Mexico, Lima, Veracruz and other colonial enclaves. Its distribution was almost entirely urban, with a token presence in rural areas,[20] and its readers included politicians and government officials as well as other members of the middle classes, first and foremost merchants but also nobles and members of the military. While most of its readers were in mainland Spain, one of the publication's unique features was its imperial dimension; it circulated widely in the colonial world and was an example to the developing journalism there. From the very first issues it acted as the main loudspeaker for the entire Spanish press for news published first in Mexico and Havana, then Buenos Aires and Lima and finally Guatemala.

The CM came out every fortnight and had three permanent sections devoted to agriculture, the arts, trade and another covering colonial trade (volume of traffic, ports, etc.), and information on crops, prices and exchange rates. Although its core topic was trade, the publication also reported on mercantile activities and traffic and the sciences made possible by trade. Its initial prospectus expressed interest in reporting news about statistics, the history of trade, the useful arts, legislation and public law, as well as converting theoretical information into practical guidelines. The CM's role in the modernisation of knowledge aimed at merchants has already been discussed.[21] The paper used book reviews, memoirs and articles from the foreign press in a similar way to

18 On the CM, see Enciso, *Prensa económica*.

19 Part of this material appeared in the *Almanak Mercantil* (1795–1808), the annual volume that Gallard published for fourteen years as a complement to the CM; see ch. 9 below.

20 Larriba, *El público*, 74–78.

21 See ch. 9 below.

disseminate up-to-date information, serving merchants as well as policy makers and political authorities.

Although the CM always retained its original internal structure, it went through two distinct stages in terms of content. The turning point came in 1799, when Gallard resigned from his position at the Balance of Payments Office and resumed his place at the head of the publication. By this point the *Semanario de Agricultura* had begun to publicise authors (Franklin, Chaptal, Sinclair, Parmentier, Rumford, Fabbroni and Young) and to carry articles on agricultural topics and the arts (rejection of fallow land, common land and the Mesta and support for enclosures and the mechanisation of agricultural work, etc.) that were already covered by the CM, which was then free to increase the amount of space it devoted to trade and open up unreservedly to theoretical discussions. A feature that clearly distinguished this stage from the first was thus established; the CM barely touched on theoretical issues at the beginning, probably because of Larruga's strong influence on the publication's identity: its inductive approach and the inclusion of plentiful case studies brought its profile closer to Larruga's *Memorias políticas y económicas* (1787–1800, 45 vols.). Between 1792 and 1798 the CM published innumerable reports from all over Spain, endorsed by guilds, companies with links to the Board of Trade, trade consulates — the consulate in Galicia was especially active — and individual producers, detailing the structure of different industrial and trade sectors. The paper thus placed itself at the service of the creation of a market that included not only peninsular Spain, but also the empire, always on the basis of maintaining colonial monopoly. The reports mainly focussed on the textile industry but also covered other basic goods exported from Spain to its enclaves across the Atlantic, such as spirits, paper, iron and soap. The reports laid bare the factors affecting competitiveness in the chosen sectors, thus creating a kind of x-ray of the production structure in Spain. The CM fulfilled many social functions by showing this wide range of case studies. Firstly, it created a stable information network between Spain and the colonies, and secondly it encouraged emulation among its readers: farm owners and tenant farmers, on one hand; merchants, "entrepreneurs" and "capitalists," on the other; and, finally, policy makers. The third was an eminently educational task: the CM explained how the institutions of the trading economy worked: the market, the pricing system, public granaries and finally trusts, while the fourth outlined the publication's initiatives. The CM operated first and foremost as an instrument for homogenising weights, measures, coins and guild ordinances and for creating a single imperial market, organised around an extensive road and canal network and a broad naval base. At the same time, it carried a great deal of propaganda in support of a development model that balanced agriculture and industry. While the first could not flourish without the second, industry could only thrive under a regime of customs protectionism; instead, in the domestic market the general rule should be the free trade: arguments against indiscriminate exclusive privileges, guilds, inland customs barriers, monopolies, corporate companies and technological stagnation proliferated in its pages: the CM was the first Spanish publication to carry news of the steam engine in December 1794.[22]

During its second phase, which began in 1799, theoretical and academic content increased, adopting its readers' familiarisation with "the good principles of political economy" as a key objective.[23] The translation of material from a wide range of sources, overwhelmingly from France, redoubled during this period. Extracts from treatises, reviews and press articles — the *Journal de Paris* was one of its most important sources — rubbed shoulders with news about parliamentary debates and reports from the chambers of commerce and the *Conservatoire des Arts et Métiers* in Paris, which had previously been rare in the Spanish press. The CM reported on texts devoted to the history of travel and trade and economic geography, aiming to facilitate Spanish trade's penetration of new markets; one of these was the new Republic of the United States of America, which was portrayed as a strong competitor to European powers. However, what really distinguished the CM was its work showcasing economic literature, especially post-Smithian, at the turn of the century. The benchmark for this educational task was theoretical plurality. The fact that the publication was official did not mean that it was used as a tool for ideological indoctrination but rather to encourage the pluralism that emerged in its pages as a factor for forming "opinion." Extracts from Smith (1792), Sinclair (1796, 1801), Morellet (1799), Saint Aubin (1799, 1800, 1802), Verri (1800), Diannyère (1800), Guiraudet (1800), Forbonnais (1800), Herrenschwand (1800), Roederer (1800), Young (1801), Saint Clair (1801), Canard (1802), Garnier (1802), Page (1802), Sismondi (1803), Micoud d'Umons (1803), Colquhoun (1807) and Spence (1808) were reviewed or inserted. Numerous passages from Say were also published from 1804 to 1808, anticipated the work's subsequent huge success. The publication's applied aspect was covered by information about public finance and monetary issues and the debate surrounding taxation structure and the public debt repeatedly posed alternatives to the positions held by Smith and the Physiocrats. The importance of theory was particularly clear in numerous news items covering the legislative modernisation of the French

22 CM, no. 232 (29-12-1794), 826–28.

23 CM, no. 9 (1-11-1808), 54.

banking system and the accompanying debates. Authors such as J. H. Manières (1801), A. N. Isnard (1801), St. Aubin (1801), J. C. Simonne (1804) and Monbrion (1806) were given large amounts of space in the publication, which kept its readers informed about details of changes in legislation and the parliamentary disputes in France regarding the banking laws to tackle the monopoly on banknote issue.

Despite the profusion of articles on post-Smithian economics, the CM was a long way from embracing doctrinaire liberalism. Physiocratic ideas were introduced through authors such as Morellet and Young, but the *économistes* were repeatedly refuted, mainly because the publication continued its unwavering support for a development model that balanced agriculture and industry. The CM looked to the British model, whose example would enable a "permanent national" trade system to be created in Spain. Protectionism again emerged as a cornerstone in the publication's second phase. From 1802 onwards the CM published every detail of the intense debate in France between the pro-free trade *laissez faire* economists and the protectionists or prohibitionists, although it did show a clear tendency to prefer clearly these last two;[24] customs barriers were essential to protect "infant industry" and domestic employment, as well as to prevent any repetition of the dire effects on France of its free trade agreement with Great Britain (1786).[25] The approach of replacing imports with national goods was everywhere, although luxury goods posed a problem as they required capital and specialised craftsmen, which Spain lacked. The challenge was to increase self-sufficiency in consumer staples both in the country itself and the colonies, especially labour-intensive goods and those using local raw materials.[26] Moreover, if there was one factor that had held back economic growth in Spain it was the lack of active public policies. It is highly significant that in 1808 the British economy should still be identified as one rooted in intervention, but also whose policies had been properly applied.[27] Wise policy should intertwine "favour" with "freedom," as was the case in Britain,"[28] and while the principle of competition was the general rule, there had "to be limits on its application, however right it was in theory."[29] The programme defended in the CM in 1808, shortly before it was closed down, advocated implementing freedom of trade, consumption and manufacture, limiting impediments to

24 See, for example, CM, no. 2 (4-I-1806), 10–12; no. 3 (7-I-1806), 19–20.
25 CM, no. 10 (3-II-1806), 74–76.
26 CM, no. 10 (4-II-1808), 74–78.
27 Reinert, *Translating Empire*, 6–8.
28 CM, no. 45 (6-VI-1808), 354–57.
29 CM, no. 6 (20-I-1806), 42.

growth and the submission of the guilds and all kinds of corporations, so that economic activity reverted to the hands of private "entrepreneurs." However, this was accompanied by a robust set of state interventions including selective tax reductions, control of grain exports, subsidies for the production and export of industrial goods, the creation of publically-owned factories, and trade consulate-founded applied art schools. In short, these interventions represented limitations to the principle of free competition in the internal market. The "freedom" and "favour" policy thus established direct links with the Spanish Enlightenment's industrial programme; in short, this led to the scheme's modernisation, including aspects backed by leading lights with connections to the Board of Trade (Uztáriz, Argumosa, Ward, Barberi and Larruga).

3 The *Semanario de Agricultura y Artes dirigido a los párrocos* (1797–1808)

The CM's rapid establishment prompted the publication of the first Spanish periodical devoted solely to agriculture: the *Semanario de agricultura y artes dirigido a los párrocos* (SAP),[30] which was designed in the *Dirección de Fomento* at Manuel Godoy's initiative. Godoy gave Virio the task of devising a plan for economic and political education in 1796.[31] Virio proposed creating a weekly publication, which, with help from Juan Antonio Melón (1758–1743),[32] soon took shape as the SAP. Melón had trained as a priest and held a doctorate in Theology from the University of Salamanca. When recruited by Virio, he was firmly embedded in the Bourbon government, for whom he had previously worked on the creation of a prestigious collection of classical Latin authors. In fact, it was Melón who was really responsible for producing the SAP, as Virio was appointed head of the *Dirección de Fomento* in May 1797, five months after the first issue appeared.

The SAP was mainly aimed at rural parish priests. The publication's main objective was to enlist their help to create an "opinion" that was favourable to agricultural innovations in these areas. Enlightenment culture had already

30 There are two detailed studies on the history of this publication: Fernando Díez Rodríguez, *Prensa agraria en la España de la Ilustración. El Semanario de agricultura y artes dirigido a los párrocos (1797–1808)* (Madrid: Ministerio de Agricultura, 1980); Larriba and Dufour, *El Semanario de agricultura*, 9–61.

31 AHN, *Estado*, bundle 3.242–1.

32 Board of Commerce chemist Domingo García Fernández (1759–1829) also participated in the creation of the SAP.

permeated towns and cities to a reasonable degree, but it was not easy to reach rural parts, which were generally poor, isolated and with a scattered and illiterate populace. Although the SAP prospectus evoked the work parish priests did in such settings in Protestant countries, its purpose in fact already formed part of the Spanish Enlightenment mainstream. Campomanes, Jovellanos, Díaz Valdés and Griselini, whose essay Josefa Amar y Borbón had translated in 1784 under the auspices of the Aragon Society, advocated converting parish priests into culture and education mediators, and the SAP, whose profile was undeniably semi-official, gave shape to this idea. Although the journal eventually operated independently from the *Dirección de Fomento*, it received exceptional support from Godoy.[33] The first issue of the *Semanario* was advertised in the main Spanish newspapers of the day, and this was accompanied by an unusually large print run of 23.000 copies of the prospectus, which was distributed among prelates and mayors in Spain and the Indies. A large number of copies — around 3.000 — of the first few issues were also printed. The government aimed to create a stable readership, recruited not only from among churchmen but also state employees in local councils, courts, consulates and economic societies. The publication's official nature became clearer in 1805; partly as a result of financial problems, funding and management passed into the hands of the Madrid Botanical Garden. It became the Botanic Garden's official mouthpiece, which strengthened its profile as a science weekly, and published the lectures on botany, agriculture and the rural economy given by scientists working there, including Francisco Antonio Zea (1776–1822), Simón Rojas (1777–1827) and the Boutelou brothers, Claudio and Esteban.

However, the SA failed to establish the hoped-for broad stable readership. Unlike the CM, it mainly took root in non-urban settings, in sparsely populated towns and villages in inland regions such as Aragon and Extremadura, places with archaic agriculture, weak industry and rudimentary trade. Institutions made up a significant proportion of subscribers, and where the Church was concerned, it was the authorities that predominated rather than the parish clergy.[34] The first issues of the SAP were read out in public to parishioners, doubtlessly to encourage emulation,[35] but this did little to increase the number of readers, and there were other major handicaps such as the high subscription price and the publication's rather too specialised profile. In spite of the SAP's prevailing rhetoric of mistrusting speculative writing, the publication disseminated a utilitarian culture that agricultural labourers found difficult to

33 La Parra, *Manuel Godoy*, 183.

34 Larriba, *El público*, 78–81.

35 See, e.g., SAP, no. 21 (25-V-1797), 336; no. 23 (8-VI-1797), 368.

understand. Nonetheless, it made commendable efforts to broaden its readership: from 1801 it began to pay special attention to women, carrying chemistry and botany compendia and news about women's associations to combat begging.[36] However, the lack of readers caused endemic financial problems and other ambitious original objectives were never entirely fulfilled. As its initial prospectus explained, the SAP aspired to become a powerful focus for agricultural development, distributing new seeds, complementing economic societies, promoting a selected library on agricultural matters and establishing a new scientific vocabulary for agriculture.

Always open to readers' contributions, the SAP carried news from all over Spain and the two Spanish archipelagos — the Balearics and the Canary Islands —, although items from Spanish America were few and far between. The paper viewed itself as a real showcase for Spain's great agricultural diversity, disseminating news of local agricultural improvements on a national scale. Some regions were particularly well-represented; one of these was Aragon, whose local economics society and its pioneering Agriculture Chair supplied a great deal of information. This geographical diversity also had an international dimension and the SAP published news and books reviews not only from across the entire European spectrum, but also concerning agriculture in China, the French colonies and the ancient Arab world, including extensive extracts from Abu Zacharia's renowned treatise on agriculture (1803). This was aided by the fact that, unlike the CM with its rigid format, the SAP was a real *vade mecum* of different ways of popularising knowledge, where dialogues and primers mingled with dictionaries and almanacs.

The newspaper also produced excellent translations of articles from foreign publications, usually through the medium of French — Young's *Annals of Agriculture*, Rozier's *Journal de Physique*, Tessier's *Annales de l'agriculture française* or the *Bibliothèque britannique* —. It redoubled the information coming from European agricultural societies, not only from the pioneers in Dublin and Paris, but also from others in France and the centre of Europe (Saxony, Westphalia and Luxemburg). Information on the uses of agricultural land in the prosperous English counties of Suffolk and Norfolk was supplied via the Bath and Sussex societies.[37] Guided by Young and Sinclair, it also carried news from the Royal Society in London, inviting readers to follow its example and purchase pieces of land close to large urban centres to promote agricultural experiences.[38] The

36 On the emergence of the women's public around the Spanish press, see Bolufer, "*Espectadores* y lectoras," 23–57.

37 SAP, no. 87 (30-VIII-1798), 129–39; no. 88 (6-IX-1798), 145–56.

38 SAP, no. 224 (16-IV-1800), 233–39.

series of authors that were reviewed or translated included agronomists like Chaptal, Rozier, Tillet, Cadet de Vaux, Kirwan, Tessier, Daubenton, Valmont de Bomare, Fabbroni and, especially, Young. It was also the spokesperson for the new generation of Spanish scientists and agronomists such as the Boutelou brothers, Álvarez Guerra, Celestino Mutis (1732–1808) and Ignacio de Asso (1742–1814). Under their influence, interest in the old Castilian agricultural customs declined even further.

The entire SAP was built around the idea that agriculture took priority over other sectors of the economy, especially industry. It was the country's chief source of wealth and thus merited priority attention in public policy, as well as possessing moral benefits vis-à-vis other sectors, protecting the social virtues that underpinned good habits.[39] The defence of the simple, healthy and industrious life was presented as linked to the rejection of phenomena that were inherent to commercial society, such as luxury, big cities and indebtedness. It is not surprising that the SA should have published numerous extracts from Benjamin Franklin's works, which illustrated perfectly the unique union of the new Enlightenment ideas and the old virtues of frugality, self-restraint and thrift.[40] These were fostered not only by agriculture itself, but also by a suitable combination of this and domestic rural industry, the model of industry endorsed in the SAP. The journal abounded with articles devoted to hemp, linen and other materials that lent themselves to cottage industries in which families worked together at home, had little capital, and the priority of agricultural work was respected. There is a sharp contrast between these articles and pieces on other industrial sectors; the SAP dealt with wool manufacture only cursorily, supporting the consumption of Spanish goods and showing an attitude of open mistrust towards luxury articles, trading companies and "large factories."

Agriculture was presented as a science, reliant on veterinary science, natural sciences, chemistry and physics, to which the SA also gave centre stage.[41] As a science, agriculture required a well-regulated education system, and the SAP constantly carried favourable publicity for schools of rural economics, agriculture chairs and agrarian societies, praising these institutions while at the same time insisting that they should promote practical knowledge. The examples given cut across the entire Spanish and European spectrum; where Spain was concerned, the Workers Mutual Society and the Agriculture Chair of Saragossa (1784), both founded by the Aragon Society, were held up as models from

39 SAP, see, e.g., no. 33 (17-VIII-1797), 94–100.
40 SAP, see, e.g., no. 66 (5-IV-1798), 217–21.
41 There is a quantified analysis of the topics in the SAP in Díez, *Prensa agraria*, 65ff.

the very beginning.[42] However, close attention was also paid to topics such as public health and hygiene — the journal carried the news of the invention of vaccinations in the early nineteenth century, the drafting of the French Rural Code and education, above and beyond strictly agricultural subjects — news on Catherine the Great's education reform, devised by Ivan I. Betzky.

The most important issue, however, was charity. At the time of the SAP's creation, the pressure of the population on subsistence was becoming a structural problem in Spain, pushing state policy against unemployment and begging into the limelight. The SAP therefore frequently published news about the regulation of Spanish hospices (Vitoria and La Rioja, for example) and it became one of the gateways into the country for works by Rumford, the polymath and ex-soldier from the United States. The first news of these appeared in 1800,[43] at the height of the subsistence crisis, when the Sociedad Matritense published the first translation of his writings.[44] The SAP provided its readers with a very broad spectrum of his ideas and experiences; much of this dealt with the creation of charity boards in Hamburg, London, Verona and other European cities, which ensured that alms were distributed efficiently, centralised collection and were useful for funding public works. More specifically, the money collected was used to convert hospices into centres for learning to manufacture basic textiles under a regime of unrelenting discipline: in Rumford's words, they were "military workhouses." Numerous pages were also devoted to his popular "economy soup;"[45] once again, this was linked to an initiative of the government, which in 1803 had enacted a law stating that economic societies should promote popular dishes of this kind, as the Matritense Society did for the next two years. There were detailed examples, frequently Rumford's own ideas, of how the soups could be introduced in Munich, Geneva and London through public kitchens managed by charity boards. Also included were extracts from his works describing additional strategies for combatting the subsistence crisis through saving fuel and fighting against usury. Finally, there was also space for Rumford's scientific side. The SAP covered his initiatives for mechanics museums and a range of experiments in mechanisation carried out under the aegis of the Royal Institution in London, which he presented as a model to follow.[46]

42 Its history, in the SAP, no. 32 (10-V-1797), 78–82.

43 SAP, no. 160 (23-I-1800), 54–64; no. 161 (30-I-1800), 71–80.

44 Benjamin Thompson Rumford, Count of Rumford, *Ensayos políticos, económicos y filosóficos* (Madrid: Imprenta Real, 1800–1801). The work was translated by Domingo Agüero and it was a partial version of Rumford's *Essais politiques, économiques et philosophiques* (1799–1806, 6 vols.).

45 The first was published in the SAP, no. 165 (27-II-1800), 132–38.

46 SAP, no. 193 (11-IX-1800), 166–76.

However, it was Chaptal's innovations at the *Institut de France* that provided the main reference in this field.[47]

The SAP approached agriculture's role within the economy as a whole through talks and reviews devoted to Lavoisier (1798), Arnould (1801), Bentham (1803) and Smith. The entries taken from the *Wealth of Nations* created a unique reading of this work: they emphasised the notion that agriculture was more productive than industry, the rejection of monopolies, trade privileges and other factors that distorted the trading system and, contrary to Smith, opposed free trade, including free trade in grain with the foreign countries.[48] In any event, most of the publication's articles aimed to support more intensive and mechanised agriculture through providing information on new crops, uses and agricultural techniques. British scientist Arthur Young — "the wisest farmer in Europe"[49] — was the SAP's star turn on these matters. From 1798 and especially after 1801, numerous articles from Young's *Annals of Agriculture* were translated, as well his many travel books describing journeys through rural Europe, particularly those devoted to England (1770–1771) and Ireland (1776–1778). Young pointed an accusing finger at the British government in his writings, arguing that the preference it had long shown towards industry and trade fostered a set of public policies that encouraged "mercantile greed" and led to such harmful consequences as prohibitions, monopolies and other similar *Colbertiste* privileges. Indeed, a "purely mercantile government" was the worst of all,[50] not only encouraging luxury, public debt, war and begging, but also depressing agriculture, the real source of wealth and the cause — not the effect — of the development of industry and trade. British growth was nurtured by the false assumption that industrial competitiveness was achieved thanks to the low price of grain, as this was the main factor regulating wages and therefore the price of goods. However, this only stimulated industrial growth artificially to the detriment of agriculture, preventing capital from flowing to the latter, which was the economic sector that generated the highest returns.[51]

Young's articles in the SAP also informed a significant set of institutional reforms, which had to a large extent brought about both English prosperity and

47 See Elsa Bolado and Lluis Argemi. "Jean Antoine Chaptal: from Chemistry to Political Economy," *The European Journal of the History of Economic Thought* 12, no. 2 (2005): 215–239.

48 The clearest example of this agrarian reading of the *Wealth of Nations* was the translation, in four installments, of the first part of *An Essay of the Best Means of Providing Employment for the People* (1793), written by Irish scientist Samuel Crumpe, which was published in 1802.

49 SAP, no. 217 (26-II-1801), 121.

50 SAP, no. 243 (27-VIII-1801), 130.

51 SAP, no. 244 (3-IX-1801), 154–59.

the relative economic buoyancy of Protestant countries in Ireland in comparison with Catholic areas. Young recommended reducing the tax burden on agriculture, eliminating tithes and setting a single tax for every bushel produced. At the same time, crop intensification would force the elimination of fallow land, the control of new divisions, the creation of artificial meadows and new crop rotation systems. Young's influence on the SAP was particularly noticeable in connection with two other issues. The first was agrarian individualism, which entailed fighting against common and fallow land and defending enclosures and long-term direct tenancies; and the second was establishing an optimum size for agricultural property. Young's position, with its echoes of the Physiocrats and economists like Jean Herrenschwand, a Swiss, whose work *De l'économie politique moderne* (1786) had been translated into Spanish in 1800,[52] opposed smallholdings on the basis that they hindered the mechanisation of agriculture and kept rural families on the poverty line, forcing them to fall back on industrial work to supplement their incomes. Against this background, there were clear advantages to large farms and estates: they facilitated capitalisation, the complementary nature of agriculture and livestock, as well as mechanisation, although Young preferred using oxen to horses for agricultural work, in contrast to the Physiocrats.[53] Finally, as opposed to what was traditionally believed, large-scale land ownership harmonised agricultural growth with the interests of the rural working classes, converting them into day labourers and thus guaranteeing better wages and greater well-being. It also favoured the disappearance of cottage industries, whose existence hampered agricultural growth. For this to act as a real incentive to industry, there had to be an unmistakably clear division of labour between the two sectors, and manufacturing activities had to be concentrated into large towns and cities.[54]

Young therefore orientated the Spanish Enlightenment towards capitalist agriculture much more clearly than the theoretical and reforming tradition of 1760s Spain had. Nonetheless, the SAP did not represent a break of any kind with these ideas. It is highly significant that in 1808 the publication should have ended its twelve-year existence with two wide-ranging reports rooted in the tradition of Campomanes and Jovellanos. The first, framed in the context of agriculture in Andalusia, posed the solution of the necessary division of large estates in very similar terms to the *Expediente* of Agrarian Law opened forty years before. The second, which referred to Castile, took up the set of reforms proposed by Jovellanos in his *Informe de Ley Agraria*, which especially insisted

52 Jean Herrenschwand, *Principios de economía política* (Madrid: Vega y Compañía, 1800).

53 SAP, no. 220 (19-III-1801), 169–83.

54 SAP, no. 246 (17-IX-1801), 190.

on the overriding need to solve the problem of entailed estates and mortmain to make land ownership "circulate." At its core, the SAP thus remained loyal to the Bourbon reforms characterising the reign of Carlos III and Carlos IV.

4 Final Remarks

Overall, the CM and the SAP remained faithful to the doctrinal bases and Bourbon reforms that characterised the reigns of Carlos III and Carlos IV. While they were proponents of the priority of industry and agriculture respectively, both publications argued that Spain's economic development should be built on a system of free trade within its borders — although with exceptions —, protectionism through tariffs and a monopoly over colonial possessions. The official impetus that had inspired their creation was thus very present in both these publications; however, this proximity to power to the monarchy, specifically to the Public Finance's Balance of Trade Office, did not entail absolute doctrinal or reformist uniformity, and it must be stressed newly that these two journals, the most emblematic of the Spanish Enlightenment with economic content, were essentially pluralist. This is a particularly noteworthy with regard to the CM, which emerged as an effective showcase for the diversity of internal currents; as Almenar explains so clearly, this was essential for the development of the economic culture opened up by Adam Smith's *The Wealth of Nations*. Among other issues this meant spreading the ideas of those who favoured reducing the sovereign's economic activity to a minimum, including the defenders of free trade with the outside world. Nevertheless, in spite of the fact that the CM was published at the very same time as Spain was assimilating first Smith's ideas and then Say's, it shows no signs of any special sympathy towards Smith's "system of natural liberty." In contrast, its combined defence of the industrial system, mechanisation, intervention in manufacturing and tariff protection positioned it close to various French authors, especially Chaptal, and economists that are now deemed of secondary importance such as Ferrier and Ganhil were styled as defenders of the "national economy" and set up a deeply-drawn line of nuances and even opposition to the classical economics mainstream.[55]

55 Almenar, "El desarrollo," 25–26; Lluch and Almenar, "Difusión e influencia," 154. On Say's simultaneous dissemination in Spain, see Menudo and O'Kean, "La recepción," 117–42.

Epilogue

In the last week of June 1808, the *Semanario de Agricultura* and then the *Correo Mercantil* published their final issues just a few days apart. The *Memorial Literario*, which was still active at the time, managed to survive until November. The closing of the three emblematic eighteenth century publications marked a hiatus in the "golden age" of the Spanish press, which had begun so successfully in 1780. Although it was not overtly stated, the papers were closed down because Spain was now a country at war and with an awkward problem of political sovereignty. After years of unrelenting economic decline and months of political uncertainty, the popular mutiny of Aranjuez — the royal seat a few kilometres from Madrid — had forced Carlos IV to dismiss his despised prime minister Manuel de Godoy and then to abdicate a few days later in favour of Fernando VII. A month later, Fernando also abdicated in favour of Joseph Bonaparte, who had the backing of a large number of French troops who were already on Spanish soil. From then on the Peninsula War (1808–1814) created a diabolical mix of armed conflict and a climate of extreme political instability. Spain was split between Bonaparte's government, which was supported by pro-France liberals and enshrined in the July 1808 Bayonne Constitution, and the *Junta Central* — Central Board —, the body representing a wide range of provincial boards, on which conservative and radical patriot factions were united in their support for restoring Fernando VII. In September 1810 the deposed King's supporters convened the *Cortes* of Cadiz (1810–1814), and in March 1812, after a year and a half of intense parliamentary activity, the famous Political Constitution of the Spanish monarchy was enacted.

The Constitution of Cadiz was a short-lived affair, interrupted by long periods in which absolutism was restored (1814–1820 and 1823–1833) and only in force from 1812–1814 and 1820–1823 during the Liberal Triennium *Cortes*. In spite of this, its enactment represented a real turning point in the history of Spain and the Enlightenment itself. Spain's early nineteenth century constitutional experiences were in fact wrought by authorities, intellectuals and reformers that had been the architects of the Enlightenment's development during the preceding decades. In the new context created by the War they spread their principles through the press, propaganda and the other expressions of culture and political activism that emerged during the conflict, while also transferring these principles to parliamentary debates and the articles of the Bayonne and Cadiz constitutional charters. These fathers of *early* Spanish constitutionalism were not only connected to the economic institutions discussed in this book: they were their real creators on all fronts. They founded

 | DOI:10.1163/9789004442894_013

or participated in institutions aimed at fostering economic growth, such as the economic societies and trade consulates; they promoted new entities whose purpose was to modernise the country's economic management — the Board of Trade, the Bank of San Carlos and the Department of General Development for the Country —; they established pioneering university chairs in political economy and commerce designed to teach the new Enlightenment sciences; and, finally, in the print culture sphere, they were behind the blossoming of the press and the first dictionaries and teaching materials covering commerce and economics. In short, thanks to them, Spain built an institutionalised economic culture, of which there had been very few signs at the beginning of the eighteenth century and which continued into the constitutional period.

This new culture represented a genuine fermentation of Enlightenment ideas. It was a real product of Spain's interconnection with Enlightenment Europe, without which it could not have existed. While the models for these economic institutions originated in several countries and were not always filtered and reshaped through France, the institutions themselves were not a simple mechanical translation of these foreign experiences but the outcomes of a process of innovation with added value. They were hybrids that had involved adapting these external experiences to Spain's unique framework,[1] and were so important during the years before Spain's first constitutional era that this period cannot be interpreted without analysing the mark left by both political economy and its institutions on the main actors during these crucial years. Attention needs to be paid to the remarkable circulation of ideas and the economic institutions that had enabled Spain to reconnect with countries that were more developed culturally and economically in previous decades. As this book has shown, after the War against the French all these economic institutions, without exception, survived the meandering path through constitutional and absolutist phases to mature as entities within the new structure of the Liberal state.

The economic institutions played a major role in spreading and implementing the principles of the science of political economy during the eighteenth century. They created the fabric that was needed for the social diffusion and intergenerational transmission of an economic culture that was pluralist from the very start. Although its sources reveal a debt to the main internal strands of European Enlightenment political economy, from the Gournay circle and the Physiocrats to the German cameralists and Neapolitan and Scottish economists, the "alter-economists," whose positions were a long way from those of

1 See, for a broader analysis, Burke, *Cultural Hibridity*.

the brilliant Physiocrat school, formed a clear majority, as they did across most of the Continent. Wholly indebted to all these currents, economic institutions in eighteenth century Spain endorse Robertson's approach regarding the desirability of addressing national variants of the Enlightenment on the basis of a unitary concept of the movement.[2] At the same time, this approach revives the importance of moderate currents in the origin and development of the European Enlightenment, as against the interpretative premises of Israel's Radical Enlightenment.[3] In fact, these currents underlay the process by which political economy matured all over Europe from the late seventeenth century onwards; as it eventually became one of the main disciplines of Enlightenment movements in Spain and other European countries, the intellectual history of the Enlightenment can still be constructed on the basis of Montesquieu, Hume, Genovesi, Smith, Filangieri and other moderate thinkers. These less extreme, liberal and empiricist authors occupied intellectual ground that was far removed from materialist, atheist and radical currents of thought, dominating and cementing the Enlightenment mainstream on large parts of the Old Continent. The Spanish Enlightenment represented a selection of these ideological strands, which Israel would class as "moderate" and which were mainly formulated in the French, British and Italian movements. On the grounds that the Catholic faith and membership of the enlightened Republic of Letters were compatible, the main actors tried to temper these currents' contents so that they could be not only useful but also viable in a closed political and religious context like eighteenth century Spain. The main challenge in the country was to bring about the gradual transformation of this cumbersome political and religious legacy; the dilemma did not consist of a sort of "intellectual drama," as Israel terms it,[4] which emerged during the *early* Enlightenment based on a choice between supposedly "radical" and "moderate" Enlightenments, but of the very possibility that a pragmatic movement of socio-cultural ideas, reforms and practices that were not only "enlightened" but were also essential in the ideological struggles of the time could exist. They were based on foreign ideology, as they were interwoven with European ideas, whose very names fed the aversion of powerful and well-oiled machines of reactionary and counter-Enlightenment sectors in Spain. The end result was that in general terms the Spanish Enlightenment had no need to base itself on an "abstract body of basic values" that were rational, secular and materialist and, according to Israel, exclusive to the "radical" Enlightenment, in order to develop regalist policies,

2 Robertson, *The Case*, 377ff.
3 Israel, *Radical Enlightenment*, 3–22.
4 Israel, *Radical Enlightenment*, 528–40.

eliminate privileges, combat the power of the Church, open up participation in the public sphere, activate the circulation of "useful" writings, found new centres of learning, promote the press, contribute to the professionalisation of men of letters and the secularisation of art and its representations, support trade's good repute and universalise education. In other words, they aimed to structure a more egalitarian society that was less conditioned by Catholicism and the Church, less bound by class structure and progressively more open to freedom of expression, transparency and public information vis-à-vis state affairs and socio-political participation, and finally, to open up a political culture that emerged at the beginning of the nineteenth century and placed Spain before the first constitutional experiences in its history. These transforming initiatives pointed in the direction of modernity, and political economy and its institutions played an irreplaceable role: as Schumpeter highlighted, the individuals at the head of these institutions, such as Campomanes or Jovellanos, developed an economic culture that was characterised by its pragmatic and applied approach.[5]

Political economy was gradually accepted as the basis of modern politics during the 1740s and 1750s. Like a science of the state, it was first embraced by small groups of political and intellectual elites, after which the economic institutions used print culture and education in the decisive role they played in spreading the principles of political economy to increasingly large and more diverse audiences. Over the last thirty years of the eighteenth century, which essentially coincided with the reign of Carlos III, the men of the Spanish Enlightenment retained their close connection with the monarchy's bureaucratic apparatus, but a generation of intellectuals and reformers that were more independent from the centres of power began to emerge. The individuals who wrote about the government were no longer only those who governed, and these two groups began to develop distinct sociocultural practices. The main economic institutions of the Spanish Enlightenment were created at their hands; these in turn housed all possible formats of spreading and popularising knowledge, from the press to memoirs, letters and dictionaries. At the end of the eighteenth century, the Enlightenment was far from being only a tool in the hands of a limited group of intellectuals and reformers associated with the court. By that time these institutions had inspired the creation of a new "public" that was interested in political economy and aware of its importance for the country's survival.

5 Schumpeter, *History of Economic Analysis*, 172–73.

It is no accident that the main hub of economic institutions should have emerged and become established geographically in the last third of the eighteenth century, during the decisive period which began all over Enlightenment Europe after the Seven Years' War. Although this occurred later than in Britain or France, during the 1760s political economy and the public sphere began to interweave in Spain. As in other absolutist countries, this contributed decisively to the weakening of these countries' characteristic machinery that was designed to conceal the arcanes of power and control the public sphere and opinion via censorship. This "public," which in 1808 was emerging as a decisive political player for the first time, was forged thanks to the interposing of two processes that was led by the economic institutions: first, the appearance of a more individualistic and egalitarian sociability that emerged around entities like the economic societies, and, second, the development of an intellectual sociability that used the press and other forms of print culture to create a new type of communication that was characterised by the use of reason and criticism in traditionally untouchable fields such as religion and the state. The economic institutions thus played a leading role in the gradual politicisation process undergone by the Spanish Enlightenment around the emergence of the public sphere and public opinion, which really came to fruition in the movement of political and cultural ideas that blossomed in the shadow of the Peninsula War. In short, the Spanish Enlightenment cannot be understood without appreciating the intellectual contribution made by political economy and its institutions, as well as the many social functions that they fulfilled.

Over and above its contribution to the diffusion of the principles of the political economy and the emergence of the "public," the economics institutions played also a key role in the circulating of information and knowledge, which in other countries had clearly been shown to be a decisive factor for promoting economic development processes. Furthermore, they also helped to structure national and regional markets in many ways; reducing uncertainty about the situation of these markets; creating a more uniform and better-trained bureaucracy that contributed to the articulating of state structure; dignifying productive occupations, including trade; fighting against fraud; involving local elites in developing the Enlightenment programme; encouraging the circulation of news from local spheres to the national sphere; standardising the system of coins, weights and measures; passing on professional techniques; and finally, publicising innovations in trade and production techniques through the entire country. This had direct implications for the organisation of economic activity, knowledge and political life, and all these aspects reveal these institutions' functioning in the country's political structure. Their multi-faceted nature equipped them with a noticeably modernising sense; achieving a more structured state, as an essential pre-requisite for emerging from longstanding cultural and economic backwardness, was a symbol of the Spanish Enlightenment and was also certainly a leitmotif of the economic institutions' activity. But, in light of events outside Spain, the fact that these institutions were created later contributed to the slowness of economic development.

However, on the brink of 1808, the legacy left by the *long* century since 1700, during which four Bourbon monarchs had reigned, was a state that was still some way from being centralised, uniform or having a unified domestic market. A wide range of monetary, tariff and fiscal systems persisted, and the old duality between the lands of Castile and the Crown of Aragon was still very much to the fore. Jurisdictional fragmentation was rife, not only because of the continued existence of the ecclesiastical state and seigniorial jurisdictions, but also due to the impact of privileged and semi-autonomous bodies, either municipal authorities or regions with *fueros* such as the Basque provinces and the Kingdom of Navarre. These exempt areas had a large set of economic powers and were well-positioned inside a chain of internal customs barriers, which only exacerbated the problems of the lack of uniformity and fractured domestic market. The state structuring project had made slow progress since the centralising urge manifested in the 1707 and 1714 *Nueva Planta* decrees: as an anonymous government official explained, under Carlos III reign, Spain was still "a body made up of smaller separate bodies that competed with each other, oppressed and despised each other and were in a state of perpetual struggle against each other;" it was a type of "monstrous republic" made up of "small republics that were pitched against one another because each one's individual interest was contrary to the common interest."[6]

This dismal diagnosis certainly laid bare Spanish absolutism's shortcomings, but assessing the real tools that it possessed to resolve them is another question. In this regard it is important to bear in mind the fact that as the century progressed the "absolute" exercise of political power was neutralised — or at least strongly conditioned — by such new factors such as the appearance of the "public," the consolidation of better-educated and informed court and regional elites, and the hidden presence of a public opinion with an increasing ability to distinguish good public policies from bad. The serious problem of political stability triggered by the Esquilache Riots (1766), which began as a reaction of court elites to the first measures to liberalise the grain trade enacted by the government just a year earlier, marked a symbolic boundary with respect to the possibility of being able to impose reforms by means of

6 Marcelin Defourneaux, *Pablo de Olavide ou l'afrancesado (1725–1803)* (Paris: PUF, 1959), 84–85.

the sheer exercise of authority. The disputes that subsequently surfaced in the public sphere regarding the implementation of the José de Gálvez's free trade scheme in the colonies (1778), integrating the Basque-Navarre customs system into the common state-wide regime (1778–1782) and Lerena's Treasury reform (1785–1787) were clear reflections of the fact that any reforms would require a more complex strategy than that used in previous decades in cases such as the enactment of the *Nueva Planta* decrees (1707 and 1714) and the introduction of Ensenada's *única contribución* (1749). This strategy operated both in the sphere of the "top-down" imposition royal sovereignty and this sovereignty's political assimilation of the new "bottom-up" Enlightenment-inspired expressions that were emerging. Public opinion had to be listened to if it were to be modulated, and also in order to win the support of the normally minority reformist sector at state council level, and local political authority level — the courts and the magistrates — and the regional elites, who would be responsible for embracing the reforms and attempting to implement them. Ensuring their success as far as possible required intensive use of "Enlightenment" deterrent instruments; as the "absolutism" path in its purest sense was no longer feasible, all that remained was "enlightened absolutism."

It was in this precise area that the economic institutions were active during the last thirty years of the eighteenth century. Firstly, they encouraged an enlightened economic culture with both regional and national dimensions, which transcended the heritage received via the old *arbitrismo* tradition that was entrenched in the ancient kingdoms and merchants handbooks linked to local trade usages. Meanwhile, as channels for the new patriotism that extolled the fact of being part of Spain, they were designed to overcome the traditional primacy of local ties and belonging to pre-nation communities. Achieving the Enlightenment ideal of "public happiness" required breaking with the political tradition inherited from the Hapsburgs, particularly as, with the exceptions of the Basque provinces and Navarre, the last flickers of the *austracistas* had been extinguished in the 1740s, and the *fueros* were fading away like a forgotten dream in Catalonia and the old Aragonese kingdoms. Above all, achieving this ideal required unifying the different and diverse parts making up the country around a common project; this was especially important since, as previously stated, the Spanish Enlightenment was more than a simple intellectual and reformist project associated with the court in Madrid. It had also taken root in the regions, and not only as the result of decisions made by the country's central power, but also through autonomous initiatives led by enlightened groups at local level. If the Enlightenment programme were to materialise, centralising and unifying elements needed to be combined with others with decentralising tendencies. However, both of these required devising a unifying programme that was designed to reunite the elites, local authorities and regions around it with the aim of attaining a state that was more and better structured and would enable the regions to carry out their economic programmes in conjunction with the common country-wide programme.

There are clear lessons to be drawn from eighteenth century Spain in this respect. One of the most illuminating examples is to be found in the different fates of Catalonia and the Basque Country. Both regions had a well-established and structured industrial tradition, the first focussing on textiles and the second on iron. Both also benefitted from robust Enlightenment movements, which grew up around the Barcelona Board of Trade and the Bascongada Society. They were also distinguished by their support for industry as the hub of economic development. However, while Catalonia witnessed the beginning of the most successful economic growth process in the entire Hispanic Enlightenment in the eighteenth century on the basis of its powerful textile industry, it was decades before this process materialised in the Basque Country. The root cause of this difference lies in the fact that Catalan entrepreneurs and manufacturers were able to operate unhindered in the Spanish empire's domestic and colonial markets. Meanwhile, the refusal to move the internal *foral* customs barriers to the country's borders, as the court in Madrid and the enlightened sectors in the Basque provinces and Navarre intended, was followed by an egregious process of deindustrialisation and impoverishment, which was only reversed in the 1830s via their integration into the common customs system.[7] The Spanish Enlightenment's support for a more structured state was not mere rhetoric, therefore. In contrast with the Basque Country, Catalonia's experience highlights the advantages of an economic programme that united court backing with local entrepreneurship.

The poor results achieved by the empire-wide market, in the short term at least, were affected by the fact that its creation was weak, slow and delayed. The intellectual bases for converting Spain into a new "trading empire" had been established in the 1740s,[8] but its real articulation was essentially brought about by the 1765 free trade Decree and gathered speed significantly after the

7 There are parallels with the dilemma created by the passing of the Act of Union in 1707, especially from the Scottish point of view. The bill was designed to resolve a critical problem for Scotland: the potentially contradictory relationship between the established political institutions and the conditions required for economic development or, in other terms, the political cost of creating a framework that facilitated economic growth; see John Robertson, "The Scottish Enlightenment at the limits of the civil tradition," in *Wealth and Virtue. The Shapping of Political Economy in the Scottish Enlightenment*, eds. Istvan Hont and Michael Ignatieff (Cambridge: CUP, 1983): 137.

8 Tavárez, "La invención," 56–76

José de Gálvez's reform of 1778. The first economic policies that were adapted to a transatlantic scale date back to that year, as does the 1778–1782 tariff rate. It was the notable increase in trading activity resulting from this legislation that gave rise to the spread of trade consulates, the creation of the first economic societies and the appearance of the periodical press and a series of economic and political treatises in the colonies during the 1780s and 1790s that were similar to those produced in the metropolis itself. The outcome was the forging of an economic culture and a network of economic institutions that were not only associated with the peninsula but also covered the empire: the clearest example was the *Correo Mercantil*. However, these new institutions on both sides of the Atlantic were created at a particularly devastating economic juncture, when the country had reached its economic growth ceiling, a new war was erupting against England (1796–1802) and the Treasury had gone into an irreversible decline. It was virtually impossible to consolidate the imperial market and the economic culture underpinning it in these circumstances, and the War of 1808 and the pro-independence movement in the colonies dealt the death blow to Spain's endeavours to create a large trade and maritime base built on a shared economic culture through which to secure its colonies.

The delay in creating a nationwide economic policy had an especially decisive influence on this set of circumstances. The starting point, against the backdrop of composite Hapsburg Spain, was certainly not the best: when Felipe V came to the throne in 1700 the country was far less structured in economic terms than either its model Britain, whose parliament had been acting as a catalyst for national economic policy since the end of the seventeenth century, or France, which had benefitted from a centralised economic policy with the capacity to intervene anywhere in the country since at least the days of Louis XIV and his minister Colbert. To this were added the problems deriving from the fact that the institutions devoted to economic growth lacked clearly defined powers, and from the late consolidation of elements of the print culture — mainly the press — which were efficient channels for transmitting information. These problems were certainly not exclusive to Spain, but were shared by all Ancien Regime governments; however, the issue of founding a centralised body to promote economic development with sovereignty over all national territory and freed from Royal Treasury oversight was another matter. In Spain this issue essentially concerned the Board of Trade and the contrast with Britain and France was very telling in this aspect as well. Differences between these two countries are usually based on their governments' tendencies to intervene or not, with Britain generally assumed to intrude less in private enterprise. Spain had a different type of problem, however: how to set up a centralised body with these characteristics. The Board of Trade was created later than those in both Britain and Bourbon France, which was its main model. Unlike the *Conseil de commerce* (1700) — then the *Bureau de commerce* (1722) — the Board lacked the capacity to intervene in the economic situation: with its powerful body of manufactured goods inspectors, the French agency benefitted from centralised management with clearly-defined and hierarchical competences.[9] In contrast, the Spanish Board was genuinely inefficient: during a large part of the eighteenth century, it endured unresolved issues relating to its internal composition, poor funding and negligible powers that were intruded on by the influential Councils, which still held controlled Spain's economic management, albeit in a disorganised fashion. In short, as Grafe has highlighted, sweeping generalisations about constitutional and absolutist models are of limited usefulness:[10] Spain was not nearly as politically, economically and culturally centralised as France, and this hindered its economic growth. However, the real stumbling block was not the design of its economic institutions: although they were created later, they were rooted in Enlightenment culture and similar to those in countries that were more advanced politically and culturally. The main problem was the political construction of a robust and efficient centre, capable of supporting these institutions and uniting elites and local authorities around them in a programme that would overcome the burdensome Hapsburg legacy while respecting regional diversity. Eighteenth century Spain's flaws were due not to a lack of "enlightenment" but to the weakness of its "absolutism."

However, this somewhat unequivocal analysis needs to be qualified: it is important to identify when this *long durée* enlightened century started, but perhaps more so to pinpoint its end. As this idea is generally accepted by current European historiography, there is no reason why it should not also apply to Spain; in fact, the question of how *long* the Enlightenment survived there is fundamental. The first consideration is to challenge the identification of the Enlightenment with revolution, which is misleading and, more importantly, uncertain, and then, contrary to what Israel maintains,[11] the notion that Enlightenment's only possible outcome was not a radical democratic and republican project. This path cannot be presented as excluding enlightened absolutism; if it were, most European nations, including Spain, would be left off the Enlightenment map. Just as the enlightened ideas were received relatively late there, once the delaying effect caused by the revolution in France had been overcome, they also came to fruition later. This issue is especially interesting

9 Minard, *La fortune*, 212–24.
10 Grafe, *Distant Tyranny*, 11ff.
11 Israel, *Radical Enlightenment*, 21.

because the benefits were reaped when the country's economic survival was in serious doubt due to the halt in economic growth after 1790, the bankruptcy of the Treasury and the imminent break-up of the empire. In spite of this, and backed by the freedom of the press and of expression in general, the Liberal Triennium (1820–1823) was undoubtedly one of Spain's great periods, together with the reformist reign of Fernando VI, with the Marquis of Ensenada at its head (1748–1754), the reign of Carlos III (1759–1788) and the broad movement of political ideas and practices before and during the drafting of the Constitution of Cadiz (1808–1814). If, in line with Mokyr's analysis,[12] the effect of enlightened political economy ideas are assessed not in the area of technological advances, but instead in terms of the institutional changes that impacted directly on economic growth, the struggle initiated by the regalists and political economists in eighteenth century Spain did not culminate until very late. The nineteenth century liberals accepted that centralisation was the route to political and economic modernisation, and in 1833 they finished the work that the *Cortes* of Cadiz and the Triennium Liberal had begun in order to organise the country geographically on the basis of the hierarchy of municipalities and provinces. Likewise, in the period from 1833 to 1850, monetary integration was achieved, internal customs barriers were eliminated and the tax system was unified; all in all, the basic machinery of the Ancien Regime was dismantled during this time. The framework provided by *a long durée* approach therefore gives additional reasons to better appreciate the task begun by members of the Spanish Enlightenment during the eighteenth century and to ensure that Spain participated fully in the enlightened Europe that adjusted itself to the creation of new economic institutions and political economy's emergence as a science. The overview set out in this book confronts the well-worn clichés of Spain as a decrepit and fading country that was left out of the European Enlightenment. Spain had its own unique Enlightenment, which requires attention and study and can be analysed using the traditional categories of ideas, institutions and reforms of the enlightened absolutism.

12 Mokyr, *The Enlightened Economy*, 63–78.

Appendix

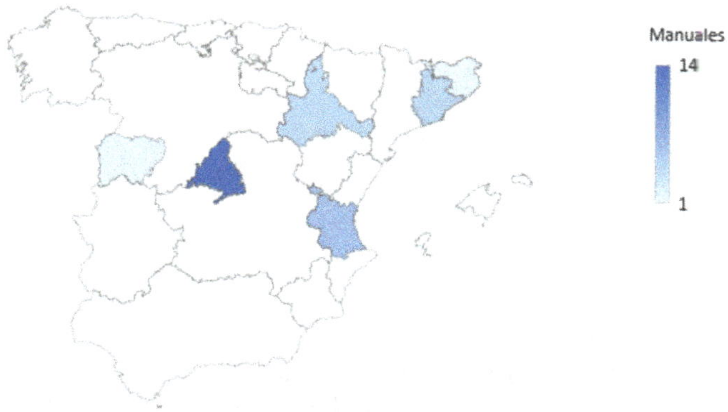

MAP 1 Place of publication of the Spanish Merchant Handbooks' first editions (1699-1759)
SOURCE: JESÚS ASTIGARRAGA ON HIS OWN RESEARCH DATA

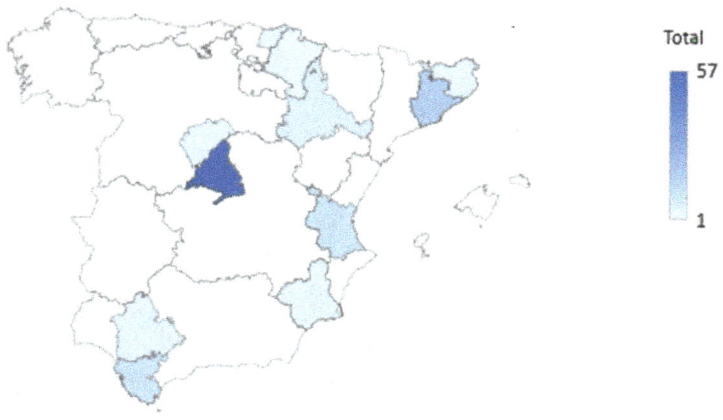

MAP 2 Place of publication of Spanish Merchant Handbooks' first editions (1760-1808), total publications
SOURCE: JESÚS ASTIGARRAGA ON HIS OWN RESEARCH DATA

 DOI:10.1163/9789004442894_014

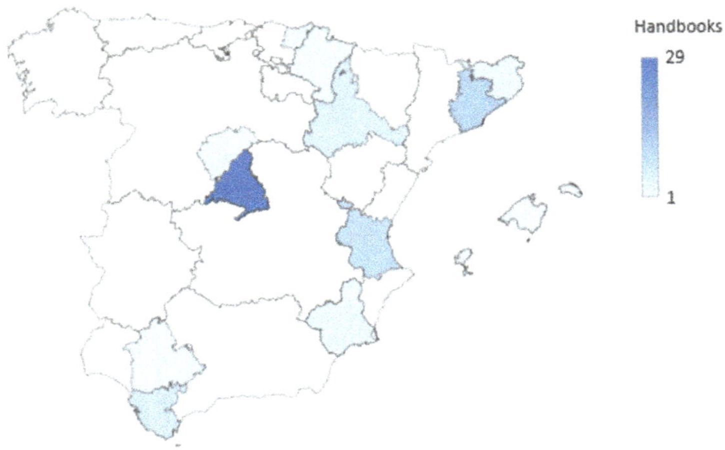

MAP 3 Place of publication of Spanish Merchant Handbooks' first editions, except the compendiums of *vales reales and the Almanak Mercantil* (1760-1808)
SOURCE: JESÚS ASTIGARRAGA ON HIS OWN RESEARCH DATA

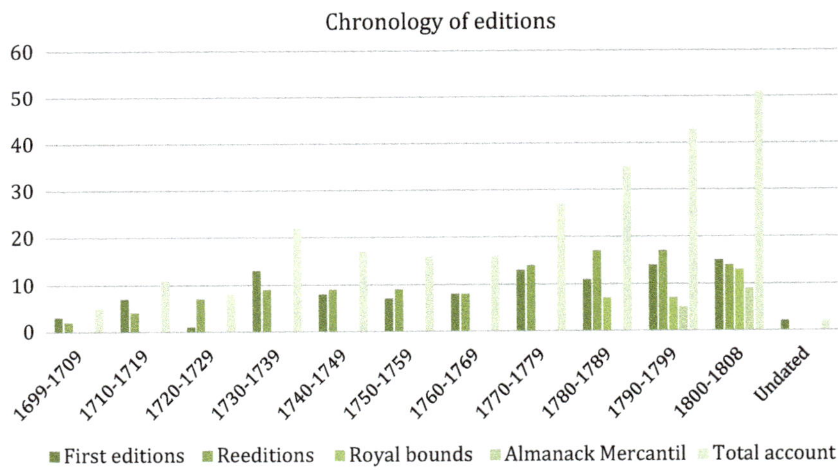

FIGURE 1 Chronology of the editions of the Spanish Merchant Handbooks (1699-1808)
SOURCE: JESÚS ASTIGARRAGA ON HIS OWN RESEARCH DATA

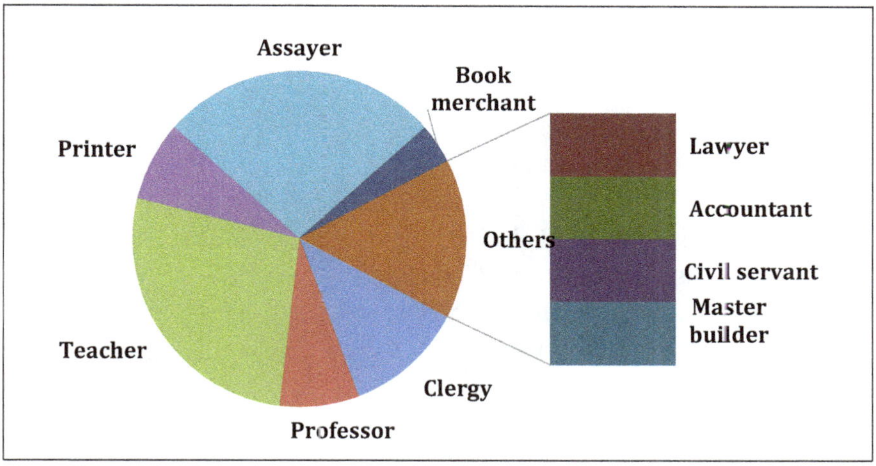

FIGURE 2 Occupations of Spanish Merchant Handbooks' authors (1699-1749)
SOURCE: JESÚS ASTIGARRAGA ON HIS OWN RESEARCH DATA

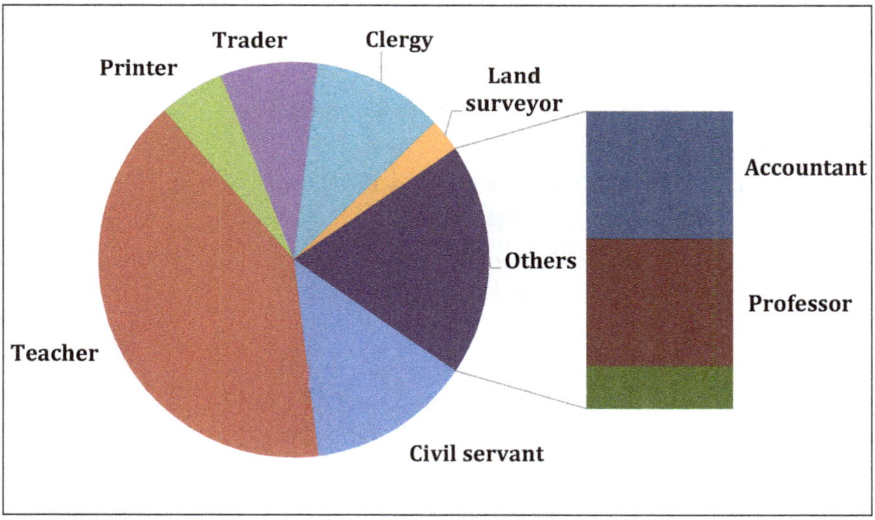

FIGURE 3 Occupations of Spanish Merchant Handbooks' authors (1750-1808)
SOURCE: JESÚS ASTIGARRAGA ON HIS OWN RESEARCH DATA

Bibliography, Sources and Abbreviations

1 Abbreviations

(Archives, Libraries, Publishing Houses)

AC: Archivo Campomanes (Madrid).
AHN: Archivo Histórico Nacional (Madrid).
ASA: Archivo Real Sociedad Aragonesa (Saragossa).
ASM: Archivo Sociedad Matritense (Madrid).
BAE: Biblioteca de Autores Españoles.
BCMH: Biblioteca Central del Ministerio de Hacienda (Madrid).
BNE: Biblioteca Nacional de España (Madrid).
BUS: Biblioteca Universitaria (Sevilla).
CEPC: Centro de Estudios Políticos y Constitucionales.
CNRS: Centre National de la Recherche Scientifique.
CROMOHS: Cyber Review of Modern Historiography.
CSIC: Centro Superior de Investigaciones Científicas.
CUP: Cambridge University Press.
CV: Casa de Velázquez.
EHESS: École des Hautes Études en Science Sociales.
FCE: Fondo de Cultura Económica.
FUE: Fundación Universitaria Española (Madrid).
IEF: Instituto de Estudios Fiscales.
IFC: Institución Fernando El Católico.
INED: Institut National d'Études Démographiques.
OUP: Oxford University Press.
PUF: Presses Universitaires de France.
RACMP: Real Academia de Ciencias Morales y Políticas.
RAH: Real Academia de la Historia (Madrid).
RHE: Revista de Historia Económica.
SEESXVIII: Sociedad Española de Estudios del Siglo XVIII.
VF: Voltaire Foundation.

2 Press

Aduana crítica (1763–1765; ed. Miguel de la Barrera).
Almacén de frutos literarios inéditos de nuestros mejores autores antiguos y modernos (1804; ed. Antonio Valladares de Sotomayor).

Annales de l'agriculture française (1797–1873; ed. Henri-Alexander Tessier).
Annales politiques, civiles et littéraires du Dix-Huitième siécle (APC, 1777–1792; ed. Simon-Nicholas-Henri Linguet).
Annals of Agriculture and Other Useful Arts (1784–1815; ed. Arthur Young).
Biblioteca española económico-política (1801–1821; ed. Juan Sempere).
Biblioteca periódica anual para utilidad de los libreros y literatos (1784–1791; ed. Joaquín Ezquerra).
Cajón de sastre (1760–1761; ed. Francisco Mariano Nifo).
Correo de Madrid o de los ciegos (CMC, 1786–1791; ed. José Antonio Manegat).
Correo general de España (1770; ed. Francisco Mariano Nifo).
Correo general histórico, literario económico de la Europa (CGH, 1763; ed. Francisco Mariano Nifo).
Correo literario de la Europa (1781–1782, 1786–1787; ed. Francisco Antonio Escartín).
Correo mercantil de España y sus Indias (CM, 1792–1808; ed. Diego María Gallard).
Descripción natural, geográfica, y económica de todos los pueblos de España (1771; ed. Francisco Mariano Nifo).
Diario curioso, erudito, económico y comercial (1786–1787; ed. Jacques Thevin).
Diario curioso, histórico, erudito, comercial, civil y económico (1762, 1772–1773, ed. Pedro Ángel de Tarazona).
Diario de Barcelona (1792- ; ed. Pedro Pablo Ussón).
Diario de los literatos (1737–1742; ed. Francisco Manuel de Huerta).
Diario extranjero (1763; ed. Francisco Mariano Nifo).
Discursos mercuriales (DM, 1752, 1755–1756; ed. Juan Enrique Graef).
Diario noticioso, curioso, erudito, y comercial, público y económico (1758; ed. Francisco Mariano Nifo).
Diario pinciano (1787–1788; ed. Mariano Beristain).
El apologista universal (1786–1788; ed. Pedro Centeno).
El Censor (1781–1787; ed. Luis García del Cañuelo and Luis Marcelino Pereira).
El corresponsal de El Censor (1786–1788; ed. Manuel Rubín de Celis, pseud. Ramón Harnero).
El duende de Madrid (1787; ed. Pedro Pablo Trullench).
El duende especulativo sobre la vida civil (1761; ed. Juan Antonio Mercadal).
El filósofo a la moda o el maestro universal (1788).
El hablador juicioso y crítico imparcial (EHJ, 1763; ed. J. Langlet).
El Observador (1787; ed. Juan Marchena).
El Pensador (EP, 1762–1767; ed. José Clavijo y Fajardo, pseud. José Álvarez Valladares).
El Pensador Matritense (EPM, 1780; ed. Pedro Ángel de Tarazona).
Espíritu de los mejores diarios literarios que se publican en Europa (EMD, 1787–1791; ed. Cristóbal Cladera).
Estafeta de Londres (EL, 1762; ed. Francisco Mariano Nifo, pseud. Mariano de la Gija).

État politique actuel de l'Angleterre (EPA, 1757–1759; ed. Edme Jacques Genet).
Gabinete de lectura española (1787–1793; ed. Isidro Bosarte).
Gaceta de Madrid (1661-).
Journal d'agriculture, du commerce et des finances (1765–1783).
Journal de commerce (JC, 1759–1762; ed. Jacques Accarias de Serionne).
Journal de Paris (1777–1840).
Journal de physique (1771–1783, ed. François Rozier).
Journal des Savants (1665–1792).
Journal Encyclopédique (JEN, 1756–1794, ed. Pierre Rousseau).
Journal Oeconomique (JOE, 1751–1767).
La Espigadera (1790–1791; ed. Alfonso Bravo).
L'Epilogueur moderne, (1750–1755, ed. Jean Rousset de Missy).
L'Esprit des journaux (EDJ, 1772–1818; ed. Jean-Louis Coster and Jean-Jacques Tutot).
Le vrai patriote hollandais (1748–1749, ed. Jean Rousset de Missy).
Magazin des événements de toutes sortes, passés, présents et futurs (1741–1742, ed. Jean Rousset de Missy).
Memorial literario, instructivo y curioso de la Corte de Madrid (ML, 1784–1808; ed. Joaquín Ezquerra).
Memorias instructivas y curiosas (MIC, 1778–1791; ed. Miguel Gerónimo Suárez).
Mercurio histórico y político (1738–1830).
Miscelánea instructiva, curiosa y agradable (1796–1800; ed. Diego María Gallard, Francisco Pinilla and Matías Pinilla).
Miscelánea política (MP, 1763–1764; ed. Mateo Antonio Barberi).
Noticia periódica de los precios corrientes de la semana (1779–1820).
Semanario de agricultura y artes dirigido a los párrocos (SAP, 1797–1808; ed. Juan Antonio Melón).
Semanario económico (SE, 1765–1767, ed. Pedro Saura, pseud. Pedro Araus).
Semanario económico (SE, 1777–1778, ed. Juan Cubié, pseud. Juan Viceu).
Semanario erudito (SEV, 1787–1791; ed. Antonio Valladares de Sotomayor).
Variedades de ciencia, literatura y artes (1803–1805; ed. Manuel José Quintana).

3 Spanish Merchants' Handbooks

Alonso de Barba, Álvaro. *Arte de los metales en que se enseña el verdadero beneficio de los de oro y plata por azogue, el modo de fundirlos todos, y cómo se han de refinar y apartar unos de otros* (1640). Madrid: Bernardo Peralta, 1770.
Asensio y Mejorada, Francisco. *Nuevo uso y provechoso para reducir a reales de vellón, conforme a la Real Pragmática de 17 de mayo de 1737, todo género de moneda corriente.* c. 1758.

Atienza, José. *Método nuevo, fácil, breve, y curioso de aritmética, teórica y práctica; con el que cualquiera podrá, sin maestro, aprender a contar desde el alfabeto hasta lo más sublime de la facultad, con muchas reglas nuevas y curiosas*. Madrid: Alfonso López, 1748.

Ávila, Andrés de. *Modo fácil para la cobranza, y pago de cualquiera cantidades en los cuatro reinos de Castilla, Aragón, Valencia, y Cataluña. Con la correspondencia que tienen entre sí todas las monedas de oro, y plata en cada uno de ellos, y las provinciales que respectivamente usan*. Valencia: Tomás Santos, 1769.

Badelles, Mariano. *Descanso de comerciantes: principalmente para los que tratan con la seda*. Valencia: José Tomás Lucas, 1754.

Bails, Benito. *Aritmética para negociantes*. Madrid: Viuda de Ibarra, 1790.

Barrême, François. *Llibre fácil de comptes fets, ab lo qual se pot traurer tota especie de comptes de tota moneda, per enter ó trencat, tenint present los exemples que á est fi se han añadit* (1703). Gerona: Jaume Brò, 1750.

Barrême, François. *Libro de cuentas hechas: útil para toda clase de personas; sacado de las obras de Barrême*. Barcelona: Francisco Genéras, 1765.

Bernaldo de Quirós, Carlos. *Tabla demostrativa de diferentes sumas y cuentas, hechas para lo mercantil, principalmente para la seda*. Valencia: Antonio Batle, 1740.

Bes y Labet, Ignacio de. *Tratado útil, y provechoso para los comerciantes, y demás personas que quieran saber la reducción de cambios de las libras tornesas, sueldos y dineros, moneda imaginaria de Francia, a reales de vellón, moneda efectiva de estos reinos de España*. Madrid: Gabriel Ramírez, 1768.

Bes y Labet, Ignacio de. *Manual de comerciantes. Tratado utilísimo para los banqueros, mercaderes y demás personas que negocian, libran o toman letras de cambio para Holanda, Francia, Inglaterra y Génova, con explicación de las monedas efectivas e imaginarias de estos reinos de España*. Madrid: Joaquín Ibarra, 1775.

Biel y Aznar, José. *Aritmética especulativa, y práctica para lo mercantil, con el valor y correspondencia de las monedas, pesos y medidas, de estos reinos* (1762). Zaragoza: Medardo Heras, 1789.

Blainville, Miteau de. *Instrucción para la teneduría de libros en partida doble, que contiene los principios de esta ciencia [...] Escrita en francés, por M. Miseau Blamville, y traducida al castellano, por D. José de Cabredo*. Madrid: Viuda de Ibarra, 1800.

Bordázar de Artazu, Antonio. *Proporción de monedas, pesos y medidas, con principios prácticos de aritmética y geometría para su uso*. Valencia: Imprenta de Antonio Bordázar, 1736.

Bordázar de Artazu, Antonio. *Reducción de monedas antiguas, y corrientes de toda Europa, sacada del libro de monedas, pesos, y medidas, escrito por Antonio Bordázar de Artazu. Según el nuevo aumento de la plata y con tarifas convenientes*. Valencia: Simón Faure, 1736.

Cantos Benítez, Pedro de. *Escrutinio de maravedises y monedas de oro antiguas, su valor, reducción y cambio a las monedas corrientes. Deducido de escrituras, leyes y pragmáticas antiguas y modernas de España*. Madrid: Antonio Marín, 1763.

Capmany, Antonio de. *Código de las costumbres marítimas de Barcelona, hasta aquí vulgarmente llamado Libro del Consulado*. 2 vols. Madrid: Antonio de Sancha, 1791.

Carratalá, Esteban. *Aplicación de la aritmética a las operaciones más usuales del comercio, según la práctica y uso de esta plaza de Cádiz. Escrito en virtud de acuerdo de la Junta de Gobierno del Estudio de Bellas Artes de esta ciudad*. Cadiz: Juan Jiménez, 1799.

Casamayor, María Andrea (pseud. Casandro Mamés de la Marca y Araioa). *Tyrocinio aritmético, instrucción de las cuatro reglas llanas*. Zaragoza: José Fort, 1738.

Castelar, Emilio. *Cambios sobre las más principales plazas de Europa; operados y puestos en práctica según los cálculos, monedas de cambio, y otros particulares que en cada una de ellas se usan*. Madrid: Andrés de Soto, 1785.

Ciscar y Ciscar, Gabriel. *Memoria elemental sobre los nuevos pesos y medidas decimales fundados en la naturaleza*. Madrid: Imprenta Real, 1800.

Coll y Alsina, Pedro Mártir. *Norma en que se presentan varias fórmulas de contratas de fletamentos, conocimientos, pólizas de seguros, letras de cambio, patronías de buques, facturas, libros de cuentas, balances […] para gobierno de un hijo suyo comerciante*. Barcelona: Compañía de Jordi, Roca y Gaspar, 1803.

Corachán, Juan Bautista. *Aritmética demostrada teórico-práctica, para lo matemático, y mercantil: explícanse las monedas, pesos, y medidas de los hebreos, griegos, romanos, y de estos reinos de España, conferidos entre sí* (1699). Barcelona: Pablo Campins, 1735.

Cortés, Jerónimo. *Aritmética práctica muy útil y necesaria para todo género de tratantes y mercaderes* (1604). Zaragoza: Herederos de Diego Larumbe, 1724.

Crean, Eduardo. *Cálculo general de todos los cambios corrientes en estos reinos de España, con Francia, Inglaterra, Holanda, Portugal e Italia; compuesto en once cuadernos de tablas*. Madrid: Francisco Martínez Abad, 1737.

Domínguez Vicente, José Manuel. *Discursos jurídicos sobre las aceptaciones, pagas, intereses, y demás requisitos, y cualidades de las letras de cambio*. Madrid: Herederos de Juan García Infanzón, 1732.

Ezpeleta, Martín de. *Libro de cuentas extraordinarias*. Zaragoza: Gaspar Martínez, 1704.

Fernández, Gaspar. *Compendio para hacer todos los cambios y descuentos por el nuevo cálculo decimal, en que se facilitan las operaciones que exige este ramo*. Madrid: Imprenta Real, 1804.

Fernández de Anuncibay Urreta Basurto, José. *Pláticas de aritmética y palestra de contadores. Divididas en tres libros. En el primero y segundo se ejemplifican todas las demandas y requisitos necesarios para el que lo aficionare, consiga ser perfecto contador. En el tercero, las conducentes a los tratados de compañías, valimientos de juros, cobranza de diezmos, censos, alcabalas, y otras muchas curiosidades, que hallarán los novicios traficantes en los comercios, y algunos artífices, acomodadas a su deseo.* Madrid: Juan Muñoz, 1732.

Gallardo, Diego María. *Almanak mercantil o guía de comerciantes.* 14 vols. Madrid: Viuda de Joaquín Ibarra and Imprenta de Vega y Compañía, 1795–1808.

García, Francisco Javier. *Aritmética especulativa, y práctica, y arte mayor, o álgebra.* Zaragoza: Luis de Cueto, 1733.

García Caballero, José. *Teórica, y práctica de la arte de ensayar oro, plata, y vellón rico. Dánse reglas para ligar, religar, alear y reducir cualesquiera cantidades de oro, y plata a la ley del reino. Corrígense las reglas, y tablas de Juan de Arphe, y auméntase otras nuevas, para mayor claridad de los que quisieren aprender esta facultad.* Madrid: Imprenta de Agustín Fernández, 1713.

García Caballero, José. *Breve cotejo, y balance de las pesas, y medidas de varias naciones, reinos, y provincias, comparadas, y reducidas a las que corren en estos reinos de Castilla. Declárase también la ley, peso, y valor de algunas monedas hebreas, griegas, romanas, y castellanas, y de otros reinos, y señoríos.* Madrid: Viuda de Francisco del Hierro, 1731.

García de la Fuente, Félix. *Voz aritmética práctica para todos. Principios geométricos, con reglas para medir los campos, y para formar todo género de cuentas, con las circunstancias que puedan ocurrir.* Salamanca: Imprenta de Santa Cruz, 1736.

Gerard, Juan. *Tratado completo de aritmética, o método para aprender a contar por principios. Obra útil a toda especie de personas particularmente a los que se dedican al comercio.* Madrid: Imprenta de Vega y Compañía, 1798.

González Cañaveras, Juan Antonio. *Aritmética especulativa y práctica.* Cadiz: Manuel Espinosa de los Monteros, 1777.

González de la Torre, Manuel. *Cartilla aritmética o rudimentos de las cuatro reglas con la reducción de monedas, pesos y medidas de los cinco reinos.* Valencia: Gerónimo Conejos, 1749.

González de la Torre, Manuel. *Libro de cuentas hechas útil para toda clase de personas.* Gerona: Jaume Bró, 1750.

González de la Torre, Manuel. *Instrucción para las cobranzas de letras de cambio y vales de comercio.* Valencia: Francisco Burguete, 1774.

González de la Torre, Manuel. *Descanso de comerciantes, principalmente para los que tratan en seda, que hallarán las cuentas hechas por el precio de 10 reales la libra de seda, hasta el de 50 desde media onza, por menor, hasta 70 lib. y por mayor hasta 2000: que en el año 1754 se imprimió a nombre de Mariano Badelles; y ahora nuevamente añadido por su verdadero autor Manuel González de la Torre.* Valencia: Francisco Burguete, 1774.

Guardamino y Sáinz, Diego de. *Prontuario y claves de las correspondencias, que, entre sí, tienen las monedas, medidas de granos, de palmos, y peso sutil de Castilla, con las de varios reinos, y provincias de la Europa, Señorío de Vizcaya, y demás continentes de España.* Madrid: Antonio Marín, 1757.

Guerra, Francisco. *Valor y reduccio de la moneda de or y de plata a altres especies de moneda: conforme al aument que té la moneda de or, en virtut de la Real Prágmatica de 17 de Juliol de 1779, declarada por la Real Audiencia de est Principat de Cathalunya à 9 de Agost de dit any*. Gerona: Narcis Oliva, 1779.

Herranz y Quirós, Diego Narciso. *Aritmética pura y comercial, dividida en dos partes: la primera instruye a los principiantes en lo perteneciente a la aritmética pura; la segunda trata de los cambios o reducciones de monedas de la mayor parte de las principales plazas de comercio de la Europa*. Madrid: Benito Cano, 1790.

Hualde, Miguel de. *El contador lego, especulativo y práctico, sobre varios asuntos de aritmética civil y astronómica. Incluye 3 cuadernos. 1. Es útil para los pueblos, ganaderos, escribanos, contadores, moralistas, juristas y comerciantes.* Madrid: Francisco Javier García, 1758.

Ifern, Francesc. *Compendi breu de las quatre reglas generals de la arismetica practica: que son sumar, restar, multiplicàr y partir: ab algunas reglas necessarias per los negociants; ab una taula al fi, à rahò de tant lo any, á quant vé per lo mes y lo dia* (1746). Gerona: Narcís Oliva, 1753.

Iturburu, Joaquín de. *Nuevo método para las operaciones de cambios de España con las principales plazas extranjeras de comercio*. 2 vols. Madrid: José del Collado, 1805–1806.

Jócano y Madaria, Sebastián de. *Disertación crítica y apologética del arte de llevar cuenta y razón contra la opinión del Barón de Bielfeld, acerca del arte en general y del método llamado partidas dobles en particular*. Madrid: Gerónimo Ortega y Herederos de Ibarra, 1793.

León, Andrés de. *Extracto de reducciones de monedas, de pesos, de medidas y de números quebrados, con la cuenta de raciones de armada, noticia de los individuos de un ejército, sueldos que gozan al mes, y al día e inválidos que se descuentan, con otras noticias provechosas.* Zaragoza: Joseph Fort, 1743.

Luque y Leyva, Luis de. *Arte de la partida doble* (1774). Cadiz: Imprenta del autor, 1783.

Luque y Leyva, Luis de. *Aritmética de escritorios de comercio, en que se comprenden todos los cambios, aneajes, reducciones y toda otra especie de cuenta que pueda ocurrir.* Cadiz: Imprenta del autor, 1780.

Martínez Gómez, Vicente. *Manual de comercio, en que se halla la descripción de las monedas, pesas y medidas que se usan en los reinos de España*. Madrid: Benito Cano, 1795.

Medrano, Felipe. *Tablas de reducción, que comprenden cuantas comparaciones puedan hacerse entre el pie, y vara de Castilla, y pie de Rey, y toisa de París, en longitud cuadrado, y cúbico; las del peso específico de los pies cúbicos de Castilla de agua dulce, madera de pino [...] las de la diferencia del aparente al verdadero nivel en medida de Castilla, y de París*. 1748.

Molledo y Martín, Jerónimo. *Nuevo manual de comerciantes. Tratado utilísimo para los banqueros, mercaderes y demás personas que negocian, libran o toman letras de cambio para Holanda, Génova, Hamburgo, Francia e Inglaterra.* 2 vols. Madrid: José del Collado, 1805.

Muñoz de Amador, Bernardo. *Proporción aritmética-práctica de la plata. Tablas generales, en que se demuestra el peso y valor de la plata en todas leyes reducido a las últimas, que por la Real Pragmática del año pasado de 1728 se observa; y todo puesto según práctica de ensayadores, contrastes y mercaderes, muy útil para todos los comerciantes en plata.* 2 vols. Madrid: Antonio Marín, 1741.

Muñoz de Amador, Bernardo. *Arte de ensayar oro y plata, con breves reglas para la teórica y la práctica, en la que se explica también el oficio de ensayador y marcador mayor de los reinos.* Madrid: Antonio Marín, 1755.

Pérez de Moya, Juan. *Aritmética práctica y especulativa* (1562). Barcelona: Rafael Figueró, 1703.

Poy y Comes, Manuel. *Elementos de aritmética y álgebra, para la instrucción de la juventud.* Barcelona: Francisco Suriá y Burgada, 1786.

Poy y Comes, Manuel. *Llave aritmética y algebraica.* Barcelona: Francisco Suriá y Burgada, 1790.

Poy y Comes, Manuel. *Rudimentos de la razón y proporción en común y en particular, con aplicación del álgebra a varias cuestiones de comercio.* Barcelona: Francisco Suriá y Burgada, 1790.

Puig, Andrés. *Aritmética especulativa y práctica y arte de álgebra: en la cual se contiene todo lo que pertenece al arte menor o mercantil y a las dos álgebras, racional e irracional: con la explicación de todas las proposiciones y problemas de los libros* [...] *de la matemática Euclides* (1672). Barcelona: Giralt, 1715.

Reguera Valdelomar, Juan. *Recopilación de todas las providencias respectivas a vales reales expedidas desde MDCCLXXX.* Madrid: Viuda e Hijo de Marín, c. 1802.

Rendón y Fuentes, Francisco. *Prontuario aritmético o breve reducción de unas monedas a otras: en que se comprenden todas las que se usan en este reino en las casas de comercio, y oficinas, para pagos y cobros.* Cadiz: Espinosa de los Monteros, 1763.

Rodríguez, Antonio. *Arte sutilísima, práctica y teórica, para contar guarismo de repente. Por lo cual se harán con mucha facilidad todas las reglas y reducciones de monedas, pesos y medidas, censos, rentas, pechos, alcabalas y aduanas, a tanto por ciento, que se usan en Castilla y otros reinos.* Madrid: Juan Esteban, 1719.

Rodríguez, Antonio and Pedro Enguera. *Arte útil y compendioso para facilitar el método de las cuentas de compras, ventas, censos, alcabalas, pesos, medidas y reducciones de monedas, según las Pragmáticas que se observan en este reino de Castilla y otros. Añadido nuevamente las faltas y aumentos del oro. Compuesto por el maestro Antonio Rodríguez, profesor de aritmética en la Universidad de Salamanca. Enmendado y *añadido por don Pedro Enguera, maestro de matemáticas del Rey y alarife de Madrid. Añadido nuevamente las faltas del oro y de la plata* (1730). Madrid: 1740.

Sage, Balthazar Georges. *Arte de ensayar oro y plata: bosquejo o descripción comparativa de la copelación de las substancias metálicas por medio del plomo o del bismuto* [...] *traducido y añadido con algunas notas por* [...] *Casimiro Gómez de Ortega*. Madrid: Joaquín Ibarra, 1785.

Santa Cruz, Miguel Jerónimo de. *Dorado contador. Aritmética especulativa y práctica. Contiene la fineza, y reglas de contar oro, y plata, y los aneajes de Flandes* (1594). Madrid: Joaquín Ibarra, 1754.

Solá, Manuel. *Aritmética teórico-práctica mercantil dispuesta en forma de diálogo*. Barcelona: Compañía Jordi, Roca y Gaspar, 1801.

Souza Brito, Gabriel de. *Norte mercantil y crisol de cuentas, dividido en tres libros* (1706). Amsterdam: Casa de Juan ten Houten, 1770.

Taboada y Ulloa, Juan Antonio. *Antorcha luciente: que con su claridad alumbra, para registrar el más breve modo de reducir a reales de vellón doblones, y pesos efectivos de a diez reales de plata provincial* (1725). Madrid: Imprenta y librería de Gabriel Ramírez, 1751.

Taboada y Ulloa, Juan Antonio. *Antorcha aritmética práctica, provechosa para tratantes y mercaderes. Instruye a los principiantes con reglas del arte menor, y muchas nuevas para reducir las monedas de Castilla unas en otras. Declara modo seguro de comerciar con dichas monedas, la cobranza de vales y letras de todas partes y otras curiosidades* (1731). Madrid: Imprenta de José Otero, 1784.

Torralba y Campos, Mariano. *Descanso de comerciantes: principalmente para los que tratan en seda* [...]: *que en* [...] *1754 se imprimió a nombre de Mariano Badelles y ahora nuevamente añadido por Mariano Torralba y Campos*. Valencia: Francisco Burguete, 1784.

Tramullas y Ferreras, José. *Prontuario y guía de artífices plateros, en que se dan reglas para ligar, religar y abonar y reducir cualesquiera cantidad de oro y plata a la ley y quilate que su S. M.* [...] *manda en la Real Pragmática de 28 de febrero de 1730*. Madrid: Herederos de Francisco del Hierro, 1734.

Tramullas y Ferreras, José. *Puntual correspondencia, y reducción verídica de la moneda de vellón de Cataluña a la de Castilla, y la de Castilla a la de Cataluña: y asimismo la reducción legítima de todas las monedas corrientes de oro y plata, a reales de vellón de Castilla, según la realidad de su valor, con la explicación correspondiente de entrambas monedas*. Madrid: Juan de Oliveras, 1734.

Tramullas y Ferreras, José. *Guía, y desengaño, de artífices plateros, y marcadores de oro, y plata. En el cual se prescribe la obligación de los fabricantes plateros en preparar las materias de oro, y plata antes de construir con ellas las obras*. Barcelona: Herederos de María Martí, 1743.

Verbedel, Valero. *El contador moderno, o sea práctica moderna de contadores, en el modo de conocer los géneros, diferencias y extracciones de la cantidad redituable, según el sentido de sus contratos.* Madrid: Antonio Sanz, 1734.

Villar, Bartolomé. *Libro de cuentas para todo género de mercaderes, en el que toparán, luz los que quisieren aprender de cuenta, y claridad, para los que no saben contar.* Valencia: José García, 1716.

Zubiaur, Manuel de. *Aritmética práctica para instruir la juventud.* Bilbao: Antonio Zafra, 1718.

4 Primary Sources

Abeille, Louis-Paul. *Effets d'un privilège exclusif en matière de commerce, sur les droits de la propriété, etc.* Paris-Rouen: A.-L. Regnard, 1765.

Abeille, Louis-Paul. *El trigo considerado como género comerciable.* Madrid: Imprenta de la Gaceta, 1764.

Accarias de Serionne, Jacques. *Historia y descripción general de los intereses de comercio de todas las naciones de Europa en las cuatro partes del mundo.* 4 vols. Madrid: Miguel Escribano, 1772–1774.

Actas y Memorias de la Real Sociedad Económica de los Amigos del País de la Provincia de Segovia. 4 vols. Segovia: 1785–1793.

Aguirre, Manuel de. *Indagación y reflexiones sobre la geografía.* Madrid: Joaquín Ibarra, 1782.

Aguirre, Manuel de. *Sistema de sociedades patrióticas.* Madrid: Joaquín Ibarra, 1785.

Álamo, Manuel Romero del. *Efectos perniciosos del lujo* (1789). Rev. ed. by Elvira Martínez. Oviedo: Universidad de Oviedo, 1985.

Alcalá-Galiano, Vicente and Diego María Gallard. *Colección alfabética de los aranceles de Francia, precedida de observaciones preliminares sobre los derechos de aduanas de aquel Reino, y de las ordenanzas con que se gobiernan; y añadida de algunos otros reales decretos que rigen al presente en Francia sobre la materia.* 3 vols. Madrid: Lorenzo de San Martín, 1789.

Amat, Jaume. *Observaciones de un comerciante sobre la nota XVII del Elogio del Excelentísimo Señor Conde de Gausa.* Barcelona: Pla, 1789.

Arancel de la Gran Bretaña del año de 1802. Madrid: Imprenta Real, 1803.

Arancel de los derechos de aduanas y navegación en Francia, publicado en París en el año de 1800. Madrid: Antonio Espinosa, 1805.

Argumosa, Teodoro Ventura de. *Erudición política.* Madrid: 1743.

Arias, Antonio Sandalio de. *Cartilla elemental de agricultura acomodada a nuestro suelo y clima.* Madrid: Gómez Fuentenebro y Compañía, 1808.

Arriquíbar, Nicolás de. *Recreación política. Reflexiones sobre el Amigo de los Hombres en su Tratado de Población, considerado con respecto a nuestros intereses* (1779). Rev. ed. by Jesús Astigarraga and José Manuel Barrenechea. Vitoria: Instituto Vasco de Estadística, 1987.

Banqueri, Justo José. *Discurso sobre la libertad, facilidad y utilidad del comercio interior* (c. 1801). RAH, mss. 9/4729.

Barberi, Mateo Antonio. *Cartas político-instructivas sobre varios puntos de la felicidad pública.* Madrid: Imprenta de Francisco Javier García, 1770.

Beawes, Wyndham. *Lex mercatoria rediviva.* 2 vols. London: Baldwin and Crowder, 1751.

Beawes, Wyndham. *A Civil, Commercial, Political, and Literary History of Spain and Portugal.* 2 vols. London: R. Faulder, 1793.

Bielfeld, Jakob Friedrich von. *Institutions politiques.* 2 vols. The Hague: Pierre Gosse, 1760.

Bielfeld, Jakob Friedrich von. *Instituciones políticas.* 6 vols. Madrid: 1767–1801.

Bielfeld, Jakob Friedrich von. *Instituciones políticas.* Bordeaux: Francisco Mor, 1781.

Butel-Dumont, Georges Marie. *De la histoire et commerce des colonies angloises dans l'Amerique septentrionale.* London: 1755.

Cabarrús, Francisco. *Elogio del Exmo. Sr. Conde Gausa.* Madrid: Viuda e hijos de Ibarra, 1785.

Cabra, Jerónimo José de. *Pruebas del Espíritu del Sr. Melon y de las Proposiciones de economía civil y comercio del Sr. Normante.* 2 vols. Madrid: Isidoro de Hernández Pacheco, 1787.

Campillo, José del. *España despierta* (c. 1743). Rev. ed. by Dolores Mateos. Oviedo: Principado de Asturias, 1993.

Campomanes, Pedro Rodríguez, Count of. *Discurso sobre el fomento de la industria popular.* Madrid: Antonio de Sancha, 1774.

Campomanes, Pedro Rodríguez, Count of. *Discurso sobre la educación popular de los artesanos y su fomento.* Madrid: Antonio de Sancha, 1775.

Campomanes, Pedro Rodríguez, Count of. *Apéndice a la educación popular.* 4 vols. Madrid: Antonio de Sancha, 1775–1777.

Cantillon, Richard. *Essai sur la nature du commerce en général* (1755). Rev. ed. by Richard van den Berg. New York: Routledge, 2015.

Cartilla rústica dispuesta para instrucción de labradores. Salamanca: Imprenta de Francisco de Tóxar, 1799.

Cary, John. *Storia del commercio della Gran Bretagna scritta da John Cary* (1758). 2 vols. Rev. ed. by Maria Luisa Perna. Naples: Istituto Italiano per gli Studi Filosofici, 1984.

Cavanilles, Antonio José. *Observaciones sobre la historia natural, geografía, agricultura, población y frutos del Reino de Valencia.* 2 vols. Madrid: Imprenta Real, 1795–1797.

Child, Josiah. *Traités sur le commerce.* Amsterdam-Paris: 1754.

Cistué, José Benito. *Elogio del Ilustrísimo Señor D. Juan Antonio Hernández Pérez de Larrea, Obispo de Valladolid y Director de la Real Sociedad Aragonesa*. Zaragoza: 1803.

Cliquot de Blervache, Simon. *Dissertation sur les effets que produit le taux de l'intérêst de l'argent sur le commerce et l'agriculture*. Amiens: Veuve Godart, 1754.

Code de commerce. Paris: 1807.

Código de comercio de Francia con los discursos de los oradores del Consejo de Estado y del Tribunado. Madrid: Imprenta de la Calle de la Greda, 1808.

Condillac, Étienne Bonnot de. *El comercio y el gobierno considerados por sí mismos y sus relaciones recíprocas*. In *Memorias instructivas y curiosas*, edited by Gerónimo Suárez y Núñez, II, 219–386; IV, 3–116. Madrid: Pedro Marín, 1778–1780.

Coyer, Gabriel-François, Abbé. *La nobleza comerciante*. Madrid: Joaquín Ibarra, 1781.

Crumpe, Samuel. *An Essay of the Best Means of Providing Employment for the People*. London: 1793.

Davenant, Charles. "Del uso de la Arismética Política en el comercio y rentas." In Nicolás de Arriquíbar, *Recreación política. Reflexiones sobre el Amigo de los Hombres en su Tratado de Población, considerado con respecto a nuestros intereses* (1779). Rev. ed. by José Manuel Barrenechea and Jesús Astigarraga, 77–86. Vitoria: Instituto Vasco de Estadística, 1987.

Diderot, Denis and Jean le Rond D'Alembert, eds. *Encyclopédie ou Dictionnaire raisonné des sciences, des arts et des métiers*. Vol. I. Paris: 1751.

Duhamel de Monceau, Henri-Louis. *Tratado del cultivo de granos*. Madrid: José Ortega, 1751.

Elgueta, Antonio de. *Cartilla de agricultura de moreras*. Madrid: Gabriel Ramírez, 1761.

Essais de la Société de Dublin. Paris: Frères Estienne, 1759.

Estatutos aprobados por S. M. para gobierno de la Real Sociedad Bascongada de Amigos del País. Vitoria: Robles, 1773.

Estatutos da Aula do Commercio ordenados por el Rey. Lisbon: Miguel Rodrigues, 1759.

Filangieri, Gaetano. *Scienza della legislazione*. 7 vols. Naples: 1780–1791

Filangieri, Gaetano. *Ciencia de la legislación*. 6 vols. Madrid: Manuel González, 1787–1789.

Foronda, Valentín de. *Cartas escritas por Mr. De Fer al autor del Correo de Europa*. Bordeaux: Louis Boudrie, 1783.

Foronda, Valentín de. *Cartas sobre los asuntos más exquisitos de la economía* política, *y sobre las leyes criminales* (1789–1794). Rev. ed. by José Manuel Barrenechea. Vitoria: Gobierno Vasco, 1994.

Foronda, Valentín de. *Miscelánea o colección de varios discursos*. Madrid: Imprenta de Manuel González, 1793.

Foronda, Valentín de. "Disertación sobre la libertad de escribir." In *Miscelánea o colección de varios discursos*, edited by Valentín de Foronda, 176–98. Madrid: Imprenta de Manuel González, 1793.

Fougeret de Montbron, Louis-Charles. *Préservatif contre l'anglomanie.* Minorca: 1757.

Galiani, Ferdinando. *Diálogos sobre el comercio de los granos, atribuidos al Abate Galiani.* Madrid: Joaquín Ibarra, 1775.

Gándara, Miguel Antonio de la. *Apuntes sobre el bien y el mal de España* (1804). Rev. ed. by Jacinta Macías. Madrid: IEF, 1988.

Gee, Joshua. *Consideraciones sobre el comercio y la navegación de la Gran Bretaña.* Madrid: Imprenta de Juan de San Martín, 1753.

Genovesi, Antonio. *Delle Lezioni di comercio o sia di economia civile* (1765–1767). Rev. ed. by Maria Luisa Perna. Naples: Istituto Italiano per gli Studi Filosofici, 2005.

Genovesi, Antonio. *Lecciones de comercio, o bien de economía civil.* 3 vols. Madrid: Viuda de Ibarra, 1785–1786.

Griselini, Francesco. *Discurso sobre el problema de si corresponde a los párrocos y curas de las aldeas el instruir a los labradores en los buenos principios de la economía campestre.* Zaragoza: B. Miedes, n. d. [1784].

Herbert, Jean-Claude. *Essai sur la police générale des grains, sur leurs prix et sur les effets de l'agriculture.* London: 1753.

Herbert, Jean-Claude. *Discurso sobre el comercio de los granos en que se demuestran la utilidad y necesidad de un libre comercio, para que tenga siempre un precio cómodo, y para fomento general de la agricultura.* Madrid: Miguel Escribano, 1765.

Herbert, Jean-Claude. *Ensayo sobre la policía general de los granos, sobre sus precios y sobre los efectos de la agricultura.* Madrid: Antonio Espinosa, 1795.

Heros, Juan Francisco de los. *Discursos sobre el comercio* (1790). Rev ed. by José Manuel Barrenechea. Madrid: Banco Bilbao Vizcaya, 1989.

Herrenschwand, Jean. *Principios de economía política.* Madrid: Vega y Compañía, 1800.

Hume, David. *Political Discourses.* Edinburgh: 1752.

Hume, David. *Discursos políticos del señor David Hume.* Madrid: Imprenta de González, 1789.

Instituciones económicas de la Sociedad de Amigos del País de la ciudad y Reino de Valencia. Valencia: Benito Monfort, 1777.

Jovellanos, Gaspar Melchor de. "Introducción a un discurso sobre el estudio de la economía civil" (1776). In *Obras de Don Gaspar Melchor de Jovellanos* (BAE, vol. LXXXVII), edited by Miguel Artola, 7–17. Madrid: 1956.

Jovellanos, Gaspar Melchor de. "Discurso económico sobre los medios de promover la felicidad de Asturias dirigido a su Real Sociedad" (1781). In *Obras completas. Vol. X. Escritos económicos*, edited by Vicent Llombart and Joaquín Ocampo, 267–304. Gijón: KRK ediciones, 2008.

Jovellanos, Gaspar Melchor de. "Dictamen sobre la oportunidad de publicar una gaceta económica" (1786). In *Obras completas. Vol. X. Escritos económicos*, edited by Vicent Llombart and Joaquín Ocampo, 648–51. Gijón: KRK ediciones, 2008.

Jovellanos, Gaspar Melchor de. "Dictamen que dio la Clase de Agricultura de la Sociedad Económica [...] sobre las causas de la decadencia de estos cuerpos" (1786). In *Obras completas. Vol. X. Escritos económicos*, edited by Vicent Llombart and Joaquín Ocampo, 652–60. Gijón: KRK ediciones, 2008.

Jovellanos, Gaspar Melchor de. "Informe de la Sociedad Económica de esta Corte al Real y Supremo Consejo de Castilla en el Expediente de Ley Agraria" (1795). In *Gaspar Melchor de Jovellanos. Escritos económicos*, edited by Vicent Llombart, 189–359. Madrid: RACMP, 2000.

Jovellanos, Gaspar Melchor de. "Introducción a un discurso sobre la economía civil y la instrucción pública" (1796–1797). In *Obras completas. Vol. X. Escritos económicos*, edited by Vicent Llombart and Joaquín Ocampo, 886–901. Gijón: KRK ediciones, 2008.

Jovellanos, Gaspar Melchor de. "Plan para la educación de la nobleza y las clases pudientes" (1798). In *Obras de Don Gaspar Melchor de Jovellanos* (BAE, vol. LXXXVII), edited by Miguel Artola, 295–332. Madrid: 1956.

Jovellanos, Gaspar Melchor de. "Bases para la formación de un plan de educación pública" (1808). In *Obras publicadas e inéditas de G. M. Jovellanos* (BAE, vol. XLVI), edited by Cándido Nocedal, 268–71. Madrid: Rivadeneyra, 1858.

Kruse, Jürgen Elert. *Allgemeiner und besonders hamburgischer contorist* (1753). Hamburg: 1771.

Larruga, Eugenio. *Historia de la Real y General Junta de Comercio, Moneda y Minas y Dependencias de Extranjeros*. 13 vols. Madrid: c. 1788. BCMH, mss. 479A, 479B, 479C.

Larruga, Eugenio. *Memorias políticas y económicas sobre los frutos, comercio, fábricas y minas de España*. 45 vols. Madrid: Benito Cano, 1787–1800.

Mably, Gabriel Bonnot de. *Derecho público de la Europa, fundado en los Tratados concluidos hasta el año de 1740*. 2 vols. Madrid: Viuda de Diego de Peralta, 1746.

Magnier Grandprez, Jean-Charles. *Code des douanes de la République Française*. Strasbourg: 1802.

Marien y Arróspide, Tomás Antonio de. *Tableau des droits et usages de commerce relatifs au passage du Sund*. Copenhagen: M. Moller, 1776.

Marien y Arróspide, Tomás Antonio de. *Catálogo de los derechos y usos del comercio relativos al paso del Sund*. Madrid: Imprenta Real, 1789.

Marien y Arróspide, Tomás Antonio de. *Tratado general de monedas, pesas, medidas y cambios de todas las naciones reducidas a las que se usan en España*. Madrid: Benito Cano, 1789.

Melon, Jean-François. *Essai politique sur le commerce* (1734). 1736.

Mémoires et observations recueillies par la Société Oeconomique de Berne. 33 vols. 1762–1773.

Memorias de la Real Sociedad Económica Mallorquina de Amigos del País. Palma de Majorca: Ignacio Sarrá, 1784.

Memorias de la Real Sociedad Patriótica de Sevilla. Seville: Vázquez, Hidalgo y Compañía, 1779.

Memorias de la Real Sociedad Tudelana de los Deseosos del Bien Público. Madrid: Imprenta Real, 1787.

Memorias de la Sociedad Económica. 5 vols. Madrid: Antonio Sancha, 1780–1795.

Mirabeau, Riqueti, Victor, Marquis of. *L'Ami des Hommes, ou Traité de la population*. 3 vols. Avignon: 1758–1760.

Mirabeau, Riqueti, Victor, Marquis of. *Disertación sobre el cultivo de trigos, que la Academia de Agricultura de la ciudad de Berna, en Suiza, premió en el año de 1760*. Madrid: Joaquín Ibarra, 1764.

Molloy, Charles. *Derecho marítimo y naval, o tratado de los negocios marítimos y del comercio. Obra escrita en inglés por el Señor Carlos Moloy, y traducida al castellano por D. Cesáreo de Nava Palacio, con varias adiciones*. 4 vols. Madrid: Imprenta Real, 1793.

Morellet, André. *Prospectus d'un nouveau dictionnaire de commerce*. Paris: Frères Estienne, 1769.

Morellet, André. *Mémoires inédits de l'Abbé Morellet, sur le Dix-huitième siècle et sur la Révolution*. 2 vols. Geneva: Slatkine Reprints, 1967.

Navia Osorio, Álvaro, Marquis of Santa Cruz de Marcenado. *Reflexiones militares*. 10 vols. Turin: Juan Francisco Mairesse and Alexandro Vimercato, 1724–1727.

Navia Osorio Álvaro, Marquis of Santa Cruz de Marcenado. *Rapsodia económico-política- monárquica*. Madrid: A. Marín, 1732.

Necker, Jacques. *Sobre la legislación y el comercio de los granos*. In *Memorias instructivas y curiosas*, edited by Gerónimo Suárez y Núñez, VIII, 3–237. Madrid: Pedro Marín, 1786.

Normante, Lorenzo. *Discurso sobre la utilidad de los conocimientos económico-políticos, y la necesidad de su estudio metódico*. Zaragoza: Blas de Miedes, 1784.

Normante, Lorenzo. *Proposiciones de economía civil y comercio*. Zaragoza: Blas de Miedes, 1785.

Normante, Lorenzo. *Espíritu del Señor Melon en su Ensayo político sobre el comercio*. Zaragoza: Blas de Miedes, 1786.

Ordenanzas para el Real Colegio de San Telmo de Sevilla. Madrid: Viuda de Ibarra, 1786.

Panckoucke, Charles-Joseph, ed. *Encyclopédie méthodique. Économie politique et diplomatique*. 4 vols. Paris-Liège: Panckoucke and Plomteux, 1784–1788.

Panckoucke, Charles-Joseph, ed. *Enciclopedia metódica. Fábricas, artes y oficios, traducido del francés al castellano por Don Antonio Carbonell y Borja*. 2 vols. Madrid: Sancha, 1794.

Patullo, Henri. *Discurso sobre el mejoramiento de los terrenos*. Madrid: Antonio Sancha, 1774.

Plan de una Sociedad Económica o Academia de agricultura, ciencias y artes útiles, y comercio (1763). San Sebastián: 1985.

Pluche, Nöel-Antoine. *Espectáculo de la naturaleza, o conversaciones acerca de las particularidades de la historia natural.* 16 vols. Madrid: Gabriel Ramírez, 1753–1755.

Plumard de Dangeul, Louis-Joseph. *Remarques sur les avantages et les désavantages de la France et de la Grande Bretagne par rapport au commerce et aux autres sources de la puissance des états.* Leyden: 1754.

Plumard de Dangeul, Louis-Joseph. *Observaciones sobre las ventajas, y desventajas de la Francia y de la Gran Bretaña, en orden al comercio, y la agricultura y demás recursos de la soberanía de los estados.* Madrid: Blas Román, 1771.

Proyecto de Mr. Colbert al rey Luis XIV de Francia sobre el comercio. Traducido del francés. Madrid: Imprenta Real, 1801.

Quintana, Francisco de la. *Dos discursos sobre el gobierno de los granos, y cultivo de las tierras.* Madrid: Francisco Xavier García, 1755.

Quintana, Manuel José. "Informe de la Junta creada por la Regencia para proponer los medios de proceder al arreglo de los diversos ramos de la instrucción pública" (1813). In *Obras completas del Excmo. Sr. D. Manuel José Quintana*, 175–91. Madrid: M. Rivadeneyra, 1852.

Raynal, Guillaume-Thomas-François. *Historia política de los establecimientos ultramarinos de las naciones europeas.* 5 vols. Madrid: Antonio Sancha, 1784–1790.

Ricard, Samuel. *Traité général du comerce* (1700). 2 vols. Amsterdam: J. Changuion, 1781.

Romá y Rossell, Francisco. *Las señales de la felicidad de España y medios de hacerlas eficaces* (1768). Rev. ed. by Ernet Lluch. Barcelona: Alta Fulla, 1988.

Rozier, François, Abbé. *Cours complet d'agriculture* [...] *ou Dictionnaire universel d'agriculture.* 10 vols. Paris: 1781–1800.

Rozier, François, Abbé. *Curso completo, o Diccionario universal de agricultura teórica, práctica, económica, y de medicina rural y veterinaria.* 16 vols. Madrid: Imprenta Real, 1797–1803.

Rubín de Celis, Manuel. *El Corresponsal del Censor.* Rev. ed. by Klaus-Dieter Ertler, Renate Hodab and Inmaculada Urzainqui. Madrid: Iberoamericana, 2009.

Rumford, Benjamin Thompson, Count of. *Ensayos políticos, económicos y filosóficos.* 2 vols. Madrid: Imprenta Real, 1800–1801.

Savary des Brûlons, Jacques and Philémon-Louis. *Dictionnaire universel de commerce.* 3 vols. Paris: J. Estienne, 1723–1730.

Say, Jean-Baptiste. *Tratado de economía política o exposición simple del modo cómo se forman, distribuyen y consumen las riquezas.* 3 vols. Madrid: Pedro María Caballero-Gómez Fuentenebro, 1804–1807.

Seigneux de Correvon, Gabriel. *Essais sur l'esprit de la législation, favorable à l'agriculture, à la population, au commerce, aux arts, aux métiers.* Paris: Dessaint, 1766.

Seixo, Vicente del. *Lecciones prácticas de agricultura y economía que da un padre a su hijo.* 5 vols. Madrid: Pantaleón Aznar, 1792–1795.

Seixo, Vicente del. *Reflexiones cristianas y políticas sobre el estado religioso y el celibato, comparado con el del matrimonio*. Madrid: Pantaleón Aznar, 1795.

Seixo, Vicente del. *Compendio de observaciones que forman el plano de un viaje político y filosófico que debe hacerse dentro y fuera del reino en que nacemos*. Madrid: Pantaleón Aznar, 1796.

Seixo, Vicente del. *Reflexiones sobre los progresos de agricultura y pastoría*. Madrid: Pantaleón Aznar, 1797.

Seixo, Vicente del. *Cartilla de labradores*. Madrid: 1800.

Sempere y Guarinos, Juan. *Ensayo de una biblioteca de los mejores escritores de Carlos III*. 6 vols. Madrid: Imprenta Real, 1785–1789.

Smith, Adam. *An Inquiry Into the Nature and Causes of the Wealth of Nations* (1776). 2 vols. Rev. ed. by Roy H. Campbell, Andrew S. Skinner and William B. Todd. Oxford: OUP, 1976.

Smith, Adam. *Investigación de la naturaleza y causas de la riqueza de las naciones*. 4 vols. Valladolid: Viuda e Hijos de Santander, 1794.

Suárez y Núñez, Gerónimo. *Tratado legal teórico y práctico de letras de cambio*. Madrid: José Doblado, 1788.

Targa, Carlos. *Reflexiones sobre los contratos marítimos*. Madrid: Javier García, 1753.

Terreros, Esteban. *Diccionario castellano con las voces de ciencias y artes*. 4 vols. Madrid: Viuda de Ibarra, Hijos y Compañía, 1786–1793.

Thomas, Antoine-Léonard. *Elogio de Maximiliano de Béthune, Duque de Sully*. Madrid: Imprenta Real, 1763.

Torres, Pedro de. *Diversión honesta, en que se forman cinco conversaciones rústico-económicas, para entretenimiento decente*. Granada: Imprenta Real, 1785.

Tratado del contrato de cambio. Madrid: Benito Cano, 1788.

Turgot, Anne-Robert-Jacques. *Reflexiones sobre la formación y distribución de las riquezas*. In *Memorias instructivas y curiosas*, edited by Gerónimo Suárez y Núñez, XII: 3–100. Madrid: Pedro Marín, 1791.

Ulloa, Bernardo de. *Restablecimiento de fábricas y comercio español*. 2 vols. Madrid: Antonio Marín, 1740.

Uztáriz, Gerónimo de. *Teórica y práctica de comercio y de marina* (1724). Rev. ed. by Gabriel Franco. Madrid: Aguilar, 1768.

Uztáriz, Gerónimo de. *Théorie et pratique du commerce et de la marine*. Hamburg: Chrétien Herold, 1753.

Valcárcel, José Antonio. *Agricultura general, y gobierno de la casa del campo*. 10 vols. Valencia: 1765–1795.

Véron de Forbonnais, François. *Le négociant anglois, ou traduction libre du livre intitulé: The British Merchant, contenant divers mémoires sur le commerce de l'Angleterre avec la France, le Portugal et l'Espagne*. 2 vols. Dresde: 1753.

Véron de Forbonnais, François. *Considérations sur les finances d'Espagne*. Paris: 1753.

Véron de Forbonnais, François. *Elementos de comercio*. 2 vols. Madrid: Imprenta de Francisco Xavier García, 1765.

Vidal y Cabasés, Francisco. *Conversaciones instructivas en que se trata de fomentar la agricultura por medio del riego de las tierras*. Madrid: Antonio de Sancha, 1778.

Villava, Victorián de. *Discurso preliminar del traductor de las Lecciones de comercio del Genovesi, en que se da razón de la obra y se la califica con imparcialidad*. Huesca: Viuda de Miguel de Larumbe, n. d. [1786].

Virio, Juan Bautista. *Colección alfabética de los aranceles de la Gran Bretaña, y extractos de las leyes, reglamentos, órdenes y providencias expedidas en aquel reino para el régimen de sus aduanas, y fomento de su comercio*. 4 vols. Madrid: J. Ibarra, 1792.

Ward, Bernardo. *Obra pía*. Valencia: Salvador Faulí, 1750.

Ward, Bernardo. *Proyecto económico*. Madrid: Joaquín Ibarra, 1779.

Zavala y Auñón, Miguel de. *Representación al R. N. Señor D. Phelipe V*. Madrid: 1732.

Zuazo, Ramón María de. *Memoria económica sobre el comercio y la navegación, origen de los juzgados consulares, su organización, y reformas de que son susceptibles* (c. 1796). BNE, mss. 9515.

Zuazo, Ramón María de. *Tratado de comercio y de la jurisdicción consular* (c. 1796). BUS, mss. 32–218.

5 Secondary Sources

Addy, George M. *The Enlightenment in the University of Salamanca*. Durham: Duke University Press, 1966.

Aguilar Piñal, Francisco. *La prensa española en el siglo XVIII. Diarios, revistas y pronósticos*. Madrid: CSIC, 1978.

Aguilar Piñal, Francisco. *Bibliografía de autores españoles del siglo XVIII*. 10 vols. Madrid: CSIC, 1981–2001.

Aguilar Piñal, Francisco. "Un traductor de la ciencia ilustrada: Suárez y Núñez." *Cuadernos Dieciochistas* 7 (2006): 87–112.

Albareda, Joaquim. *Felipe V y el triunfo del absolutismo. Cataluña en un conflicto europeo (1700–1714)*. Barcelona: Generalitat de Catalunya, 2002.

Albareda, Joaquim. *La guerra de Sucesión de España (1700–1714)*. Barcelona: Crítica, 2010.

Albertone, Manuela. "Fondements économiques de la réflexion du XVIIIe siècle autor de l'homme porteur de droits." *Clio@Themis* 3 (2010), http://www.cliothemis.com/Clio-Themis-numero-3.

Alimento, Antonella. "La concurrence comme politique moderne: la contribution de l'école de Gournay à la naissance d'une sphère publique dans la France des années 1750–1760." In *L'économie politique et la sphère publique dans le débats des Lumières*, edited by Jesús Astigarraga and Javier Usoz, 213–27. Madrid: CV, 2013.

Alimento, Antonella. "Beyond the Treaty of Utrecht: Véron de Forbonnais' French Translation of *The British Merchant* (1753)." *History of European Ideas* 40, no. 8 (2014), 1044–66. DOI: http://dx.doi.org/10.1080/01916599.2014.968331.

Alimento, Antonella and Koen Stapelbroek. "Trade and Treaties: Balancing the Interstate system." In *The Politics of Commerce Treaties in the Eighteenth Century. Balance of Power, Balance of Trade*, edited by Antonella Alimento and Koen Stapelbroek, 1–43. Cham: Palgrave MacMillan, 2017. DOI: http://dx.doi.org/10.1007/978-3-319-53574-6_1.

Almenar, Salvador. "El desarrollo del pensamiento económico clásico en España." In *Economía y economistas españoles. Vol. IV. La economía clásica*, edited by Enrique Fuentes Quintana, 7–92. Barcelona: Galaxia Gütenberg-Círculo de Lectores, 2000.

Almodovar, António and Jose Luis Cardoso. "Textbooks and the Teaching of Political Economy in Portugal 1759–1910." In *The Economic Reader. Textbooks, Manuals and the Dissemination of the Economic Sciences During the 19th and Early 20th Centuries*, edited by Massimo Augello and Marco E. L. Guidi, 190–213. London-New York: Routledge, 2012.

Almuiña, César. "Estudio Preliminar." In *Diario Pinciano, primer periódico de Valladolid (1787–88)*, edited by César Almuiña, 5–74. Valladolid: 1978.

Álvarez Barrientos, Joaquín. "El periodista en la España del siglo XVIII y la profesionalidad del escritor." *Estudios de Historia Social* 51–53 (1999): 29–39.

Álvarez Barrientos, Joaquín, ed. *Se hicieron literatos para ser políticos*. Madrid: Universidad de Cádiz, 2004.

Álvarez Barrientos, Joaquín. *Los hombres de letras en la España del siglo XVIII. Apóstoles y arribistas*. Madrid: Castalia, 2006.

Álvarez de Miranda, Pedro. *Palabras e ideas: el léxico de la Ilustración temprana en España (1680–1760)*. Madrid: Real Academia Española, 1992.

Álvarez de Miranda, Pedro. "Los proyectos enciclopédicos en el siglo XVIII español." In *Europa: proyecciones y percepciones históricas*, 91–6. Salamanca: Universidad de Salamanca, 1992.

Álvarez Morales, Antonio. "La difusión del derecho natural y de gentes europeo en la universidad española de los siglos XVIII y XIX." In *Doctores y escolares. II Congreso Internacional de Historia de las Universidades hispánicas*, I, 49–60. Valencia: Universidad de València, 1995.

Anes, Gonzalo. "Coyuntura económica e 'Ilustración': Las sociedades de amigos del país." In *Economía e Ilustración en la España del siglo XVIII*, 11–41. Barcelona: Ediciones Ariel, 1969.

Anes, Gonzalo. "*L'Encyclopédie ou Dictionnaire raisonné des sciences, des arts et des métiers* en España." In *Homenaje a Xavier Zubiri*, 123–30. Madrid: Moneda y Crédito, 1970.

Anes, Gonzalo. "La *Encyclopédie Méthodique* en España." In *Ciencia social y análisis económico,* edited by José Luis García Delgado and Julio Segura, 105–52. Madrid: Tecnos, 1978.

Anes, Gonzalo. *La Ley Agraria*. Madrid: Alianza, 1995.

Anes, Gonzalo. "La Inquisición en la *Encyclopédie*: una censura inédita de Jovellanos." In *El siglo que llaman ilustrado*, edited by Joaquín Álvarez Barrientos and José Checa, 87–97. Madrid: CSIC, 1996.

Argemí, Lluis, ed. *Agricultura e Ilustración*. Madrid: Ministerio de Agricultura, Pesca y Alimentación, 1988.

Arrieta, Jon. "L'antitesis pactisme-absolutisme durant la guerra de Successió a Catalunya." In *Del patriotisme al catalanisme: societat i política (segles XVI-XIX)*, 105–28. Vic: Eumo, 2001.

Arrieta, Jon. "Austracismo, ¿qué hay detrás de ese nombre?" In *Los Borbones. Dinastía y memoria de nación en la España del siglo XVIII*, edited by Pablo Fernández Albaladejo, 177–216. Madrid: Marcial Pons-CV, 2001.

Astigarraga, Jesús. "Estudio Preliminar." In *Ilustración y economía en Navarra (1770–1793): el pensamiento económico de José María Magallón y Francisco Javier de Argáiz*, edited by Jesús Astigarraga, XIII-CXXX. Vitoria: Gobierno Vasco, 1996.

Astigarraga, Jesús. *Los ilustrados vascos*. Barcelona: Crítica, 2003.

Astigarraga, Jesús. "Diálogo económico en la 'otra' Europa. Las traducciones españolas de los economistas de la Ilustración napolitana (A. Genovesi, F. Galiani y G. Filangieri)." *CROMOHS* 9 (2004), http://www.fupress.net/index.php/cromohs/article/view/15645/14511. DOI: http://dx.doi.org/10.13128/Cromohs-15645.

Astigarraga, Jesús. "La prima versione spagnola della *Scienza della legislazione*." In *Diritti e Costituzione. L'opera di Gaetano Filangieri e la sua fortuna europea*, edited by Antonio Trampus, 61–84. Bologna: Il Mulino, 2005.

Astigarraga, Jesús. "André Morellet y la enseñanza de la economía en la Ilustración española: la *Memoria sobre la utilidad del establecimiento de una escuela de Comercio*." *Cuadernos de Historia Moderna* 35 (2010): 143–73.

Astigarraga, Jesús. "La dérangeante découverte de l'autre: les (més)aventures de *l'Essai politique sur le commerce* (1734) de Jean-François Melon dans l'Espagne du XVIIIe siècle." *Revue d'Histoire Moderne et Contemporaine* 57 (2010): 91–118.

Astigarraga, Jesús. "La traduction au service de la politique. Le succès de Jacques Necker dans les Lumières espagnoles." *Annales Historiques de la Révolution Française* 364 (2011): 3–27.

Astigarraga, Jesús. *Luces y republicanismo*. Madrid: CEPC, 2011.

Astigarraga, Jesús. "Un nuevo sistema económico para la Monarquía española. Las *Reflexiones sobre el estado actual del comercio de España* (1761) de Simón de Aragorri." *Revista de Historia Industrial* 52 (2013): 13–44.

Astigarraga, Jesús. "Forbonnais and the Discovery of the Science of Commerce in Spain (1755–1765)." *History of European Ideas* 40, no. 8 (2014): 1087–107. DOI: 10.1080/01916599.2014.968333.

Astigarraga, Jesús. "Admirer, rougir, imiter. Spain and the European Enlightenment." In *The Spanish Enlightenment Revisited*, edited by Jesús Astigarraga, 1–17. Oxford: VF, 2015.

Astigarraga, Jesús. "Economic Societies and the Politicisation of the Spanish Enlightenment." In *The Spanish Enlightenment Revisited*, edited by Jesús Astigarraga, 63–81. Oxford: VF, 2015.

Astigarraga, Jesús. "Les traductions espagnoles des normes législatives et des écrits économiques de Turgot (1774–1791)." *Annales Historiques de la Révolution Française* 384 (2016): 27–51.

Astigarraga, Jesús. "Turgot et le débat sur la liberté du travail dans l'Espagne des Lumières (1776–1813)." *Mediterranea. Ricerche Storiche* 40 (2017): 343–72. DOI: 10.19229/1828-230X/4042017.

Astigarraga, Jesús. "*Oikonomia* y 'Comercio' en la versión española del *Journal Oeconomique*: los *Discursos mercuriales* (1752–1756) de Graef." *Cuadernos de Historia Moderna* 42, no. 1 (2017): 239–60. DOI: 10.5209/CHMO.56662.

Astigarraga, Jesús. "Prensa económica de la Ilustración española (1758–1792)." *Studia Historica- Historia Moderna* 40, no. 2 (2018): 199–232. DOI: 10.14201/shhmo20184021992321.

Astigarraga, Jesús. "Spreading the Official Economic Enlightenment in Spain: the *Memorial Literario* (17684–1808)." *Bulletin of Spanish Studies* 96, no. 10 (2019): 1607–25. DOI: 10.1080/14753820.2019.1678318.

Astigarraga, Jesús and José Manuel Barrenechea. "Estudio Preliminar." In Nicolás de Arriquíbar, *Recreación política*, edited by Jesús Astigarraga and José Manuel Barrenechea, 9–57. Bilbao: Instituto Vasco de Estadística, 1987.

Astigarraga, Jesús and Javier Usoz. "Una alternativa fisiócrata al *Informe de Ley Agraria* de Jovellanos." *RHE* XXV, no. 3 (2007): 427–58. DOI: 10.1017/S0212610900000197.

Astigarraga Jesús and Javier Usoz. "From the Neapolitan A. Genovesi of Carlo di Borbone to the Spanish A. Genovesi of Carlo III: V. de Villava's Spanish Translation of *Lezioni di Commercio*." In *Genovesi economista*, edited by Bruno Jossa, Rosario Patalano and Eugenio Zagari, 193–220. Naples: Istituto Italiano per gli Studi Filosofici, 2007.

Astigarraga, Jesús and Javier Usoz. "Algunas puntualizaciones sobre la fisiocracia en la Ilustración *tardía* española." *RHE* XXVI, no. 3 (2008): 489–97. DOI: 10.1017/S0212610900000434.

Astigarraga, Jesús and Javier Usoz. "El pensamiento político y económico ilustrado y las cátedras de la Sociedad Económica Aragonesa." *Anuario de Historia del Derecho Español* 78–79 (2008–2009): 423–48.

Astigarraga, Jesús and Javier Usoz. "The Enlightenment in Translation. Antonio Genovesi's Political Economy in Spain, 1778–1800." *Mediterranean Historical Review* 28, no. 1 (2013): 24–45. DOI: 10.1080/09518967.2013.782672.

Astigarraga Jesús and Juan Zabalza. "La fortuna del *Essai sur la nature du commerce en général* (1755), de Richard Cantillon, en la España del siglo XVIII." *Investigaciones de Historia Económica* 7, no. 3 (2007): 9–36.

Astigarraga, Jesús and Juan Zabalza. "Los diccionarios de comercio y economía en el siglo XVIII español." *Revista de Historia Industrial* 35 (2007): 13–46.

Augello, Massimo, Marco Bianchini, Gabriella Gioli and Piero Roggi, eds. *Le cattedre di economia politica in Italia.* Milan: F. Angeli, 1988.

Augello, Massimo, Marco Bianchini and Marco E. L. Guidi. eds. *Le riviste di economia in Italia (1700–1900). Dai giornali scientifico-letterari ai periodici specialistici.* Milan: F. Angeli, 1996.

Augello, Massimo and Marco E. L. Guidi, eds. *The Spread of Political Economy and the Professionalization of Economists.* London-New York: Routledge, 2003.

Augello, Massimo and Marco E. L. Guidi. *Economisti e scienza economica nell' Italia liberale (1848–1922). Una storia istituzionale.* Milan: F. Angeli, 2019.

Ausejo, Elena. "Las matemáticas en la Ilustración hispana: estado de la cuestión." In *Ilustración, ilustraciones*, edited by Jesús Astigarraga, María Victoria López-Cordón and José María Urkia, II, 693–713. San Sebastián: Real Sociedad Bascongada de Amigos del País and Sociedad Española de Conmemoraciones Culturales, 2009.

Baker, Keith Michael. "Politics and Public Opinion under the Old Regime: Some Reflections." In *Press and Politics in Pre-Revolutionary France*, edited by Jack R. Censer and Jeremy D. Popkin, 204–46. Berkeley-Los Angeles: University of California Press, 1987.

Baker, Keith Michael. *Au tribunal de l'opinion: essais sur l'imaginaire politique au XVIIIe siècle.* Paris: Payot, 1993.

Barrenechea, José Manuel. *Valentín de Foronda, reformador y economista ilustrado.* Vitoria: Diputación Foral de Álava, 1984.

Barrenechea, José Manuel. "Prólogo." In Juan Francisco de los Heros, *Discurso sobre el comercio* (c. 1775), edited by José Manuel Barrenechea, XV-LXXXV. Madrid: Banco Bilbao Vizcaya, 1989.

Barrenechea, José Manuel. "Estudio Preliminar." In Valentín de Foronda, *Cartas sobre los asuntos más exquisitos de la Economía Política y sobre las leyes criminales*, edited by José Manuel Barrenechea, xvii-CXX. Vitoria: Gobierno Vasco, 1994.

Barrenechea, José Manuel. "Estudio Preliminar." In *Moral y economía en el siglo XVIII*, edited by José Manuel Barrenechea, 9–58. Vitoria: Gobierno Vasco, 1995.

Barrenechea, José Manuel and Jesús Astigarraga. "*Estudio Preliminar*." In Francisco Joaquín de Villarreal y Ecenarro, *Elementos políticos*, edited by José Manuel Barrenechea and Jesús Astigarraga, XIII-CX. Vitoria: Gobierno Vasco, 1997.

Belissa, Marc. "What Trade for a Republican People? French Revolutionary Debates About Comercial Treaties (1792–1799)." In *The Politics of Commerce Treaties in the Eighteenth Century. Balance of Power, Balance of Trade*, edited by Antonella Alimento and Koen Stapelbroek, 421–38. Cham: Palgrave MacMillan, 2017. DOI: 10.1007/978-3-319-53374-6_16.

Berg, Richard van den. "Introduction." In Richard Cantillon, *Essai sur la nature du commerce en général*, edited by Richard van den Berg, 1–43. New York: Routledge, 2015.

Berg, Richard van den. "'A Judicious and Industrious Compiler': Mapping Postlethwayt's Dictionary of Commerce." *The European Journal of the History of Economic Thought* 24, no. 6 (2017): 1167–213.

Berkvens-Stevelinck, Christiane and Jeroom Vercruysse, eds. *Le métier de journaliste au XVIIIe Siècle*. Oxford: VF, 1993.

Bernal, Antonio Miguel. *España, proyecto inacabado. Costes/beneficios del imperio*. Madrid: Marcial Pons, 2005.

Bolado, Elsa and Lluis Argemí. "Jean Antoine Chaptal: from Chemistry to Political Economy." *The European Journal of the History of Economic Thought* 12, no. 2 (2005): 215–39. DOI: 10.1080/09672560500112512.

Bolufer, Mónica. "*Espectadores* y lectoras: representaciones e influencia del público femenino en la prensa del siglo XVIII." *Cuadernos de Estudios del siglo XVIII* 5 (1995): 23–57.

Bolufer, Mónica. "Femmes et hommes dans la société idéale. Les sociétés économiques des amis du pays dans l'Espagne des Lumières." *Dix-Huitième Siècle* 43 (2011): 487–504.

Bolufer, Mónica. "Civilizar las costumbres: el papel de la prensa periódica dieciochesca." *Bulletin of Spanish Studies* 91, no. 9–10 (2014): 97–113. DOI: 10.180/14753820.2014.96.2864.

Bolufer, Mónica. *Arte y atificio de la vida en común*. Madrid: Marcial Pons, 2019.

Bolufer, Mónica. "The Enlightenment in Spain: Classic and New Historiographical perspectives." In *Routledge Companion to the Hispanic Enlightenment,* edited by Elizabeth Franklin Lewis, Mónica Bolufer and Catherine M. Jaffe, 3–15. Abingdon-New York: Routledge, 2020. DOI: https://doi.org/10.4324/9781315180281.

Bourde, André J. *Agronomie et agronomes en France au XVIIIe siècle*. 3 vols. Paris: Service d'Edition et de Vente des Publications de l'Education Nationale, 1967.

Burke, Peter. *Cultural Hibridity, Cultural Exchange, Cultural Translation: Reflections on History and Theory*. Cambridge: Polity, 2010.

Callahan, William J. "A Note on the Royal y General Junta de Comercio, 1679–1814." *The Economic History Review* XXI, no. 3 (1968): 519–28.

Carrera, Jaume. *La enseñanza profesional en Barcelona en los siglos XVIII y XIX*. Barcelona: Bosch, 1958.

Castro, Concepción de. *El pan de Madrid.* Madrid: Alianza, 1987.

Castro, Concepción de. *Campomanes. Estado y reformismo ilustrado*. Madrid: Alianza, 1996.

Censer, Jack R. *The French Press in the Age of Enlightenment*. New York: Routledge, 1994.

Censer, Jack R. and Popkin, Jeremy D., eds. *Press and Politics in Pre-Revolutionary France*. Berkeley-Los Angeles: University of California Press, 1987.

Cervera, Pablo. *El pensamiento económico de la Ilustración valenciana*. Valencia: Generalitat Valenciana, 2003.

Cervera, Pablo. "En los orígenes del reformismo: Ilustración y agronomía en Valencia (1765–1812)." *Áreas. Revista Internacional de Ciencias Sociales* 26 (2007): 12–29.

Cole, Arthur H. *The Historical Development of Economic and Business Literature*. Boston: Baker Library, Harvard Graduate School of Business Administration, 1957.

Comín, Francisco and Bartolomé Yun. "Spain: from Composite Monarchy to Nation-State, 1492–1914. An Exceptional Case?" In *The Rise of Fiscal State: a Global History 1500–1914*, edited by Bartolomé Yun, Patrick K. O'Brien and Francisco Comín, 233–66. Cambridge: CUP, 2012. DOI: 10.1017/CBO9781139004237.013.

Coquelin, Charles and Gilbert Guillaumin. *Dictionnaire de l'économie politique* (Paris: Guillaumin, 1852–1853). 2 vols. Brussels: Meline, Cans et Compagnie, 1853–1854.

Charles, Loïc, Frédéric Lefebvre and Christine Théré, eds. *Le cercle de Vicent de Gournay*. Paris: INED, 2011.

Chartier, Roger. *The Cultural Uses of Print in Early Modern France*. Princeton, NJ: Princeton University Press, 1987.

Chartier, Roger. *Les origines culturelles de la Révolution française* (Paris: Le Seuil, 1990). Spanish trans., *Espacio público, crítica y desacralización en el siglo XVIII: los orígenes culturales de la Revolución francesa*. Barcelona: Gedisa, 1995.

Chartier, Roger. *Libros, lecturas y lectores en la Edad Moderna*. Madrid: Alianza, 1993.

Checa, Antonio. "La terminología periodística: sus orígenes y su consolidación." *Cuadernos de Ilustración al Romanticismo* 16 (2010): 1–10.

Cheney, Paul. *Revolutionary Commerce. Globalization and the French Monarchy*. Cambridge, Mss-London: Harvard University Press, 2010.

Darnton, Robert. *The Business of Enlightenment*. Cambridge-London: Harvard University Press, 1982.

De Hoyos, José Carlos. *Léxico económico en la lengua española de principios del XIX. El 'Epítome' de Jean-Baptiste Say*. San Millán de la Cogolla: Cilengua, 2018.

Defourneaux, Marcelin. *Pablo de Olavide ou l'afrancesado (1725–1803)*. Paris: PUF, 1959.

Defourneaux, Marcelin. *Inquisición y censura de libros en la España del siglo XVIII*. Madrid: Taurus, 1973.

Delgado, José Miguel. *Fomento portuario y compañías privilegiadas*. Madrid: CSIC, 1998.

Delgado, José Miguel. *El proyecto político de Carvajal*. Madrid: CSIC, 2001.

Delgado, Josep M. *Dinámicas imperiales (1650–1796)*. Barcelona: Bellaterra, 2007.

Demerson, Jorge and Paula Demerson. *La decadencia de las reales sociedades económicas de amigos del país*. Oviedo: Centro de Estudios del Siglo XVIII, 1978.

Di Battista, Francesco. "Per la storia de la prima cattedra universitaria d'economia. Napoli, 1754–1866." In *Le cattedre di economia politica in Italia*, edited by Massimo Augello, Marco Bianchini, Gabriella Gioli and Piero Roggi, 31–46. Milan: F. Angeli, 1988.

Díez Rodríguez, Fernando. *Prensa agraria en la España de la Ilustración. El Semanario de agricultura y artes dirigido a los párrocos (1797–1808)*. Madrid: Ministerio de Agricultura, 1980.

Domergue, Lucienne. *Jovellanos à la Société Économique des Amis du Pays de Madrid (1778–1795)*. Toulouse: Université de Toulouse-Le Mirail, 1971.

Domergue, Lucienne. *Censure et Lumières dans l'Espagne de Charles III*. Paris: CNRS, 1982.

Domergue, Lucienne. "La prensa periódica y la censura en la segunda mitad del siglo XVIII." *Estudios de Historia Social* 52–53 (1990): 141–49.

Donoso, Rafael. *Una contribución a la historia de la contabilidad*. Sevilla: Universidad de Sevilla, 1996.

Dopico, Fausto. *A Ilustración e a sociedade galega. A vision de Galicia dos economistas ilustrados*. Vigo: Galaxia, 1976.

Dubet, Anne. "Les calculs des gens d'argent: des traités d'arithmétique pour marchands et financiers en Espagne au XVIIIe siècle." In *Des marchands entre deux mondes*, edited by Jean-Pierre Clément, Béatrice Pérez and Sonia V. Rose, 323–38. Paris: Université Paris Sorbonne, 2007.

Dubet, Anne and Sergio Solbes. *El rey, el ministro y el tesorero*. Madrid: Marcial Pons, 2019.

Dziembowski, Edmond. *Un nouveau patriotisme français, 1750–1770*. Oxford: VF, 1998.

Dziembowski, Edmond. "Le peuple français instruit: Edme-Jacques Genet et la traduction des écrits politiques britanniques pendant la Guerre de Sept Ans." In *Cultural Transfers: France and Britain in the Long Eighteenth-Century*, edited by Ann Thomson, Simon Burrows and Edmon Dziembowski, 175–88. Oxford: VF, 2010.

Egido, Teófanes. *Opinión pública y oposición al poder en la España del siglo XVIII (1713–1759)*. Valladolid: Universidad de Valladolid, 1971.

Elliott, John H. *Imperial Spain 1469–1716* (London: 1963). Spanish trans., *La España imperial, 1469–1716*. Barcelona: Vicens Vives, 1986.

Elliott, John H. "A Europe of Composite Monarchies." *Past and Present* 137, no. 1 (1992): 48–71.

Elorza, Antonio. *La ideología liberal en la Ilustración española*. Madrid: Taurus, 1970.

Elorza, Antonio. "Estudio Preliminar." In Manuel de Aguirre, *Cartas y Discursos del Militar Ingenuo al Correo de los Ciegos de Madrid*, edited by Antonio Elorza, 11–68. San Sebastián: Izarra, 1974.

Enciso, Luis María. *Nipho y el periodismo español del siglo XVIII*. Valladolid: Universidad de Valladolid, 1956.

Enciso, Luis María. *Prensa económica del XVIII: El Correo mercantil de España y sus Indias*. Valladolid: Universidad de Valladolid: 1958.

Enciso, Luis María. "La recepción de la *Enciclopedia* en España." In *Las Enciclopedias en España antes de l'Encyclopédie*, edited by Alfredo Alvar, 501–45. Madrid: CSIC, 2009.

Enciso, Luis María. *Compases finales de la cultura ilustrada en la época de Carlos IV*. Madrid: RAH, 2013.

Escolano, Agustín. *Educación y economía en la España ilustrada*. Madrid: Ministerio de Educación y Ciencia, 1988.

Estrada-Rius, Albert. *La casa de la moneda de Barcelona*. Lleida: Pagès, 2015.

Étienvre, Françoise. "Traducción y renovación cultural a mediados del siglo XVIII en España." In *Fénix de España*, edited by Pablo Fernández Albaladejo, 93–117. Madrid: Marcial Pons, 2006.

Fernández Albaladejo, Pablo. *Fragmentos de monarquía*. Madrid: Alianza, 1992.

Fernández Albaladejo, Pablo. "Dinastía y comunidad política: el momento de la patria." In *Los Borbones. Dinastía y memoria de nación en la España del siglo XVIII*, edited by Pablo Fernández Albaladejo, 485–532. Madrid: Marcial Pons-CV, 2001.

Fernández Díaz, Roberto. "Burguesía y consulados en el Siglo XVIII." In *Mercado y desarrollo económico en la España contemporánea*, edited by Tomás Martínez, 1–39. Madrid: Siglo XXI, 1986.

Fernández Díaz, Roberto. *Cataluña y el absolutismo borbónico. Historia y política*. Barcelona: Crítica, 2014.

Fernández Durán, Reyes. *Jerónimo de Uztáriz (1670–1732). Una política económica para Felipe V.* Madrid: Minerva, 1999.

Fernádez Sarasola, Ignacio. "Estudio Preliminar." In Valentín de Foronda, *Escritos políticos y constitucionales*, edited by Ignacio Fernández Sarasola, 9–94. Bilbao: Universidad del País Vasco, 2002.

Fernández Sarasola, Ignacio, ed. *Proyectos constitucionales en España (1786–1824)*. Madrid: CEPC, 2004.

Fernández Sarasola, Ignacio. "Opinión pública y 'libertades de expresión' en el constitucionalismo español (1726–1845)." *Historia Constitucional* 7 (2006): 159–86. DOI: http://dx.doi.org/10.17811/hc.v0i7.46.

Fernández Sarasola, Ignacio. "Constitution Projects During the Spanish Enlightenment." In *The Spanish Enlightenment Revisited*, edited by Jesús Astigarraga, 129–47. Oxford: VF, 2015.

Fernández Sebastián, Javier. "Estudio introductorio: Ibáñez de la Rentería y el pensamiento político de la Ilustración." In *La Ilustración política*, edited by Javier Fernández Sebastián, 17–151, 205-42. Bilbao: Universidad del País Vasco, 1994.

Fernández Sebastián, Javier. "Toleration and Freedom of Expression in the Hispanic World Between Enlightenment and Liberalism." *Past and present* 211 (2011): 166–76.

Fernández Sebastián, Javier. "From the 'Voice of the People' to the Freedom of the Press: the Birth of Public Opinion." In *The Spanish Enlightenment Revisited*, edited by Jesús Astigarraga, 203–33. Oxford: VF, 2015.

Ferrone, Vincenzo. *Scienza Natura Religione. Mondo newtoniano e cultura italiana nel primo Settecento*. Naples: Jovene Editore, 1982.

Ferrone, Vincenzo. *La società giusta ed equa. Repubblicanesimo e diritti dell'uomo in Gaetano Filangieri.* Roma-Bari: Laterza, 2003.

Fontana, Josep. *La crisis del Antiguo Régimen, 1808–1833*. Barcelona: Crítica, 1979.

Fontana, Josep. *Historia de Catalunya: La fi de l'Antic Règim i la industrialització (1787–1868)*. Barcelona: Edicions 62, 1998.

Forniés, Juan Francisco. "La Cátedra de economía civil y comercio de la ciudad de Zaragoza en el período de la Ilustración (1784–1808)." *Información Comercial Española* 512 (1976): 108–18.

Franco, Gloria. "El ejercicio del poder en la España del Siglo XVIII. Entre las prácticas culturales y las prácticas políticas." *Mélanges de la Casa de Velázquez* 35, no. 1 (2005): 51–77.

Franco, Gloria. "Captar súbditos y crear ciudadanos, doble objetivo de los 'Amigos del País' en el siglo XVIII." *Historia social* 64 (2009): 3–23.

Fumaroli, Marc. *La República de las Letras*. Barcelona: Acantilado, 2013.

Fuentes, José Franciso. *José Marchena. Biografía política e intelectual*. Barcelona: Crítica, 1989.

Fuentes, José Francisco. "*El Censor* y el público." *Estudios de Historia Social* 52–53 (1990): 221–30.

Fuentes Quintana, Enrique, ed. *Economía y economistas españoles. Vol. III. La Ilustración*. Barcelona: Galaxia Gutenberg-Círculo de Lectores, 2000.

García Cárcel, Ricardo. *Felipe V y los españoles: una visión periférica del problema de España*. Barcelona: Plaza y Janés, 2002.

García Garrosa, María Jesús. "Translation in Enlightenment Spain." In *Routledge Companion to the Hispanic Enlightenment,* edited by Elizabeth Franklin Lewis, Mónica Bolufer and Catherine M. Jaffe, 258–70. Abingdon-New York: Routledge, 2020.

García Guerra, Elena María. "Los manuales de mercaderes y contadores durante la Edad Moderna." In *Las Enciclopedias en España antes de l'Encyclopédie*, edited by Alfredo Alvar, 319–33. Madrid: CSIC, 2009.

García Pérez, Guillermo. *La economía y los reaccionarios al surgir la España contemporánea*. Madrid: Cuadernos para el Diálogo, 1974.

Gauci, Perry. *The Politics of Trade: the Overseas Merchant in State and Society, 1660–1720*. Oxford: OUP, 2001.

Gembicki, Dieter. "Le journalisme à sensation: *L'Epilogueur moderne* (1750–1754) de Rousset de Missy." In *Le Journalisme d'Ancien Régime,* 241–55. Lyon: Presses universitaires de Lyon, 1982.

Glaisyer, Natasha. *The Culture of Commerce in England, 1660–1720*. Suffolk: The Boydell Press, 2006.

Gómez de Enterría, Josefa. *Voces de la economía y el comercio en el español del siglo XVIII*. Alcalá de Henares: Universidad de Alcalá de Henares, 1996.

Gómez Urdáñez, Jose Luis. *El proyecto reformista del marqués de Ensenada*. Lérida: Milenio, 1996.

Gómez Urdáñez, José Luis. *Fernando VI*. Madrid: Arlanza, 2001.

González, José María. "El sevillano Luis de Luque y Leyva, *reintroductor* de la partida doble en la bibliografía española." *Cuadernos de investigación contable* 4, no. 1–2 (1992): 81–148.

González Enciso, Agustín. *War, Power and the Economy Mercantilism and State Formation in 18th Century Europe*. London-New York: Routledge, 2016.

González Enciso, Agustín. "Between Private and Pubic Interests: the *Moral Economy of Collaboration* in Eighteenth-Century Spain." In *The War Within. Private Interests and the Fiscal State in Early-Modern Europe*, edited by Jöel Félix and Anne Dubet, 171–93. Cham: Palgrave Macmillan, 2018.

Goodman, Dena. *The Republic of Letters. A Cultural History of the French Enlightenment*. Ithaca-London: Cornell University Press, 1994.

Grafe, Regina. *Distant Tyranny: Market, Power, and Backwardness in Spain, 1650–1800*. Princeton-Oxford: Princeton University Press, 2012.

Grieder, Josephine. *Anglomania in France, 1740–1789*. Geneva: Droz, 1985.

Guasti, Niccolò. "Il 'ragno di Francia' e la 'mosca di Spagna': Forbonnais e la riforma della fiscalità all'epoca di Ensenada e Machault." *CROMOHS* 9 (2004): 1–38.

Guasti, Niccolò. *Lotta politica e riforme all'inizio del regno di Carlo III. Campomanes e l'espulsione dei gesuiti (1759–1768)*. Florence: Alinea, 2006.

Guasti, Niccolò. "Campomanes' Civil Economy and the Emergence of the Public Sphere in Spanish *Ilustración*." In *L'économie politique et la sphère publique dans le débat des Lumières*, edited by Jesús Astigarraga and Javier Usoz, 229–44. Madrid: CV, 2013.

Guasti, Niccolò. "Introduzione. Nomante e Genovesi: l'economia civile nell *Ilustración* spagnola." In Lorenzo Normante, *Proposiones de economía civil y comercio*, edited by Niccolò Guasti, 7–108. Florence: Alinea, 2013.

Guiard, Teófilo. *Historia del Consulado y Casa de Contratación de Bilbao y del comercio de la Villa*. 2 vols. Bilbao: José de Astuy, 1913–1914.

Guinard, Paul-J. *La presse espagnole de 1737 à 1791. Formation et significance d'un genre*. Paris: Centre de recherches hispaniques, 1973.

Guidi, Marco E. L. "*Economy* and *Political Economy* in Italian Dictionaries and Encyclopaedias (1726–1861)." In *Political Economy and National Realities*, edited by Manuela Albertone and Alberto Masoero, 147–75. Turin: Fondazione Luigi Einaudi, 1994.

Guidi, Marco E. L. and Marco Cini, eds. *Le avventure delle 'Aventures'. Traduzioni del 'Télémaque' di Fénelon tra Sette e Ottocento*. Pisa: Edizioni ETS, 2017.

Habermas, Jürgen. *Strukturwandel der Öffentlichkeit. Untersuchungen zu einer Kategorie der bürgerlichen Gesellschaft* (Suhrkamp: Frankfurt am Main, 1962). Spanish trans., *Historia y crítica de la opinión pública. La transformación estructural de la vida pública*. Barcelona: Gustavo Gill, 2004.

Hamilton, Earl. *War & Prices in Spain, 1651–1800*. New York: Russell & Russell, 1947.

Hasquin, Hervé. "Jacques Accarias de Serionne, économiste et publiciste français au service des Pays-Bas Autrichiens." In *Études sur le XVIIIe siécle*, edited by Roland Mortier and Hervé Hasquin, 159–70. Brussels: Éditions de l'Université, 1974.

Hernández, Esteban. "A Spanish Treatise of 1706 on Double Entry Bookkepping: *Norte Mercantil y Crisol de Cuentas* by Gabriel de Souza Brito." *Accounting and Business Research* 15 (1985): 291–96.

Hernández, Esteban. "Origins and Development of Accounting in Spain (from the 13th to the 19th Century)." In *Accounting in Spain*, edited by José A. Gonzalo. Madrid: Asociación Española de Contabilidad, 1992.

Herr, Richard. *The Eighteenth Century Revolution in Spain* (Princeton: Princeton University Press, 1958). Spanish trans., *España y la revolución del Siglo XVIII*. Madrid: Aguilar, 1964.

Hont, Istvan. *Jealousy of Trade. International Competition and the Nation-State in Historical Perspective*. Cambridge-London: Harvard University Press, 2005.

Hoock, Jochen. "Discours commercial et économie politique en France au XVIIIe siècle: l'échec d'une synthèse." *Revue de Synthèse* 108, no. 1 (1987): 57–73.

Hoock, Johan. "Le phénomène Savary et l'innovation en matière commerciale en France aux XVIIe et XVIIIe siècles." In *Innovations et renouveaux techniques de l'Antiquité à nos jours*, edited by Jean-Pierre Kintz, 113–23. Strasbourg: Oberlin, 1989.

Hooch, Johan, Pierre Jeannin and Wolfgang Kaiser, eds. *Ars Mercatoria. Handbücher und Traktate für den Gebrauch des Kaufmanns, 1470–1820*. 3 vols. Paderborn: Schöningh, 1991–2001.

Hormigón, Mariano. "Las matemáticas en la Ilustración española. Su desarrollo en el reinado de Carlos III." In *Ciencia, técnica y Estado en la España ilustrada*, edited by Joaquín Fernández Pérez and Ignacio González Tascón, 265–78. Zaragoza: Ministerio de Educación y Ciencia, 1990.

Hutchison, Terence W. *Before Adam Smith. The Emergence of Political Economy, 1662–1776*. Oxford: Blackwell, 1988.

Iglesias, Nieves and Ana María Mañá. *Correo de Madrid o de los Ciegos, 1786–1791*. Madrid: Hemeroteca Municipal, 1968.

Isenmann, Moritz. "*Égalité, Réciprocité, Souveraineté*: the Role of Comercial Treaties in Colbert's Economic Policy." In *The Politics of Commerce Treaties in the Eighteenth Century. Balance of Power, Balance of Trade*, edited by Antonella Alimento and Koen Stapelbroek, 77–103. Cham: Palgrave MacMillan, 2017. DOI: http://dx.doi.org/10.1007/978-3-319-53574-6_2.

Israel, Johathan. *Radical Enlightenment: Philosophy and the Making of Modernity, 1650–1750*. Oxford: OUP, 2002.

Israel, Jonathan. *Democratic Enlightenment: Philosophy, Revolution, and Human Rights, 1750–1790*. Oxford: OUP, 2011.

Ives, Robin J. "Political Publicity and Political Economy in Eighteenth Century France." *French History* 17, no. 1 (2003): 1–18.

Jaffe, Catherine and Elizabeth Franklin Lewis, eds. *Eve's Enlightenment: Women's Experience in Spain and Spanish America, 1726–1839*. Baton Rouge: Lousiana State University Press, 2009.

Jakob, Margaret. *Radical Enlightenment. The Origins of Freemasonry: Facts and Dictions*. Philadelphia: University of Pensilvania Press, 2006.

Johnson, Edgar Augustus Jerome. *Predecessors of Adam Smith* (New York: Prentice Hall 1937). New York: A. M. Kelley, 1965.

Jüttner, Siegfried. *Espíritu de los mejores diarios literarios que se publican en Europa (1787–1791). Indices (onomástico y de fuentes, de obras y toponímico)*. Frankfurt am Main: Peter Lang, 2009.

Kafker, Frank A. "Les traductions de *l'Encyclopédie* au XVIIIe siècle: quelle fut leur influence?" *Recherches sur Diderot et sur l'Encyclopédie* 12 (1992): 165–73.

Kaiser, Wolfgang. "Ars Mercatoria. Möglichkeiten und grenzen einer analytischen bibliographie und datenbank." In *Ars Mercatoria. Handbücher und Traktate für den Gebrauch des Kaufmanns, 1470–1820*, edited by Johan Hooch, Pierre Jeannin and Wolfgang Kaiser, 3, 1–36. Paderborn: Schöningh, 2001.

Kamen, Henri. *The War of Succession in Spain, 1700–1715* (London: Weidenfeld & Nicolson, 1969). Spanish trans., *La Guerra de Sucesión en España*. Barcelona: Grijalbo, 1974.

Kaplan, Steve. L. and Sophus A. Reinert. "The Economic Turn in Enlightenment Europe." In *The Economic Turn. Recasting Political Economy in Enlightenment Europe*, edited by Steven L. Kaplan and Sophus A. Reinert, 1–33. London: Anthem, 2019.

Lafuente, Antonio and José Luis Peset. "Las actividades e instituciones científicas en la España ilustrada." In *Carlos III y la ciencia de la Ilustración*, edited by Manuel Sellés, José Luis Peset and Antonio Lafuente, 29–79. Madrid: Alianza, 1988.

La Parra, Emilio. *El Regente Gabriel Ciscar. Ciencia y revolución en la España romántica*. Madrid: Compañía literaria, 1995.

La Parra, Emilio. *Manuel Godoy. La aventura del poder*. Barcelona: Tusquets, 2002.

Larrère, Catherine. *L'invention de l'économie au XVIIIe siècle. Du droit naturel à la physiocratie*. Paris: PUF, 1992.

Larrère, Catherine. "L'*Encyclopédie Méthodique*: une économie très politique." In *L'Encyclopédie Méthodique (1782–1832). Des Lumières au Positivisme*, edited by Claude Blanckaert and Michel Porret, 215–39. Geneva: Droz, 2006.

Larriba, Elisabel. "Inquisición y prensa periódica en la segunda mitad del siglo XVIII." *Cuadernos de Ilustración y Romanticismo* 13 (2005): 77–92.

Larriba, Elisabel. "La última salida al ruedo del *Memorial Literario* (10 Octubre-20 Noviembre 1808)," *Cuadernos de Ilustración y Romanticismo* 16 (2010): 1–88.

Larriba, Elisabel. "Las aspiraciones a la libertad de imprenta en la segunda mitad del siglo XVIII." In *El nacimiento de la libertad de imprenta*, edited by Elisabel Larriba and Fernando Durán, 19–41. Madrid: Sílex, 2012.

Larriba, Elisabel. *El público de la prensa en España a finales del siglo XVIII (1781–1808)*. Zaragoza: Prensas Universitarias de Zaragoza, 2013.

Larriba, Elisabel and Gérard Dufour. *El Semanario de agricultura y artes dirigido a los párrocos (1797–1808)*. Valladolid: Ámbito, 1997.

Lasso Gaite, Juan Francisco. *Crónica de la codificación española –6–. Codificación mercantil*. Madrid: Ministerio de Justicia, 1998.

Le Guellec, Maud. *Presse et culture dans l'Espagne des Lumières*. Madrid: CV, 2016.

Letwin, William. *The Origins of Scientific Economics*. London: Methuen, 1963.

Levy, Darline Gay. *The Ideas and Careers of Simon-Nicolas-Henri Linguet: A Study in Eighteenth-Century French Politics*. Urbana: University of Illinois Press, 1980.

López-Cordón, María Victoria. "Secretarios y secretarías en la Edad Moderna: de las manos del Príncipe a relojeros de la Monarquía." *Studia Historica. Historia moderna* 15 (1996): 107–31.

López-Cordón, María Victoria. "Instauración dinástica y reformismo administrativo: la implantación del sistema ministerial." *Manuscrits* 18 (2000): 93–111.

López-Cordón, María Victoria. "Vida privada, asuntos públicos." In *Felipe V y su tiempo*, edited by Eliseo Serrano, 447–76. Zaragoza: IFC, 2004.

López-Cordón, María Victoria. *Condición femenina y razón ilustrada: Josefa Amar y Borbón*. Zaragoza: Prensas Universitarias de Zaragoza, 2005.

López-Cordón, María Victoria. "The Enlightenment and its Interpreters: Nobility, Bureaucrats, and Publicists." In *Routledge Companion to the Hispanic Enlightenment*, edited by Elizabeth Franklin Lewis, Mónica Bolufer and Catherine M. Jaffe, 203–17. Abingdon-New York: Routledge, 2020. DOI: 10.4324/9781315180281-15.

López-Cordón, María Victoria. "El bien público y el *sistema político de la Europa*." In *Bajo el velo del bien público*, edited by Jesús Astigarraga and Javier Usoz, 249–78. Zaragoza: IFC, 2020.

López Piñero, José María. *Ciencia y técnica en la sociedad española de los siglos XVI y XVII*. Barcelona: Labor, 1979.

López Piñero, José María and Víctor Navarro Brotons. *Història de la ciéncia al País Valencià*. Valencia: Generalitat Valenciana, 1995.

López-Vidriero, María Luisa. "Censura civil e integración nacional: el censor ilustrado." In *El mundo hispánico en el Siglo de las Luces*, II, 855–67. Madrid: SEESXVIII, 1996.

Lorenzo, Elena de. "Jovellanos: desde la censura dieciochesca hacia la libertad de imprenta." In *Hacia 1812, desde el siglo ilustrado*, edited by Fernando Durán, 991–1007. Gijón: Trea, 2013.

Lorenzo, Elena de. "Notas sobre la actividad censora de la Real Academia Española en el siglo XVIII." In *Instituciones censoras*, edited by Fernando Durán, 199–241. Madrid: CSIC, 2016.

Llombart, Vicent. "El sorgiment de les societats economiques i llur conflict amb les institucions comercials." *Recerques* 11 (1981): 181–98.

Llombart, Vicent. *Campomanes, economista y político de Carlos III*. Madrid: Alianza, 1992.

Llombart, Vicent. "Estudio Preliminar." In Manuel Sisternes, *Idea de una Ley Agraria española*, edited by Vicent Llombart. Barcelona: Alta Fulla, 1993.

Llombart, Vicent. "La política económica de Carlos III: ¿fiscalismo, cosmética o estímulo del crecimiento?" *RHE* 11 (1994): 11–39.

Llombart, Vicent. "El pensamiento económico de la Ilustración española." In *Economía y economistas españoles. Vol. III. La Ilustración*, edited by Enrique Fuentes Quintana, 7–89. Barcelona: Galaxia Gutenberg-Círculo de Lectores, 2000.

Llombart, Vicent. "El *Informe de Ley Agraria* de Jovellanos: núcleo analítico, programa de reformas y fuentes intelectuales." In *Economía y economistas españoles. Vol. III. La Ilustración,* edited by Enrique Fuentes Quintana, 421–46. Barcelona: Galaxia Gutenberg-Círculo de Lectores, 2000.

Llombart, Vicent. "Estudio Preliminar." In Gaspar Melchor de Jovellanos, *Escritos económicos*, edited by Vicent Llombart, 3–179. Madrid: RACMP, 2000.

Llombart, Vicent. "Traducciones españolas de economía política (1700–1812): catálogo bibliográfico y una nueva perspectiva." *CROMOHS* 9 (2004), http://www.fupress.net/index.php/cromohs/article/view/15644/14764. DOI: www. cromohs.unifi.it/92004/llombart. html.

Llombart, Vicent and Jesús Astigarraga. "Las primeras antorchas de la economía: las aociedades económicas de amigos del país en el siglo XVIII." In *Economía y economistas españoles. Vol. III. La Ilustración,* edited by Enrique Fuentes Quintana, 699–705. Barcelona: Galaxia Gutenberg-Círculo de Lectores, 2000.

Llopis, Enrique. "España, la 'revolución de los modernistas' y el legado del Antiguo Régimen." In *El legado del Antiguo Régimen en España*, edited by Enrique Llopis, 11–76. Barcelona: Crítica, 2004.

Llopis, Enrique and Sonia Sotaca. "Antes, bastante antes: la primera fase de la integración del mercado español de trigo, 1725–1808." *Historia Agraria* 36 (2005): 225–62.

Lluch, Ernest. *El pensament econòmic a Catalunya (1760–1840)*. Barcelona: Edicions 62, 1973.

Lluch, Ernest. *Las Españas vencidas del siglo XVIII. Claroscuros de la Ilustración.* Barcelona: Crítica, 1999.

Lluch, Ernest. *La alternativa catalana (1700–1714–1740)*. Vic: Eumo, 2000.

Lluch, Ernest. *Aragonesismo austracista (1734–1742). Conde Juan Amor de Soria.* Zaragoza: IFC, 2000.

Lluch, Ernest and Lluis Argemí. *Agronomía y fisiocracia en España (1750–1820)*. Valencia: Alfonso el Magnánimo, 1985.

Lluch, Ernest and Salvador Almenar. "Difusión e influencia de los economistas clásicos en España (1776–1870)." In *Economía y economistas españoles. Vol. IV. La economía clásica*, edited by Enrique Fuentes Quintana, 93–170. Barcelona: Galaxia Gütenberg-Círculo de Lectores, 2000.

Lynch, John. *Bourbon Spain, 1700–1808* (Oxford: Basil Blackwell, 1989). Spanish trans., *La España del siglo XVIII*. Barcelona: Crítica, 1991.

Maestre, José María, Manuel Antonio Díaz and Alberto Romero, eds. *Francisco Mariano Nipho. El nacimiento de la prensa y de la crítica literaria periodística en la España del siglo XVIII*. Alcañiz-Madrid: CSIC, 2015.

Maravall, José Antonio. *Antiguos y modernos. La idea de progreso en el desarrollo inicial de una sociedad*. Madrid: Sociedad de estudios y publicaciones, 1966.

Martín, Manuel. "Estudio preliminar. La institucionalización de los estudios de economía política en la universidad española (1784–1857)." In Marqués de Valle Santoro, *Elementos de Economía Política con aplicación particular a España*, edited by Manuel Martín, IX-CCXXXIV. Madrid: IEF, 1989.

Martínez Shaw, Carlos. "La Cataluña del siglo XVIII bajo el signo de la expansión." In *España en el siglo XVIII*, edited by Roberto Fernández, 55–131. Barcelona: Crítica, 1985.

Martínez Shaw, Carlos. "Las vías del desarrollo regional en la España del siglo XVIII." In *El mundo hispánico en el Siglo de las Luces*, I, 176–92. Madrid: SEESXVIII, 1996.

Martucci, Roberto. "La *Méthodique* di Panckoucke e il suo dizionario di *Économie politique and diplomatique*," *Storia del pensiero económico* 41 (2001): 213–30.

McCulloch, John Ramsay. *The Literature of Political Economy* (London: 1845). New York: A. M. Kelley, 1991.

McCusker, J. J. and C. Gravestein. *The Beginnings of Commercial and Financial Journalism*. Amsterdam: Netherlands Economic History Archives, 1991.

Meijide, María Luisa. "Un agrónomo del siglo XVIII: el orensano Vicente del Seixo." *Boletín de la Real Academia Galega* 359 (1977): 183–206.

Meijide, María Luisa. "Vicente del Seixo y la Sociedad Económica de Amigos del País de Madrid." *Boletín da Real Academia Galega* 360 (1980): 355–72.

Melton, James van Horn. *The Rise of the Public in Enlightenment Europe* (Cambridge: CUP, 2001). Spanish trans., *La aparición del público durante la Ilustración europea*. Valencia: Universidad de Valencia, 2009.

Menudo, José Manuel and Jose María O'Kean. "La recepción de la obra de Jean-Baptiste Say en España: la teoría económica del empresario." *RHE* 23, no. 1 (2005): 117–42. DOI: 10.107/50212610900011836.

Menudo, José Manuel and Jose María O'Kean. "Ediciones, reimpresiones y traducciones en español del *Tratado de economía política* de Jean-Baptiste Say." *RHE* 37, no. 1 (2019): 169–92. DOI: 10.107/50212610918000186.

Mestre, Antonio. *Despotismo e Ilustración en España*. Barcelona: Ariel, 1976.

Mestre, Antonio. *Mayans y la España de la Ilustración*. Madrid: Instituto de Espasa Calpe, 1999.

Meyssonnier, Simone. *La balance et l'horloge. La genèse de la pensée libérale en France au XVIIIe siècle*. Paris: Les éditions de la passion, 1989.

Minard, Philippe. *La fortune du Colbertisme*. Paris: Fayard, 1998.

Mokyr, Joel. *The Lever of Riches* (New York-Oxford: OUP, 1990). Spanish trans., *La palanca de la riqueza*. Madrid: Alianza, 1993.

Mokyr, Joel. *The Enlightened Economy. Britain and the Industrial Revolution, 1700–1850*. New Haven-London: Yale University Press, 2009.

Molas, Pere. "La Junta General de Comercio y Moneda: la institución y los hombres." *Cuadernos de Historia. Anexo de la Revista Hispania* 9 (1978): 1–36.

Molas, Pere. *Hombres de leyes, economistas y científicos en la Junta General de Comercio, 1679–1832*. Barcelona: CSIC, 1981.

Munck, Thomas. *The Enlightenment. A Comparative Social History, 1721–1794* (New York: OUP, 2000). Spanish trans., *Historia social de la Ilustración*. Barcelona: Crítica, 2001.

Murphy, Antoin. "Le développement des idées économiques en France (1750–1756)." *Révue d'histoire moderne et contemporaine* XXXIII (1986): 521–41.

Murray, Glen. "Guía de los marcos acuñados y ensayadores de la Casa de Moneda de Madrid." *Numisma* 233 (1993): 295–387.

Nava, María Teresa. *Reformismo ilustrado y americanismo: la Real Academia de la Historia, 1735–1792*. Madrid: Universidad Complutense de Madrid, 1989.

Nava, María Teresa. "El poder y su precio: los orígenes de la Secretaría del Despacho de Hacienda (1700–1724)." In *Gobernar en tiempo de crisis*, edited by María Victoria López-Cordón and José Manuel Nieto, 109–32. Madrid: Sílex, 2008.

Nava, María Teresa. "Ciencia y académicos de la Historia en la Ilustración española: la emergencia del autor colectivo." *Revista Historia Autónoma* 10 (2017): 67–85. http://dx.doi.org/10.15366/rha2017.10.004.

Ocampo, Joaquín. "El *Semanario Económico* (1765–1767): a la Ilustración por la utilidad." *El Argonauta español* 10 (2013), http://argonauta.revues.org/1926.

Orain, Arnaud. "Le *Journal Oeconomique*, le cercle de Gournay et le pouvoir monarchique: quelques preuves matérielles d'un lien organique." *Dix-Huitième Siècle* 45 (2013): 565–83.

Ozouf, Mona. "L'opinion publique." In *The Political Culture of the Old Regime*, edited by Keith Michael Baker, I, 419–34. Oxford: Pergamon Press, 1987.

Pampliega, Víctor. "*Empleo oscuro y penoso.* El trabajo del censor." In *Instituciones censoras*, edited by Fernando Durán, 113–58. Madrid: CSIC, 2016.

Paquette, Gabriel B. *Enlightenment, Governance, and Reform in Spain and its Empire, 1759–1808.* New York: Palgrave MacMillan, 2008.

Perdices, Luis. *Pablo de Olavide (1725–1803). El ilustrado*. Madrid: Editorial Complutense, 1992.

Pérez Magallón, Jesús. *Construyendo la modernidad: la cultura española en el tiempo de los novatores (1675–1725)*. Madrid: CSIC, 2002.

Pérez-Samper, María Ángeles. "Luces, tertulias, cortejos y refrescos." *Cuadernos de Estudios del Siglo XVIII* 10–11 (2001): 107–53.

Pérez Sarrión, Guillermo. "La formación de la política manufacturera de la Ilustración española en la primera mitad del siglo XVIII. Una aproximación." In *Más estado y más mercado*, edited by Guillermo Pérez Sarrión, 181–233. Madrid: Sílex, 2011.

Pérez Sarrión, Guillermo. *La península comercial. Mercado, redes sociales y estado en España en el siglo XVIII*. Madrid: Marcial Pons, 2012.

Pérez Sindreu, Francisco de Paula. *La casa de la moneda de Sevilla*. Seville: Universidad de Sevilla, 1991.

Perona, Dionisio A. *Notas sobre el proceso de la codificación mercantil en la España del siglo XIX*. Madrid: Dykinson, 2015.

Perrot, Jean-Claude. *Une histoire intellectuelle de l'économie politique*. Paris: EHESS, 1992.

Peset, Mariano and José Luis Peset. *La universidad española (siglos XVIII y XIX)*. Madrid: Taurus, 1974.

Peset, Mariano and José Luis Peset. *Gregorio Mayans y la reforma universitaria*. Valencia: 1975.

Petit, Carlos. *La compañía mercantil bajo el régimen de las Ordenanzas del Consulado de Bilbao, 1737–1829*. Seville: Universidad Hispalense, 1980.

Pimentel, Juan. *Testigos del mundo. Ciencia, literatura y viajes en la Ilustración*. Madrid: Marcial Pons, 2003.

Pincuss, Steve and James Robinson. "Wars and State-Making Reconsidered." *Annales: Histoire, Sciences Sociales* 71, no. 1 (2016): 5–36.

Porter, Roy S. and Teich Mikula´sˇ , eds. *The Enlightenment in National Context*. Cambridge: CUP, 1981.

Portillo, José María. *Revolución de nación*. Madrid: CEPC, 2000.

Portillo, José María. "Constitucionalismo antes de la Constitución. La economía política y los orígenes del constitucionalismo en España," *Nuevo Mundo-Mundos nuevos* 7 (2007), https://doi.org/10.4000/nuevomundo.4160.

Pradells, Jesús. "Juan Bautista Virio (1753–1837): experiencia europea y reformismo económico en la España ilustrada." *Revista de Historia Moderna* 8–9 (1990): 223–71.

Raven, James. *Publishing Business in Eighteenth-Century England*. Suffolk: The Boydell Press, 2014.

Reinert, Sophus A. *Translating Empire. Emulation and the Origins of Political Economy*. Cambridge-London: Harvard University Press, 2011.

Ringrose, David R. *España, 1700–1900: el mito del fracaso*. Madrid: Alianza, 1996.

Robertson, John. "The Enlightenment Above the National Context: Political Economy in Eigtheenth-Century Scotland and Naples." *The Historical Journal* 40, no. 3 (1997): 667–97.

Robertson, John. "The Scottish Enlightenment at the Limits of the Civil Tradition." In *Wealth and Virtue. The Shapping of Political Economy in the Scottish Enlightenment*, edited by Istvan Hont and Michael Ignatieff, 137–78. Cambridge: CUP, 1983.

Robertson, John. *The Case for the Enlightenment. Scotland and Naples, 1680–1760*. Cambridge: CUP, 2005.

Robertson, John. "Enlightenment, Public Sphere and Political Economy." In *L'économie politique et la sphère publique dans le débat des Lumières*, edited by Jesús Astigarraga and Javier Usoz, 9–32. Madrid: CV, 2013.

Rojo, Ángel. "José Bonaparte (1808–1813) y la legislación mercantil e industrial española." *Revista de Derecho mercantil* 143–144 (1977): 121–82.

Rothkrug, Lionel. *Opposition to Louis XIV. The Political and Social Origins of the French Enlightenment*. Princeton: Princeton University Press, 1965.

Rus, Salvador. "Una versión del 'estado de naturaleza' en la España del siglo XVIII: el texto de Joaquín Marín y Mendoza." *Cuadernos Dieciochistas* 1 (2000): 257–82.

Sáiz, María Dolores. *Historia del periodismo en España. Vol. 1. Los orígenes. El Siglo XVIII*. Madrid: Alianza, 1983.

Salavert, Vicent L. "L'aritmetica practica de Geronimo Cortés i la vida mercantil al País Valencià a les darreries del segle XVI." *Estudis. Revista de Historia Moderna* 8 (1982): 105–24.

Salavert, Vicent L. "Introducción a la historia de la aritmética práctica en la Corona de Aragón en el siglo XVI." *Dynamis* 10 (1990): 63–91.

Sánchez, Alfonso, José Luis Malo and Luis Blanco. *La cátedra de economía civil y comercio de la Real Sociedad Económica Aragonesa de Amigos del País (1784–1846)*. Zaragoza: Ibercaja and Real Sociedad Económica Aragonesa de Amigos del País, 2003.

Sánchez Blanco, Francisco. "Los *Discursos mercuriales* (1752–1756) de Juan Enrique Graef." *Estudios de Historia Social* 52–53 (1990): 477–89.

Sánchez Blanco, Francisco. *Europa y el pensamiento español del siglo XVIII*. Madrid: Alianza, 1991.

Sánchez Blanco, Francisco. "Introducción." In *Discursos mercuriales económico-políticos (1752–1756)*, edited by Francisco Sánchez Blanco, 19–76. Seville: Fundación El Monte, 1996.

Sánchez Blanco, Francisco. *El Absolutismo y las Luces en el reinado de Carlos III*. Madrid: Marcial Pons, 2002.

Sarrailh, Jean. *L'Espagne éclairée de la seconde moitié du XVIIIe siècle* (Paris: Impr. Nationale, 1954). Spanish trans., *La España ilustrada de la segunda mitad del siglo XVIII*. Méjico: FCE, 1957.

Scott, H. M., "Introduction: The Problem of Enlightened Absolutism." In *Enlightened Absolutism. Reform and Reformers in Later Eighteenth-Century Europe*, edited by H. M. Scott, 1–35. Michigan: University of Michigan Press, 1990.

Schabas, Margaret. *The Natural Origins of Economics*. Chicago: University of Chicago Press, 2005.

Schaffer, Robert Jones. *The Economic Societies in the Spanish World (1763–1821)*. Syracuse: Syracuse University Press, 1958.

Schaub, Jean-Frédéric. *La Francia española. Las raíces hispanas del absolutismo francés*. Madrid: Marcial Pons, 2004.

Schumpeter, Joseph A. *History of Economic Analysis*. New York: OUP, 1954.

Sgard, Jean, ed. *Dictionnaire des journalistes (1600–1789)*. Grenoble: 1976,.

Sgard, Jean, ed. *Dictionnaire des journaux (1600–1789)*. Paris: 1991, http://dictionnaire-journaux.gazettes18e.fr/journal

Shovlin, John. *The Political Economy of Virtue. Luxury, Patriotism and the Origins of the French Revolution*. New York: Cornell University, 2006.

Smith, Robert Sidney. *The Spanish Guild Merchant: a History of the Consulado, 1250–1700*. Durham: Duke University, 1940.

Smith, Robert Sidney. "The *Wealth of Nations* in Spain and Hispanic America, 1780–1830." *Journal of Political Economy* 4 (1957): 104–25.

Stapelbroek, Koen, ed. *Trade and War. The Neutrality of Commerce in the Inter-State System*. Helsinki: Collegium for Advanced Studies, 2011.

Stapelbroek, Koen and Jani Marjanen, eds. *The Rise of Economic Societies in the Eighteenth Century: Patriotic Reform in Europe and North America*. Basingstoke: Palgrave Macmillan, 2012.

Stein, Stanley J. and Barbara Stein. *Apogee of Empire: Spain and New Spain in the Age of Charles III, 1759–1808*. Baltimore: John Hopkins University Press, 2003.

Steiner, Philippe. "Les grandes revues économiques de langue française au XVIIIe siècle (1751–1776)." In *Les revues françaises d'économie politique XVIIIe-XIXe siècle*, edited by Luc Marco, 33–78. Paris: L'Harmatan, 1996.

Steiner, Philippe. *La 'science nouvelle' de l'économie politique*. Paris: PUF, 1998.

Tavárez, Fidel J. "La invención de un imperio comercial hispánico, 1740–1765." *Magallánica* 2, no. 3 (2015): 56–76, http://fh.mdp.edu.ar/revistas/index.php/magallanica/article/view/1509/2215.

Tavárez, Fidel J. "Colonial Economic Improvement: How Spain Created New Consulates to Preserve and Develop its American Empire, 1778–1795." *Hispanic American Historical Review* 98, no. 4 (2018): 605–34. DOI: http://dx.doi.org/10.1215/00182168-7160336.

Tedde de Lorca, Pedro. *El Banco de San Carlos (1782–1829)*. Madrid: Banco de España-Alianza Editorial, 1988.

Terjanian, Anoush Fraser. *Commerce and its Discontents in Eighteenth-Century French Political Thought*. Cambridge: CUP, 2013.

Théré, Christine. "Economic Publishing and Authors, 1566–1789." In *Studies in the History of French Political Economy*, edited by Gilbert Faccarello, 1–56. London-New York: Routledge, 1998.

Torres, Rafael. *La llave de todos los tesoros. La Tesorería General de Carlos III*. Madrid: Sílex, 2012.

Torres, Rafael. *El precio de la guerra. El estado fiscal-militar de Carlos III (1779–1783)*. Madrid: Marcial Pons, 2013.

Tortarolo, Edoardo. "Opinion publique tra Antico Regime e rivoluzione francese. Contributo a un vocabolario storico della política settecentesca." *Rivista Storica italiana* CII, no. 1 (1999): 5–23.

Tortarolo, Edoardo. "Public Opinion and the Italian Enlightenment. Approaches to a Historical Vocabulary." In *Concepts and Symbols of the Eighteenth Century in Europe: Opinion*, edited by Peter-Eckhard Knabe, 34–44. Berlin: Arno Spitz, 2000.

Tribe, Keith. *Governing Economy. The Reformation of German Economic Discourse, 1750–1840*. Cambridge: CUP, 1998.

Tsuda, Takumi. "Un économiste trahi, Vincent de Gournay (1712–1759)." In Jacques-Claude-Marie Vincent de Gournay, *Traités sur le commerce de Josiah Child avec les Remarques inédites de Vicent de Gournay*, edited by Takumi Tsuda, 445–85. Tokyo: Kinokuniya Company, 1983.

Ugarte, Juana. *Discurso Historia Informática. La palabra economía en los textos económicos españoles del siglo XVIII*. Oviedo: Universidad de Oviedo, 1996.

Urzainqui, Inmaculada. "Los redactores del *Memorial literario* (1784–1808)." *Estudios de Historia Social* 52–53 (1990): 501–16.

Urzainqui, Inmaculada. "Crítica teatral y secularización: el *Memorial Literario* (1784–1797)." *Bulletin Hispanique* 94 (1992): 203–43.

Urzainqui, Inmaculada. "Un nuevo instrumento cultural: la prensa periódica." In *La República de las Letras en la España del Siglo XVIII*, edited by Joaquín Álvarez Barrientos, François Lopez and Inmaculada Urzainqui, 125–216. Madrid: CSIC, 1995.

Urzainqui, Inmaculada. "La prensa en la época de Carlos IV: continuidades y cambios." In *La época de Carlos IV (1788–1808)*, edited by Elena de Lorenzo, 87–112. Oviedo: SEESXVIII, 2009.

Urzainqui, Inmaculada. "Periodista-*espectador* en la España de las Luces. La conciencia de un género nuevo de escritura periodística." *El argonauta español* 6 (2009), https://argonauta.revues.org/516.

Urzainqui, Inmaculada. "Libertad de imprenta y prensa crítica a fines del siglo XVIII." In *El nacimiento de la libertad de imprenta*, edited by Elisabel Larriba and Fernando Durán, 43–78. Madrid: Sílex, 2012.

Urzainqui, Inmaculada. "Diálogo entre periodistas (1737–1770)." In *Francisco Mariano Nipho. El nacimiento de la prensa y de la crítica literaria periodística en la España del siglo XVIII*, edited by José María Maestre, Manuel Antonio Díaz and Antonio Romero, 375–418. Alcañiz-Madrid: CSIC, 2014.

Usoz, Javier. *Pensamiento económico y reformismo ilustrado en Aragón (1760–1800)*. PhD. Zaragoza: Universidad de Zaragoza, 1996.

Usoz, Javier. "Mateo Antonio Barberi: el ideario de la Junta General de Comercio en Aragón." *Cuadernos Aragoneses de Economía* 8, no. 2 (1998): 501–23.

Usoz, Javier. "El enfoque regional del pensamiento económico de la Ilustración española y su aplicación elemental a Aragón." In *Nación y Constitución. De la Ilustración al Liberalismo*, edited by Cinta Canterla, 223–42. Seville: SEESVIII, 2006.

Usoz, Javier. "La 'nueva política' ilustrada y la esfera pública: las introducciones a la economía en el siglo XVIII español." *Revista de estudios políticos* 153 (2011): 11–46.

Usoz, Javier. "Política y economía en la Ilustración: la Real Sociedad Económica Aragonesa y las instituciones territoriales de la Monarquía borbónica." In *Más estado y más mercado*, edited by Guillermo Pérez Sarrión, 261–96. Madrid: Sílex, 2011.

Usoz, Javier. "Political Economy and the Creation of the Public Sphere during the Spanish Enlightenment." In *The Spanish Enlightenment Revisited*, edited by Jesús Astigarraga, 105–27. Oxford: VF, 2015.

Valles, José Manuel. *Ciencia, economía política e Ilustración en Vicente Alcalá-Galiano*. Madrid: CEPC, 2008.

Varela, Eulogio. *Espíritu de los mejores diarios literarios que se publican en Europa, Madrid 1787–1791*. Madrid: Sección de cultura "Nora," 1966.

Velasco, Eva. *La Real Academia de la Historia en el siglo XVIII*. Madrid: CEPC, 2000.

Velasco, Eva. "Las censuras de la Real Academia de la Historia (1746–1772)." In *Instituciones censoras*, edited by Fernando Durán, 113–58. Madrid: CSIC, 2016.

Venturi, Franco. "Economisti e riformatore spagnoli e italiani del'700." *Rivista Storica Italiana* 74 (1962): 532–61.

Venturi, Franco. "Il movimiento riformatore degli illuministi meridionale." *Rivista Storica Italiana* 74 (1962): 5–26.

Venturi, Franco. *Settecento riformatore*. 5 vols. Turin: 1969–1984.

Venturi, Franco. *Utopia and Reform in the Enlightenment*. Cambridge: CUP, 1971.

Vilar, Jean. "Des idées, des mots pour 'des choses': l'économie savoir sans nom de l'Espagne classique." In *Les mentalités dans la Péninsule Ibérique et en Amérique Latine aux XVIe et XVIIe siècles*, 33–59. Tours: Université de Tours, 1978.

Vilar, Pierre. *La Catalogne dans l'Europe moderne*. 3 vols. Paris: SEVPEN, 1962.

Vilar, Pierre. *Oro y moneda en la historia, 1450–1920*. Barcelona-Caracas-Méjico: Ariel, 1969.

Witthaus, J.-H. "Los *Discursos mercuriales* de Juan-Enrique Graef. Acerca de la constitución de la esfera pública a mediados del siglo XVIII." In *Redes y espacios de opinión pública*, edited by Marieta Cantos, 51–65. Cadiz: Universidad de Cadiz, 2006.

Index

www.ingramcontent.com/pod-product-compliance
Lightning Source LLC
Chambersburg PA
CBHW071325230926
51849CB00002B/320
* 9 7 8 9 0 0 4 4 4 2 3 8 2 *